Marilyn Monroe

Marilyn Monroe

MAURICE ZOLOTOW

Updated and Expanded Edition

PERENNIAL LIBRARY

Harper & Row, Publishers, New York
Grand Rapids, Philadelphia, St. Louis, San Francisco
London, Singapore, Sydney, Tokyo, Toronto

PN
2287
.M69
Z6
1990

The first edition of this book was published in 1960 by Harcourt, Brace & Company.

MARILYN MONROE, *Updated and Expanded Edition*. Copyright © 1960 by Maurice Zolotow. Prologue and Epilogue copyright © 1990 by Maurice Zolotow. All rights reserved. Printed in the United States of America. No part of this book may be used or reproduced in any manner whatsoever without written permission except in the case of brief quotations embodied in critical articles and reviews. For information address Harper & Row, Publishers, Inc., 10 East 53rd Street, New York, NY 10022.

First PERENNIAL LIBRARY edition published 1990.

LIBRARY OF CONGRESS CATALOG CARD NUMBER 88-45578
ISBN 0-06-097196-7

90 91 92 93 94 DT/MPC 10 9 8 7 6 5 4 3 2 1

To my daughter,
CRESCENT DRAGONWAGON

Contents

(Photographs follow pages 190 and 336)

Preface and Acknowledgments

This is not an authorized biography. Neither is it an unauthorized biography. On certain phases of Marilyn Monroe's early life and later career, I have received first-hand information from Marilyn herself; on others, she has been silent. Toward this work as a whole, she has a friendly neutrality, I hope, but I have written it without either her guidance or approval.

The actress, as subject, is elusive. All actresses, by reason of their natural gifts and their professional habits, are able to put on a great number of *personae*. They can, if they wish, change faces so rapidly, so often, and so persuasively that the biographer gets dizzy. This is especially true of the motion-picture actress. And the problem is complicated by the eerie quality of her habitat: Hollywood. The Hollywood *ambiance* is remote from common human experience. Even so sensitive and skillful a writer as F. Scott Fitzgerald could not make it real. The only books that have spoken to me truly of Hollywood have been *grands guignols:* Nathanael West's *The Day of the Locust,* Norman Mailer's *The Deer Park,* and Evelyn Waugh's *The Loved One.* In no foreign city have I felt such a sense of strangeness as I feel in Hollywood.

I have sought, with great care, to capture the elusive, taking, as my justification, that remark of Hamlet's about actors being "the abstracts and brief chronicles of the time." Even if they do not change the world as scientists and statesmen do, even if their influence, unlike that of the novelist, is transitory, yet while they live they touch our emotions more directly than other celebrities. In rare cases, an actor or an actress comes to satisfy the fantasies of millions. Such a rare creature is Monroe, and therefore her "brief chronicle" has seemed to me to be worth telling seriously.

At times in this book, there are dialogues, scenes of action, and occasional descriptions of my heroine's states of mind and feeling. I did not invent them. They are based on interviews with the participants or on published material. Most of the direct quotations from Monroe are drawn from my conversations with her. Quotations identified by the phrase "she wrote" are generally taken from one of the three autobiographical pieces to which she has put her name. These are "The Truth About Me" (as told to Liza Wilson), "Wolves I Have Known" (as told to Florabel Muir), and a series of 13 articles that were published weekly in the *Empire News* (London) from May 9 through August 1, 1954. These last were extracts from a book which had been "told to" Ben Hecht. That autobiography has never been published except in this fragmentary form. I have drawn very sparingly from the three short books about Miss Monroe that have been published: *The Marilyn Monroe Story*, by Joe Franklin and Laurie Palmer (New York, 1953); *Marilyn,* by Sidney Skolsky (New York, 1954), and *Will Acting Spoil Marilyn Monroe?,* by Pete Martin (New York, 1956).

I owe special gratitude to two motion-picture directors: Joshua Logan and Billy Wilder. They took time out of their crowded lives to answer patiently my questions about film technique. I had made up my mind that this biography of a movie star would be unique in at least one respect: it would deal seriously with her acting problems and her acting work and describe concretely what happened on a set and why. And if this book conveys some authentic sense of the experience of playing before a movie camera, it is largely due to the help of these two men.

To Lee Strasberg, the most celebrated teacher of acting in this period, I am indebted for valuable insights, not only into one of his most gifted pupils, but into the challenge that faces all actors. The private conversations I have had with him, as well as the observations I have heard him make during meetings at the Actors' Studio, have enlightened me on the creative process in acting.

To Herbert Mayes and Margaret Cousins I am grateful for the

Prologue (1990)

I met Marilyn Monroe in 1952.

After trudging with Dean Martin while he played eighteen holes of golf at Lakeside, I had come back to the Beverly Hills Hotel. I showered. I looked forward to an evening by myself. I changed into Daks slacks, a linen shirt, and Peal shoes. I went down to the small bar in the Polo Lounge. I sipped an extra-dry martini with a twist. I sighed. I relaxed. I felt good.

"Call for Maurice Zolotow."

I took it on the phone at the bar.

"Zolly?"

"Yeah . . ."

"It's Herb, Herb Stein. Got anything on for tonight?"

"No."

"I'll pick you up in ten, fifteen minutes. I'm taking you to a dinner for Walter Winchell. At the Ambassador."

"I don't like Winchell," I said.

"The L.A. Press Club is throwing it. 20th Century-Fox is picking up the tab. Jet Fore asked me to bring you. You'll meet Zanuck. You'll meet Marilyn Monroe."

"I'm dead tired, Herb."

"You got to come. Jet Fore asked me to bring you."

Jet Fore was one of the sixty-three publicists at 20th. A good guy. A jovial fat guy. Herb Stein, who was a *Hollywood Reporter* columnist, told me he owed Jet Fore a favor. And I owed Herb Stein a

1

favor. When I began coming out to the West Coast in 1947 to do magazine articles about movie and radio stars, Herb had helped me find sources and taken me around to dinner parties and orgies. Herb was a popular man-about-town, tall and handsome and saturnine. He knew everybody. He was an intimate friend of Carl (Junior) Laemmle, son of Carl Laemmle, founder of Universal Pictures. He was an intimate friend of Bryan (Brynie) Foy, producer and director, and one of the Seven Little Foys, children of the fabulous Eddie Foy, musical comedy star . . .

"So what about it, Zolly?"

"Yes," I said.

He picked me up about half past six. He was driving a white three-hole Buick convertible. He drove downtown to the old Ambassador Hotel. It was opposite the original Brown Derby on Wilshire. This Brown Derby was the one shaped like a gargantuan brown derby. We went to a private dining room. Jet Fore greeted me. He led me to a place beside a man in a gray flannel suit and a plaid vest with a Phi Beta Kappa key on a watch chain. The man looked to be fifty, maybe fifty-five. He had a moustache and an air of culture about him.

"Maurie," said Jet Fore, "this is Charlie Brackett!"

The great Charles Brackett. Writing partner of Billy Wilder. Writers of *Bluebeard's Eighth Wife, Midnight, Ball of Fire,* and *Ninotchka.* Brackett and Wilder, who became the greatest writing, producing, and directing team in movie history. I loved all their pictures, from the first, *The Major and the Minor,* to the last, *Sunset Boulevard.* They separated in 1950. Charles Brackett was now producing pictures at 20th Century-Fox. He had co-written the still-unreleased *Niagara.* He had produced it. Directed by Henry Hathaway. Starring Joseph Cotten and, in her first important role, the blonde starlet Marilyn Monroe, who had made a breakthrough of a sort playing dumb sexpots in *The Asphalt Jungle* (she was Louis Calhern's darling) and *All About Eve* (she was George Sanders's darling).

So I sat down next to Charles Brackett. Little did I know that my life was about to take a magnificent deviation. Our conversation began with gossip about the New York stage (he missed it so much and he knew I was a part of it) and about surviving members of the Algonquin Round Table who had remained in New York, like George S. Kaufman and Marc Connelly. I knew a side of Charles Brackett that few persons in Hollywood were aware of. He had been the first drama encouragement they gave me during a crucial period in the writing of this book.

I am indebted to Evelyn Pain, editor, and Ken Cunningham, art editor, of *Photoplay Magazine* for permission to use several exclusive photographs in their collection.

I owe special thanks to Jane Wilkie, who helped me gather and interpret much of the material in the book, particularly the information about Miss Monroe's first marriage and the incidents that occurred during the making of her two recent films. I am also grateful to Gerald McKnight, who gathered much of the data and made suggestions about the treatment of her adventures in England; to Edward J. Brash, who collated the reviews of her films; to the Museum of Modern Art for the use of their excellent film library; to the Theatre Room of the New York Public Library. I am grateful to the 20th Century-Fox Film Studios for screening Miss Monroe's early films for me, as well as for giving me every possible assistance without demanding that I permit censorship of the manuscript or submit it in advance of publication.

The following persons also assisted me in ways both great and small: Bill Batchelor, Dorothy Blair, Charles Brackett, Harry Brand, Reginald Carroll, Phoebe Brand Carnovsky, Jack Cardiff, Jack Cole, Roy Craft, Tony Curtis, Frank Delaney, Jim Denton, Leila Fields, Sidney Fields, Frank Goodman, Amy Greene, Milton H. Greene, Eileen Heckart, Betsy Holland, Nunnally Johnson, Elia Kazan, Fred Karger, Tom Kelley, Ernest Lehman, Jack Lemmon, Natasha Lytess, Norman Mailer, David March, Kevin McCarthy, Tess Michaels, Cameron Mitchell, Inez Melson, Jean Negulesco, Lionel Newman, Sir Laurence Olivier, Jack Podell, James D. Proctor, Gladys Rasmussen, Jane Russell, Robert Ryan, Sidney Skolsky, Emmeline Snively, Leon Shamroy, Alan Snyder, John Springer, Herb Stein, Maureen Stapleton, Paula Strasberg, George Solotaire, Daniel Taradash, Earl Theisen, Dame Sybil Thorndike, Linn Unkifer, Jerry Wald, Eli Wallach, Leo Wilder, Florence Williams, and Sonia Wolfson.

MAURICE ZOLOTOW

Marilyn Monroe

critic of *The New Yorker*. And he had written a series of dry, crisp, witty novels: *Week End, Counsel of the Ungodly, That Last Infirmity, American Colony,* and *Entirely Surrounded.* The last one was about Alexander Woollcott and his circle, which included the Lunts. I recently reread *Week End.* Brackett wrote in the sophisticated cruel vein of Ronald Firbank and the early Aldous Huxley *(Crome Yellow* and *Antic Hay).* He could have been one of our great men of letters if he had not become one of our greatest screenwriters.

So you can see why, out of my immense respect, my awe, for the taste and wisdom of this man, I listened when Mr. Brackett spoke of Marilyn Monroe.

Yes, he wanted me to write an article about her for *The Saturday Evening Post.* Yes, he wanted publicity for his picture. I knew that. But I also listened to him when he started speaking in his low cultivated voice—he came from a respectable family in Saratoga Springs, had fought in World War I, and had been a Paris expatriate and one of the brave literary experimenters of the golden 1920s, one of the very first *New Yorker* contributors. He spoke of Marilyn Monroe as the human being. He was the first person who understood and explained to me the contradiction between the inner waif and the external "sexpot" and how these two persons came together in her photographs and made her irresistibly compelling. He wanted to screen *Niagara* for me, and we made a date for the following Thursday morning. And it was Mr. Brackett who told me those few first intriguing facts about her mysterious provenance, her year in an orphanage, her struggle to make herself a serious actress, her conflicts with Harry Cohn at Columbia and with Darryl Zanuck at Fox. He knew he could trust my discretion . . .

Suddenly there was a stirring in the room like a rustling of feathers.

It was Marilyn. She was seated at the head table—flanked by Zanuck on her right and Winchell on her left. Winchell was a short, ugly little man with an etiolated complexion and little evil black eyes. His Broadway gossip column appeared in four hundred papers. His Sunday night fifteen-minute radio program was listened to by all America. He was a powerful man, not only in show business circles but in politics. He could make you and break you. Or at least he would try to break you if you crossed him. Marilyn was his "date" for the evening. Zanuck, yes, even the mighty Zanuck, genuflected before the mightier Winchell. Zanuck put Winchell in many of his films, playing

Walter Winchell. He even made a movie about Winchell, *Broadway Through a Keyhole*. Zanuck paid Irving Hoffman $25,000 a year just to keep Zanuck in good with Winchell. Hoffman was, in Marxian verbiage, a lackey and a lickspittle. When I see these words, usually in Chinese propaganda, I always think of the oleaginous Hoffman. Tony Curtis played Hoffman and Burt Lancaster played Winchell in Ernest Lehman's now classic *Sweet Smell of Success*. Lehman and I had once been Broadway press agents. We also had once had to play the unctuous toadies to Winchell. We hated ourselves for it. Lehman got his own back, though, and Winchell tried desperately to destroy him and failed—though he did drive Lehman to Tahiti for several months to escape.

And now here he was on a dais and there was Marilyn Monroe.

I looked at her in the flesh. I gawked and I gaped. I had seen many great women stars in the flesh, but she was different. On my first trip to Hollywood, a friend had taken me on the set of a Rita Hayworth movie and I had shaken hands with the raven-tressed Hayworth. On this same trip I had met Marlene Dietrich, Barbara Stanwyck, and Claire Trevor. I knew well the greatest stage actresses of my time.

Marilyn Monroe was different.

A silver blonde with a face heavily cosmeticized. Wearing a skin-tight green sequined gown with a thrilling *décolletage*. A strange smile on her mouth.

And Charles Brackett talked about her while we ate our shrimp cocktails, our avocado salads, our prime steaks, our sherberts. Then there were praises for Winchell. Zanuck spoke. Marilyn spoke. Winchell acknowledged the tributes.

Afterwards, I went over to Walter and we talked about Broadway and the Stork Club. I was one of those who was admitted to the Stork Club, an elegant watering hole on East 53rd Street that is now Paley Park. There was a time when only a few of the cognoscenti could gain admittance. And to be allowed to go into the hallowed Cub Room of the Stork—and to sit at Table 50, Winchell's favorite table—ah, that was indeed an accolade.

I have sat at Table 50.

How many of you reading this remember the name of Walter Winchell? How many of you have ever heard of Sherman Billingsley? He was the owner of the Stork. He was the *arbiter elegantarium* of New York café society.

That autumn night in 1952 in Mid-Wilshire Los Angeles, Marilyn Monroe posed for a photograph between me and Winchell. I would give a lot to have that print. I have lost it.

After the flash exploded, I looked into her eyes. She looked into my eyes. A contact was made. I shivered.

Under the make-up mask, I saw a soul in hell.

A voice in my mind said, "You must write a book about this woman."

Now, remember, this is not 1990. Marilyn Monroe was just another one of a score of beautiful "starlets."

As for me, I had never written a book-length biography of an actress. You didn't see many books published about stars of the stage or screen in the 1950s. Nobody wanted to read about their lives. Nobody wanted to read their confessions. I had published four books with E.P. Dutton and Random House: two novels and two collections of my profiles and essays about show business celebrities. *No People Like Show People,* which contained a long and realistic portrait of Tallulah Bankhead, was a best-seller. I was now with Harcourt, Brace . . .

I had told my editor, Julian Muller, that I wanted to write a biography of Alfred Lunt and Lynn Fontanne. He said the house was interested. He said I should write a chapter by chapter outline. I said I would write an outline and a sample chapter.

That was before my fateful encounter with Marilyn Monroe and before I went to 20th Century-Fox and saw a screening of *Niagara.* Marilyn Monroe illuminated the screen. Marilyn Monroe possessed the screen. Marilyn Monroe radiated like a burning star, a literal *étoile.* Henry Hathaway was at the screening and told me about her need for retakes. Joe Cotten was there. I had known him from his Mercury Theatre days with Orson Welles in New York. I was a friend of Orson Welles's. Cotten said she did not wear lingerie. There was no brassière or slip under her dress. In the opening shots of the film when she awakens naked under the sheets in the motel room, she was actually naked. (Monroemaniacs now make sacred tours of Niagara Falls and look for the motel in which the scenes were shot. They were shot on location and in an actual motel. The motel has since been levelled to make way for a shopping center. But "The Maid of the Mist" boat still sails.)

Cotten said something that made a profound impression on me. He said there were certain women who, even when clothed, emitted an aura of nudity. He said that this was the secret of Marilyn Monroe's movie magnetism.

And he was right. I now believe that there are certain women who haunt us because they project The Implicit Nude. From Theda Bara on—I think of Gloria Swanson and Clara Bow and Louise Brooks, of Claudette Colbert and Jean Harlow, Barbara Stanwyck, Rita Hayworth, Ginger Rogers . . .

Marilyn Monroe. . . . Implicit Nudes.

Back in New York, I now told Julian Muller I planned to write a book about Marilyn Monroe.

"Who?"

"Marilyn Monroe."

"Why Marilyn Monroe?"

He looked puzzled. I could not explain why I had become obsessed by my vision of uncovering the secret life of Norma Jean Baker. But I had. It was out of my control. Harcourt, Brace passed on the project. They wanted Lunt and Fontanne. My agent, Helen Straus, head of the William Morris literary department, told me to write another book. Nobody wanted Marilyn Monroe. She tried. She tried hard. She was a good salesperson. Lisel Eisenheimer, who then ran the magazine sector of the literary department at William Morris, tried to peddle a story on Marilyn Monroe to the magazines for which I customarily wrote and to others. She failed. I made a pitch directly to Stuart Rose of *The Saturday Evening Post* (by this time some forty or fifty pieces of mine had appeared in it), to David Brown, editor of *Cosmopolitan,* and to De Witt Wallace, editor of the *Reader's Digest.* Of course, magazines, even those of general circulation, were already publishing personality pieces about movie stars, but not too often, and usually your subject had to be a long-established star: Humphrey Bogart, Robert Taylor, Garbo, Katharine Hepburn.

And, keep in mind, even though we are now moving beyond 1952, Marilyn Monroe had still not started to make her way in such glitzy films as *Gentlemen Prefer Blondes* and *How to Marry a Millionaire.* Her great years of fame and artistic distinction had still to come, and who could have foreseen them back in 1952?

I remember David Brown (who was ultimately to marry Helen Gurley and who became an executive at 20th himself and a movie producer) taking me to lunch and gently urging me to stop pestering editors with Marilyn Monroe. He assumed I was having an affair with her. As did many persons. I got used to the leer, the shrugging shoulders, the changing of the subject.

By now, in my spare time, I was phoning people in Hollywood or talking to them when I was out there and finding out more and more about the elusive Norma Jean Baker.

A dossier on Monroe was growing. I worked in the *grenier* of an old three-story Victorian house on Elm Place in Hastings-on-Hudson, New York. In Hollywood, my "dilatory domicile" was always the Beverly Hills Hotel.

And then came the break.

Ernest V. Heyn, newly appointed editor of *The American Weekly,* a Sunday newspaper supplement in competition with *Parade* and *This Week,* decided he wanted to buy my byline. Lisel (she's now managing editor of *McCall's*) arranged a meeting at his office. He said they would meet my best price and also that I could choose my subjects.

"Who do you want to write about?"

"Marilyn Monroe."

He didn't flinch. He didn't leer. He didn't shrug.

"How many installments could you give us?"

"How much?"

Liesel shook her head. Clients weren't supposed to discuss such tawdry matters as money but I didn't care. I was desperate to get the seed money I needed to really give me time in Los Angeles to do my biographical excavations.

He said they paid $1,500. I said I was getting $2,500. At the time, I was one of the highest-paid magazine writers.

He said *American Weekly* would pay $1,500 an article and they would take five articles. In addition, he would give me $2,500 for expenses. He drew up a contract. I signed it.

Within a few weeks I had cleaned up all the unfinished work, and I, my wife, and our two children (aged two and eight) were taking the nine-hour coast-to-coast flight. We settled down at the Del Capri Motel on Wilshire in the Westwood area for a stay of six weeks.

By now Marilyn Monroe was on suspension from 20th Century. By now she was one of the most famous women in the United States.

Every morning I left the Del Capri in our rented Oldsmobile. I went south on Westwood Boulevard, swung into Pico, and pulled into 20th Century-Fox. It was like walking inside a medieval walled city. The kingdom of 20th Century-Fox, like the kingdoms of MGM and Universal, covered an immense terrain of a thousand acres—all that is now Century City, all those high apartment buildings and office towers, hotels, theaters, did not exist in 1955 and 1956, because this was the country of the great studio and the reigning monarch was Zanuck. In the course of the weeks that followed I was to interview many of the actors and actresses with whom Marilyn had worked—including Jane Russell and Betty Grable and Lauren Bacall, Cary Grant, Cameron Mitchell, Robert Ryan, even Clark Gable, who was working on a film with Jane Russell and who told me he wanted someday to work with Monroe. He was a gallant man and a kind person. I talked to Zanuck himself (whom I had first met in 1952 when I was researching a profile of George Jessel for *The Saturday Evening Post*). I interviewed directors like Jean Negulesco and cinematographers like Leon Shamroy, who had shot her screen test. And I went to other lots, like RKO, which had not yet been taken over by Desilu Productions (the company owned by Lucille Ball and Desi Arnaz). I talked to persons who had known Marilyn when she was a little child, who had known her mother. I went to the Los Angeles orphanage. I stood in the very room in which Norma Jean Baker had once slept and I looked out of the window she had looked out of and saw the RKO water tower. I went to the Studio Club, where she had lived for a year. And I had a long afternoon with photographer Tom Kelley.

And then, in New York, I spoke with Marilyn Monroe herself and with so many of the persons in her life—Lee Strasberg and Milton Greene and Arthur Miller. I even lunched with Norman Mailer at the Algonquin. Mailer had written in one of his essays that she was the person in Hollywood whom he most wanted to meet. Who would have dreamed that years later he would publish a biography of Monroe and he would quote from the book I had written?

I first met Arthur Miller in 1937 in a narrow corridor outside a bank of elevators at 49 East 33rd Street, a small building occupied by the publishers Harper and Brothers. We were both courting ladies who worked in secretarial positions at Harper's. We were both waiting for our girlfriends. He was waiting for Mary. I was waiting for Charlotte. He was tall and thin and wore glasses and I was tall and thinner and wore glasses. Soon the ladies for whom we were waiting would emerge from an elevator after 5 P.M. Subsequently Arthur and I began speaking of what we were doing and what we hoped to accomplish. And years later, as a reporter covering the Broadway beat, I was to speak to him and to know his director, Kazan, and some of the actors who worked for him.

But who could have foreseen that he would fall in love with Marilyn Monroe and that their love would become an international sensation and that I would be in the throes of composing a biography of her? Even as I was writing the book, new events would be happening and I would have to change the pages, but finally it had to be finished, and when I finished it and became anxious to start working on the book about the Lunts, I did not know that *The Misfits* (which had not been completed and released when I wrote the original manuscript) would be her final film and Gable's final film.

And among those who shared their painful experiences of working with Marilyn Monroe was Billy Wilder. To have been able to meet and to know persons like Wilder and Charles Brackett, these experiences I feel have made all the anguish of trying to encapsulate a human life worth the endless drudgery and the frustrations of cancelled appointments and refusals of valuable sources to be interviewed.

And to have made contact with Marilyn Monroe was an experience charged with high tension. I have said she was different from all other movie stars I have known or heard about or read about—except Garbo. Let me tell you what I mean by "different." I mean this: that Monroe was an infinity of character and mystery that it was impossible for me, or anybody else, to explore because it was so vast. There is always more and more and more. And it is in her films. The camera captures it always—whether in still photographs or moving pictures. But it was so in a room. There was always more and more and more. You could never come to the end of her. I think it must sometimes have been painful for her to live with this infinity. It was why, I believe, she resorted to alcohol and sedating pills—though her menstrual agonies drove her to seek chemical relief.

And I collected the photographs, including the two Kelley nudes, *Golden Dreams* and *A New Wrinkle,* and collected the permissions and got John Baumgarth, the calendar publisher, to let me use the nudes, and then Julian Muller and Bill Jovanovich, the CEO of Harcourt (his name wasn't part of the corporate title then) approved the manuscript and approved the pictures—some about her life and others stills from her films. All the photographs with two exceptions.

The nudes! I mean—the Explicit Nudes. Because, as I now know, she was always the Implicit Nude. Was it a coincidence that, in 1953, as I was getting more involved with the biography of Marilyn Monroe that nobody wanted, a young man in Chicago quit his job in the advertising department of *Esquire* and started making a dummy for a new magazine? He would call the magazine *Playboy*. His first inside nude, what would become the Playmate of the Month, was Marilyn Monroe in *A New Wrinkle*. And that her photograph, partly clothed, was on the cover! She wasn't the playmate of the month because there was no month on the cover—Hugh Hefner didn't know when there would be a second issue! Once, on a visit to his mansion in Chicago, it was back in 1963, I talked with Hefner, who was attired in a robe and pyjamas while I was having a scotch-and-soda and he was imbibing Pepsi-Cola, about the mystery of Marilyn Monroe, and I asked him why he had selected Marilyn Monroe—a relatively unknown creature—out of the hundreds of nude subjects he had considered.

And he puffed on his pipe. And he shook his head in wonderment.

"I couldn't tell you," he said slowly. "I wish I knew what made me choose her. I just don't know."

And I told him I had the same feeling of mystery about my own motivations in writing the book about her that was published in 1960 —without the nudes, for Jovanovich believed that it would be indelicate for a serious publisher to print them. Well, that was thirty years ago!

Though *Marilyn Monroe* was published in many countries, including France, only the British edition (W.H. Allen) published the nudes.

For the first time in the U.S., this new edition contains the beautiful Tom Kelley portraits of Marilyn *desnuda*.

Besides the original illustrations, this edition has twelve new photographs of Marilyn. I am grateful to Greg Schreiner and Ray Van Goeye, two dedicated admirers of Monroe and collectors, for these hitherto unpublished stills and studio publicity shots—now so rare to find.

The French edition, published by Gallimard in 1961, had an "Epilogue" written at the request of Pierre Lazareff, the great French journalist and editor of *L'Air du Temps*, the series in which *Marilyn Monroe* appeared. After the American edition was in print, Miller and Monroe divorced. Lazareff asked me to write my thoughts about the divorce and her future.

This French chapter has been added to this edition. It is the first time it appears in English.

The last time I saw Marilyn Monroe was in the summer of 1962.
Like our first meeting it was fortuitous.

On Tuesday and Friday mornings I used to go to the Actors' Studio
to attend Lee Strasberg's informal seminars. A few journalists and
playwrights were invited to sit in as auditors. On this Friday morning
I was sitting in the last row, against the back wall. I was waiting for
the first scene to begin. Then there would be discussion by the group,
most of them actors and actresses, and finally commentary and analysis by Strasberg (and may I say, parenthetically, that Strasberg was
a teacher of noble visions and powerful clarity and he illuminated
whatever subject arose). I had a particular reason this Friday. Kevin
McCarthy, Anne Jackson, and Clifton James were doing a scene I had
written from a play I was writing entitled *The Enigma Variations*.
Nobody except Strasberg knew I had written it and nobody knew the
author was in the audience. *The Enigma Variations,* though often
optioned, was never produced; none of my other playscripts were ever
produced. And my only screen credit is for "original story" on a 1950
Paramount film, *Let's Dance,* starring Fred Astaire and Betty Hutton.

As I was nervously awaiting "my" scene, I felt a nudge. I looked
over to my left. Marilyn Monroe had come in and was sitting beside
me. She was grinning. Her eyes were laughing also. She was in jeans
and a blouse. Looking like the little girl she always carried around
inside her. An adolescent rather than a woman of thirty-two.

She said she hadn't read my book. She said her friends had read it.
Then she said well, she *had* read some pages—the "good" pages. She
suddenly said, "Well, thanks." She put her hand in mine and our
fingers interlaced. I felt very close to her, as if I had found the real
person who had been hiding inside the tight green gown that night in
1952 at the Ambassador Hotel.

So much had happened in those ten years.

The scene was played and the discussion ensued. Only actors could
participate. Marilyn Monroe did not speak. I did not ask her how she
liked the scene. I did not tell her I had written the words. I did not
feel good about it anyway. And I certainly wasn't about to have her
mentally compare me to some other writers she had known (and one
she had married). After all, she had spoken lines written by William
Inge, Terence Rattigan, Billy Wilder, I. A. L. Diamond, and Arthur
Miller.

11

We walked down 44th Street. She was looking for a cab. I suggested we head over to 43rd or 45th because on 44th we would pass Sardi's, with the usual paparazzi outside and the fans, and she might be bothered, but she said nobody ever recognized her unless she wanted them to recognize her.

She put on her kerchief. She put on dark glasses. And she, by some trick, perhaps it was a kind of acting in everyday life, assumed the mien and the stride of an adolescent girl, threw off the emanation of the glamour queen.

We walked down 44th and all the taxis were taken. We passed Sardi's. Nobody paid attention to her. Finally, past Seventh Avenue, a taxi stopped. I opened the door for her. She looked thin—she must have lost fifteen pounds or more. She had a certain wanness. I kissed her goodbye. I closed the door. The taxi went down 44th Street.

I saw the back of her head receding. She had taken off the kerchief. She did not turn around.

M.Z.
Hollywood, California
October 9, 1989

1 A Quiet Child

On a September day in 1938, Norma Jean Baker, twelve-year-old resident of a slum neighborhood in Los Angeles, went to school in a borrowed sweater a size too small for her. Her first class was in mathematics, and her effect on the class, especially on the boys in it, was devastating.

A few days later, Norma Jean began to experiment in beautifying her face. She had no money for cosmetics, so she walked to and from school—four miles a day—and hoarded bus fares until she had saved 50 cents. Then she bought a cylinder of lipstick and an eyebrow pencil—surely one of the best financial investments a girl ever made. She colored her lips a bright scarlet. Her eyebrows—which were scraggly and mouse-brown—she darkened into curving slashes above her deep gray eyes. "My arrival in school," she later wrote, "with painted lips and darkened brows, and still encased in the magic sweater, started everybody buzzing."

The tight white sweater revealed the possibilities to Norma Jean. She thought that she had a lever with which to move the world. She knew, even then, that the world she wanted to move was the world of the cinema.

She moved it. She achieved worldwide fame, wealth, and artistic success. She became beautiful. She became Marilyn Monroe.

Marilyn Monroe was born on June 1, 1926, in the maternity ward of Los Angeles General Hospital. The name on her birth certificate was Norma Jeane Mortenson, but the name she went by was Norma

Jean Baker. Her mother was Gladys Baker. Her father was Edward Mortenson. They were not married, at least not to each other.

At the time of Norma Jeane's birth, her mother was twenty-four, and resided at 5454 Wilshire Boulevard, in the western part of Los Angeles. Her father's occupation was given as baker, his age as twenty-nine, his address as "unknown."

We know little about Norma Jeane Mortenson's ancestors. They were poor people and their lives went unreported in the newspapers and are blurred in the memories of surviving friends. The fragments of available data compose a mosaic of misery, mental disorder, and violent death. On her mother's side, both grandparents were committed to mental institutions. An uncle killed himself. Her father died in a motorcycle accident. Here is what Marilyn herself once told me about her background:

"My father's occupation is listed as 'baker' on my birth certificate, but that isn't why they called me Norma Jean Baker. My mother was married when she was fifteen, in Mexico, and Baker was her first husband's name. My grandfather was a painter, housepainter, in Mexico City. He also at one time worked in the oil-fields. I never heard of any acting talent in the family. My grandmother was beautiful I have heard. My mother not as beautiful as her. My grandmother's maiden name was Hogan. She came from Ireland. I am part Irish, part Scotch, and part Norwegian to the best of my knowledge. My grandfather was born in Scotland. My mother always spoke with a little of a Scotch accent. My mother had two children with Baker. My half-brother is dead. I never see my half-sister. We have nothing in common. She is married to an airplane engineer. I am not sure where she lives. It's in Florida, Clearwater or St. Petersburg. I never saw my father or him me. My mother told me he was killed in an accident when I was little. When I was eight, she took me to her small furnished room once and she stood me on a chair and showed me a picture of a handsome man. It was in a gold frame, hanging on the wall. She said it was my father. He was wearing a slouch hat cocked on one side of his head. He had a little mustache and a smile. He looked kind of like Clark Gable—you know, strong and manly."

Those who knew Gladys Baker at the time she was living with Mortenson say they never met him and did not know of him. Through a curious chain of circumstances, I was able to find out a few facts about the handsome stranger. In 1956, a Danish picture magazine published a translation of an article I had written about Marilyn. A farmer of Seeland, Denmark, was a subscriber, and his wife, Malene Nielsen, read my article. ("Malene," by the way, is the Danish form of "Marilyn.") Malene Nielsen, now forty, has a slight physical resemblance to Marilyn Monroe. In my description of Edward Mortenson, Mrs. Nielsen recognized her father, and in this way the facts came to light and were documented in the Norwegian and Danish press.

Mortenson was born in Haugesund, Norway, in 1897 and apprenticed to a baker in his youth. He later opened his own bakeshop in Haugesund. It is still functioning. He married in 1917. He had three children, including Malene. Mortenson had a taste for fast motorcycles and fast women. He deserted his family in 1923 and came to the United States. He became an itinerant baker, working for a few hours in one city and then traveling on to another. He was also an itinerant lover, striking up romantic liaisons here and there. He wandered about on his motorcycle until late one afternoon in 1929, in Ohio. A report from the Salvation Army to the Mortenson family states:

"Our officer in Youngstown, Ohio, has called on the City Record office and learned that Edward Mortenson was killed on June 18, 1929, at 5.10 P.M. He was driving along the road leading from Youngstown to Akron. When he tried to pass a car in front of him, he crashed into a Hudson sedan. He broke both his legs and fell to the ground unconscious and paralyzed. His cycle went to pieces. When he was brought to the hospital, he passed away. Dr. Vasck attended Mr. Mortenson. His motorcycle was beyond repair. He was buried in Mt. Hope Park, Youngstown. The deceased did not leave anything of value."

Gladys Baker was one of those women who repeatedly lose their hearts to men who run out on them. The Baker family emigrated to Los Angeles after World War I. Baker worked at gasoline stations; Mrs. Baker, who had become friendly with Grace McKee, a film librarian at Columbia Pictures, found work as a filing clerk and later as a technician with Consolidated Film Laboratories, which processes film. One day Mrs. Baker came home early because she was sick. Her children were in school. Her husband was in the bedroom making love to another woman. This is the sort of thing that creates marital ill will, and Mrs. Baker ordered the hussy out of the house. Mr. Baker resented this, insulted her, and left the house. That was the last she saw of him. Not long afterward, while she was at work, Baker spirited away her children. She put detectives on his trail and traced him to a Southern state. He had divorced her and remarried and was now a prosperous insurance broker. Gladys gave up, and Baker kept the children.

When Norma Jean Baker came into the world, her mother and her circle were a vital part of the motion-picture industry, part of the broad base on which the pyramid is balanced. At the apex are the great stars, the great directors, the all-powerful studio heads. Below them are the writers, the cinematographers, the featured players. And then there are some 20,000 persons who build the scenery, sew the costumes, put on the makeup and fix the coiffures, arrange the klieg lights, print the film, cut the film.

To the outsider Hollywood may be synonymous with Los Angeles. Once, movie making dominated the town. When Norma Jean was growing up, Los Angeles was chiefly a place where movies were made for the whole world and where old people came from Kansas and Iowa to live out their declining years in the land of perpetual sunshine and oranges. Today, Los Angeles is an industrial city with aircraft plants and munitions factories, oil wells and oil refineries, garment factories, automotive plants—and symbolically as well as geographically Hollywood is only a small part of it. To the Angeleno, Hollywood denotes a specific area bounded by Beverly Hills on the west, the Freeway on the north, Wilshire Boulevard on the south, and Vermont Avenue on the east. Within this enclave are the studios of Paramount, RKO, Columbia, the Sam Goldwyn studio, Poverty Row, where the "quickie" B pictures were ground out, Central Casting, Western Costume, Consolidated Films, NBC, and CBS. Some studios are located outside of Hollywood—M-G-M in Culver City, Universal in Universal City, Warner Brothers in Burbank.

Before 1946, however, almost everyone who worked in the movie industry lived in Hollywood. The poorer ones lived on narrow palm-lined streets in cracked stucco bungalows set on 25- by 50-foot plots of land. The lives of these people revolved entirely around motion pictures, and the dream of every technician was to have a child who would grow up into another John Gilbert or Mary Pickford.

This dream was ground into Norma Jean by her mother and her

mother's friends. The idea of becoming a star was part of her daily diet, along with her milk and cereal. Her ambitions therefore arose naturally out of her environment.

By the time Norma Jean was born, Gladys Baker had become a negative cutter, first at Columbia Pictures and later at RKO-Radio Pictures. Earl Theisen, who was a crew foreman at Consolidated Films 35 years ago, remembers that when Norma Jean was born a collection was taken up to pay the doctor and to tide Mrs. Baker over until she could return to work. Reginald Carroll, now a vice-president at Consolidated, remembers Gladys Baker as a small, finely made woman, of high spirits, with a trim figure, reddish-blonde hair, twinkling green eyes. He also recalls that Mrs. Baker was proud of her daughter. When Norma Jean was old enough to walk, her mother brought her to the laboratory, and the child sat quietly while her mother worked. Carroll remembers Norma Jean as an unusual child because she was able to sit for long periods without complaining.

The most direct link I found with Mrs. Baker was Mrs. Leila Fields, a negative cutter at RKO. She had known both Grace McKee and Gladys Baker. When I talked to her, Mrs. Fields, then sixty, was working in a small one-story low-roofed cottage on the RKO lot. This was a cutting room. The walls were of thick cement. Mrs. Fields was perched on a high stool before a table. She was running strips of film from one spool onto another spool. As we talked, she wound and unwound the film. Sometimes she snipped away several frames of film and glued them to other slices of film. She wore white cotton gloves so the perspiration wouldn't spoil the negatives. The room was uncomfortably warm. There were no windows or air conditioning. A large red metal sign bore the words "NO SMOKING."

There were three other high tables and three other stools, but nobody else was in the room. Mrs. Fields was the only negative cutter left at RKO, for this was 1956 and the movie industry was staggering from the competition of television. Production had been curtailed at RKO—soon afterward the whole studio was sold to Desilu Productions Inc., which films programs for television.

"Gladys Baker worked here," Mrs. Fields said. "That's where she used to sit, right there, alongside of me. Sure, in this room, this very room."

The moment filled with a sense of the past. Like a flashback, the scene between myself and Mrs. Fields dissolved to the scenes of 1928. In the small stuffy room filled with the odors of wet film and glue, four negative cutters sat on the high stools, gossiping as they snipped film. In one corner sat a little girl watching it all, silently.

"What did Gladys look like?" I asked.

"She was a beautiful woman, one of the most beautiful women it was ever my privilege to know. She had a good heart and was a good friend and was always happy until she got this sickness. Before that, she was lively and always had a joke to make you laugh. Marilyn is the spitting image of her mother, except the hair and eyes. Her mother's eyes were green. You don't see eyes like hers often. Marilyn's are more blue."

"More gray," I said.

"My daughter went to Van Nuys High the same time with Marilyn."

"You ever meet Edward Mortenson?" I asked.

"No," she said. "No. I didn't. I don't know anything about him. Don't light that cigarette. It's against the rules. I must tell you about Grace McKee. Grace was a wonderful person. They broke the mold when they made Grace. She was one in a million. She was Gladys's best friend, and she loved and adored Norma Jean. If it weren't for Grace, there wouldn't be a Marilyn Monroe today. Grace raved about Norma Jean like she was her own. Grace said Norma Jean was going to be a movie star. She had this feeling about her. A conviction. I think Grace McKee, she's gone now, God rest her soul, should have more credit for what she did. Marilyn hardly ever mentions her. Grace paid for Norma Jean to have singing and dancing lessons when she was a child. She did. It's a fact. She even paid for her to have piano lessons. Nobody knows about that. It's a fact."

During the years of the Great Depression, when Grace McKee was laid off at Columbia and Mrs. Baker was cracking up, Miss McKee repeated the ritual formula: "Don't worry, Norma Jean. You're going to be a beautiful girl when you get big. You're going to be an important woman. You're going to be a movie star. Oh, I feel it in my bones."

On Sundays, Grace or Gladys took the child on walking tours to ogle the homes of the famous stars in the Hollywood hills. At *premières* at Grauman's Chinese, they were in the throng gaping at the kings and queens of movieland. They stood outside the Ambassador Hotel or the old Hollywood Hotel to watch. Once, they had actually seen Mary Pickford in the flesh, and Mrs. Baker recounted the saga of America's Sweetheart as another mother might tell her child of Snow White or the Sleeping Beauty. The two ladies delighted in the stories of all the great stars. They read the fan magazines devoutly and gushed over Hollywood mythology as if they had been teen-age girls living far away. The fact that they were themselves part of the Hollywood machinery didn't disillusion them. On the contrary. They believed even more strongly in the myth. They saw with their own eyes how one could become decked with furs and diamonds. Mrs. Baker was obsessed with the Pickford legend and put up her daughter's hair in curls and tried to make her mince and smile like Mary.

One of Mrs. Baker's favorite activities was taking Norma Jean to the forecourt of Grauman's Chinese Theatre. Here, hollowed in plaster, were the footprints of the great ones. It was an expedition that Marilyn would take by herself many a time before her own feet stamped their imprint, in July, 1953. During the years of her struggle in pictures, she would wander down Hollywood Boulevard and drift idly among the footprints, trying, as everyone did, to see whose prints fitted her own feet. The ones that fitted her were Rudolph Valentino's. When she began reading, her mother made her lisp out the fairy tales in the motion-picture fan magazines. Says Marilyn: "I refuse to let articles appear in movie magazines signed 'By Marilyn Monroe.' I might never see the article and it might be okayed by somebody in the studio. This is wrong, because when I was a little girl I read signed stories in fan magazines and I believed every word of them. Then I tried to model my life after the lives of the stars I read about. If I'm going to have that kind of influence, I want to be sure it's because of something I've actually said or written."

She dreamed of becoming "so beautiful that people would turn to look at me as I passed." When she was six, she imagined herself going naked into the world. This fantasy often possessed her in church. As the organ thundered out hymns, she quivered with a desire to throw off her clothes and stand naked "for God and everyone else to see." "My impulses to appear naked had no shame or sense of sin in them. I think I wanted people to see me naked because I was ashamed of the clothes I wore. Naked, I was like other girls and not someone in an orphan's uniform."

Dr. Freud, in *The Interpretation of Dreams*, states that the nakedness dream is the most universal one. But Freud adds that the dreamer who dreams of striding about naked in public feels embarrassment. The "embarrassment dream of nakedness," he says, is often a way of expressing one's fear of being unmasked. For Norma Jean it was not. She had no fear of "exposure," no qualms about it at all. On the contrary, the dream of being seen naked by a mass of spectators gave her pleasure. To be beautiful, and to be naked and beautiful, made her feel triumphant, made her feel loved. "I didn't go into the movies to make money," she once wrote. "I wanted to become famous so that everyone would like me and I'd be surrounded by love and affection."

As soon as Gladys told Mortenson that she was pregnant, sometime in 1925, the baker climbed on his motorcycle and rode away. After the infant was born, Gladys fell into spells of moodiness. She became withdrawn, silent, depressed, suspicious, and given to muttering to herself. She neglected Norma Jean. She would forget to feed the baby or change her clothes. Finally, Grace McKee moved in to take care of the child. Then one night, Gladys accused Grace of trying to poison her. She seized a kitchen knife and stabbed Grace. The police were called, and Gladys was taken to the hospital. She was confined for several months and then released when she seemed to have recovered from her paranoia.

Since Grace McKee was unable to care for Norma Jean during the day, she had the child made a legal ward of Los Angeles County. At the age of five, Norma Jean was placed in a foster home. The foster parents received $20 monthly. It still hurts her that no family wanted to adopt her permanently. "I've often wondered about this," she wrote. "I guess I wanted love more than anything else in the world at that time."

The reason she was not adopted had nothing to do with love. As a foster child, she was money in the bank. As an adopted child, she would be another mouth to feed. Most of the families who took her in lived on the poverty-stricken fringes of society. California had been hit as hard as any other state by the economic collapse in 1930. It had breadlines and unemployment riots and families on relief. It also endured the migration of hundreds of thousands of persons from other states who preferred to starve in the sunshine of southern California.

Norma Jean's first foster home was on a farm in Hawthorne County, about 15 miles south of Hollywood. Her foster mother made her scrub floors and wash dishes. The farmer and his wife were religious fanatics, who made her memorize the following pledge: "I promise, God helping me, not to buy, drink or sell, or give alcoholic liquor while I live; from all tobaccos I'll abstain and never take God's name in vain."

Since neither alcohol, nicotine, nor blasphemy tempted her, Norma Jean was faithful to her vows. The next family with whom she boarded was even more solicitous about her salvation. She was taught long prayers to intone upon awakening and before going to sleep. Should she die during the night, which they told her was possible, it would be better if she did not find herself in hell with the damned. "I always felt insecure," Marilyn says with admirable understatement.

Another foster family was equally concerned about the problem of sin and damnation. They made her attend church, one of the evangelical denominations, on Wednesday and three times on Sunday—Bible class, morning service, and evening service. During revivals, the family and Norma Jean went to meetings every night for three weeks. When she attempted to dance or sing "as little girls will, even sad little girls, they'd tell me that this was a sin, too." When she asked for ten cents to go to the Saturday matinee, she was given a warning instead: "What if the world came to an end this afternoon and you were sitting in a movie? Do you know what would happen to you? You'd burn, right along with all the bad people."

Her next foster parents, with whom she lived during 1932, were a letter carrier and his wife. Norma Jean convinced herself that these were her true parents. She used to call them "Mama" and "Daddy," but one day, the woman said, "Stop calling me Mama. I'm not your Mama. I'm not related to you at all. You just board out here." In September of that year, Norma Jean entered public school. She remembers standing in the line outside the Vine Street school. All the children, except herself, were with a parent. A teacher asked, "Where's your family?"

"I don't know."

"Is your mother dead?"

"Yes."

"Your father, too?"

"I think so."

A girl in the line overheard the conversation, and said to her mother, "Oh, look, Mummy, that girl's an orphan." Norma Jean leaned against a wall and wept.

Then one day, the postman's wife suddenly told her: "A woman is coming to see you tomorrow. She's your real mama. You can call her Mama if you want to."

Her real mother did visit her intermittently. Marilyn recalls her as "a pretty woman who never smiled. I'd seen her often before, but until this time I hadn't known who she was. That time when I said, 'Hello, Mama,' she stared at me. She had never kissed me or held me in her arms or hardly spoken to me. I didn't know anything about her then."

In one foster home, Norma Jean was accused of stealing a pearl necklace. She wrote, "I have never forgotten the shame, humiliation, and the deep, deep hurt. They left a scar that has remained." Once, Grace McKee came to see her and left her a birthday card and a 50-cent piece. The money was taken away. "You dirtied your clothes today" was the excuse.

Then she lived for a time with a family of females—great-grandmother, grandmother, mother, and three daughters. The great-grandmother hated the charity girl. When one of the daughters tore her skirt, the great-grandmother shrilled, "Norma Jean tore it," and Norma Jean went without supper. She was sometimes beaten with a hairbrush. Saturday night was bath night. Hot water costs money, and so the tub was filled only once for the whole group. First the great-grandmother took her bath. Then, in descending order of ages, the other five took their baths in the same water. Finally, Norma Jean was forced to go into the filthy water.

Marilyn once told me of an experience that has haunted her. "While I was in the second grade, the public school chose me to appear in the Easter sunrise service at Hollywood Bowl. They gave all of us a black robe. Under the black robe, we wore white tunics. The service, which is an impressive ceremony, begins before dawn. All we children were arranged in the form of a cross. Just when the sun rose we were given a signal to throw off the black robes and that changed the cross from black to white. I got so interested watching the sky, I didn't pay attention and didn't see the signal. I was the only child who forgot to throw off her black robe. I was the only black mark on a white cross."

A social-service worker came every two weeks to see how things were going. Marilyn wrote, "She never asked me any questions. She would pick up my feet and look at the soles of my shoes. If my shoes weren't worn through I was reported as doing well."

There were a few happy interludes. For instance, there was the family that wanted to get her out of the house on Saturday. She was given a quarter, a bag of Swiss-cheese sandwiches, and a Thermos bottle and told to stay in the movies until the theater closed at midnight.

She loved going to the movies. She became Bette Davis, Jean Harlow, Joan Crawford, Jean Arthur, or whatever movie heroine she was watching. Ginger Rogers was one of her favorites.

Another foster family was wealthy, and treated her kindly. They lived in a villa on Highland Avenue. They had a collection of rare tropical birds, and Norma Jean was allowed to feed the birds and talk to them. Tropical birds are excellent conversationalists, even if their vocabulary is limited. Marilyn says that these birds were much nicer to talk to than most of the human beings she had known up to that time.

The next foster family was an English couple who played character roles in movies. They were a happy-go-lucky pair, addicted to smoking, dancing, gambling, and drinking. Norma Jean enjoyed being with them, since she was never made to feel guilty about being alive, but she also suspected them of being sinners, and at night, in her bed, she prayed hard for them. They had once been vaudeville artists and they still retained some skill in such arts as knife throwing and juggling. They taught Norma Jean to throw knives, juggle oranges, and dance the hula.

Norma Jean, who was now eight, prepared dinner for the couple and washed the dishes. After that they all played rummy. The couple attempted to polish her diction. During the year she lived with them, she copied their intonations, and to this day there is a British overtone in Marilyn Monroe's diction.

In 1934, Gladys Baker was released from the hospital and returned to work as a motion-picture laboratory technician. She saved her money and, together with the English couple, bought a four-bedroom house in 1935. At an auction she secured a grand piano that had once belonged to Fredric March, and Norma Jean started taking piano lessons. Although this fact is known only to a handful of her closest friends, Marilyn can still play some of the lighter classics on the piano, "Für Elise," "The Spinning Wheel," "To a Wild Rose," and such pieces.

For a time, life flowed serenely. Then, one Saturday morning during breakfast, Gladys went into the kitchen for more coffee. Suddenly, she began laughing wildly, screaming and cursing, hurling dishes against the wall. The police came, and then an ambulance. The English couple put Norma Jean into another room so she wouldn't see what was happening. But she could hear. The front door opened, and loud voices rose in the corridor—among them, her mother's voice, protesting. Norma Jean opened the door a crack and peered out to see two men wrestling with her mother and finally overpowering her. Gladys Baker was committed to the Norwalk Hospital for Mental Diseases, where she remained until 1945.

Norma Jean's next foster home was a two-story frame house in the southeastern area of Hollywood. The landlady took in boarders as well as foster children. Norma Jean slept in a disused storage closet without windows at one end of the top floor. The star boarder was a solemn old man, a certified public accountant, who dressed in dark suits and had a gold watch in his vest pocket and a gold chain and an elk's tooth across his vest. He was the richest man in the house, so his opinions were always listened to with respect by the owner of the place and all the other boarders, and he was always called "mister." At dinner, he was the first to be served. He occupied the finest room in the place—a large front room upstairs with a private bath.

One evening, when Norma Jean had gone up to put some linens in the linen closet, the "mister" opened his door slightly and beckoned to her.

"Would you come in here for a moment?" he asked. She did. He closed the door and pushed the bolt. "Now we're alone," he said. He was smiling in a strange remote way. She had never seen him smile before, and she didn't understand it. He took off his coat and vest and hung them in the closet. Then he sat down in his club chair and told her to come and sit on his lap. She obediently did so. She was a pretty little girl, he said, and they were going to play a game, and if she would be a good little girl he would give her a present. He said the game began with a little kiss. He gave her a little kiss. She didn't cry out or resist. She had been trained to obey. When the game was over, the "mister" unlocked the door. Norma Jean was shaking and ran to her foster mother.

"I have to tell you what Mr. K. did," she stammered. "He—he—he—"

The woman interrupted Norma Jean. "Now you stop that, or I'll slap your face," she said. "I don't want to hear anything against Mr. K. He's a fine man."

"But he did something to me, he—he—"

The landlady struck her across her mouth. Norma Jean cried in bed that night and hoped she would die, although she knew that if she died she would go to hell because of what she had done. Mr. K. later gave her some money. She says she threw it away. She was obsessed by her guilt. She had committed the unpardonable sin.

Ever since that incident, dusk and darkness have terrified Marilyn. Her sleep is uneasy. The terrors of her childhood return in twisted shapes, and therefore, as long as possible, she resists sleep by reading or talking, and when it does come she often starts out of it, aware of muffled screams in her throat. She does not use a pillow; she has an obsession about being suffocated by a pillow in her sleep.

2 How Many Dishes Did She Wash in the Orphanage?

Three months after Norma Jean's ninth birthday, on September 9, 1935, Grace McKee, with whom the child had been living recently and who had been made her legal guardian, packed up Norma's clothes. Miss McKee had married a Mr. Goddard, known as Doc Goddard in his circle. He was not a medical doctor, but an inventor, and he was called "doc" as a compliment to his brains. Doc Goddard had two children by a previous marriage.

At nine, Norma Jean was tall for her age and skinny. Her face was elongated, her hair a mass of light-brown curls. She rarely smiled. She was a quiet child. She spoke only when she was spoken to and then in stammering syllables. She had begun to stammer the night she was raped. Stammering, like baldness, is an affliction that rarely troubles women. Marilyn Monroe is one of the rare women who stutter, though she seldom does it when she is speaking lines she has rehearsed.

When she saw "Aunt Grace" putting underwear, a dress, a coat, shoes, and stockings into a box, she knew she was going away again. She knew this had been too good to last. She had tried to make Aunt Grace's new husband and her stepsisters like her. She had been dutiful and run their errands and obeyed them, but she was in the way. Aunt Grace didn't tell her where they were going. But it was not a pleasure trip, because Aunt Grace had been crying all morning.

Grace drove down to Rossmore Avenue in Hollywood, turned up Melrose, and finally came to El Centro Avenue. El Centro is only six blocks long. It is in the centre of Hollywood—the RKO Studios were a block away, and Paramount's empire on Marathon Street only a 15-minute walk. She stopped the car at 815 N. El Centro.

"This is where you will live," Mrs. Goddard said. "I hope you'll be happy here. I'll come and see you as often as I can. They'll take good care of you here—better than I can at home, but I expect soon we'll get a bigger house and then you will come and live with me again."

"Yes, Aunt G-Grace," Marilyn said.

815 N. El Centro is a handsome three-story building of old red brick, set back on a sweeping lawn. In design it is New England Colonial, not Los Angeles grotesque, and it resembles an elegant eighteenth-century mansion. A flagpole flying the American flag is the only indication that it is a public building.

Mrs. Goddard held Norma Jean's hand as they walked up to the front door and rang the bell. As they waited, the child read the words on a wooden plaque: LOS ANGELES ORPHANS HOME. Orphan! But she was no orphan. She had a mother. Her mother was sick, but she had a mother. Somebody was making a mistake.

Her body stiffened. Mrs. Dewey, superintendent of the orphanage, which is a privately endowed institution operated by the Los Angeles Orphans Home Society since 1886, opened the door.

"I won't go in there," Norma Jean cried out. "I'm not an orphan. I'm not. My mother isn't dead, is she, Aunt Grace? She's not dead."

She was forcibly carried into the orphanage. Then she was taken upstairs and shown to her quarters in the dormitory. Mrs. Goddard gave the facts about Norma Jean to a case worker. Mrs. Ingraham, the present superintendent, told me that Marilyn's case history is the most tragic she has ever read in the course of her experience.

Norma Jean lived in the orphanage for two years, until June 26, 1937. There were 57 other children there. Twenty-four were girls, ranging in age from six to fourteen. Norma Jean lived in a room in the "girls' cottage" in the south wing of the orphanage, a high-ceilinged room with enormous windows letting in air and sunlight. There were 12 beds in the room. Each girl was assigned her own small chiffonier and had space to arrange her dolls, her stuffed animals, her picture books.

Under the east window of the bedroom were two beds, placed back to back. One of these was Norma Jean's. It faced the RKO sign on the water tower, with its flashing symbol of forked lightning that glowed at night.

Waiting until all the other girls were fast asleep, Norma Jean would lean her elbows on the sill and stare up at the velvet tropical sky and the huge orange-colored California moon and see the RKO sign and dream of how it would be when she was an actress. She kept her dreams to herself. She once told me: "I just gave up talking for years. I remember in public school I used to be afraid to open my mouth. I was always in fear the teacher would call on me to give an answer and I'd stutter. Or if I got the answer out it would be stupid and wrong. I decided it was safer to keep my mouth shut. I'm still that way with strangers. That's why I don't like to go to large gatherings, cocktail parties, receptions, things like that. If I have to, I'll do it, but I've never been any good at talking."

The orphanage records on Norma Jean show that she was a docile child. Among the items in her dossier are these, culled from various months:

"Norma Jean's behaviour is normal." . . . "She is bright and sun-shiny." . . . "The school reports on her are good." . . . "She is quiet." . . . "She sleeps well and eats well." . . . "She is well-be-haved." . . . "Her grades are good." . . . "She participates in all activities willingly." . . . "She is co-operative."

Life at the Los Angeles Orphans Home, as it must in any institution, followed an unvarying pattern of group monotony. In her rebellion against punctuality and conformity, Marilyn Monroe is perhaps compensating for those years. The children were awakened at six-thirty in the morning by a clanging gong. They made their beds. Then they were herded together and marched to the refectory downstairs. The refectory was large, its walls pleasantly decorated in robin's-egg blue. Both the dining room and the kitchen were spotlessly clean. The children sat in fours at small tables. The food was comparable in quality to that in a first-rate hospital; nevertheless Marilyn has always tried to give the impression that the children were forced to eat nauseating meals, the kind that start riots in Warner Brothers' prison movies.

After some meals, the older children, including Norma Jean, were assigned to help wash dishes. She now says that she had to wash 100 plates, 100 cups, 100 knives, forks and spoons, three times a day, seven days a week. She says she was made to scrub toilets and clean bathtubs. She has given out conflicting stories of this phase of her life. Her official studio biography says she received ten cents a *month* for working in the kitchen. To one interviewer she said: "I never saw the money. It was put in a Christmas fund. It was customary for all the little girls to take their savings and on Christmas Eve buy presents for each other at the corner drugstore. Practical presents like notebooks and pencils."

She told another writer she received five cents a week for working in the kitchen—that is 20 cents a month—and ten cents a month extra for working in the pantry. "And out of these big sums," she added, "a penny every Sunday had to go into the church collection. I never could figure out why they took a penny from an orphan like that."

Interviewed, however, by a *Time* researcher in 1956, she recalculated her salary and reduced it to five cents a *month*. Out of this monthly nickel, a penny a week went for the collection plate, leaving a penny a month for spending money. Now, forgetting that in a previous version of her remembrances she had never seen a penny of the money, she said that she did have one penny and bought a hair ribbon every month. How the notebooks and pencils figured in this budget she did not explain. There is no doubt that she feels keenly that she was mistreated, yet Clarice Evans, who some years later shared a room with Marilyn Monroe, distinctly remembers Marilyn's telling her that one of the most "thrilling" experiences of her childhood was when she got her first job for "real money"—helping to set tables and wash dishes at the orphanage!

Which is true? For Marilyn, both. All actresses love to dramatize themselves, throw themselves into a role, and play it convincingly. They are never lying. They cannot contradict themselves, really, for they always believe what they are saying at the moment.

There were sports and games at the orphanage which Marilyn never mentions. Behind the building were five acres of land on which the children played every afternoon. There were swings, see-saws, exercise bars, sandboxes, and a swimming pool. Inside there was a large playroom with radio, phonograph, toys, and games. There was an auditorium and a stage. The children acted in plays and musical shows. There is no record that Norma Jean Baker appeared in any of them. She kept secret her talents at juggling, knife throwing, and hula dancing.

About four or five months after she moved into the orphanage, she fell into a depressed mood. It came on during a rainy day. Rain always made her think of her father and set up a desire to wander. On the way back from school, she slipped away from the line and fled. She didn't know where she was running to and wandered aimlessly in the slashing rainstorm. A policeman found her and took her to a police station. She was brought back to Mrs. Dewey's office. She was changed into dry clothes. She expected to be beaten. Instead, Mrs. Dewey took her in her arms and told her she was pretty. Then she powdered Norma Jean's nose and chin with a powder puff.

In 1950, Marilyn told the story of the powder puff to Sonia Wolfson, a publicity woman at 20th Century-Fox and then confided, "This was the first time in my life I felt loved—no one had ever noticed my face or hair or me before." Miss Wolfson made a written notation the day Marilyn told her the story.

On Christmas day, the children were taken to a party at the RKO Studios, where they were shown a screening of *Snow White and the Seven Dwarfs*. Afterward they were fed ice cream, cake, and fruit punch by various actors and actresses who needed a little "humanitarian-type" publicity. Then the children gathered around a huge Christmas tree, the photographers snapped pictures, and the stars, showing their most advantageous profiles, distributed presents to the children. Norma Jean got a necklace of imitation pearls.

I once asked Mrs. Ingraham, "Why did the orphanage make Marilyn wash dishes and pay her so little and then keep the money or make the children put it in the collection plate?"

Mrs. Ingraham sighed. "Well," she said, "I really don't know why Miss Monroe tells these terrible stories about us. And people print them, whatever she says. We don't *have* to give the children any work assignments. We have a staff of twenty-one here, including a housemother for every ten children. We have a staff in the kitchen fully capable of attending to the dishes. But we do give the children small jobs and pay them for it. We do this deliberately to give the child a feeling of being useful, of her own importance, and to give her money to spend as she wants to spend it. Now this story of Marilyn's that we made her wash dishes three times a day is just plain silly. It would take a child four hours to wash that many dishes. How would Marilyn have had time to go to school and do homework and be in bed by nine, which is lights-out time, if she was washing that many dishes three times a day?"

"How many dishes did she wash?"

"Oh she never washed any dishes and she never scrubbed toilets. The most she did was to help dry the dishes an hour a week, one hour. That's all. She had to make her own bed and keep her section of the girls' cottage tidied up, is all."

"How much did you pay her?"

"It wasn't really payment. It would be much easier for us just to give the children a dime a week and let it go at that, because it actually makes it harder for us in the kitchen when we have them helping out. They get in the way. But it's our theory that giving the child five cents a week, which was what Marilyn received, is good for a child's morale. She feels she has a place in the world. No institution can ever take the place of a family or a good foster home. We know that. We know the children here do suffer from feelings of rejection. The idea of having them do little tasks and giving them money is to make them feel proud of themselves. We do it even now."

Like organized labor, the inmates of the Los Angeles Orphans Home have been given a cost-of-living increase in their take-home pay. They now receive ten cents a week.

Just as she invariably speaks with hatred of the orphanage, so Marilyn Monroe rarely speaks with love of Grace McKee Goddard, and seldom mentions her at all. Yet, each Saturday, Mrs. Goddard came to see her and brought her presents of candy and toys. It seems strange that Marilyn would tell Miss Wolfson that Mrs. Dewey was the first person to give her a sign of love. Aunt Grace had loved her dearly—since her birth; there were moments of love from her mother; there were moments of love from the English actor and actress.

The last entry in the file is dated October 4, 1947, ten years after Marilyn left the orphanage. Norma Jean Baker had recently become twenty-one and was no longer a county ward, but Mrs. Dewey still cared enough about her to write Mrs. Goddard a letter asking how she was. Only two sentences are recorded from Mrs. Goddard's reply: "Norma Jean Baker has great success in pictures and promises to be a star. She is a very beautiful woman and is now acting as Marilyn Monroe."

3 *In Loco Parentis*

When Norma Jean was eleven, in 1937, Aunt Grace kept her promise and liberated her from the orphanage. She came for her one afternoon, and they drove to an outlying neighborhood in the Sawtelle district, a part of Los Angeles that lies between Santa Monica and Culver City. In those days, before the emergence of low-cost ranch homes and general prosperity, it was a slum, with dilapidated one-bedroom hovels and unpaved streets that became swamps during the January rainstorms. Sawtelle was inhabited by poor people on relief. Norma Jean went to live in one of these decaying bungalows, with Miss E. Ana Lower, a spinster of sixty-two, and an aunt of Mrs. Goddard's. Norma Jean called her "Aunt Ana." She believes that Aunt Ana was the most important of the forces that molded her. Aunt Ana not only listened to Norma Jean's fantasies but also believed in her beauty and talent, and she was sure that Norma Jean could do what she wanted to do.

Aunt Ana did not believe in the reality of sickness, of disease, of evil, of failure, of death. She did believe in the infinite power of the mind to achieve anything it wished to achieve. Aunt Ana, in short, was a believer in the doctrines of Mary Baker Eddy. She earned her living as a Christian Science practitioner, treating the sick with prayer. "God is All and God is Love." Norma Jean, by now a narcissist and the heroine of complicated inner dramas of her own invention, took this to mean that God loved her and would surely help her to become a movie star, which she had been preparing to be from the time her mother and Grace McKee had given her the dream.

To anybody for whom the "hysterical" way of life has become the most practical method of surviving in a hostile environment, the tenets of Christian Science are, if not always efficient in curing disease, useful in other ways. The "hysteric" tends to think that external reality is what he makes it in his mind. Mrs. Eddy herself was a prime example of the "hysteric."

The "hysterical" component is the *sine qua non* of the acting personality. An actress can manage without sensitivity, without beauty, without a commanding voice—but she cannot communicate imaginary experiences to us without the "hysterical" gift. Since the word "hysteria" suggests a human being out of control, I want to make it clear that in using it in relation to Marilyn Monroe's character I am not implying that she is or ever was given to uncontrollable seizures. In fact, her self-control is evident even to those who know her slightly. What I am referring to is a quality of temperament that is essential, not only to actors, but to all creative persons who have to deal with the emotions of fictional characters. The "hysterical" gift is what enabled Tolstoy, a middle-aged man with a beard, to put himself in the place of the adolescent Natasha and feel the stirrings of first love. It is what makes an actress reach out her hand for a glass of water in such a way that we believe she is dying of thirst— when, in fact, she may have had several glasses of water before making her entrance.

I once asked Lee Strasberg, the leading theoretician of the acting art in our time, what he regarded as the essential ingredient of the acting personality. He said, "It is the ability to respond to imaginary stimuli with the same intensity as one does to real stimuli. It is rising to imaginary situations as if they are real. One feels them as real, they are real to the actor while he is acting them out."

Harry Stack Sullivan, a psychiatrist, illustrates the "hysterical" temperament with the following incident. When he was a schoolboy, he once poured red ink into water and told a girl it was wine. She drank some of it and promptly became drunk. He explained to her that it was just ink—not wine. She immediately became sick! Sullivan believes that the "hysterical" behavior pattern develops in the first two years of infancy and that it occurs "most frequently in self-absorbed people who have met insuperable difficulties in living. These folk live rather as if the world were a stage on which each performs, assisted by shadowy figures, for a shadowy audience, including one luminously real person, the actor." Of course, while all actors, to some degree or another, like all writers, are "hysterical," few hysterics in the clinical sense succeed in becoming professional actors or writers.

Marilyn Monroe has always spoken of Ana Lower with affection. She told me: "She changed my whole life. She was the first person in the world I ever really loved and she loved me. She was a wonderful human being. I once wrote a poem about her and I showed it to somebody once and they cried when I read it to them. It was called 'I Love Her.' It was written about how I felt when she died. She was the only one who loved me and understood me. She showed me the path to the higher things of life and she gave me more confidence in myself. She never hurt me, not once. She couldn't. She was all kindness and all love. She was good to me."

Ana Lower once gave Norma Jean a copy of Mrs. Eddy's *Science and Health, with Key to the Scriptures.* She knew she was going to die soon, and on the flyleaf she wrote, "Norma, dear, read this book. I do not leave you much except my love, but not even death can diminish that; nor will death ever take me far away from you."

In 1937, Norma Jean transferred to Emerson Junior High School on Selby Avenue in Westwood Village. Since it was north of the Santa Monica railroad tracks, it was on the "right side," socially speaking. Norma Jean lived on the "wrong side," and she was acutely conscious of belonging to an inferior class. Her entire wardrobe at the time was two orphanage navy-blue skirts and two middy blouses. In September, 1941, she entered Van Nuys High School, but she left it in February, 1942, failing to complete her sophomore year. She was a C student, poor in all subjects except English, and particularly weak in arithmetic. She liked reading romantic novels and writing poetry and prose. She once won a fountain pen for an essay on "Dog, Man's Best Friend." She became interested in Abraham Lincoln and read many books about him. She idolized him, and she once told me that she thought of Lincoln as her father. A photograph of Lincoln always hung over her bed. Arthur Miller, her third husband, has an extraordinary resemblance to photographs of Lincoln.

Curiously enough, despite her desire to be an actress, she made only a few random stabs at it during her school years. Usually girls who've gotten it into their heads that they are fated to be actresses become active in school plays. You can't keep them away from grease paint and rehearsals. But Marilyn's shyness deterred her. She recalls only two attempts. Both were at Emerson Junior High School. She played in something called *Petronella* and in a musical put on for Valentine's Day. She played a king in one and a prince in the other. She said to me: "It may seem weird to you, but I looked very boyish then. I shot up to my present height when I was ten. I was skinny. In the Valentine's Day play I played a prince who disguised himself as a beggar in order to win the princess. They never had enough boys to act the boy parts, so I got the boy parts. At Van Nuys I tried out for the Dramatic Society. I read for *Art and Mrs. Bottle* [a comedy by the English playwright Benn W. Levy], but I was not acceptable. I wanted to be in it because a boy I had a crush on, Warren Peek, was playing the lead."

Van Nuys High has an extensive schedule of drama, including courses in the history of the theatre and in acting technique. Although many stories in the fan magazines have described Marilyn as acting at Van Nuys, she did not appear in any productions there. Mrs. Esther Matthews, present secretary to the principal, Thomas Dyer, states, "We are proud to claim Jane Russell, but we do not claim Marilyn Monroe. She didn't learn anything about acting while she was at Van Nuys High."

It was during her first year with Aunt Ana Lower that Norma Jean reached puberty. It is necessary, at this point, to say something about the effects of this process on Marilyn, for they played, and continue to play, a decisive part in her emotional as well as her physical life. Simone de Beauvoir estimates that 85 per cent of all women experience distress during menstruation. But Marilyn has the misfortune to belong to that small group for whom the process is excruciatingly painful and long drawn out. Some of the tantrums of which her colleagues complain may be traced to this "curse," as many women call it.

One day I visited Marilyn's dressing room in the Star Building on the 20th Century-Fox lot. The Star Building is a two-story Alcazar of beige stucco and Moorish pillars. The suite she had occupied, dressing room M, is on the ground floor. It had been Betty Grable's during her reign as 20th's Queen of Sex. Marilyn inherited it when she began playing in *No Business Like Show Business* (1954).

The windows had not been opened for a long time; the rooms were stuffy and the blinds were drawn. I flicked a switch in the small reception room, a rococo den containing red-upholstered Queen Anne furniture, a mirrored fireplace, and a crystal chandelier. Beyond was the combined living room-bedroom. There were mirrors everywhere, on the walls, on the tables, on the dresser. One wall was all mirrors. Behind this mirrored wall was a deep closet, which I investigated. There wasn't much there—a pair of faded blue dungarees, some gray flannel slacks in a heap on the floor, a red silk blouse, a white Empress Eugenie tricorne with its saucy feather. On the hat shelf there were also a lot of little boxes, fourteen of them, with the Schwab Pharmacy label on each. The labels read:

"Take 1 or 2 tablets every three hours for pain."

"Ergotrate. Take 1 tablet every 4 hours when menstrual flow is heavy."

"Take 1 tablet for pain."

"Take 1 tablet 4 times a day for menstrual pain."

"Empirin with codeine for pain. Take 1 tablet when needed."

Mary Baker Eddy had maintained that "What is termed disease does not exist. . . . The fact that pain cannot exist where there is no mortal mind to feel it is a proof that this so-called mind makes its own pain—that is, its own belief in pain."

I once asked Marilyn whether she used Christian Science to alleviate pain.

She smiled thoughtfully. "Aunt Ana used to pray with me," she said. "But it seems I had such a strong belief of pain that she couldn't overcome it. I've read Mrs. Eddy and tried to put some of her ideas into my life, but it doesn't work for me. I believe more in Freud than in religious mysticism, and yet there's a mystical side in Freud, isn't there? I do not believe I could ever take the road of religion, and yet I believe in many things that can't be explained by science. I know that I feel stronger if the people around me on the set love me, care for me, and hold good thoughts for me. It creates an aura of love, and I believe I can give a better performance."

Gladys Rasmussen, one of her hairdressers, says that before she goes out to do a scene, Marilyn will say, "Please hold a good thought for me, Gladys." I asked Miss Rasmussen what sort of thought she holds and she replied, "My thought usually is, Dear God I pray everything will work out the way Marilyn wants it to work out."

Out of her experience of pain Marilyn came to equate love with pity. She believes that a man who doesn't feel sympathy for her pain cannot love her, and her own love for people is strongly linked with pity—more so than with lust or romantic idealization. Her concept of love finds an interesting and moving expression in the plays and novels of Graham Greene. For instance, in *The Heart of the Matter*, the central character, Major Scobie, has an affair with a woman because her great sufferings arouse his passion; and he returns to his wife because his wife's agony is greater than that of his mistress. The idea is that one loves a human being when one feels sorry for him; one is loved when compassion is felt for one by another.

Because this idea is so fundamental with her, Marilyn can never convincingly portray a *femme fatale* on the screen, even when she tries to, as she did in *Niagara* and *Don't Bother to Knock*.

In his essay "On Acting," the psychoanalyst Otto Fenichel remarks that the good actor cannot really play an emotion he has not experienced. "The good actor believes that he plays his parts; actually he plays himself," writes Dr. Fenichel.

And when the actress is cast in a part whose chief motivations are in contradiction to her nature, she must convert the character into her own way of being. Marilyn Monroe was supposed to play a fortune hunter in *Gentlemen Prefer Blondes* and *How to Marry a Millionaire*, a night-club floozie in *Bus Stop*, an abstracted essence of sex in *Seven Year Itch*, a hard-boiled chorus girl in *The Prince and the Showgirl*, an alcoholic band vocalist in *Some Like It Hot*. But invariably a soft sweetness pervades all her characterizations.

4 A Convenient Husband

Norma Jean was returned to her legal guardian, Aunt Grace, in 1938. Aunt Ana was sick and could not look after her. By now the Goddards were living in a larger house, and there was room for her. It was at this time that Norma Jean borrowed the white sweater and discovered her power. She did not connect the excitement she aroused with her need for affection. Her naïveté about sex at this time and, indeed, up to the time of her first marriage was Victorian. Then, for a long time, sex for her was a power operation. Once, in a burst of candor, she confessed to Hollywood correspondent Florabel Muir, "If you are born with what the world calls sex appeal, you can either let it wreck you or use it to your advantage in the tough show-business struggle, and it isn't always easy to pick the right route."

Even before she got into show business, she was already consciously using "sex appeal" in the struggle for a more abundant life. At twelve she had caused a sensation in a sweater. By the summer of 1939, she was dating regularly. Nowadays it has become fairly common for a girl of thirteen to go out with a neighborhood boy on a formal date. But before World War II this sort of thing was unusual. Norma Jean's unorthodox habits shocked her girl friends. She went to school heavily made up. When criticized, she would angrily reply, "What do you care? It's my face, isn't it?" She was a ring-a-ding girl and dated older boys of seventeen or eighteen. Her figure had rounded out precociously, and at thirteen she looked eighteen. The gossips accused her of getting drunk and engaging in all-night petting orgies on the beaches of Venice, Ocean Park, and Santa Monica. She didn't resent the gossip. "I couldn't feel angry with the scandal makers. Girls being jealous of me! Girls frightened of losing their boy friends because I was more attractive! These were no longer daydreams made up to hide lonely hours. They were truths!"

How she reveled in the sensation of being the center of attraction, of being treated with deference by gentlemen callers, one of whom was an aged roué of twenty who thought she was a mature young lady! She did carry herself like an experienced lady of affairs. She had already cultivated a "fancy" style of walking. She began mastering the rhythmic rotation of her hips in a tight skirt.

On visits to the beach, she borrowed Bebe Goddard's swimsuit. (What would have happened or not have happened to Marilyn if her foster sister had not been a size smaller?) Marilyn recalls how she pirouetted before a mirror in the bedroom, rehearsing a voluptuous slink. The hubbub caused by the sweater was nothing compared to the riots induced by the swimsuit. Old men went out of their minds. Young men yelled and whistled. Women stared and resented her.

Norma Jean was balling it up. She was out on the town or on the beach seven nights a week. She says she was "wooed" as if she were the only girl on the block. Her admirers were unanimous in their praise. Yet she didn't connect her magnetism with the sexual experience. "The truth was that with all my lipstick and mascara and precocious curves I was as unresponsive as a fossil. . . . I used to lie awake at night wondering why the boys came after me."

Aunt Grace and Aunt Ana, not realizing that Norma Jean was as safe with her suitors as Penelope had been with hers, not knowing that their foster niece went no further than a clasp of the hands and a good-night kiss and never permitted her escorts any contact more intimate than a friendly hug around the waist or a playful bout of wrestling on the beach, were worried.

Norma Jean got to be fourteen and fifteen and her adorers increased. The two women held conferences daily. They had visions of parked cars on Mulholland Drive, of, to paraphrase T. S. Eliot, dates in one-night cheap motels. What if Norma Jean were following in her mother's footsteps?

Like Aunt Ana, Aunt Grace was a Christian Scientist. The ladies went to Mary Baker Eddy's text for instruction. In her peculiar literary style, Mrs. Eddy had stated that "Chastity is the cement of civilization and progress." She urged all those who wished to give "new pinions" to joy "to happify existence" by marriage. By the time Norma Jean was fifteen, the aunts knew they had to find a suitable man to "happify" their niece.

After considering various possibilities, their choice fell upon a twenty-one-year-old resident of Van Nuys, James Dougherty. The Doughertys and the Goddards had been friends for many years. Dougherty was earning a good salary in the Lockheed plant. He occasionally drove Norma Jean and Bebe Goddard home from Van Nuys High School. Jim had never responded to Norma Jean's charms because he thought of her as a little girl.

Dougherty was a slim, suave, nattily dressed man, who was popular with the girls. At Van Nuys, he had been president of the senior class. At the very moment when Mesdames Goddard and Lower were plotting their matrimonial schemes, Jim's steady girl friend was a lovely thing who had been named Queen of the Santa Barbara Festival.

Now there are few pastimes so pleasing to women as the arranging of other people's marriages. The first step was to convince Norma Jean that she should "happify" her existence. One night, the girl confided to Aunt Grace how sad she was because all the girls accused her of being a "man-trap." Norma Jean said she couldn't help it, could she, if other girls' beaux were irresistibly drawn to her? What could one do about it?

This was the perfect opening. "What you have to do is get married," said Aunt Grace.

"But I'm too young," Norma Jean replied.

"Only in years, honey," Aunt Grace said. "You're really quite mature as a woman."

Norma Jean mulled over this point. "Who'll marry me?" she inquired, reasonably enough.

"There's Jim," Aunt Grace said.

"Jim?"

"Jim Dougherty. How do you feel about Jim?"

"I don't feel anything," she said. "I mean he's like the other boys, except he's older and taller and more polite."

"Well," Aunt Grace said, "that's a fine quality in a husband—politeness."

There was more to Mrs. Goddard's plan than met the eye. The Goddards were planning to move to West Virginia. Doc Goddard didn't want Norma Jean Baker along, and Aunt Ana, ill with a "belief of heart trouble," was too feeble to chaperone the siren of the San Fernando Valley.

The aunts now paid a call on Mrs. Dougherty, and began their campaign to persuade her that their niece would make her son a fine helpmeet. Norma Jean was healthy, clean, hard-working, good-looking, conscientious, and good fun to have around. Mrs. Dougherty brought up Norma Jean's reputation for loose living, and the aunts laughed and said it was just animal spirits. She was healthy and she was young but she was a decent girl, a home girl.

But wasn't she too young for matrimony? Not at all, countered the aunts. Norma Jean was mature for her years. She wasn't one of your giggly adolescents. She was quiet, well-mannered, intelligent, and her feet were on the ground. She had the figure of a twenty-year-old woman. And above all she *was* well-mannered.

"Politeness," Aunt Grace pointed out, "is a fine quality in a wife."

Mrs. Dougherty finally agreed to approve the nuptials provided that Jim liked Norma Jean.

One Friday in January, 1942, Jim awakened at his usual time of three in the afternoon—he was on the midnight-to-eight shift at Lockheed. He found a note pinned to his pillow. It was a message from Aunt Grace. She wanted him to take Norma Jean out that evening and to find a suitable date for Bebe. Dougherty complied, although, as he says, "until the evening got started I thought I was robbing the cradle."

The evening turned out to be quite different from what he'd expected. Norma Jean borrowed a red-silk party dress from Bebe, and Jim was vulnerable, of course. Staring up at him with her liquescent blue-gray eyes, her lips tremulously parted, this girl made him feel, he has said, "like a big shot." When they danced, he discovered a soft helplessness in her body. He describes her as "sweet and innocent." He believed she had a "crush" on him.

By March, they were going steady, and by May they were engaged. Dougherty insists Marilyn was "head over heels in love" with him. Marilyn has always claimed that it was a marriage of convenience. She had to do it or be sent back to the orphanage. She wrote, "My marriage brought me neither happiness nor pain. My husband

and I hardly spoke to each other. This wasn't because we were angry. We had nothing to say."

Marilyn violently denied to Pete Martin that she had had a "crush" on Jim. In her statements to the Hollywood bureau of *Time*, she took an even more pessimistic view of her first marriage. It had not only brought her pain, it had brought her despair. She had even made an attempt at suicide—"not a very serious one"—during her marriage. To Clarice Evans she confided that she regarded Jim more as a brother than as a husband. Yet Jim's sister, Mrs. Elyda Nelson, was convinced that it was the real thing. She recalls, by the way, that when her brother and his fiancée went to the jeweler's to select two rings for the double-ring ceremony, Jim chose an expensive set and that Marilyn said, "Oh, no, Jimmy, not that one. It's too expensive. Please get the cheaper set." According to Mrs. Nelson, all Marilyn wanted was to be near Jim. "She didn't need a big diamond to show to her friends. She had Jim and that was enough."

According to Dougherty, Marilyn loved him so much that she used to say that if he ever stopped loving her, she'd go to Santa Monica and jump off the pier. He would laugh and say, "Why always the Santa Monica pier, baby? Couldn't you use some other pier?"

Marilyn had two shocks before her marriage. The first was finding out that she was illegitimate, and that her real name was Norma Jeane Mortenson. The second was finding out about the "facts of life." (Not that she didn't have some vague intimations of immorality based on the recollections of early childhood.) In one of her premarital chats with Aunt Grace, Marilyn asked whether she and Jim could be "just friends" or whether she had to go any further and if so exactly how much further. She admitted she was frightened of what a husband might "do." These questions came as a surprise to Aunt Grace, who had assumed that her niece was sophisticated. Aunt Grace told Aunt Ana. Aunt Ana bought Marilyn one of those manuals containing helpful hints for the bride-to-be. Marilyn read it through and was rather appalled at the complications of biology. She told Aunt Grace she didn't feel confident of being a good wife. She thought she was too cold. Dougherty says, "She needn't have given it a second thought; she was a most responsive bride—a perfect bride in every respect—except the cooking department."

They were married on Friday, June 19, 1942, at half past eight in the evening, at the home of Mr. and Mrs. Chester Howell of 432 S. Bentley Avenue, in the West Los Angeles district. The Howells were friends of the Doughertys. Aunt Ana gave away the bride. In the wedding invitations, Norma Jean Baker is described as "her niece," a sentimental piece of fiction. During the ceremony, Norma Jean was trembling with fear. Outwardly she looked like a dream, in a white embroidered gown which Aunt Ana had sewn and which Marilyn kept for many years. One historian of the event reports that she did not throw away her bridal bouquet because it meant so much to her; she took it home to keep "forever and ever."

After the wedding, the Doughertys, with several other couples, repaired to the Florentine Gardens, a Hollywood night club, for supper and the floor show. During the show, the patrons were exhorted to go onstage and join the conga line. Mrs. Dougherty, who was high on champagne, jubilantly jounced her hips in the conga number. When she returned to the table, her new husband was furious.

"You made a monkey out of yourself," he told her.

Later she was to say that being married to Jim was "like being retired to a zoo." Possibly this simile came to her mind because he often compared her to a monkey. Another interpretation may be that she felt like a caged animal, locked up for the amusement of a husband.

Mrs. Dougherty hated cooking, cleaning, and dishwashing. It was foster-home life all over again. Girl friends had warned her that marriage tended to narrow a girl's variety of romantic experiences. Alas, it was true. The men lost interest in Mrs. Dougherty. "The rose," she wrote, "seemed to have fallen out of my teeth."

It was a boring existence for a Lorelei. What it took years of married life to do for Madame Bovary was accomplished for Madame Dougherty in a few months.

But, while waiting for opportunity to come knocking at her door, she tried to be a conscientious wife. Dougherty reports that "she was a wonderful housekeeper and didn't have a lazy bone in her body. She darned socks and sewed on missing buttons like a veteran housewife." Somehow the image of Marilyn Monroe sitting in the tiny one-room furnished bungalow at 4524 Vista Del Monte Street in Van Nuys, humming a happy song as she blissfully sews a white button on her husband's shirt, is incongruous. I mean, it's like trying to picture Helen of Troy washing Menelaus' socks or Cleopatra scrubbing the deck of her barge.

Of what dreams and desires were seething in his wife, Dougherty had no more suspicion than Dr. Bovary. Jim thought her an adoring wife. She packed a lunch for him before he went to work, and she "tucked little love notes in between the sandwiches. They were always sweet and brought a glow to me when I read them in the middle of the night. I remember one that went, 'Dearest Daddy, when you read this I'll be asleep and dreaming of you. Love and kisses. Your baby.' "

While Marilyn was no Elizabeth Barrett Browning when it came to counting the ways of her love, this certainly is the sort of *billet-doux* calculated to please any man, especially if he doesn't know anything about the father complexes of young girls.

It should have become clear to Jim, early in his marriage, that he had taken to his heart a sprite, a water spirit, a creature of mistiness and romance, an undine. But how many of us know an undine when she is in our house?

Once, feeling close to Jim, she confided her aspirations to be a Hollywood star. He thought she was crazy. "There are thousands of beautiful girls that can sing, dance, and act," he said. "They're walking the streets of Hollywood without a job. What makes you think you can do any better?"

He just didn't see it. He didn't feel it. He didn't understand or want to understand. He loved Norma Jean very much, and he wanted children and a woman who felt contented repairing socks and mending shirts.

Only gradually did it dawn on him that she inhabited a different world from his. Her cooking was surrealistic. Once, when she brewed some coffee, he asked her what she had put in it to make it so bitter. She said she had heard that salt brought out the flavor of coffee and had put a teaspoonful in the cup!

The Doughertys once lived on Bessemer Street in an area in the San Fernando Valley in which there were farms. Their neighbors owned a cow which was pastured in a field across the way. One day, during a heavy rainstorm, the cow was grazing. The farmer and his wife had gone somewhere. Marilyn's heart was moved by the sight of the wet bovine. She got some clothesline and tied it around the cow's neck. She led the beast up the steps of the house and tried to drag it into the parlor, but the cow resisted. Marilyn was wrenching one way, the cow the other. At this crisis, Dougherty came home.

"What are you doing?" he asked, though the situation seemed clear enough.

"Help me, Jim," she said. "It's been standing out in all that rain. You push from the back and I'll keep on pulling."

"But, honey," he said, "it isn't our cow. Don't worry about it."

"But we just can't leave the poor thing out in this awful weather," Marilyn said.

Dougherty found life with Marilyn disturbing.

He once asked her to make highballs for some friends. She dropped some ice cubes into each glass and filled the glasses with straight whiskey. After one round of drinks, everybody was drunk.

Another time, Jim, who was a fisherman, brought home a mess of catfish. He asked Mrs. Dougherty to prepare them. There are many Japanese living in southern California, and somewhere Norma Jean had heard about *sashimi*, raw fish, and she thought it might be fun. She skinned and boned the catfish and served it *au naturel*. Dougherty spat out the first mouthful.

"When the hell are you gonna learn how to cook?" he shouted.

"You're a brute," she cried, and flung a garbage pail at his head. The spirit of a Petruchio filling him, Jim seized his wife, placed her under the shower, and gave her a good drenching with ice-cold water.

"This will cool you off, baby," he said.

Another time, when she was alone at home, a wire short-circuited in the living room and threw up a shower of sparks. Marilyn put out the fire by pouring a potful of coffee on the sparks. Then she hid in the bedroom and locked the door.

But it was the peas-and-carrots routine that really confused Jim. Eight years after their divorce, the peas-and-carrots still haunted him. He was now on the Van Nuys police force. He had married again and was the father of three daughters. When he was asked by an INS reporter if he had any theories why Joe di Maggio and Marilyn had come to a parting of the ways, he suggested that it might have been her cooking. He figured a guy like Joe, well, he likes a thick steak, something a real man can get his teeth into. "But she never broiled steak for me. The only thing I remember is peas-and-carrots. That's all she ever cooked. Neither of us liked them, but I had to eat them. Marilyn thought they looked pretty on the table."

In 1944, Dougherty enlisted in the U.S. Merchant Marine. After boot camp, he was sent to the Catalina Island base as a physical-training instructor. Norma Jean joined him. Here, for the first time since her marriage, Mrs. Dougherty found herself in her most congenial element—men. As she once said, "I don't mind this being a man's world—as long as I can be a woman in it." Catalina Island was swarming with men—sailors, marines, Seabees, Coast Guardsmen. And there weren't too many girls about. Dougherty says bitterly, "She knew she had a beautiful body, and she knew men liked it, and she didn't mind showing a little bit of it."

Mrs. Dougherty, inspired by the whistles and the stares, regressed to tight sweaters and tight skirts. At other times, she went in for white shorts and a white blouse. On the beach, she would wear what he calls "skimpy" bathing attire. Her husband lectured her about her clothes and the incendiary effects of her hip swinging and her bosom joggling. She shrugged his arguments away. It destroyed him to watch other men looking at her and to know the thoughts burning in their minds. He wanted her to be beautiful and exciting, but for him only.

To be married to such beauty is an ordeal for a husband. Yeats, in praying for his daughter, prayed that she might be beautiful—but not too beautiful. Marilyn was not too beautiful, but she was more provocative than girls who were more beautiful than she. At a dance for servicemen on the island, with Stan Kenton's band playing, she was the belle of the ball. Dougherty was able to have no more than one dance with her. As he stood on the sidelines watching, men nearby, not knowing he was her husband, made ribald comments about her anatomy. Dougherty couldn't endure it. He cut in and said they had to go home. She said it wasn't even midnight yet. She suggested that she walk home with him and wait until he was asleep, and then come back and dance the hours away.

"Where would you sleep?" he asked.

"What do you mean, honey, where would I sleep?" she repeated.

"What I mean is, baby, if you go back to this dance, then don't come home—tonight or any other night."

It's the sort of narrow-minded attitude that inhibits a girl's *joie de vivre*, you know. Monogamy, Mrs. Dougherty thought, was perfectly all right in its place, but one didn't have to carry it to insufferable extremes.

On October 2, 1946, while her spouse was overseas, Norma Jean was granted a divorce in Reno, Nevada. She got custody of a beat-up Ford car and an old phonograph. By then, opportunity had come knocking at her door. It was a timid knock. But Norma Jean answered it.

5 She Becomes a Model— and a Blonde

In the lives of those men and women who rise high in the world, the moment when they pass from obscurity into greatness is perhaps the most satisfying they ever experience. The difficulties of the old life are being abandoned; the difficulties of the new are still unknown. The future looms ahead as a thing of infinite promise. For Marilyn Monroe, this sweet moment took place on a bright, hot June morning in 1945.

She had an appointment at eleven with the head of one of the largest model agencies in Hollywood.

The break had finally come. Jim wasn't there to get in the way. He was on a supply boat in the South Pacific. She was living with his parents and brothers in Van Nuys.

She couldn't sleep the night before and got out of bed when it was still dark outside. She was too excited to eat any breakfast. She took a long bath and massaged cologne into her skin. Then she made up her face. Had she made her lips too large? Too much mascara? Should she comb her hair out? She rubbed cold cream over her face and removed the make-up. She studied her face in the mirror, like an artist squinting at an unfinished portrait on the easel. It took her an hour until she was satisfied with the look of her face. Now what should she wear? She didn't have many clothes. A few pairs of dungarees, two sweaters, a white dress with an orange yoke, a teal-blue tailored suit. She tried on the suit. No, not right. She liked herself better in the dress. She brushed her white suède shoes. Her only good pair. Then she brushed her hair. She couldn't do anything with it. Let it fly loose. Maybe she should try the suit again. Out of the dress and into the suit. Then back again into the dress. She slipped it over her head. Reaching behind her, she buttoned it up. It was tight around the waist, and the hemline was above her knees. She couldn't tell how it looked, really, because she didn't have a full-length mirror. Someday there would be a maid and a full-length mirror and a room of her own. She went downstairs and was polite to the family and drank a cup of coffee with them. They didn't know where she was going. They thought she was on her way to the defense plant where she'd been working since last year.

She put on her smoked glasses and got into the old coupé. It was a long drive from Van Nuys to the Blue Book Models Agency in the Ambassador Hotel. She drove in a dreamy way, hardly seeing the other traffic, giving herself up to her reveries and shifting gears unconsciously, trusting that the other cars wouldn't hit her. (This trust in other cars is a characteristic of Los Angeles drivers.) She cruised down Van Nuys Boulevard through the town of Sherman Oaks and cut over to Ventura Boulevard, going east until she came to Coldwater Canyon. She turned into the canyon and began the long series of winding, precipitous rises and falls that took her from the San Fernando Valley into the splendor of Beverly Hills. On Mulholland Drive—which is midway between both points and at the summit of the Santa Monica Mountains—she braked the car and got out. The view was exhilarating. That's what she felt about herself—she was on top of the mountain. She got in again, and now it was downhill, and soon she was in the region of estates and lavish homes. At Sunset Boulevard, the Beverly Hills Hotel stood in mock-Moorish grandeur. Someday, she speculated, eyeing the giraffe-like palms that fringed the grounds of the hotel, she would be a movie star and go to parties at the Beverly Hills Hotel, lunch on the Patio Terrace, and sip cocktails in the late afternoon in the Polo Lounge. She had often walked through the lobby and cafés of the hotel, dreaming herself Betty Grable or Lana Turner, re-experiencing some social gathering she had read about in the gossip columns. At Wilshire Boulevard, she turned again and drove another five miles in a downtown direction to the Ambassador Hotel. In her childhood, this had been the epitome of Hollywood *luxe et volupté*. Movie stars used to lounge around its pool. On Friday evenings, in formal clothes, they crowded into the famous Cocoanut Grove and danced to the music of Abe Lyman's band.

She left the car at the porte-cochere. An attendant gave her a ticket. He turned up his nose at the old car, but his eyes, consuming her, expressed great admiration. She felt good about this. Beautiful women, more than any other kind, need to be constantly assured that they are beautiful.

In the lobby she saw by a clock that she was 15 minutes early. She wandered about the shops in the arcade, picturing herself in the expensive sports clothes on display. Faint memories rose in her mind, like wisps of morning fog rising from the earth, of times when she, her mother, and Aunt Grace had sat here in the lobby, in the hope that a movie celebrity would pass, and of how the two ladies would argue whether a certain man who looked like Ronald Colman or Spencer Tracy really was Ronald Colman or Spencer Tracy.

She thought about her job—she was working at the Radio Plane Parts Company in Burbank. She had started out as parachute inspector and had been promoted to the "dope room," where she sprayed a liquid mixture, "dope," on parts of fuselages.

She worked in overalls. Some attractive women might have been sick at the idea of putting on overalls. But Norma Jean rose to the challenge. "Putting a girl in overalls," she wrote, "is like having her work in tights, particularly if a girl knows how to wear overalls." She knew how to wear overalls. As usual, all the men in the factory were after her. And once in a while she went out and had a beer with one of them. But she was not unfaithful to Jim.

One day, the Army sent a photographer, David Conover, to do a picture layout of the plant. Among other things, he was asked to get morale-boosting pictures of beautiful home-front girls, showing how they too were taking part in the war effort in defense plants. The pictures were to be sent out to hundreds of camp papers, to *Yank* magazine, to *Stars and Stripes*.

From the beginning, Marilyn has had an almost instinctual affinity with photographers. The first photographer in her life was Conover, a Pfc. in Army public relations. He was the first of a series of photographers who helped her make camera history. The others include Potter Hueth, Earl Theisen, Phillipe Halsman, Anthony Beauchamp, Tom Kelley, Sam Shaw, Cecil Beaton, Andre de Dienes, Hans Knopf, Milton H. Greene, and Richard Avedon.

Conover was scouting the plant for photogenic subjects. He passed Norma Jean's table. He breathed hard as he watched her body move. Her face had the clean-cut scrubbed look of the ideal American girl. There was virginity in the eyes, passion in the mouth. He came over and told her he had been shooting pictures around the plant since the day before yesterday.

"I haven't seen you before," he said. "Where have you been all my life?"

She laughed. "I was on sick leave."

"Come on outside," he said. "I'm going to take your picture."

She shook her head. She said the other women in the "dope" room would make trouble for her if she stopped working and "goofed off." She wouldn't pose until Conover got written permission from the foreman. Then she went out and posed in her overalls. He shot a roll of black-and-white. He asked, "Don't you have a sweater? I mean, in your locker?"

"Sure," she said, "I always have a sweater."

"You mind changing into it?"

She changed into it. He shot a roll of Kodachromes. Eating a sandwich. Spraying. Punching the time-clock. She asked him when the pictures would come out, and he said they'd be in Army papers but he didn't know when. He asked for her phone number. She gave it to him.

The 1945 pictures of Monroe show her full face and, usually, looking over her left shoulder. Her hair is dark and unruly. She gives the impression of a sweet, healthy girl. Yet something else in her comes alive in the print.

About two weeks later, Conover phoned and said he had gotten the color prints back from the laboratory. He said the man at Eastman Kodak had asked him, "Who's your model, for goodness sake?" and he told her she ought to be a model. He himself was being shipped out of the country on an Army assignment, but he'd shown his prints of her to Potter Hueth, a commercial photographer, and he suggested she see Hueth. She could make $5 an hour modeling. That was nearly as much as she made in a whole day spraying "dope." Norma Jean called Hueth and went to see him in his studio on Pico Boulevard. He told her he thought she looked swell in Conover's pictures and said that there was a demand for pictures of pretty, natural-looking girls like her in the magazines. It was the heyday of the cover girl, the Rheingold girl, the glamour girl, and there were magazines like *See, Click, Pic, Laff, Salute, Sir,* whose contents consisted mainly of voluptuous girls in interesting poses and shreds of clothing.

"The usual fee for modeling is five dollars or ten dollars an hour," Hueth said. "I can't pay that right now. Would you work with me on speculation? If I sell any pictures of you to magazines, I'll pay you."

During the following weeks, she went to Hueth's studio several nights a week and posed. The sexuality in these early shots is amorphous. There was sex there, of course, for, as director Jean Negulesco remarks, Marilyn cannot do anything without giving off an animal aura—Negulesco once told me that she can look sexy eating mashed potatoes. But Hueth's pictures mainly show her with a healthy clean-cut girl-next-door appeal. He posed her with a Dalmatian; in a sloppy-joe sweater and a plaid skirt; in a tight sweater and slacks; on a bale of hay, bare legs dangling. Hueth showed the pictures to Emmeline Snively, of the model agency, and an appointment was made.

At exactly eleven o'clock that June morning, Norma Jean Dougherty gathered herself together and walked into the reception room of the model agency. While she waited, she looked at the pictures on the wall, pictures of sleek, well-groomed, self-possessed women in advertisements or on magazine covers. Miss Snively booked all sorts of models, ranging from artists' models to high-fashion models, those gaunt, chic creatures with hipless and breastless bodies. Since 1925, when John Robert Powers, a former model, had started the Powers agency, modeling had become a $150,000,000 industry. Business had discovered that, in a commodity culture, beauty was a commodity that could be used to promote the sale of other commodities.

Norma Jean was ushered into Miss Snively's office. Miss Snively is a small effervescent lady. She rose and pumped Norma Jean's hand. Norma Jean started to sit down, but Miss Snively said, "My dear, please walk to the door and back." Norma Jean didn't walk well—too unevenly. The hair was bad. A "California blonde"—light on top and dark underneath. Needed a good coiffure. Should cut it short and bleach it. But the smile was friendly, the legs marvelous, the bosom excellent, and there was a general air of sweetness about her. In the white dress, thought Miss Snively, she looked demure, like a "cherub in a church choir."

"Potter Hueth's been saying the nicest things about you," Miss Snively said. "I can see how true they are. Do you want to be a model?"

Norma Jean knew how to be shy and humble when she had to. "I don't know," she said. "I thought I could be one and then—I mean, s-seeing all those pictures of the models, I don't know if I'm beautiful enough. But if you would g-give me a chance, I'd like to try."

"Try—that's the spirit, honey. If you've got the will power to work hard, you've got to be a success, because you've got one thing, honey, and it's one of the rarest gifts in this world, and that's charm, charm's what you've got."

Norma Jean lowered her eyes modestly.

"How old are you?"

"Nineteen this month."

"Size?"

"I wear a size twelve."

"Height?"

"Oh, five feet, five."

"Bust?"

"Thirty-six."

"Waist?"

"Twenty-four."

"Hips?"

"Thirty-five."

Miss Snively was writing it down. "Now, Miss Dougherty—"

"It's M-Mrs. Dougherty, ma'am."

"Well, Mrs. Dougherty, modeling today is a science. It's not something a girl can walk off the street and do without the proper training and knowledge. You've got to have the know-how, honey."

By a fortunate coincidence, Miss Snively also ran a school for modeling as well as an agency. For $100, she offered a three-month course of training.

"I guess that lets me out," Norma Jean said. "I don't have it."

"Well, that's all right, Mrs. Dougherty, that's perfectly all right. You don't have to pay any money now. You'll pay for it out of what you earn as a model. Do you want to get down to hard work?"

"Oh, yes."

"You've got a lot of work ahead of you. Your smile isn't right. You're smiling up instead of down and it makes your nose too big. And you'll have to get your hair straightened and bleached. You'll be a marvelous blonde. So dramatic-looking."

"I wouldn't ever want to be a bleached blonde, Miss Snively."

The next day Norma Jean quit her job at the plant and started attending modeling school. She studied fashion modeling with Mrs. Gavin Beardsley, make-up and grooming with Maria Smith, and the fine art of posing with the head of the academy, Miss Snively herself. Norma Jean's first modeling job was as a hostess at an aluminum exhibit at the Los Angeles Home Show in the Pan-Pacific Auditorium. She got $10 a day for nine days. Every cent went to pay Miss Snively for the course. Her second job turned out badly. She was sent, together with a group of models, on location to Malibu Beach to model sports clothes for the Montgomery-Ward catalogue. But after two days, she was sent home. She never succeeded as a fashion model. She never showed off the clothes she was modeling. All the attention was drawn to the model, not the clothes. Her first advertising assignment was posing for a new Douglas airliner that was being put into service by American Airlines. Photographs were shot at the Douglas plant. Dressed in a sheer black negligee, she was pictured enjoying the delights of reposing in a sleeping compartment of a DC-4 flagship. Miss Snively realized her pupil had more than the usual amount of sex appeal when word got back to her that work had slowed down at Douglas for a week because every executive found some excuse to go into the studio where the pictures were being shot and regale himself with a sight of Mrs. Dougherty.

Looking back, Miss Snively says: "She was the hardest worker I ever handled. She never missed a class. She had confidence in herself. Quit her job at a factory without anything except her confidence and my belief in her. She did something I've never seen any other model do. She would study every print a photographer did of her. I mean she'd take them home and study them for hours. Then she'd go back and ask the photographer, 'What did I do wrong in this one?' or 'Why didn't this come out better?' They would tell her. And she never repeated a mistake. Photographers liked her because she was co-operative. She knew how to take directions. She had a lot of location jobs, where they go out for the whole day and get twenty-five dollars for the day. She was in great demand for bathing-suit pictures.

"A lot of models ask me how they can be like Marilyn Monroe and I say to them, honey, I say to them, if you can show half the gumption, just half, that little girl showed, you'll be a success, too. But there'll never be another like her."

She was stubborn about changing her hair. Miss Snively kept telling her, "If you intend to go places, you've got to bleach, honey. The biggest demand is for blondes. A blonde can be photographed light, medium, or dark by controlling the light. The way your hair is now, you always come out more dark than light."

"I wouldn't look natural," she kept protesting.

Then photographer Raphael Wolff offered her a six-hour job at $10 an hour posing for a series of shampoo advertisements. It is often minor episodes that lead to fateful changes. Wolff wouldn't hire her unless she became a blonde. He said he would pay for the bleach himself. It was against her better judgment that she became a blonde. It is hard for a woman to understand why a difference in the color of her hair can influence men so much. But she gave in and was sent to Frank and Joseph, the Hollywood hair stylists. Her hair was cut short, given a straight permanent, and then bleached a golden blonde, quite unlike the platinum tinge she later acquired. Her hair was styled in a sophisticated upsweep. She thought it looked artificial. She was uneasy when she first saw herself in the mirror. "It wasn't the 'real me.'" Then she saw that it worked. Being a pragmatist, she remained blonde, through varying shades of yellow and silver.

She couldn't get used to the strange, exotic image that stared back at her from a glass. But she knew she was becoming more of a siren than she had ever been before. The very artificiality of it, she realized, meant that it was a created thing and she would have to create a personality to go along with the new face and the new hair. A bleached blonde is not natural; therefore she cannot wear ordinary clothes or make-up, or *be* ordinary. She becomes, in a sense, an assembled product. To be artificially put together by modistes, couturiers, cosmeticians and coiffeurs, leads to a profound loss of one's identity. Motion-picture actresses often lose all sense of who and what they really are. They are wraiths, reflections in a mirror, existing only in an audience's reaction to them. They hardly exist

55

apart from an audience. If they lose the appeal, because of a change in type or because they have gotten middle-aged, they, as it were, die.

Whether she knew it or not, the moment Marilyn bleached her hair, she made a serious commitment. One is never the same afterward, and it is a question only of the degree to which one lives up to the commitment.

She saw clearly that her future as a model lay not in fashion work or in advertising but in glamour poses, in "cheesecake." The ability to contort one's body into interesting poses and the concentration necessary to hold the poses for long, tiresome periods are important. A knowledge of the body is important. So she studied anatomy textbooks. She exercised for an hour each day—bending and stretching exercises, bicycling, walking at a fast tempo. She studied her face in the mirror and practiced expressing a range of emotions. She tirelessly taught herself how to think sex and project it.

Photographer Earl Theisen told me: "I remember a series I shot with Marilyn, oh back in nineteen forty-six or nineteen forty-seven. I picked her up at her place and I saw a big book * on the human anatomy open and all marked up, and I said what was the idea, and she said, 'I'm studying the bone structure of the body. Your body does what your bones do. Did you know that?' Anything she does is calculated and is based on a more scientific knowledge of the human body than anybody has except doctors.

"She's built kind of like a sex machine. She can turn it on and off. I've seen her turn the sex machine into operation. I'll focus on her, get ready to shoot, and then looking in the finder I can actually see the sex blossoming out, like it was a flower. If I'm in a hurry and want to shoot too quickly, she'll say, 'Earl, you shot it too quick. It won't be right. Let's do it over.' You see, it takes time for her to create this sex thing. And don't let anybody tell you it's in her hips or in her bosom."

I asked him where it was located.

"I'll tell you where it's located," he said. "It's in her mind, that's where it is."

In 1949, Phillipe Halsman was asked by the editors of *Life* Magazine to provide them with several pages of photographs of "starlets."

* A modern edition of *De humani corporis,* by Andreas Vesalius, 1543, with drawings by von Kalkar, a painter of the Titian school. Marilyn still studies this book.

Halsman conceived a charming notion. He invited eight "starlets" to his studio, Marilyn among them. He told them that he would take their pictures *en masse*. He wanted them, at his command, to project the emotions they experienced in four "basic situations." Halsman described these "basic situations" as "enjoying a delicious but invisible drink, hearing the funniest but inaudible joke, being frightened by the most horrible but invisible monster, and being kissed by the most wonderful lover." Marilyn, as Halsman recalls the incident, was a failure in the first three poses, but when she pretended that she was being kissed "she gave a performance of such realism and dramatic intensity that not only she, but even I, was utterly exhausted."

Jerry Wald, who produced *Clash by Night,* in which Marilyn co-starred, says, "Her sexuality, well, it's something she has corked up in a bottle. She opens the bottle and uses some when she needs it for a scene and then she puts the cork back in the bottle and puts the bottle away until she needs it again."

By 1946, she was being featured regularly in all the men's magazines. She once defined a "man's magazine" as a periodical with cover girls who are not flat-chested. One month she was on the cover of five such magazines.

6 "A Kind of Fantastic Beauty"— the Model Becomes a Starlet

Howard Hughes, the proprietor of RKO-Radio Pictures and a fervent admirer of the non-flat bosom, was laid up in Cedars of Lebanon Hospital. He had recently crashed in his private plane. He was encased in plaster from feet to neck, but his eyes had not been injured. His eyes were in excellent condition. Hughes was whiling away the monotony of hospital life by examining photographs of well-stacked girls in the magazines. In the course of this harmless diversion, he kept running across the same blonde dish. She was not identified by name. He called his office and told one of his associates to find out the girl's name and give her a screen test. One of the master's aides eventually got in touch with Miss Snively and said in the solemn voice reserved for great questions of state that Howard Hughes had decided to give Norma Jean Dougherty a screen test.

Miss Snively was properly elated. A mighty event impended. All models hope to become movie stars. To be screen-tested is the ambition of every model. And now it was about to happen to Norma Jean. Miss Snively kept herself under control. She had not been born yesterday. She realized that the pupil had outgrown the teacher. Norma Jean needed an agent. She needed what they call on Sunset Boulevard "representation." Howard Hughes was too formidable a prospect for her to cope with. To protect Norma Jean's interests, Miss Snively called in Helen Ainsworth. Miss Ainsworth immediately justified her 10-per-cent commission by getting in touch with 20th Century-Fox, which was looking for "new faces." She rang up

Ben Lyon, who had been a popular movie hero during the 1920's and 1930's but was now a talent scout at the studio, and told him about the interest at the Hughes office. Lyon was interested. Miss Ainsworth said she would bring Norma Jean Dougherty over immediately.

Norma Jean had no time to shop for a new dress or to get her hair done. They went to the Fox lot. Well, she was inside the gates at last. A major studio is like one of those walled cities of the Middle Ages, protecting the *haute bourgeoisie* from the hordes outside. The outpost is the Administration Building, which can be freely entered from the outside world. At 20th, the Administration Building has a back door which leads to the walled city with its lanes. Here there are bungalows and writers' building and stars' building and sound-stage buildings and the fascinating back lot with a New York street and small-town streets and foreign locales and a lake where naval battle scenes are shot and rugged mountain terrain and Western bad-lands and the frontier street with its Last Chance saloon and the hitching post.

Marilyn and her agent entered by the front door of the Adminis-tration Building. Lyon's office was there. He was an amiable man. He didn't embarrass her by asking her to read a scene. He didn't ask about her experience. The mere fact that Hughes was interested was enough for him. She had a good face and a good body.

"I think she's got good bones in her face," Lyon said.

"Let's get down to cases, Ben," Miss Ainsworth said. "Can you test her tomorrow?"

"You know I can't do that. I don't want to test her in black and white. I want to do a color test. Darryl Zanuck has to approve every color test. It will take a little time to get Mr. Zanuck's okay on it."

"But Hughes wants to screen-test her."

"I'll screen-test her."

"If you're not going to do it fast, then we're going over to RKO from here, Ben."

"Will you give me two days?"

Norma Jean sat silent, not speaking one word, holding her breath and praying that nothing would go wrong. Two days later, Lyon had arranged a screen test. It was unauthorized. Zanuck, one of the most autocratic of all the studio bosses, ran 20th Century-Fox with an iron fist. Lyon decided to risk Zanuck's wrath. A screen test runs about 12 minutes. Usually the person being tested plays opposite an experienced actor or actress in a dramatic scene, and the candidate gets a chance to study the part and rehearses before the shooting. But Lyon didn't dare give away the game by asking the casting department for a contract player to do the scene with the newcomer. He was going to gamble on Norma Jean's ability to project sex without words. She would do a test by herself. In color. No dialogue. A silent test. He had the help of one of the best cameramen on the lot: Leon Shamroy, a large Rabelaisian polar bear of a man. Shamroy loves a good intrigue, and he fears neither man, beast, nor executive producer. The conspirators decided to make the test on the set of *Mother Wore Tights,* a film starring Betty Grable, then in production. They got on the scene at half past five in the morning. On the set, Marilyn prepared herself in a portable dressing room. Lyon had sneaked out of wardrobe a sequin evening gown for the scene. Shamroy lighted the set himself. He loaded his film, framed the scene between his fingers, and then operated the camera. Marilyn walked out and crossed to the set. She was wearing spiked shoes, and she stumbled and almost fell down crossing over the tangle of cables as she went from her dressing room across the stage and onto the set. In that short walk Norma Jean Dougherty became Marilyn Monroe.

Lyon told her that when he cued her with the word "Action," she was to walk across the set. Sit down. Light a cigarette. Put it out. Go upstage. Cross. Look out a window. Sit down. Come downstage and exit.

Shamroy signaled he was ready.

"Action," Lyon said.

The arc lights blinded her. The giant eye of the camera seemed to suck her into its pupil. She lost all sense of where she was, all the strain and fear left her, she didn't see the anxious faces on the periphery of the set. She didn't see anything finally, but was lost in the experience, letting her sexuality blossom out as she had learned to do for photographs. Shamroy shot two reels.

The print was ready that afternoon. Shamroy looked at it in a movieola, a small hand-cranked device in which strips of film can be studied for editing and cutting. He told me, "I got a cold chill. This girl had something I hadn't seen since silent pictures. She had a kind of fantastic beauty like Gloria Swanson, when a movie star had to look beautiful, and she got sex on a piece of film like Jean Harlow. This is the first girl who looked like one of those lush stars of the silent era. Every frame of the test radiated sex. She didn't need a sound track to tell her story. That was what made her test so great to me. She was creating her effects visually. She was showing us she could sell emotions in pictures—that's what pictures have to be— moving pictures are pictures that move, not just characters talking. . . ."

Every technician and creative artist in films, whatever their critical opinion of Monroe as an artist, feel what Billy Wilder calls her "flesh impact." Wilder says, "Flesh impact is rare. Three I remember who had it were Clara Bow, Jean Harlow, and Rita Hayworth. Such girls have flesh which photographs like flesh. You feel you can reach out and touch it."

Every day after seven, Zanuck looked at the "rushes" of all the films in production. The rushes are the scenes or parts of scenes shot that day. Lyon had sneaked Norma Jean's color test in with the daily rushes. When the color test had run, Zanuck pressed a button signaling the projectionist to hold up the next scene.

"Who's the girl?" he barked at Lyon.

"Her name's Norma Jean Dougherty, Mr. Zanuck. She's a model."

"Did I authorize this test?"

"No, sir."

"That's the *Mother Wore Tights* set, isn't it?" Zanuck knew everything that went on in his empire. He worked 15 hours a day. The lights in his office were the last to black out.

"Yes, sir."

Zanuck didn't smile. "It's a damn fine test. Sign her up."

A contract was drawn on August 26, 1946. Lyon told Norma Jean that the name "Norma Jean Dougherty" was obviously unsuitable for a movie actress. It was too long and sounded insipid. He said he had been an admirer of musical-comedy star Marilyn Miller, and suggested that Marilyn would be a good first name. Norma Jean went along with him. He told her to try to find a euphonious last name. He gave her the contracts to take to her legal guardian, Grace Goddard, for co-signing. The Goddards had moved back to Los Angeles.

She rushed into their house, waving the contracts. "I've got it," she said. "I'm an actress. I'm with the finest studio in Hollywood. They liked my screen test. I'm really on the payroll. Look!"

Her aunt signed the contracts. They embraced each other and wept with joy. Marilyn—that was her new name—promised Aunt Grace that soon she would buy her a big house and hire a full-time maid for her. And did she like the new name Marilyn?

"That's a nice name, Marilyn," Aunt Grace said. "And it fits your mother's maiden name, Monroe. She was related to President Monroe. Marilyn Monroe. That sounds real pretty, Norma J—I mean, Marilyn."

That was the first Marilyn had ever heard of any relationship between herself and the propounder of the Monroe Doctrine. She didn't tell anybody, but she hated the name Marilyn. She says she has never liked it. "I've often wished," she says, "that I had held out for the name Jean Monroe."

In her own mind, Marilyn Monroe was on the threshold of stardom. To the studio, however, she was a starlet, and a starlet, in those days when beautiful young girls and handsome young men were signed up by the dozen, had about as much significance to a major studio as an individual herring has to a fisherman in the North Sea. A starlet is bought for the bloom of youth. She plays walk-ons, maybe a few speaking bits. When the bloom fades, she fades. She gets married or becomes a car-hop at a drive-in, a beautician, a hat-check girl, a call-girl. Starlets rarely become stars, and those who are gifted with the ineffable aura of a star usually don't do well as starlets. You can't play Charmian when God has meant you to play Cleopatra. But the studio gives all the starlets the "treatment," and the starlet thinks it has a meaning that it does not have. There is, first, publicity. The mighty engine of studio propaganda begins squeaking out a few little column items about her; maybe her picture is planted in a fan magazine. It seems terribly exciting to the starlet, but it isn't the real build-up. A "build-up," that's when the engine begins roaring, and it only roars for the star or for those who, in the opinion of the front office, have "star quality." For the starlet it only whispers. The studio publicity department sent over one of its younger men to talk to Marilyn Monroe, to dredge up a few facts for a studio biography—one of those two-page mimeographed life stories which recite succinctly the birth, background, education, and dramatic experience of the subject and list her physical dimensions, marital status, favorite foods, sports, and games. It is filed in a cabinet and, 99 times out of a hundred, forgotten.

Roy Craft, who was to become Marilyn's most trusted liaison with the press, was the man who was sent to interview her. To him it promised to be just another boring day's work, for every starlet told the same tale, signifying nothing but an itch for money and fame. But as Marilyn began to talk, Craft sat up. She unfolded the story of her life—no father and no mother. The poor, lonely, orphan girl. She had decided to lie about her mother, tell everybody her mother had died long ago. It was a foolish thing to do. (At this very time, her mother, who had been released from the mental hospital in 1945, had, after living with Marilyn for a year, fallen in love and remarried. She suffered another setback in 1948 and had to be committed again.) Craft, hearing the story of the orphanage and the foster homes, was naturally both saddened and delighted. Saddened for Marilyn, but pleased that he had a nice hook on which to hang some publicity. Usually somebody in the press department had to invent a Cinderella story. But here was one ready made. The trouble was that Marilyn kept on talking, telling more and more of her troubles, and it became too much of a bad thing. This wasn't Cinderella. This was Oliver Twist in girl's clothing. How could you sell the customers sex with all this tragedy? So in his first short studio biography, Craft played down the miseries of her past. "I thought it would do her more harm than good," he says. "It wasn't until nineteen fifty-two that we played the orphan bit for all it was worth. By then, she was becoming a solidly established sex symbol, and the story of her unhappy childhood got space because it was a terrific switch."

The latest version of her studio biography begins: "Roll all the Cinderella stories into one. Summon up the copy writer's extravagant superlatives. Take the drama and pathos from the greatest novels. Stand her beside the loveliest beauties of all time. Do all these things and they won't compare with the Hollywood phenomenon, Marilyn Monroe, whose sudden fame and frenetic following have never been equalled in or out of motion pictures. . . . Strong men grow misty-eyed when she tells her life story."

But in 1946 she was a name on a roster of contract players, one among many. She thought, as all starlets do, that she was being groomed for stardom. She attended classes in pantomime, dancing, and singing. On her own, she searched out deserted sound stages and recited lines to the four walls, making herself be at ease. She took old scripts home and studied them. At night, she went to studio screenings to see what other actresses did and why certain scenes in a movie came across and others didn't. She was in the gallery for hours, posing for stills. If the publicity department sent her out to the beach or the mountains to pose, she went and posed. She rode in parades in a costume. She stood in floats, one of a bevy of float-riding starlets, smiling artificially. She didn't see any sense to it, but she was getting a salary every week, and she obeyed the higher powers. When she rang up her agent or Ben Lyon or the casting department, she was told that they were waiting for the right part to turn up. After six months her option was picked up and her salary raised to $150 a week. Another starlet told her she ought to get some new clothes. She opened a charge account at I. Magnin's. It was her second charge account. Her first had been at Marian Hunter's bookstore in Beverly Hills. A saleswoman at Magnin's took her in hand, telling her that she knew exactly "how a starlet should dress." She had helped Betty Grable, Rita Hayworth, and many other aspiring Venuses dress right. Marilyn bought $500 worth of expensive finery, the first well-made clothes she ever owned.

Finally, she got a part, a small part, in *Scudda Hoo! Scudda Hay!* a movie about a farmer's troubles with a team of mules. June Haver was to play the lead. Marilyn reported to the set in her costume. An assistant director told her she was one of a group of extras. She was to break out of a crowd, cross over, say "Hello" to June Haver, and then walk out of camera range. That was the extent of her contribution to the epic. And even that didn't stay in. It was cut out of the final edition of *Scudda Hoo! Scudda Hay!*

She waited patiently for the next role. It didn't come. Whatever "flesh impact" she had seemed to have been forgotten. No director wanted her for a story he was doing. No producer was interested in her. And then, as abruptly as it had come, her glory was taken away. Her option was not picked up in August, 1947.

Sidney Skolsky's theory is interesting. "Marilyn Monroe was not rushed into stardom and given good roles in important pictures for a simple reason which can be told in two words: Betty Grable. Betty Grable was not only 20th Century-Fox's big moneymaker but also the actress rated as box-office champion of the entire industry in its official poll."

Marilyn went back to modeling. She moved into a cheaper apartment. She shampooed, bleached, and set her own hair. She mended her stockings and wore them until they disintegrated. She became an amateur seamstress, lengthening hems and letting waists out or in as styles and her figure changed. She often went without breakfast and lunch to save money for acting lessons. Sometimes two or three days went by and all she ate was milk and crackers. Usually, however, there was a man around to buy her a dinner.

To survive in the velvet jungle of Hollywood, one had to reckon with wolves. A starlet could survive by taking on a lover—a married man, of course—who would pay her rent and buy her meals. Or she might be the mistress of an old man who was a studio power and who not only supported her but subtly advanced her career. For Marilyn Monroe, the men were usually important as meal tickets, a way of enabling her to survive until she could break through. During the next few years, her adventures in the sexual underworld of the movie colony were bizarre and pathetic.

7 The Wolves, the Foxes, and the Lovers

During the years between 1945 and 1951 when she was trying to stay alive long enough to establish a firm foothold in the movies, Marilyn Monroe clung stubbornly to her romantic attitude toward love. By the standards of other starlets, she was peculiar. They could take love as it came. Sometimes it was amusing or profitable, sometimes interesting, sometimes useful to one's advancement. Marilyn was unable to play the game like the others. She reacted with loathing to men she met who made a coarse play for her at once. The men she rejected thought her either naïve or frigid. Her romantic innocence was something they did not usually run across in the picture business. And yet her illusions seem anachronistic only if you think that Los Angeles is a city of emancipated women and sexual sophistication.

It isn't. Except for small groups of sophisticates, little oases of worldliness in the sands of conventional morality, the 7,000,000 persons who inhabit the 120 square miles of greater Los Angeles compose perhaps the largest concentration of "hicks" in the country, the reason being that Los Angeles draws to itself the outstanding "hicks" of every "hick" community, the ones who are most ignorant about life, the ones who expect a paradise on earth with perpetual sunshine and oranges in the back yard. There are more primitive religious cults, health cults, and food cults in Los Angeles than anywhere else, even in the most backward rural sections of the deep South. Los Angelenos can be conned into crack-brained schemes of spiritual and economic salvation that no other group in this country would take seriously. Los Angeles has been called Iowa with palm trees, but this is unfair to Iowa, a state of educated and cultivated people, with fine universities, museums, theatres, symphony orchestras, and one of the best daily newspapers in the United States. Los Angeles is without the cultural and intellectual ferment which is to be found in any other large city in the world. Its greatest boast is that it has more automobiles per capita than any other place on earth—and the fumes emanating from these automobiles create the thickest miasma of smog in the world. Los Angeles has also contributed to American life such cultural achievements as the square-block supermarket, the one-level and multi-level ranch house, the back-yard barbecue, laundromats and drive-in hamburger joints, banks, and shoe-repair shops. Make-believe and fakery epitomize its tourist attractions, such as Disneyland with its pseudo-Mississippi River, its pseudo-African jungle, its pseudo-Alps; or Forest Lawn Cemetery with its pseudo-grottoes and its pseudo-Michelangelos and pseudo-Raphaels.

So much for the assumed sophistication of Los Angeles. Marilyn was a native of this innocent town, and she was reared in its innocent air. Part of her exaggerated horror of men can be traced to the simplicity that is the real Los Angeles and part to her traumatic experience in that foster mother's boardinghouse. Her disgust at the way she was exploited by her foster mothers had left her with a permanent resolve never to be "used." She refused to let anybody "use" her body sexually, even to advance her career. It is standard for a starlet to go out on dates with available young actors. That's part of the publicity build-up. The dates are arranged by the studio. The couple dine at important restaurants, dance at the right night clubs; the studio pays all the expenses. In this way the girl and the boy are "seen" and become items for the gossip columns. The fan magazines can speculate on the romantic possibilities of the "twosome."

Marilyn has never co-operated in studio-managed romances. She almost never went out with a man she didn't want to go out with. She often went out with men she didn't love; she often went out with men she didn't want to go to bed with; she often went out with men she was not especially wild about because they bought her a good dinner; but she was the one who made the choice. She would not exchange sexual compliance for a line in Hedda Hopper or Louella Parsons or a story in *Photoplay Magazine*.

And she never submitted to sexual advances even if they could help her career. I've been told this many times, often by persons who had tried to seduce her in bygone years, men, often, who were in a position to put her in good parts if she went on a weekend with them to Palm Springs, Tia Juana, or Las Vegas. The conclusion of these men is summed up in this statement by a producer: "Marilyn never slept with a man who could do her any good."

In the movie colony such virtue is as infrequent as it is admirable. One reason is that there are about six females to every man and these females are of a rare delectability. More women than men have always been drawn to acting because acting is one of the principal ways in which a woman can use her femininity to win a place in a male-oriented society. The girls who come to Hollywood are consumed by ambition, and usually they will do anything to get a role or a contract. They exist in a milieu in which sex is regarded as a product, manufactured in reels of film, and as artificial as capped teeth or bleached hair. They don't have any aversion to exchanging a few moments of pain or boredom for an improvement in their professional status.

Hollywood psychoanalysts will tell you that a "sex binge" is usually the first recourse of an actor or an actress suffering from anxiety. Writing in *State of Mind: A Review of Emotional and Psychiatric Problems in Everyday Practice,* an anonymous psychiatrist made these statements:

"Three quarters of the Hollywood acting population is either insane, just getting over being insane, or about to go insane. Psychiatric episodes are daily events on movie sets. . . . Sex in Hollywood is hardly a stabilizing force . . . you have the Don Juans and nymphomaniacs who bounce like pingpong balls from paramour to paramour, never pausing to give themselves a chance at maturing love experience. . . . The goings-on behind the walls of some Hollywood homes are like scenes that may be observed in the violent wards of psychiatric institutions. In short, the emotional problems of Hollywood stars are as bad as they are commonly pictured. They are, in fact, worse."

Marilyn took herself and acting too seriously to play the sex game the way it is played in Hollywood. She was willing to suffer for the sake of becoming a better actress. During periods of unemployment when she had the choice between paying a dollar for a speech lesson or buying dinner or a pair of stockings, she chose the lesson. Stockings or a hamburger will never make you an actress, she reasoned, but speech lessons may. Her weapons of survival were, like those of Stephen Dedalus in Joyce's *Portrait of the Artist as a Young Man,* silence, exile, and cunning. The exile was not geographical; yet she seemed to others to be far away from them, to be, as they now recall, "shy and reserved," "different," "cukey," "lost in her dreams." Even Natasha Lytess, with whom Marilyn lived periodically for many years, could not penetrate the wall of privacy around her. Miss Lytess describes the "veiled look" that would glaze her eyes suddenly at any suspicion of an intrusion, and the automatic gesture she employed during conversation when she would extend her right arm, which then began weaving "to the left and right like a serpent's head. It was a gesture of evasiveness. . . ." * She says Marilyn concealed everything in her personal life. "I dared not ask her the simplest questions about her life," writes Miss Lytess. "Even an inquiry as to where she might be going on a certain evening would be regarded as unpardonable prying." Her need for autonomy was so strong that she was willing to forego the use of sex as a means of advancement.

Marilyn was always on her guard against being "used," yet during her modeling years, she fell for one of the stalest approaches in the repertoire of seduction—the screen test. She got a call, one evening, from a man who represented himself as a talent scout for Samuel Goldwyn Pictures. He said they were casting a musical and they were looking for a girl like her. He said he wanted to test her. She didn't tell him to get in touch with her agent. She didn't wonder why he was calling at night. She asked, "When?"

"Right now," the caller replied, "because we're in a hurry. I'll pick you up in fifteen minutes and we'll head over to the studio."

He called for her in a Cadillac. Although it was past eight, she didn't suspect any hanky-panky. They drove to the Goldwyn studio. The lot was deserted. He took her in through a back entrance. They entered an office building. He went into one of the offices. He sat behind a desk and gave her a script. He pointed to a long speech. He told her to read it. Her fingers trembled. It was the first real movie script she had ever touched! She read the lines.

From *My Years with Marilyn* by Natasha Lytess (as told to Jane Wilkie) which I was able to read in manuscript through the kindness of Miss Lytess and Miss Wilkie.

"Would you please raise your dress a few inches?" he asked.

She absently did so. She went on reading.

"Higher," he said.

She went on reading.

"Just a little higher," he repeated, now standing quite close to her and placing his hands on her shoulders. Now even Marilyn suddenly saw through the "line." It wasn't his office. He didn't work for Goldwyn. She wasn't going to be tested. She sprang up. She hit him in the face and kicked his shins. Then she ran out of the building.

Another gentleman once asked her to his place, not to view etchings but to partake of a good home-cooked meal. He said he was a splendid chef. He would make her a meal she would never forget. It turned out to be an omelette of kisses. She developed a bad headache. Her friend tenderly offered her aspirins, but she said she had to go home.

Another man, with whom she had gone on a date to the beach, kept pressing his fingers into her flesh so he could feel the bones. He said she had admirable bones. He liked girls with good bones. She stood up and said, "Well, if you like my bones so much, I'll have an X ray made and send it to you."

One of her more interesting propositions was from a man who said he knew a sick seventy-eight-year-old multimillionaire. The multimillionaire had a large collection of Monroe pin-ups. He also had $2,000,000 and high blood pressure and a feeble constitution. He had only six months or a year to live. He wanted to marry Miss Monroe. Now, proposed the emissary, if she married the man, she'd inherit the $2,000,000; she could keep one million and give him the other.

8 A Contract at Columbia; First Coach, First Love

After she was cast adrift by 20th Century-Fox on August 25, 1947, Marilyn didn't land a contract at another studio for six months. Having lost many of her photographic contacts during the previous year, she found modeling jobs hard to get. She lived on her unemployment insurance, and when that ran out she borrowed money and gave notes for the loans. She never stopped taking drama lessons. She studied at the Actors' Lab, a school devoted to Stanislavsky's theories of acting. The Actors' Lab had been set up, in 1939, by Roman Bohnen, J. Edward Bromberg, and Morris Carnovsky, who found themselves living in luxurious exile in the motion-picture colony, but longed for the artistic and political activity of the Group Theatre, a quasi-revolutionary group which had arisen on Broadway during the Depression. The Group developed a superb acting ensemble. It introduced the plays of Clifford Odets, and nurtured the talents of Lee Strasberg, Elia Kazan, and Harold Clurman.

Uninformed scholars of Monroviana—and The Monroe herself has not assisted them by clarifying her true history—tend to regard her publicized intellectuality as a pose, and a recent pose at that. They take a skeptical view of her interest in Dostoevski and her work at the Actors' Studio. But Marilyn has never been a frivolous soul. A persistent strain of seriousness underlies her feeling about life. Because she was deprived of higher education and is inarticulate, she may often sound idiotic or naïve in conversation. She mispronounces and misuses words. She makes hapless errors in literary references.

But she has a genuine hunger for knowledge and a true love of artistic beauty.

During her last few months at 20th Century-Fox, Marilyn had been shipped to the Actors' Lab, with several other 20th Century fledgling players. The Lab, which had begun as a workshop for professional actors, had broadened out to become a school with a formal curriculum and a faculty of 12 teachers. It was located on Crescent Heights Boulevard, off Sunset, in Hollywood proper. After she was dropped by the studio, Marilyn continued her classes at the Lab, paying tuition in preference to eating. She studied speech with Margaret McLean and elementary acting with Phoebe Brand. Miss Brand—in private life, Mrs. Morris Carnovsky—remembers Marilyn only as a very young-looking, shy, self-conscious girl, who sat in a corner in the back of the classroom and never spoke up in class. "I never knew what to make of her," she says. "I didn't know what she thought of the work. She didn't tell me what her acting problems were. But she came to classes on time and did all her assignments conscientiously. Frankly, I never would have predicted she would be a success. I remember her for her beautiful long blonde hair, which was usually in need of a good combing. I tried to get through to her and find out more about her, but I couldn't do it. She was extremely retiring. What I failed to see in her acting was her wit, her acting sense of humor. It was there all the time—this lovely comedic style she has, but I was blind to it."

For Marilyn, the Actors' Lab opened the door to a world of wisdom and dramatic beauty, and she tasted as much of it as she could. She often sat with the other young actors and actresses—the fervent dreamers, the angry idealists—at the old Schwab's drugstore on Sunset, just a few steps from the Lab. Sidney Skolsky had renamed it the Schwabadero, to indicate it was the pauper's equivalent of the Trocadero, a chic cabaret on the Sunset Strip. Marilyn didn't take part in the political and artistic arguments that raged in the Schwabadero, in the delicatessen across the street, or in the Lab commissary. She listened and learned. Sometimes, if one of the students made some money, he would take her out for a good meal at Barney's Beanery on Santa Monica or Musso Frank's on Hollywood Boulevard. These were all hangouts of the *jeunes gens*.

The Actors' Lab had a leftward political orientation. Communists, socialists, anarchists, and other radicals made their voices heard on issues of the day. A child of the Depression herself, Marilyn was sympathetic to these dreamers of a new social order, although she is not an ideologue by nature. She was a political liberal long before she met Arthur Miller.

For example, during the shooting of *All About Eve,* she was engrossed in the autobiography of Lincoln Steffens. She brought it to the sound stage one day. During the shooting of a film, there are long stretches of waiting while a new scene is being set up and lighted. Marilyn liked to find a deserted corner of the stage, spread a folding chair, and settle down with a book. One of the studio executives happened to see her absorbed in Steffens. He told her it was dangerous to be seen reading such "radical" books in public. Marilyn didn't bring the dangerous book to the studio any more. "But," she wrote, "I continued to read the second volume secretly, and I kept both volumes hidden under my bed. I think hiding Lincoln Steffens under my bed was the first underhanded thing I had ever done."

One day her agent induced Max Arnow, head of the talent department at Columbia Pictures, to run Marilyn's screen test. Her flesh impact hit Arnow between the eyes. Columbia signed her to the usual six-month option contract on March 9, 1948. She was paid $125 a week. They had no vehicle for her, but Arnow suggested that she keep herself tuned up by studying with the studio acting coach, Natasha Lytess. In April, 1948, Marilyn walked into Miss Lytess's cottage on the Columbia lot. Miss Lytess tutored her charges in a book-lined room whose principal decoration was a large photograph of Max Reinhardt. She had been a member of Reinhardt's acting ensemble in Germany and worshipped him. When the Nazis took power, she and her husband, the left-wing novelist Bruno Frank, migrated to Hollywood. After the war, Frank had returned to Germany, and she had remained in Hollywood with her daughter. Miss Lytess is a slender, taut, volatile woman, with flashing eyes and a mop of graying hair.

In Lytess, Marilyn found the first ally she made in any studio—the first person of some authority who believed in her. In Marilyn, Lytess found an eager disciple, who was responsive, ambitious, and eager to work.

Marilyn was late at their first meeting, 25 minutes late. She was wearing white tailored slacks and a white shirt tied around the middle. She looked, to Lytess, typically artificial and vulgar, like just another empty-headed starlet that the studio expected her to transform into an artist in two weeks. Lytess picked up an old Rita Hayworth script and asked her to read a speech. Marilyn's voice was almost a squeak.

"I can't hear you, my dear," Lytess said. "When you speak, your mouth closes up. You will have to work on diction. Diction, diction, diction—this is right now most important for you."

"I will do whatever you tell me," said Marilyn.

"Then first you must remember the lines. Do not dare to come on the set without knowing perfectly the lines. Know them backwards and forwards so you can even throw away the words and speak the soul of the lines. But first we must work on your diction. Now, say the same lines as before—but open your mouth, wider, even more— that is good, that is better—louder—louder. . . ."

The two became inseparable friends and allies. Marilyn, when she reached a position of power, had Lytess put on the studio payroll. She would never do a scene, after 1951, unless Lytess was on the set. Lytess encouraged Marilyn's intellectual curiosity. She urged her on in her ambitions to play roles of more depth and variety, and she was at her side in the conflicts Marilyn had with the front office. At 20th later, it became a tradition that if you wanted to make an important change in a script or overcome Marilyn's objection to a scene, you could succeed only if you first persuaded Natasha Lytess.

Marilyn Monroe had grasped an important principle of advancement in Hollywood: One needed allies. She already had allies in the press corps—Sidney Skolsky and Roy Craft, now an important press agent, were on her side. She was to find others as time went on. She learned how to arouse their sympathy, how to cultivate them, how to use them, how to learn from them. She never lost an ally—she only discarded him.

Miss Lytess gave glowing reports on the acting skill of her new pupil, and the production department gave her the lead in a B picture, *Ladies of the Chorus,* a hackneyed backstage musical that was shot in 11 days. Marilyn played Peggy Martin, a strip-teaser in a burlesque show. Peggy Martin falls in love with a youth whose family is in the social register. Her mother is opposed to the marriage because she feels that rich boys are up to no good. The rich boy's mother is against the marriage because she doesn't think strip-teasers are nice. Everything turns out happily, of course. Marilyn sang two musical numbers in the picture—one with a chorus of eight beautiful chorines, each holding a Raggedy Ann doll as they sang "Every Baby Needs a Da-Da-Daddy"; and a love duet with the hero, "Anyone Can Tell I Love You." The producer of the movie sent her to Fred Karger for coaching.

Karger was musical director of Columbia Pictures. He is a composer, an arranger, and a bandleader. He asked Marilyn if she had ever sung professionally before, and she said no but that she had taken vocal lessons. He asked her to demonstrate a number, and she sang the verse and chorus of "Love Me or Leave Me." He thought she was terrible but not hopeless. She could carry a tune— not well, but she could carry it, and that was more than you could say of some of the tone-deaf characters the front office sent his way.

Her vocal range was tiny, her volume small, her phrasing trite— but she did give the illusion that she was singing, and the sound engineer could bring up the volume when she recorded the music. With some coaching, she would be able to get by. Karger had seen her screen test. He saw that she had "camera magic."

He played over for her, several times, the rhythm number she would sing in *Ladies of the Chorus,* the one about every baby's need for a da-da-daddy. When she was able to remember every note of the melody and sing it back to him without hearing it first on the piano, he gave her a copy of the lyrics. Each night she worked on the song, and in the morning she came to his office and polished her rendition.

Karger spoke to her in a soft voice. He is a gentle, kindly person. He is also a handsome man. She began to look forward to her music lesson each day. She began to like Freddy Karger a great deal, and she found herself thinking of him more and more. Marilyn was dating a lot, as usual, but nobody she liked. Love seemed to be an experience that eluded her.

She didn't realize it, but she had been living beyond her resources, emotionally and financially. She had been putting all her emotions into getting ahead, but she was starved for personal fulfillment. Financially, she was in debt, and she had moved into a dingy one-room flat—with her pet chihuahua. Most of her salary went to pay off old debts. One day she failed to report to Karger for her lesson, and he found out that she had phoned in to say she was ill. On his way home, Karger looked in on Marilyn to see if there was anything he could do. He was struck by her air of "helplessness." When he began talking to her, he realized she was not sick but hungry. Karger, at that time, lived with his mother and sister in a house off the Sunset Strip. He invited her to come home with him for dinner. The Karger women were charmed by Marilyn's naturalness, and Freddy was pleased by her beauty, her *gaucherie,* her curiosity about life and art.

She and Freddy began to see each other after working hours. The first thing, he said, she would have to move out of the "dump" in which she lived. There was an excellent residence hotel for women, not far from Columbia, the Hollywood Studio Club, and properly qualified young career women could live there for $10 to $15 a week, room and board. Freddy telephoned Florence Williams, the managing director of the Studio Club, and was able to reserve a place for Marilyn for $12 a week. She moved in on June 3, 1948.

Located at 1215 N. Lodi Street, the Studio Club was a few blocks away from her old orphanage. It is a lovely four-storied Moorish-style building with bougainvillea creeping over the walls. Operated by the national council of the Young Women's Christian Association since 1915, it is available to girls in the arts of films, theatre, music, painting, dancing. The rooms are light and large, decorated in pastel colors, and gaily furnished. There are parlors in which the girls may receive guests, a handsome restaurant, and a patio with a fountain and tropical flowers. Marilyn's first roommate was a tall, striking brunette, Clarice Evans, who was studying opera. Miss Evans was struck by the fact that Marilyn Monroe was "as interested in the capacity of the bookshelves as in the size of the closets." Karger helped her move all her things over; her baggage included 200 books. "She had enough books," says Miss Evans, "to start a circulating library." Few residents of the Studio Club owned any books. Marilyn also brought two suitcases of clothes, a bathroom scale, a bicycle, and a huge professional hair dryer. Miss Evans recalls her spending a great deal of time washing and brushing her hair. Even on the first day, Marilyn didn't waste time in small talk with her roommate because she had a singing and an acting lesson and a make-up test at Columbia, and was getting fitted for a costume. As the weeks went by, Miss Evans found her roommate a curiously quiet girl who had more telephone calls and more dates than anybody in the Studio Club and yet never got a letter from the folks back home. She never got a letter from anybody. When the girls sat around the patio and talked about their beaux and their love affairs, Marilyn never said anything. She listened. Sometimes she smiled appreciatively. Sometimes she stared off into space. She was generous—with her money when she had it, with her Ford convertible if anybody needed a car, with advice to less experienced girls about make-up and coiffure.

If the girls at the Studio Club so often found Marilyn abstracted, it was because she was falling in love with Freddy Karger. He had given her his tenderness and his pity, and this had aroused all the emotions she had so neatly and carefully wrapped up and stored away. He had cared about her as a human being rather than as a "dame" to be "made." He had wanted her to live in a nice room, and he had taken her to his home and introduced her to his family.

Her days and nights were filled with thoughts of Freddy and the ache of loneliness. The whole world had narrowed down to one human being. When she met Freddy in a crowd, she saw his face only. She was awkward and blushed when she was with him. She felt she did the wrong things and spoke stupidly when they were together. "My heart ached so much, I wanted to cry all the time," she writes. She could not fathom Karger's attitude. He liked her. He genuinely cared for her. He delighted in improving her mind with uplifting conversations about literature and classical music. He took her to concerts at the Hollywood Bowl. He frequently telephoned her and was the epitome of courtliness when they went out riding in his car or dancing at the Palladium (she was a superb ballroom dancer). Yet for all his attentiveness, he did not burn with a passion like hers. His attitude was ambiguous and ironic. There was always a bittersweet smile on his face when they were together.

Karger had recently been divorced and had been granted the custody of his six-year-old son. When he talked above love, as he sometimes did, it was to express a world-weary hopelessness about the honor of women and the depth of their feelings. He said that women were not capable of genuine love. He believed that no woman could give herself honestly and entirely up to a man for whom she cared. Women, he said, were too shrewd, too practical. A man was a fool to believe in any woman. Listening to his tirades, Marilyn resolved to show him true love. But he didn't give her a chance. He put up a barrier of irony between them. He laughed at her linguistic lapses. He teased her about her ignorance of history and culture. He once told her, with a smile on his lips, "Your mind isn't developed. Compared to your body, it's embryonic."

No, he couldn't love her—he couldn't love her as she loved him. On the other hand, if he didn't love her, why was he so kind to her? No man had ever been so kind to her. Sometimes he would smile at her "as if I were a joke." At other times, the smile would go away, as his face grew somber. One night, at his place, they were alone. He was playing the piano for her—a Chopin nocturne. Suddenly, he put on his glasses in order to read the music. She had never seen him with glasses on before.

"I don't know why," she has recalled, "but I had always been attracted to men who wore glasses. Now when he put them on, I felt suddenly overwhelmed."

And Karger—he too was suddenly overwhelmed, either by the melancholy sensuality of the music or by the heat of Marilyn's emotions. He stood up and slowly walked towards her. His eyes closed as he placed his arms around her waist. They kissed.

"A new life began for me," Marilyn wrote. "I moved from the Studio Club where I was living to a place nearer his house so he could stop on the way to work or home from work. I sat all day waiting for him. When I looked back on all the years I could remember, I shuddered. I knew now how cold and empty they had been."

When they were not together, the separation was "agony" for her; and when they were together, unless they were making love, the moments, also, were clouded over by a different agony—the agony of uncertainty whether this love she had for Freddy and the love he had for her was the "real thing." Of course, they must be married. That was what a man and woman did who were in love. But he did not seem to be anxious to marry.

One night, he said, "I've been thinking about marriage. I've been thinking maybe we should get married. But it's impossible. I have to think of my son. Suppose we were married. Suppose something happens to me—"

"Like what? What do you mean, Freddy?" she asked.

He shrugged. "Like dropping dead, or something," he said, "well, it would be terrible for the boy."

"Why do you say that?"

"Don't you see?"

"No, I don't see."

"Don't you see it wouldn't be right for him to be brought up by a woman like you? I mean, it's not that you're not capable of being a mother, but, it's, well, it's that you—it would be unfair to him."

"You hate me," she said. "You don't love me if you have that idea of me."

She said good-bye. She would never see him again.

It was painful the first day. Waiting for the telephone bell to ring. Waiting for his knock on the door. Wanting to telephone him. But she didn't. And she didn't on the second day, the third day, the fourth day, although "my heart was breaking." On the fifth day, he came to her room late one evening. She didn't open the door.

"Let me in," he pleaded, "let me in."

She would not. He pounded on the door. She says that at the moment he began to beat on her door, "I knew I was over it. The pain was still there but I knew it would go away."

She finally spoke to him from behind the closed door: "Please go away. I don't want to see you." He departed.

But soon her resolution weakened. She saw him again—and again and still again. She was not through with the affair. She was still in love with him, and he was still not as much in love with her as she was with him.

Meanwhile, at Columbia, she had finished work on *Ladies of the Chorus*. It was not a successful movie, even by B-picture standards. Such films are usually reviewed only in the motion-picture trade press. The first notice Marilyn ever got was in the *Motion Picture Herald* for October 23, 1948: "One of the brightest spots is Miss Monroe's singing. She is pretty, and with her pleasing voice and style, shows promise."

But, by then, her contract had come up for renewal. Columbia dropped her on September 8. That day her roommate asked her, "If fifty per cent of the experts in Hollywood said you had no talent and should give up, what would you do?"

Marilyn stuck out her lower lip stubbornly. "Look," she said, "if one hundred per cent told me that, all one hundred per cent would be wrong. That's why I'm studying acting and music. I believe if I make myself the best actress there is, I have to reach the top."

She started dating older men, who took her to expensive restaurants and to their Beverly Hills mansions. They were men who liked to be seen with beautiful young girls. It was a sign of their power, a success symbol. They bought a girl dinner and introduced her to people who might help her. Marilyn always hoped that Freddy would hear of her dates and be jealous and fall madly in love with her. But it was the food, also, that interested her. She says the meals at the Studio Club were "too skimpy."

Sometime in 1948, she became a friend of one of the most powerful men in the movie colony, Joseph M. Schenck, then chairman of the board at 20th Century-Fox. Schenck told her she had a glorious future—even though his own studio and Columbia had both dropped her. He enjoyed her company and liked talking to her. He invited her to his house two or three times a week, either for large dinner parties or dinner à deux.

Once, when we were talking about this phase of her life, Marilyn looked at me quizzically. She said, "I suppose you're wondering if I ever went to bed with Mr. Schenck?"

"Well," I said, "I must admit the thought had vaguely crossed my mind."

"Get this straight," she said. "Mr. Schenck and I were good friends. He gave me encouragement when I needed it. He didn't do anything for me. He let Mr. Zanuck run the studio the way Mr. Zanuck wanted to run it. I know the word around Hollywood was I was Joe Schenck's girl friend, but that's a lie. The only favor I ever asked him, Mr. Schenck, was later, when I was back at Twentieth. I wanted a decent dressing room, and I asked him about it, and he put in a good word for me and I got a good dressing room. I never asked him to help me get good parts at Twentieth, and he didn't. He knew how I felt about it, that I wanted to succeed on my talent, not any other way, and he respected my feelings. I went to his house because I liked Mr. Schenck and I liked his food and it was better than the Studio Club food. I don't mean to imply the Studio Club had bad food. I mean, let's say, that Mr. Schenck's cook was just better than their cook."

Some evenings she might sit with Schenck for hours, listening to him talk about the ancient history of Hollywood, about the grandeurs and miseries and scandals of the city of make-believe. She liked to watch his face. "It was as much the face of a town as the face of a man," she wrote. "The whole story of Hollywood was in it." She didn't tell Schenck when Columbia dropped her.

Her main source of income at this time was Earl Moran, a leading magazine illustrator. "Earl saved my life many a time," she says. "He liked to paint me with different-colored hair. Sometimes he gave me red hair, sometimes brown or brunette. I was his favorite model. He did illustrations for short stories a lot. I was able to use my acting experience in striking a good pose and holding it for him. I helped him bring out the emotions of the scene he was painting."

Schenck heard she was in trouble through Skolsky, who had heard about it from his daughter, Steffi, a student at the Actors' Lab. Schenck telephoned Harry Cohn, the president of Columbia Pictures. Cohn was a cruel, tyrannical, greedy man who not only owned his studio but ran it like a dictator. Schenck told Cohn that Columbia had made a mistake in dropping Marilyn and that he ought to give her another chance. Cohn said she should come in for an interview. When she came to his office, he showed her a picture of a yacht.

"That's my yacht," he said.

"It's beautiful," she said.

"You're invited," he said. He placed his hand on her neck. "This weekend."

"Thank you. I've never been to a yachting party before in my life."

"It's no party. I'm not inviting nobody else but you. Do you want to come?"

"I'd love to join you and your wife on the yacht, Mr. Cohn."

He glowered. "Leave my wife out of this. I said there'll be nobody there except you and me and some sailors."

She looked at him. Her face flushed.

"Whatsa matter, I insulted you or something?" he said. "Don't give me the virgin act, baby. You're just another dame to me. I know all about you. I know you're Joe Schenck's girl and he's dropping you. He called me up to do him a favor and give you a job on the lot. He's finished with you, baby. He's turning you over to me."

She forced herself to look casual. "Thanks for the invitation," she said. "It just happens I have a previous date this weekend."

His hands dropped from her body. She had never seen a man look as hateful as he did. Cohn was not used to being rejected by anybody, let alone a starlet on the make.

Standing in the doorway, Marilyn attempted one last lingering bit of casualness. "Maybe some other time I might be able to accept," she said.

"This is your last chance, baby," he said.

She closed the door behind her. Her eyes blurred with tears, she trudged downstairs and out into Beechwood Drive. Slowly, she walked to Hollywood Boulevard. She went into a drugstore that specialized in malteds so thick you had to eat them with a spoon. When she opened her purse, she found that she had a quarter and a nickel. She ordered a malted and ate it. Then she telephoned the agency to see if any modeling engagements had turned up.

"No, Miss Monroe. Sorry."

She went to her room and read Thomas Wolfe's *Look Homeward Angel*. The loneliness pictured in Wolfe's riot of language struck the note that was vibrating in her. She didn't feel hungry. She read until early morning. Then she fell into a deep sleep for two hours and awakened, filled with new hope. She went down to the lot behind her rooming house to get her car. The car was gone.

9 The Nude Calendar

She reported the theft. Two days later the police informed her that the car had been repossessed by a finance company because she was two installments in arrears. She telephoned the company and said that in Hollywood an actress without a car was paralyzed. They said she could have it back for $50. In this crisis, she thought of Tom Kelley, a photographer who had used her on several advertising jobs. He had once remarked that if she ever were interested in posing as a nude calendar girl, it paid $50. She had refused.

Now she called Kelley and said she needed $50. She said he must never tell anybody about her posing and that he must be sure to light her in such a way that she would never be recognized. He told her that nobody would ever know except himself and his wife, who was his assistant. He told her to come in the next morning, but she said she wanted to do it after dark. When night had fallen, she walked to 736 N. Seward Street, Kelley's place, a one-story pink stucco cottage, with a tiny reception room in front, a tiny office in back, and most of it a barnlike studio, with cameras, spotlights, reflectors, a prop bar in one corner, prop palm trees and prop sand, chairs, sofas, pieces of stairways.

Kelley draped red velvet on the floor, and she posed lying on it. He shot her from ten feet above. They worked two hours. Kelley says she was as graceful as an otter, turning sinuously with utter naturalness. All her constraint vanished as soon as her clothes were removed. He remembers the experience as extraordinary in its intensity. He and his wife, Natalie, who was handing him plates, one after another, didn't say a word. The childhood dream of public nakedness was consummated, at last.

After it was over, Marilyn put on her black jersey sweater, her white slacks, and her ivory polo coat. They all went to Barney's Beanery for chili and coffee. It was the first food Marilyn had eaten that day.

Like the characters in *Penguin Island,* when she put on her clothes, her shame returned. In a childish attempt at concealment, she signed the release, dated May 27, 1949, with the pseudonym "Mona Monroe."

I once talked to Kelley about the memorable picture. He's a stocky man, hard-muscled, hard-faced. He has a large face with prominent features and a thick mustache. He looks like the Ernest Hemingway of the middle years.

"You know," Kelley said, "I shot a lot of pictures of Marilyn that night, and I had trouble selling them. A lot of the companies I showed the pictures to didn't think they were so hot. The Western Lithograph Company bought one pose for two hundred and fifty dollars, and John Baumgarth bought the famous one for five hundred dollars. I sold all my rights to it for a lousy five hundred dollars. I guess he's made himself a million out of it, Baumgarth has. Marilyn, she didn't get anything much out of it either. A lousy fifty. I guess the publicity didn't hurt her any, though. My business isn't nude calendars. I'm an advertising photographer. I've got some of the top national advertisers and agencies as my clients. If I'm proud of those Monroe pictures, and I am proud of them, it's because they are works of art. Some fine artists have analyzed those pictures and judged them works of art. No matter how you look at them—upside down or sideways—the composition is so good that you get a symmetrical design."

"What kind of camera did you use?" I asked.

"An eight-by-ten Deardorff View Camera. I'll tell you something else. A lot of people, they don't know there are TWO Monroe calendars. Sure. One is *Golden Dreams* and the other is *A New Wrinkle.*"

"Who makes up the titles? Do they have people who make up titles for nude calendars?"

"I just take the pictures. The popular one, I mean the big seller, is *Golden Dreams.* That's the one with two breasts showing. That's the

84

big seller. But *A New Wrinkle* is more aesthetic. It has plastic symmetry. I guess the public doesn't appreciate plastic symmetry. They want *Golden Dreams*."

"How fast was the exposure time?"

"I took them at one-fifth of a second with the lens stopped down to f-eighteen."

"Can you definitely assure the American people that Miss Monroe was not wearing any clothes whatsoever?" I asked.

"I do," he said. "I guarantee the authenticity of it absolutely."

Once, Marilyn was asked whether she really had nothing on when she posed for *Golden Dreams*.

"Oh, I had something on," she said.

"What?"

"The radio!" she said.

So I asked Kelley what the radio had been playing.

"It wasn't a radio," he said. "It was a phonograph. I had 'Begin the Beguine,' the Artie Shaw version, on at the time. I find it's a good number for getting a naked girl in a sexual mood. In my experience, I know of no other piece of music that can arouse sexual vibrations faster than Artie Shaw's recording of 'Begin the Beguine.' " (I suddenly comprehended how maestro Shaw had won the hearts of such exquisite creatures as Ava Gardner, Lana Turner, Kathleen Winsor, Doris Dowling, and Evelyn Keyes, the current and tenth Mrs. Shaw. But what had happened afterward? Had the ladies got tired of hearing "Begin the Beguine"? Were there no recordings available to insure the permanence of passion?) "I can tell you this. Marilyn Monroe has more sexual vibrations than any woman I ever shot. I shot twenty-four poses that night. I sold two. I also shot a roll of my Rolleiflex which I gave her as a present."

"What happened to the other poses, the twenty-two, you shot with the big camera?"

"I don't know," Kelley said. "It's the damnedest thing. I had the negatives in my filing cabinet over there. Well, one night some thief broke in here. He didn't steal any of my expensive equipment. Didn't touch anything but those negatives. He stole every one of those goddam negatives. Every one. Crazy isn't it?"

10 She Walks—Fully Dressed—
for Groucho Marx

One afternoon Marilyn was having a sandwich at the Schwabadero. The girl sitting next to her at the counter said they were finishing up a Marx Brothers picture on the RKO lot. It was an independent production. They were doing retakes and needed a sexy blonde for a bit. She had been out at RKO that morning to try for it, but they had turned her down. She said Lester Cowan was the producer.

Marilyn telephoned Cowan and said she was a blonde and that she had been considered sexy at 20th and Columbia. Cowan said to come on over and meet Groucho and Harpo. They were out when she arrived. She waited three hours until they came back. They examined her, looking at her, she says, "like I was a piece of French pastry." Cowan said she didn't have any lines to speak, she would do all the talking with her body. It was a walk-on, but the walking was quite important. She would enter an office and walk in front of Groucho. Her walk had to provoke one of Groucho's most libidinous leers.

"Can you walk?" Groucho asked.

She assured him she had never had any complaints.

"But," questioned Groucho, "can you walk so you'll make smoke come out of my head?"

She walked. Just across the room, but it was enough.

"She walks like a rabbit," said Groucho, approvingly, as he brushed wisps of smoke away from his head.

"You're hired," Cowan said. "Report to make-up at seven-thirty tomorrow."

"And don't walk around like that in any unpoliced areas," Harpo cautioned.

On the set, next day, Groucho improvised some dialogue for Marilyn. Groucho played Sam Grunion, a private detective. Marilyn, in a tight, low-cut sequin gown, undulated into his office. Groucho practically swallowed his cigar at the sight of the vision. He contorted his face into a satyr's leer while Marilyn explained she needed some help from a detective.

"What can I do for you?" Groucho asked in a brisk businesslike voice. Then he shuffled downstage and looked into the camera, saying, *sotto voce,* "As if I didn't know." Then he went back into the scene, all business again. "What seems to be the problem?"

"Well," Marilyn explained, "men keep following me all the time!"

Then, with a saucy swing of her hips, she exited.

When Cowan saw the rushes he got excited and said he was going to "do something" for her. Two days later as Marilyn was casually reading Louella Parsons' column, her own name jumped out at her. She read that Cowan planned to place her under contract to him personally and build her up into starring roles. She took a taxi to RKO. It developed that Cowan didn't exactly have a contract drawn up, but he hinted that something big was in the works and she would find out about it soon. He patted her on the shoulder. He assured her she was going to be great and had nothing to worry about.

She was walking on air. The first thing she thought was that now maybe Freddy Karger would love her, maybe it would all fall into place the way she wanted it to fall into place. She went to a dollar-down, dollar-a-week jeweler's on Hollywood Boulevard. She selected a gold watch priced at $500. She showed the jeweler the item in Louella Parsons' column. She said she didn't have more than two dollars, but she was about to sign a contract and was her credit any good? It was. She gave the watch to Freddy.

Money had no meaning to Marilyn. She never thought of avoiding poverty by saving money during a prosperous period. To her the installment plan was a delightful solution to financial difficulties. Once, needing 50 cents for cab fare, she went into the Vine Street office of a chain loan company and said she wanted to borrow 50 cents. They lent her the money, after she'd convinced the manager she was serious, and she signed a promissory note. She had no qualms in 1948 about buying the new Ford convertible, an expensive radio-phonograph, an electric hair dryer—on time. She was never worried about the future. In the future, sooner or later, she would be a movie star. At this point, she didn't doubt that Lester Cowan was preparing to star her in a million-dollar picture.

After several days of uncertainty Cowan called her to his office. He didn't have a story for her right away, and he didn't want to put her under long-term contract, but he had an idea for her. How would she like to go on a publicity junket, see our great country, and put in a few words on behalf of *Love Happy*, the Marx Brothers film? It was a chance for her to get herself a lot of publicity. She'd be on salary, too. A hundred and a quarter a week, the same as Columbia had been paying her, all expenses, and she'd have herself a ball, a real vacation.

"I don't understand," she said. She felt uneasy. "What do you want me to do?"

"Do?" Cowan said. "Nothing. Just be the beautiful girl you are. One of our publicity men will meet you in New York. He'll handle everything. You just relax and have a good time. Here's a voucher. Draw yourself some money and buy some new clothes. You're going to stay at the best hotels, eat in the best restaurants. It'll be fun— and we're paying you for it."

"I have to think about it," she said.

She decided to go, on the theory that absence makes the heart grow fonder. If she went away for two months, maybe Freddy would miss her, and "it would make my sweetheart realize how much he loved me."

Marilyn inhabits a world of her own making. So she assumed that, since it was a hot June in Hollywood and New York was at the other end of the continent, it must be freezing there. She went to May's department store and purchased three tailored suits, made of heavy worsted.

When she left, the studio sent a limousine and a press agent to pick her up. Freddy didn't come to see her off. That made her sad. But she dramatized her sadness. Must not the actress suffer and suffer to become a woman?

Like most Hollywood actresses, she never ventured below Vermont Avenue. Downtown was a foreign country. So the ride downtown was exciting, and it was flattering when the porter took her bags and the press agent took her arm and handled her like a princess. She had bought on credit a fancy white rawhide suitcase and a leather overnight bag and a traveling kit for cosmetics. The press agent escorted her through the Spanish arches and patios of the Union Station to her bedroom on the Sante Fe Chief. On the way he primed her with witty comments to make,in New York. She would be called the Woo-Woo Girl. It was the time of the "girls." Ever since Lana Turner had been publicized successfully as the Sweater Girl, publicity men had put girl labels on their girls. When he said good-bye, the press agent handed her a long mimeographed treatise to study. It contained a summary of the plot of *Love Happy* and various facts and figures and anecdotes. Marilyn realized that she was just a saleswoman going on the road to sell a movie. The press agent talked to her as if she were a Mongolian idiot. She didn't disillusion him. She knew everybody assumed she was a stupid little starlet.

When the train began moving down the tracks, she settled herself in the privacy of her bedroom. She told herself she was on the way. It had to be. Then she began to read, but not the publicity release. She had brought along Freud's *Psychopathology of Everyday Life,* Wolfe's *The Web and the Rock, Swann's Way* by Proust, and *An Actor Prepares,* by Konstantin Stanislavsky. She never did study the treatise on *Love Happy.*

In the morning, she put on dark glasses and went to the diner for breakfast. It delighted her to watch the diners whispering to each other about her, knowing she was a movie star and wondering which one. She swaggered past the men in the club car, and they eyed her up and down. She still felt an intoxicating glow when she was stared at.

In Chicago, she was met by another press agent, taken to lunch at the Pump Room, and briefed all over again. She then boarded the Twentieth Century Limited. At the Harmon Station of the New York Central, about 40 minutes out of New York, still another press agent boarded the train. He had brought her a corsage of three white orchids, which she pinned to the lapel of her navy-blue suit. She was wearing a blue blouse and a choker of pearls. She adjusted her velvet beret at a cocky angle. She was ready for the press. At

Grand Central, photographers were waiting. They shot her walking down the steps of the car, showing plenty of calf. The photographers immediately knew this was no ordinary slice of "cheesecake." This was a girl who knew how to get set for a picture, how to hold a smile, how to grow a bewitching gleam in her large eyes, how to make her lips open and stay apart. . . . They kept saying, "One more, just one more, one more." . . . She was conscious of perspiring a lot. It was hot. It was very hot. She had miscalculated the weather. New York in June could be hot. As a matter of fact, New York was going through an unseasonable heat wave. The press agent seized the opportunity. He sent an assistant for ice-cream cones. She was photographed clutching three ice-cream cones in both hands. The caption: "Marilyn Monroe, the hottest thing in Hollywood, cooling off. Miss Monroe stars in the new Marx Brothers' film Love Happy." To get New York reporters to interview Marilyn and put in a plug for the picture, the press agents lied to the press and spread the false information that she was the feminine lead in *Love Happy* and was a new star, but Marilyn didn't find this out until she read the interviews that were published later.

She was ensconced in a suite at the Sherry Netherland, an elegant hotel opposite the Plaza fountain on 59th Street. She was in New York City for three days. She did not get to see the famous landmarks and museums or the latest plays or the night clubs. She had a nice view of the fountain and of the New York population scrambling about 15 stories below. All she did was pose for pictures eating ice-cream sodas, sipping tall glasses of iced tea, wearing a bathing suit. The press agents had decided to continue playing the theme of the hottest girl in Hollywood cooling off. The first important publicity break she ever got was in Sidney Fields' column in the New York *Daily Mirror,* on June 27, 1949. He wrote a column about her, and he published her photograph. This was the first time her picture had appeared in any metropolitan paper. He began his story this way: "Marilyn is a very lovely and relatively unknown movie actress. But give her time; you will hear from her. She is still very young."

I recently asked Fields why he had gone out on a limb for the unknown actress whom he had never seen in any movie. He said that her "animal vitality" was quite overpowering. He had interviewed hundreds of actresses but nobody with so much seductiveness.

Within a few days, Marilyn found the experience of being in New York frustrating. Her "sweetheart" had not called her from the Coast, not once. She was hot and sweating and bored. Except at breakfast, she was never alone. She was always being interviewed or photographed. She wasn't allowed to wander at her sweet will. The only break in the monotonous routine was a trip to Jones Beach. Andre de Dienes, a first-rank photographer, took a series of lovely pictures of her as she cavorted on the sand and in the water. Since the calendar photograph was not published for two years, these photographs are the first visual record of her transition from the awkward model of 1945 into the lovely young woman she had become. She is shown wearing a white bathing suit. Superb legs, fine ankles, slim thighs rising to a magnificent *derrière*, a beautifully formed back, slender graceful arms, wild golden hair crowning a face filled with animal *joie de vivre*. The "flesh impact" is three-dimensional. In one pose, she is shown crouching over the incoming waves, her knees balanced on a piece of driftwood, her feet slightly in the air, her torso slanting downwards as if she were slipping out of her swimsuit, her hands dug into the sand, and the spume of the waves washing over them. Her face, turned upwards, wears a look of rapture. De Dienes has said, "This is the sexiest picture I ever made."

Then it was back to Manhattan for more interviews, for radio appearances, for photographs. It was the same thing all over again in Detroit, Cleveland, Chicago, Milwaukee. In Rockford, Illinois, she had had it. The junket had another month to go, but she returned to Los Angeles in August. Now, now she would sign the new contract with Cowan. But Cowan wasn't in town. When he came back, he didn't return her calls.

Again she began the rounds of the studios, but there were no parts. Freddy had not changed. He liked her, but he didn't love her. He admired her, his mother admired her, his sister admired her, but he felt no grand passion for her. So they drifted apart. She still sends Mrs. Karger a card on Mother's Day.

It took her two years to finish paying for the gold watch. By then, Karger was married to Jane Wyman. "Music when soft voices die,/

Lingers in the memory," and her feelings for Freddy lingered on. Once, she was in Chasen's having dinner. In a private dining room, Jerry Wald was giving a dinner party for Karger and Miss Wyman. Wald happened to run into Marilyn and asked her to join the party. She became white and stammered, "N-no, I c-couldn't go in there. N-never."

11 The Love of Johnny Hyde; Marilyn Meets a Genius

At this time, she came to know a man who became her friend, her lover, and her most fervent ally in the front offices of the studios where the real decisions are made. He was Johnny Hyde, executive vice-president of the Hollywood branch of the William Morris Agency, one of the two most powerful agencies in show business. Except for one ambiguous romantic interlude in 1950, Hyde remained the most significant man in her life until he died.

"I met Johnny at Palm Springs in nineteen forty-nine," Marilyn told me. "I went with these people for a weekend, and Johnny Hyde saw me from a distance, and Bernard what's-his-name, this photographer, said he'd like to take some pictures of me, and we went to the Racquet Club, and Johnny was there and met me, but I didn't remember it but he did. He was one among many strangers I was introduced to, and it didn't take the first time. It was at the pool, he said. I was swimming in it, and we were introduced at the pool. Then he was over at these people's house I was staying with, and that's when I remember him. We had some drinks and we talked. Johnny was marvelous, he really was. He believed in my talents. He listened to me when I talked, and he encouraged me. He said I would be a very big star. I remember laughing and saying it didn't look like it because I couldn't make enough to pay my telephone bill. He said he had discovered Lana Turner and other stars and that I had more than Lana and it was a cinch I would go far. He had seen me in *Love Happy,* which was just released. He explained something to me that I didn't realize before. This was that if you are a star it is hard to find little roles. They either have to give you a star part, even if it isn't big, or nothing. I couldn't love him as much as he did me, but I did not go out with any other men during the time I was seeing him, not seriously. Isn't it sad that I loved Freddy and he didn't love me and then here's Johnny in love with me and I didn't return his love? But Johnny was kind to me, and I was faithful to him."

She was twenty-two and Johnny was fifty-three. He was a little man, almost a hunchback. His hair was thinning, and his face was lined with the tensions of a life devoted to catering to the whims of actors. He was born Ivan Haidabura in St. Petersburg in 1895. He was born into a family of acrobats. His parents, his brothers, his sisters were members of the Nicholas Haidabura Imperial Russian Troupe. The troupe came here for a vaudeville tour in 1905, and they remained, his father becoming an American citizen. During his early years in show business, Hyde produced "flash acts" for vaudeville. He became an agent in 1926, and in 1935, the Morris Agency sent him to the Coast. There he quickly became one of the most adroit intriguers in a community of two-bit Talleyrands. Hyde's flair was the recognition and fostering of new talent. He was a shrewd businessman and a sympathetic friend and, during his heyday, probably the best-loved agent in Hollywood. He drank with his clients, golfed with them, counseled them on money problems and marital difficulties, wrangled with studio executives for them. Among the stars whom he had nurtured were Lana Turner, Betty Hutton, Esther Williams, Bob Hope, and Rita Hayworth.

Probably he had fallen in love with every new girl he discovered, as he fell in love with Marilyn Monroe. But she had come at the end of his string. She was his September song, and he wanted her intensely. Did he fall in love with a real person or with an image he created out of his romantic fantasy?

I once asked one of Hyde's close friends about Johnny's intimacy with Marilyn. He said, "She was no good for Johnny. When I heard he was going with her, I felt terrible. He was a guy with heart trouble. No guy with heart trouble has any business going out with Marilyn Monroe."

A producer whom I queried about the importance of Hyde's influence in advancing her career told me: "Only one man was responsible for making her a star. That man was Johnny Hyde. He had faith in her when she was a starlet and a damned unimportant starlet. When you had Johnny in your corner, you had a pipeline to the guys who really count in Hollywood, you had the ear of Zanuck at Twentieth, of Schary at Metro, Don Hartman at Paramount, Jack Warner at Warner's. He talked her up everywhere he went, and you got to realize that a guy like Johnny, he had the entree everywhere, the best country clubs, the big parties at the best homes, and everybody sat up and listened to him because he had a hell of a track record of proven winners at the box office. He talked her up twenty-four hours a day. He made this town Marilyn Monroe conscious—and when I say this town, I mean the right circles in Bel-Air and Brentwood, where it really counts, not with the slobs. He sold her to producers and directors as another Rita Hayworth and Lana Turner.

"He taught her how to dress and talk to people. He made her sophisticated. It's the old story of Trilby and Svengali. Svengali can make a star out of Trilby, but he can't make her fall in love with him."

Usually, Marilyn doesn't betray resentment. She may feel it, but it's disguised in a mask of withdrawal. But if you suggest to her, as I once did, that Johnny Hyde or Natasha Lytess or anybody else is her "Svengali," her reaction is violent. "Johnny Hyde was wonderful," she told me. "But he was not my Svengali. Natasha Lytess was not my Svengali. Milton Greene was not my Svengali. I'm nobody's slave and never have been. Nobody hypnotizes me to do this or that. Now they write that Lee Strasberg is my Svengali. I read a thing in some column that I was on Fire Island and a photographer asked me to pose and I asked Mr. Strasberg if it was all right for me to pose. It never happened. I was never on any beach with Mr. Strasberg in the first place. And Arthur Miller isn't my Svengali. It is true that I have had coaching, advice—lessons from different teachers. Michael Chekhov. Mr. Strasberg. I believe in learning and developing myself. Why shouldn't I have a coach? I never had any acting experience before I went into the movies. Sure I used to want Natasha Lytess on the set to give me criticism of what I did wrong, and now I want Paula Strasberg. You know, I have never had the privilege of okaying any takes they do on me, contrary to what they may have told you. The directors have that power. Not me. When you're in the hands of a good director, it's good. But I not only didn't have acting experience, I worked in some pictures where I was directed by men who never directed before or didn't know a thing about character motivation or how to speak lines. Do you ever see on the screen, 'this picture was directed by an ignorant director with no taste'? No, the public always blames the star. *Me.* I had directors so stupid all they can do is repeat the lines of the script to me like they're reading a timetable. So I didn't get help from them. I had to find it elsewhere."

All actresses feel as Marilyn does about movie directors. Most directors are regarded as unimaginative mechanics who waste hours fussing over arrangements of lights and camera angles and props rather than involving themselves in the characters and the story. In her book *Hollywood, The Dream Factory,* which is based on 900 interviews with a cross section of movie workers, the anthropologist Hortense Powdermaker says that the directors themselves credit only 5 per cent of their colleagues with creative power, and the actors were even more critical.

"Many directors have little understanding of story-telling, of the movie medium, or of human beings. These emphasize lavish sets and, with enough help from cameraman, actors, editor-cutter and others, their pictures come off in some way or other, in spite of them, rather than because of them. They work mechanically and shoot from every possible angle in the hope that one will be usable. They take an almost infinite number of retakes of what they are striving for."

Marilyn saw this at the outset of her career and protected herself by having a dramatic coach on the set who had only her interests at heart.

In Johnny Hyde, Marilyn had the best agent in Hollywood on her side, and she had an excellent drama coach. All she needed was a springboard, what Skolsky calls "a good piece of film on herself." She got it by accident. One day in October, 1949, at Metro-Goldwin-Mayer, a group of talent scouts, casting agents, and directors were gathered in a projection room. They were running an unrelated series of screen tests of several dozen of the newer actors and actresses. Studios lend screen tests to each other on request.

Now it happened that Marilyn's old silent color test had *not* been one of those requested. But somebody at 20th had made a mistake and pulled her old test out of the archives and sent it to Metro with several others. When the tests were run, Lucille Ryman, a casting agent at Metro, was impressed by Marilyn's. There was no role she could recommend her for at that moment, but she was curious to know more about this blonde. She learned that Hyde represented her, and through Hyde she met Marilyn.

Her first words, uttered solemnly, were, "Miss Monroe, you have talent, great talent, talent as an actress."

This was sweet music to Marilyn's ears because Miss Ryman didn't praise her body but her talent. Marilyn told her of the discouraging events of the last three years.

"Don't lose heart, my dear," Miss Ryman said. "You're going to find every door opening soon, very soon. But until then, I want you to count on me as your friend. Come to me whenever you have any troubles or any problems and I will help you."

Miss Ryman did not know that Marilyn is the sort of person to whom troubles and problems gravitate as naturally as filings to a magnet. She called on Miss Ryman for help within a few days. Marilyn was living, at the time, in a ground-floor room. One night she was aroused from sleep by a suspicious scratching outside her window. In the shadows, she saw the head of a man. He was cutting a hole in her screen. Marilyn slipped out of bed, quietly opened the door, and was down the hall by the time the intruder had gained entrance. She phoned the police and then Miss Ryman. She was afraid to go back to sleep in her room. Miss Ryman's solution was simple. She invited Marilyn to move in with her. Marilyn lived with Miss Ryman for about six months. Miss Ryman not only gave her shelter and three meals a day but also $25 a week for walking-around money. "I can't explain the sense of well-being and security this gave me," Marilyn once remarked to Liza Wilson.

Even Marilyn's worst enemies must concede that she has a genius for collecting good Samaritans. She can make a person feel individually responsible for the hurts society had inflicted on Norma Jeane Mortenson.

Now Marilyn did not have to model or make casting rounds. She lived the life of a creative artist. She studied her lessons in drama and singing. Taking her ease *chez* Ryman, she improved the shining hours by giving her soul up to the classics of poetry and prose.

One day, Miss Ryman came home in something of a dither. John Huston was directing the movie version of W. R. Burnett's novel *The Asphalt Jungle,* a realistic tale of crime and punishment. She had just read the script. There was a marvelous part in it for Marilyn, the part she needed to make her famous. She had already talked to Huston about Marilyn. He wanted to hear her read.

"When?"

"Call Johnny Hyde. Let him talk to Huston and arrange a date, Marilyn. It's better if it comes through Johnny. You'll get a better deal that way."

Hyde himself took her to the office of the producer, Arthur Hornblow, Jr., at Metro. Here she met John Huston. She has said that Huston was the first real artistic genius she ever met face to face. His powerful self-assurance dominated the room. He turned out to be a tall man with straggling hair above a long, bony face with dark, probing eyes. A muscular, taut man, who couldn't keep still but stalked the office like a prowling animal, Huston obviously was a genius. He was not immaculately garbed, and everybody knew geniuses were sloppy dressers. He wore an old pair of corduroy pants and a dark shirt open at the collar.

He put his hands on his hips and arrogantly looked her over. He said she looked right for the part but there was more to it than looking right. She had to act. There was a scene in which she had to break up—to cry, to sob. He told her something of the plot and something of the character of Emmerich, the crooked lawyer, to be played by Louis Calhern. In the script she was called Calhern's "niece," but it was obvious she was his mistress. She called Calhern "Uncle." In those days, before the movies were freed from sexual inhibitions, they didn't call a mistress a mistress.

Huston said he didn't want to listen to Marilyn give a reading until she had thought about the part. This approach further impressed her with his genius.

"And don't just read Angela's lines," he told her. "Read Emmerich's too. Read the whole damn script. Trouble with too many of you actors, you study your own parts and don't know what the rest of it is all about. Go home now, kid. Don't come back until you know what the story's about, what Angela's about. I'll see you."

He waved good-bye to her and turned his back. She would have been shocked by his rudeness except that he was a genius. Hyde eased her out of the office. She felt choked up by the prospect before her. They came out on the steps of the Administration Building. She started to cross to the parking lot across the street and the sunlight hit her eyes and made her cry. Or at least that was what she said to Johnny. Or what she tried to say. She couldn't talk. Hyde said it was too early to go home and took her to the Retake Room, a shadowy *estaminet* on Washington Boulevard where the Metro crowd hung out because no liquor was served in the commissary. She had a daiquiri, which was her favorite drink that year. She never drank very much. She could get stoned on her own vision of herself, as any patriotic American narcissist can do.

"Look," Hyde said gently, "don't worry about it. You can do it. I know you can do it."

"I mustn't fail this time, Johnny," she said. "I mustn't let anything go wrong."

She didn't. She studied every line of that script for three days. She went over the role of Angela with Miss Lytess hour after hour. This is not the normal procedure of movie starlets. Angela, though an interesting and a vital character in the story, was not a major character. She was peripheral to the main action, and she appeared in only two long scenes, both with Calhern. That made no difference to Marilyn. With the earnest single-mindedness that characterizes her professional approach, she gave prolonged study to the role. When she had memorized the lines and worked out a definition of Angela, she rehearsed on a couch in Miss Ryman's living room, because Angela did most of her lines in a horizontal position—where mistresses usually do their lines.

When she was prepared, Hyde took her back to Culver City. Both Hornblow and Huston were waiting for her. Huston sensed her nervousness and tried to put her at her ease. She felt a sensation of near panic. She couldn't remember her lines. Her throat was dry. Her head felt as if it were made of wood and splitting open.

Huston stood by the window. He was rattling the blind. "Well, Miss Monroe, shall we roll? Bill here will cue you into your lines." He signaled to the assistant director.

She held the script close to her bosom and looked around the room. There was no couch, and she had studied her lines stretched out on a couch. A casting couch is traditional in a producer's office, but here was a producer's office with no casting couch or even a non-casting couch, not even a narrow uncomfortable couch. She didn't want to read the lines standing up. She said, "I'd like to read the scene on the floor. Do you mind?"

Everyone swung to watch Huston's reaction. He put his hands in his pockets and shrugged his shoulders. His eyes narrowed, analyzing her. He seemed to be thinking, What's the angle, baby?

"Yeah," he said, "you want to do it that way, do it that way."

She kicked off her shoes. She sat on the floor, spread out her dress, and then languidly sank upon the carpet. She placed her hands behind her head, which had the effect of making her breasts jut outward. The assistant director, who was quite happy about the way she was doing it, knelt on the floor beside her and threw her the cue for her first speech. After she finished, she said, "I want to do it again."

Huston, who had been staring out of the window the whole time, twisted the cord of the blind. "You don't have to," he said.

"Please, it's very important, let me do it again."

"What for?"

"I'd like to—please."

He shrugged. "Have it your way."

She did it again.

"You've got the part," he said. "You had it the first time. You didn't have to do it twice. Bill, get her over to Wardrobe to get measured for her clothes." He smiled at her. "You wear an evening dress in one scene with Calhern and silk lounging pajamas in another. You're on salary as of Monday. I want you on the set by nine, kid."

He abruptly turned away, dismissing her.

Marilyn found Huston an "exciting" director. He watched her and listened to her. He would let her do a scene her own way first and then, speaking to her in a low voice, criticize her, but subtly, gently. Having got involved so early in her movie career with a genuinely creative film maker, she was spoiled and could not get along happily with several of the incompetents in whose hands she later found herself.

Huston gave her one important piece of advice. He told her to forget herself when Calhern was speaking to her or gazing at her lasciviously. He showed her that acting was also reacting—listening to other actors, losing herself.

The Asphalt Jungle, played, written, and directed with sardonic realism, was a paradigm, in terms of policemen and thieves, of a competitive society. It was one of the best films of 1950. It is frequently revived, and when it is, Marilyn usually gets top billing on the marquees, although originally she was not even listed in the screen credits.

After a film is done, it goes through several stages before it is released. The first is a screening of the rough cut—without music and sound effects—before the cast and the front-office executives. Seeing herself on a screen is always an eerie experience for Marilyn. She feels that it is not she up there. She is embarrassed, and she is thrilled. Watching the rough cut of *Asphalt Jungle,* however, she knew that she had carried out her artistic intentions. Hyde was sitting next to her. He was as pleased as she was. "Honey," he whispered to her, "you're in. I can feel them reacting. They're crazy about you."

Then came the sneak preview in Westwood Village. The audience response was extraordinary. On her first entrance, they whistled and applauded and cheered, and they demonstrated whenever she came on the screen. The name "Marilyn Monroe" did not appear on the credits; many persons, filling out the usual preview cards of comment on the new film, wrote the question, "Who's the blonde with Calhern?"

After such a spontaneous public show of approval, Hyde was sure he would get a good long-term deal for Marilyn from Metro. But he didn't. He couldn't even get her another picture job. Dore Schary, who was then Metro's executive in charge of production, did not think Marilyn looked like a movie star. He didn't, of course, realize that her performance in *The Asphalt Jungle* had been acting. Later Schary dryly remarked, "There was once a genius who saw an advance screening of *Snow White and the Seven Dwarfs,* and he said nobody would pay money to see a cartoon for an hour and a half. The cartoon grossed twenty million dollars. Then this same genius was offered a chance to invest money in *A Streetcar Named Desire,* and he said it was a very poorly constructed play. *Streetcar* ran for two years on Broadway. He also had a chance to put Marilyn Monroe under contract, and he let her go. The genius who did all those things was Dore Schary."

The reviews described Monroe as "luscious," as "the most dazzling blonde since Lana Turner." The Metro board of higher strategy did not agree.

12 Some Brief Encounters: Joseph Mankiewicz, Arthur Miller, George Sanders, and Zsa Zsa Gabor

Among those who had been impressed by the blonde in *The Asphalt Jungle* was writer-director Joseph Mankiewicz. He was then working on the Darryl Zanuck production of *All About Eve* at 20th Century-Fox. The previous year he had won an Academy Award with a sparkling comedy, *Letter to Three Wives,* and he was in a position to get what he wanted. When he wanted the unknown blonde for a part in *All About Eve,* he got her. He found out the girl's name and he called Johnny Hyde and said there was a role available for Monroe—the role of Miss Casswell, a character superficially like Angela in *The Asphalt Jungle.* Miss Casswell was blonde, voluptuous, and immoral. She wanted to be a stage actress. Like Angela she was a "keptee," her keeper being, like Calhern, a man of the world, as sophisticated as Calhern—the debonair George Sanders. In *All About Eve,* Sanders played Addison de Witt, a drama critic given to uttering sardonic epigrams.

Marilyn appeared in only two sequences in the film. The first was a theatrical party given by the star, Margo Channing (Bette Davis) in honor of a director (Gary Merrill) who has just returned from Hollywood. De Witt has brought Miss Casswell as his date. At the head of the stairs, in her town house, Miss Davis receives them. "This," says Sanders, waving in Marilyn's direction, "is Miss Casswell. Miss Casswell is an actress. She is a graduate of the Copacabana School of Dramatic Arts." Marilyn was wearing a white satin evening dress. Her shoulders were bare. Her bosom was *très décolleté.* Later, during the party, a group of persons are sitting on the stairs, and a servant passes, bearing a tray. Marilyn sings out, "Oh, waiter, may I have a drink?"

Sanders informs her that the man is not a waiter, he is a butler. Marilyn's eyes grow large. "But I couldn't say, 'Oh, butler,'" she explains. "Suppose there was somebody named Butler at the party?"

In her second scene in *All About Eve,* Miss Casswell goes to a theatre to read for a part. Sanders is awaiting her out front. The audition proves a fiasco, and we see Marilyn staggering dejectedly—having just vomited because of nerves. She's in a tight cashmere sweater, trailing a fox stole along the floor. She says that the audition was terrible. She doesn't think she can stand the pressure of the theatre. Sanders suggests television as a prospect. She asks if there are auditions in television, and Sanders remarks, "My dear, everything in television is an audition."

How mean Marilyn's status was at the time is indicated by the fact that her credit was listed far down in a long catalogue of supporting players, sandwiched in between Thelma Ritter's and Barbara Bates's.

Miss Casswell's part in the plot of *All About Eve* was even more peripheral than Angela's in *The Asphalt Jungle.* Yet Marilyn worked as hard on developing Miss Casswell as she had worked on Angela. She could have done a carbon copy of Angela, and it might have satisfied Mankiewicz. She didn't. Her reading of Miss Casswell was different in its nuances. Miss Casswell is not as sensitive as Angela. She is a vacuous, self-centered moron. She reeks with animal appeal, like Angela, but the core of her motivation is an infantile pursuit of success. Sanders is a means to her end, rather than a source of pleasure, as Calhern had been to Angela.

The fine shadings that Marilyn went to such pains to achieve in two minor roles were unnoticed triumphs, but they showed she was serious about acting. They were harbingers of the future.

One day, after a morning's shooting, Marilyn was strolling to the commissary for lunch. She was overtaken by Cameron Mitchell, a young actor. The year before, he had made his mark on Broadway in the role of Happy, the younger Loman brother in *Death of a Salesman.* He had been brought out by 20th Century-Fox and was being groomed for stardom. He knew Marilyn slightly. I once asked him how she had struck him at that period of her life. He replied:

"I'd seen her around, talked to her a couple of times. At first, till you know her a little, you figure her for the standard platinum blonde, no brains, just out for money, looking for a sugar daddy to give her the minks and the diamonds. Then as you know her, you find out she's no goddam gold-plated birdbrain. She's a serious dame. At the time I first met her, she was on a big psychiatry kick. She was studying Freud, Menninger, that kind of thing. Well, I had the usual Broadway actor's attitude toward a dumb movie starlet, and she gassed me. She was a real offbeat girl."

As they were promenading, Marilyn suddenly halted. Across the walk, leaning against the concrete wall of a sound stage, were two men, deep in conversation. One was short, lean, kinetic. The other, towering above him, looked to be several inches over six feet. He was gaunt, and his sensitive face, with its high cheekbones and deeply set eyes, seemed lit with a sympathetic comprehension of human suffering. He looked like Abraham Lincoln. Marilyn felt that she was seeing an ideal in the flesh. "Who ever loved that loved not at first sight?" Marlowe wrote. Marilyn fell in love at first sight.

"Who's that?" she asked Mitchell. "You know him? The tall one?"

"Sure," he said. "I know both of them. Come on, I'll introduce you."

They went over, and Mitchell said he wanted the men to meet a young actress with a great future, Marilyn Monroe. The name rang no bells. The short man was Elia Kazan, whom Mitchell called "Gadge." Gadge, who had mounted a series of exciting productions on Broadway since 1946, had become one of the theatre's outstanding directors. Actors and actresses everywhere were spreading the word that he had a way of giving you confidence and digging out emotions in you you didn't even know you had and making them work in your acting. Kazan was one of the three founders of the Actors' Studio, which, though only two years old, had already stirred up a great ferment in acting circles. It had become recognized as the most stimulating center of acting theory and experiment in the country.

The tall man was Arthur Miller. He had won the New York Drama Critics Circle Award with his second produced play, *All My Sons*, and the Pulitzer Prize with *Death of a Salesman*. Kazan and Miller had come west with the notion of collaborating on *The Hook*, a movie about labor racketeering on the Brooklyn waterfront. It would show how the gangsters exploited honest longshoremen and how the workers finally defeat their oppressors. Miller had written a screen treatment, and Kazan had worked up a plan of production.

Miller was not as overwhelmed by Marilyn as she had been by him, but he was certainly intrigued. How far did their intimacy progress in 1950? We do not know for certain. They saw each other frequently for several weeks. Many persons in a position to know believe that Miller fell in love with her; that Marilyn expected Miller to divorce his wife and marry her; that she did not marry Johnny Hyde because she hoped to be Mrs. Miller; that it was only after she lost hope that she began going out with Joe Di Maggio, deliberately selecting the least intellectual man available.

Others say that while Miller and she were fascinated by each other, their relations were circumspect. Marilyn had a moral regard for monogamy. And Miller was no philanderer. He and his wife had been married 12 years and had two children. His family life was outwardly one of serenity.

Some persons believe that after Miller returned to his home in Brooklyn Heights late in 1950, he and Marilyn continued their liaison by telephone and letters and had secret meetings. But an opposing opinion holds that as soon as Miller left Hollywood, the friendship was terminated, for the time being. He did not reply to her letters, and he did not call her on the telephone.

As we shall see later, he was profoundly affected by the meeting with Marilyn. It was to alter the course of his life and the character of his dramatic expression.

Marilyn continued to worship him as an author. His photograph hung in her bedroom. When she was asked, at various times, to name her favorite authors, she always put Miller at the head of her list. In 1951, she told an interviewer that her favorite authors were Miller, Tolstoy, Thomas Wolfe, and Antoine de Saint-Exupéry. In 1954, Skolsky asked her to name the men she thought outstanding. It is a peculiar collection. She listed her favorite men as Marlon Brando, Michael Chekhov, John Huston, Arthur Miller, comedian Jerry Lewis, and Jawaharlal Nehru. Why she was as much impressed by Jerry Lewis as by Nehru and put both in the same list with an egocentric like Brando and intellectuals like Huston, Miller, and Chekhov, we shall never know. Skolsky did not ask her to divulge the logic of her choices, and nowadays Marilyn does not feel any need to justify or explain events in her past.

Before shooting on *All About Eve* was completed, Marilyn had an amusing bit of swordplay with Zsa Zsa Gabor, who was then married to George Sanders. It was not the first time that the two blondes had clashed. Zsa Zsa did not like Marilyn the first time she saw her. This was when Marilyn was modeling. Anthony Beauchamp, a photographer then married to Sarah Churchill, invited her to a cocktail party. Marilyn got herself up informally in a tight black skirt, white sweater and pearls, and ballet slippers. As soon as she came upon the scene, Marilyn realized that she was out of place. The other women were dressed to the teeth—or at least to the bosoms. Then Marilyn became aware of a tall, terribly chic blonde, standing not far from her, who was eyeing her clinically. Presently the chic lady, who seemed to be angry, began talking about her to the people she was with. She glared at Marilyn and remarked on the common, cheap sort of hussies one encountered so often in "Hollyvood." Suddently, she stormed out.

"That was Zsa Zsa Gabor," Beauchamp whispered to Marilyn. "My dear, what did you do to her?"

"I didn't do anything," Marilyn murmured.

"Oh come now, you must have *said* something?"

"No-no, Tony—no-nothing at all."

"Well she's in quite a state. You just drove her out of the party. *She hates you!* Refuses to be in the same bloody room with you."

Zsa Zsa was not exactly overjoyed when Marilyn was cast as Miss Casswell to Sanders' Addison de Witt. Who better than an actress knows how swiftly the romantic fictions of the cinema, or the theatre, can be converted into the realities of candlelit suppers and secret rendezvous?

One afternoon, Marilyn was lunching with Sanders in the commissary. Their being together was accidental. They were sharing a table because separate tables weren't available. He ordered a chicken salad and iced coffee. (It is disillusioning to visualize Sanders eating anything as *petit bourgeois* as chicken salad, but that is life for you.) Sanders had hardly begun on the chicken salad, when there was a telephone call for him. He returned to the table looking rather pale.

He asked for his check. He said he wasn't very hungry. Marilyn tried to talk to him, but he went away fast, very fast.

That afternoon, his stand-in gave her this message: "Mr. Sanders has asked me to request of you that hereafter when you say 'good morning' or 'good-bye' to him, you will make these salutations from afar."

Had a friend of Zsa Zsa's mistaken an innocent luncheon for a budding romance? Had the spy telephoned Zsa Zsa and made a report? Had Zsa Zsa been jealous of unfair competition? Had Sanders perhaps intimated in conversation with Zsa Zsa that his libido had been stimulated by the young blonde who was playing Miss Casswell? We have no answers from Zsa Zsa, and, of the collation, Sanders has only written: "I lunched with her [Marilyn Monroe] once or twice during the making of the film and found that her conversation had unexpected depths. She showed an interest in intellectual subjects, which was quite disconcerting. In her presence it was hard to concentrate."

13 She Refuses a Million Dollars

Because of her beauty and the *mystique* of her public image, the actress is besieged by lovers. Each lover promises to be more exciting than the last. Sometimes this leads to a persistence of the adolescent pattern of the crush, the chase, the courtship, the liaison, repeated over and over again into middle age. Falling in love is so much more theatrical than being in love. A further complication is the actress's inherent tendency to exaggerate any situation in which she's involved. Often a manufactured fantasy herself, an actress may try to live out cinematic fantasy in her personal life. Affair follows affair—with bullfighters and noblemen, with romantic frauds and fakers. As long as her lovers are content to play their parts opposite her in a film she is improvising, they will find her an exciting companion. When they weary of home movies, she wearies of them.

Marilyn Monroe is immune to this occupational disease of the actress. She takes love seriously. She takes marriage seriously. Her relationship with Johnny Hyde began as an almost classical case of the old man infatuated with young beauty. He had no doubt that she was going to become one of the great movie stars of her time, and he began looking for roles that were artistically challenging. As far back as 1950, he suggested that she play Grushenka in a movie version of *The Brothers Karamazov*, which M-G-M was planning. Julius and Philip Epstein had written the scenario. Marilyn studied the screenplay and her part in it and was ready to audition when the production was dropped from the agenda.

Hyde took delight in transforming the young girl into the sophisticated woman. She confided to him the whole story of her unhappy childhood. She won his sympathy and, winning it, she captured his love. But she did not love him. She liked him and she trusted him. But she could not love him. Everybody in the movie colony assumed that she was his mistress, and when they continued seeing each other regularly it was taken for granted that they would be married.

He told her he loved her. She wished "with all my heart" that she could return his love, but it was something she did not feel and could not make herself feel. It is usually not difficult for an actress to make herself feel any emotion she wants to feel, and Marilyn tried to make herself feel love for Johnny, but she could not. She could not go through the motions, let alone the emotions, of a love affair. He proposed marriage to her. She rejected his proposal. She had to fall in love to marry. Each time he asked her to be his wife, she made an attempt to force herself to love him, but she could not.

Hyde's need for her became so urgent that he went to various persons who knew Marilyn and asked them to intercede for him. He asked several executives at 20th Century-Fox to plead his case, which they did. Johnny's friends couldn't understand his madness for the girl. To them she was just another hard-boiled blonde on the make for an important screen credit. They tried to discourage him. They passed on every disparaging rumor they heard about her. They did everything they could to talk him out of loving her.

He loved her all the more. They saw each other every night. They were together at screenings and *premières,* at barbecue dinners on patios, at the elegant restaurants and night clubs on the Sunset Strip. And all the time he kept pressing her to marry him.

He was a sick man. He had high blood pressure and had already suffered one serious heart attack. His doctor said if he lived at this pace he would be dead within a year. He wanted one last, sweet taste of married love before he died. Hyde even used the argument that if she married him it would not be a long marriage. He told her what his doctor had told him. And still she resisted.

One evening, at Hyde's home, he started to walk upstairs to find her a book she said she wanted to read. As he reached the head of the stairs, he crumpled. He leaned against the banister, supporting himself. She ran to him. He was sitting on the landing, moaning softly and pressing his left arm. He said he hurt badly. Supporting him, she helped him to his bed and telephoned the doctor. Johnny had suffered a second coronary. The doctor said he must go away for a long rest. Hyde went to Palm Springs.

Before he left, he asked her to marry him again.

"I haven't got long to live," he said. "I've got a lot of money. Almost a million. I want you to have it. I want you to marry me and have that money."

She was weeping. "No," she sobbed. "I can't do it, Johnny. You're going to get well. Someday I'm going to fall in love with somebody and want to marry him, and it wouldn't be fair to you."

He said, "I'm not going to get well. I know it. You know it. Believe me, I'm not going to get well. Please marry me. I want to go knowing you'll have everything I have."

She shook her head.

On December 17, 1950, while he was sitting in the sun at Palm Springs, Hyde suffered another coronary occlusion. He was rushed to Cedars of Lebanon Hospital in Los Angeles. And even here, as his life was ebbing away, he begged her to marry him and she would not do it. During the night of December 20 he died. At the services, Marilyn threw herself across the coffin and cried, "Wake up, please wake up, oh my God, Johnny, Johnny." Friends took her to a place in the rear of the church. Hyde's family had refused to let her sit in the front row with them.

That day she wished she had died herself. She felt as alone as she had felt in the orphanage. "My great friend was buried," she wrote. "I was without his importance to fight for me, without his love to guide me. I cried for night after night. Sometimes I felt wrong in not marrying him and giving him what he wanted. But I also knew it would be wrong to marry a man you didn't really love. I didn't regret the million dollars I had turned down. I never stopped regretting the loss of Johnny Hyde."

14 "Mr. Zanuck Didn't Like Me"
—but the Public Did

Having impressed highly placed creative minds like John Huston and Joseph Mankiewicz with her charms, Marilyn now assumed that her studio would give her important roles.

But the days went by without a call from a producer. No director sought to interview her. She received her salary regularly, but "I just wasn't on any producer's casting list, and I didn't get a call, and I feel the reason was Mr. Zanuck didn't like me and everybody on the lot had the word he didn't like me and even if they wanted me for a good part in a picture they didn't want to offend Mr. Zanuck. He didn't have to necessarily give them orders not to cast me. It was just in the air, and every good producer and director on the lot knew the score and they wouldn't touch Marilyn Monroe with a ten-foot pole. I didn't know how to break through. I used to have night-mares about Mr. Zanuck. I used to wake up in the morning thinking I have to make Mr. Zanuck appreciate me and I'd try to get in to see him and talk it over but he wouldn't let me. Here I was, one of his employees, and I couldn't get in to see him. I couldn't get in to see anybody that counted. I didn't know any of the important direc-tors, except for Mr. Huston and Mr. Mankiewicz, and they weren't doing any productions on the lot. Mr. Zanuck had never seen me as an actress with 'star quality.' He thought I was some kind of freak. I'm not making this up. He told somebody in the front office who told me later on that I was just a freak, and he didn't want to waste time on me."

She was almost twenty-five years old now, and was still called a starlet only because that's Hollywoodese for a sexy girl who is not a star and not a character actress. Actually, in terms of Hollywood chronology, she was an old woman. By the time she reaches twenty-five, a starlet who hasn't achieved success is usually discarded, as casually as one tosses eggshells into the garbage.

The days rolled into weeks and the weeks into months, and the leaves on her calendar fell like a movie montage showing time's passing. January, February, March, April, and there was still no word from the front office. The casting department was silent. When she complained to casting, she was assured that her name was on every producer's list, of course, and they were waiting for the right part in the right vehicle. By the time April's water sprinklers had pierced the drought of a Los Angeles March to the roots, Marilyn was in a paranoid state about the front office. She felt she had about as much chance of getting a lead in a picture as she had of getting Mr. Zanuck's office as a dressing room. "And it would have made a comfortable dressing room," she remarked. "Mr. Zanuck had a very large front office."

She alternated between moods of despondency and exhilaration. In the latter moods the old reassuring voices told her that she would be famous and wonderful. She worked out a theory that she would never achieve fame by the usual Hollywood formula. She would never be "groomed for stardom." She says that the newspapers and columnists were "kept in ignorance of my existence." She says that the movie exhibitors and the film salesmen didn't get the usual titillating bulletins about her.

Marilyn elaborated a fantasy that she would not break through the wall, ever. She would have to climb over the wall. It was the public and the world who would make her greatness known to the front office instead of the other way around. "I guess I had known it all the time. I knew what I had known when I was thirteen and walked along the sea edge in a bathing suit for the first time. I knew I belonged to the public and to the world, not because I was talented or even beautiful but because I had never belonged to anyone else. The public was the only family, the only Prince Charming, and the only home I had ever dreamed about."

Considering that she had already lived, with some degree of pleasure, in the homes of Aunt Ana and Aunt Grace and of her loving

112

husband, James Dougherty, and that she had had affectionate relationships of varying intensities and satisfactions with Freddy Karger, Natasha Lytess, Lucille Ryman, and Johnny Hyde, this vision of herself as a lonely figure, doomed to walk the beaches of the world, seems curiously unreal.

Yet the vision imparted a grandeur, after all. If Darryl Francis Zanuck, one of the six most powerful men in the movie industry, went out of his way to wreck her career, it established her, at least in her own mind, as a person of some importance. The fact that Mr. Zanuck may have had other problems—of scripts, of productions, of other actresses, of budgets and profits and losses—what significance had this to Marilyn?

Were her ideas "delusions of persecution"? Zanuck was obviously not "persecuting" her, since he had no reason to persecute her. He was ignoring her because he saw no promise in her. That is not unusual. For instance, when Zanuck was head of production at Warner Brothers, he discovered Clark Gable and wanted to make him a star. But Harry Warner said, "His ears are too big," and Jack Warner said, "He's a gangster type and gangster pictures are through." Warners released Gable, and he went to M-G-M and became the most consistent box-office attraction in film history. It was neither lack of insight nor personal hatred that impelled Zanuck to ignore Marilyn; it was an honest, if misguided, judgment about the public reaction to her. And the public reaction is so unpredictable that no individual, even one as expert as Zanuck, could guess its next vagary.

But Marilyn wrote: "Studio bosses are jealous of their power. They are like political bosses. They want to pick out their own candidates for public office. They don't want the public rising up and dumping a girl they consider 'unphotogenic' in their laps and saying, 'Make her a star because we want you to make her a star.'"

Marilyn needs people to sustain her ego, and during this difficult time she relied on Sidney Skolsky, the columnist. Skolsky was unlike the other movie columnists, such as Hedda Hopper, Louella Parsons, and Sheilah Graham. The ladies specialized in tales of high-level studio intrigue, in romances among the celebrities, in "exclusive" inside stories on upcoming films and downgoing marriages. Skolsky, although he also covered the studio beat and the romance beat, took an interest in unknown actors and actresses. Almost every night he was to be found sitting at his favorite place at the counter in the Schwabadero, or he might be holding court next door in Googie's hamburger joint. He was available to anybody with talent, and he listened, with a wry sympathetic smile, while they told him about their problems.

It was to Skolsky that Marilyn turned, time and again. During the black moods, she liked to take long walks or race up the Pacific Coast Highway, the famous 101, which curves along the Pacific Ocean and is one of the loveliest automobile roads in the country.

She would telephone Skolsky at the Schwabadero and tell him that she had to see him right away. He would be waiting outside the Schwabadero, and they would drive west on Wilshire Boulevard, which, after eleven, is deserted. At 101 she would turn north and gun the engine, going 60, 70, 80 miles an hour. They usually drove as far as Malibu Beach, where they remained for hours. Skolsky recalls: "In those days I would go for long walks or long auto rides with Marilyn, and I'd listen to her talk. Mainly she talked career, and great conflict was going on inside her. She'd say that she'd keep working and that nothing—do you hear?—nothing would stop her from becoming a movie star. Then in the next breath she'd doubt that she could ever make it."

In February, 1951, she had enrolled in the adult extension division of UCLA for evening courses in art appreciation and literature. Her art teacher's lectures on the Renaissance made it "sound ten times more important than the studio's biggest epic." She learned about the works of Michelangelo, Raphael, Titian, Tintoretto, and the other masters.

"There was a new genius to hear about every day," she said. "At night I lay in bed wishing I could have lived in the Renaissance." Then a melancholy after-thought occurred to her: "Of course, if I had lived in the Renaissance I would be dead now."

Neither her teachers nor her classmates knew that the blonde who wore no make-up and came to class in a decorous skirt and blouse was a movie actress. Claire Seay, who taught Backgrounds of Literature, was amazed when, later in the year, she found out that Marilyn Monroe was in the movies. "She was so modest, so humble, so attentive, that she could have been some girl who had just come from a convent," Miss Seay stated.

Marilyn had leased an expensive studio apartment with a kitchenette at the Beverly Carlton Hotel. It was the first really elegant place of her own in which she had ever lived. The hotel had decorated it to her specifications: the ceiling and one wall oyster white; two walls gray; and one wall burgundy. The first piece of furniture she ever bought was a bed, a large triple-sized Hollywood bed, without a footboard or headboard. The bed stood close to the floor because she had a fear of falling out of bed during nightmares. The closet was filled with sports clothes and cocktail dresses. On the closet door was a full-length mirror. At the top of the mirror Marilyn had scrawled, in lipstick, the Latin word, *Nunc* (Now)—to remind herself to live in the present.

Since her modeling days, Marilyn had disciplined herself to follow a regimen of exercises. She began the day with 40 minutes of calisthenics. She did weight-lifting exercises, though these are generally not recommended for women because they tend to create unsightly biceps. Holding two five-pound dumbbells, she held out her arms horizontally, raised the weights above her head, and then lowered them. She did this 15 times. Then she extended the weights again above her head and rotated them 15 times. She says that these exercises develop good breasts and keep them firm. (Does Jayne Mansfield practice similar rituals—with ten-pound dumbbells?)

In blue jeans and sweatshirt, Marilyn went on hikes around Beverly Hills. She startled the citizenry. Nobody walks in Beverly Hills. Everybody drives everywhere—even two blocks to a newsstand. Anybody walking about Beverly Hills after 10:00 P.M. is stopped by the police and must identify himself and explain why he is walking and where.

Marilyn did not enjoy any of the popular Hollywood sports— tennis, golf, swimming, sexual promiscuity, and sun-bathing. "Despite its great vogue in California," she once said, "I don't think sun-tanned skin is any more attractive than white skin, or any healthier for that matter. I'm personally opposed to a deep tan because I like to feel blonde all over." Marilyn believes that frequent exposure to the sun hastens the aging process of the skin.

After her exercises, she took a shower. Her breakfast consisted of a concoction of warm milk, two raw eggs, and a dash of sherry, stirred to a froth, and a multi-vitamin and mineral pill. She usually did not eat lunch. On her way home from the studio, she would buy a steak, a lamb chop, or liver, and broil it in her electric Rotobroil. "I usually eat four or five raw carrots with my meat," she explained, "and that's all I have for dinner. I must be part rabbit; I never get bored with raw carrots."

Each morning Marilyn would check into the studio. She felt like an unwelcome tourist in a foreign country. If another actor asked her what she was doing, she could only say, "Waiting." She was stagnating in the actor's unique limbo of non-being. Other artists—writers, painters, sculptors, musicians, even dancers—can have some sort of private creative existence apart from an audience, at least for temporary periods. The actress has no reality unless she is acting, either for an audience in a theatre or for the camera which is the vast eye of the eventual audience of millions.

Usually, she went to the publicity department. Here, she got both consolation and active assistance from Roy Craft. He decided to embark on a photographic campaign. He would exploit her as a "pin-up." A pin-up is a photograph of a scantily clad girl who possesses certain indefinable qualities that register in a still photograph—qualities that are suggestive, amorous, friendly, provocative. Not all beautiful girls possess the *mystique* of the pin-up. A voluptuous body alone does not guarantee success in this field of endeavour. Pin-ups are highly regarded by adolescent males; by males temporarily deprived of feminine companionship because of service in the armed forces; by sailors in general; and by men of all ages, who, for one reason or another, are unable or unwilling to achieve *un contact des epidermes* with a woman. The pin-ups cater to the broadest range of interests, from 100-per-cent red-blooded American heterosexuality to every variety of fetishism. There is a considerable market—on the borderline of legality—in movie stills, printed on glossy paper, of stars in various poses which, though not so intended by the studios, please the sadist, the masochist, the foot fetishist, the latent homosexual, and so on. Merchants in Los Angeles and New York do a big business in such "exotic" prints as well as the usual "cheesecake" product. The studios, of course, only distribute the innocuous variety of pin-up. Because of the Korean War, there was, at this time, an increasing demand for pin-ups. Marilyn posed for days on end—either in the gallery, the studio's still-photography headquarters, or out at the beach or in a park. The photographs were mailed out to the editors of camp newspapers and to Army installations throughout the world. The response was gratifying. In addition, "cheesecake" photographs of Marilyn sporting at the beach, throwing a ball, climbing mountain trails, riding a horse, kicking her heels on an exercise board, were distributed to the wire services, the fan magazines, the newspapers, and the national magazines. There is an insatiable hunger for good "cheesecake" in our society. And I, for one, confess I find it one of the least degrading phases of popular culture. There are few pleasures as immediate and uncomplicated as the sight of a comely naked girl, preferably in a bedroom; secondarily, on a stage; thirdly, in great works of art, such as the paintings of Titian and Degas; and lastly, in photographs of creatures like Marilyn Monroe. As E. E. Cummings remarks in a poem:

> "a pretty girl who naked is
> is worth a million statues"

The only exception to this equation would be a statue of a naked pretty girl.

From the beginning, Marilyn's pin-ups were a smashing success—with editors, with the civilian population, and above all with the servicemen. Betty Grable had been the leading pin-up of World War II. Marilyn was the leading pin-up of the early 1950's. By the end of 1951, the studio was receiving thousands of letters a month from persons who wanted pictures of Marilyn. Only a small percentage of these art connoisseurs had ever seen her in a film.

The mail room kept a weekly check of the number of requests for pictures each star received. Soon Marilyn's name was at the top of the list. There was consternation in the front office. Zanuck wanted to know if the publicity department was secretly engaged in promoting Marilyn. Harry Brand, head of the department, assured him that the desire to own a photograph of Marilyn was a spontaneous upsurge, one of those inexplicable mass phenomena. A meeting was convened in Zanuck's office and, one by one, each member of the department was questioned. Was anybody guilty of surreptitiously conniving to get Marilyn's name and body in the newspapers? All the press agents proved their innocence.

One afternoon in March, Marilyn had an engagement at the gallery. She was going to pose for a series of pictures purporting to illustrate how she relaxed at her apartment after a hard day's work at the studio. She was supposed to wear a negligee, or, as the saying goes, a filmy negligee, about as filmy a negligee as there was in wardrobe.

Marilyn decided to be dramatic. She changed into a negligee in wardrobe, and then she walked the six blocks to the gallery. Barefooted, her long hair streaming loosely behind her, her skin clearly visible under the diaphanous negligee, she slowly floated along the studio streets. The studio messengers, on bicycles, spread the news. By the time she started back to wardrobe, after posing, the streets were lined with cheering throngs of studio employees. The next day, items about her escapade appeared in the trade papers. She was the talk of the movie colony.

A few weeks later, the studio gave a party for a group of visiting exhibitors. Marilyn, together with other starlets, had been ordered to attend. Naturally, the main attraction was such stars as Anne Baxter, Dan Dailey, June Haver, Richard Widmark, and Tyrone Power. But when Marilyn arrived, an hour and a half late, it was she who was mobbed by the theatre operators and film salesmen. The exhibitors kept asking her, "And what pictures are you going to be in, Miss Monroe?" She fluttered her eyelashes, and said, "You'll have to ask Mr. Zanuck or Mr. Schreiber about that." Soon Spyros Skouras, the president of 20th Century-Fox, became aware that his leading stars were being trampled to death in the stampede for Marilyn.

"Who is that girl?" Skouras inquired of one of his myrmidons. The myrmidon didn't know. He went to ask, and reported that her name was Marilyn Monroe and that she was a contract player. Skouras then asked the same question everybody else was asking, "What picture is she in?" Informed, rather nervously, that she was not in any forthcoming studio products, Skouras glowered. Powerful as Zanuck was, powerful as Schenck was, Skouras was even more powerful. With Joseph M. Schenck and William Goetz, Zanuck had founded 20th Century Pictures back in 1933. During a subsequent reorganization and amalgamation with William Fox Pictures, Skouras, formerly an operator of theatre chains, had emerged as the most powerful executive in the organization. Skouras growled, "The exhibitors like her. If the exhibitors like her, the public likes her, no?"

He plunged through the crowd around Marilyn. He bowed. He gallantly took her arm and led her to the head table and sat her by his right side. She stayed for dinner.

Marilyn's six-month contract, which Hyde had negotiated before his death, was due to expire on May 10. The morning after Spyros Skouras had bestowed his favors upon her, the front office entered into negotiations with the William Morris Agency. A new contract was drawn for the usual seven-year period, beginning May 11, 1951, and Marilyn's salary was raised to $500 a week. From then on she received $250-a-week raises semi-annually until she had reached the contractual ceiling of $1,500.

Zanuck gave orders that Marilyn must be worked into any film that was in production and could use a sexy blonde, and there are very few Hollywood films that can't use a sexy blonde. Supporting roles for her were found in *As Young as You Feel* and *Love Nest*. Not starring roles, for Zanuck still did not believe she had "star quality," but at least if Skouras asked any searching questions, he could be told that Marilyn was working. The publicity department was ordered to swing into action. Even if it did nothing else, the front office figured the publicity would at least sell the films in which she appeared briefly. The fan magazines began to be filled with photographs of Monroe and with stories about her dead parents and her tragic life as an orphan. All the stops were let out, and the propaganda organ boomed out the Cinderella story to end all Cinderella stories. An important breakthrough in Marilyn's rise to fame came when *Collier's* published a long feature story on her, illustrated with a delectable photograph of her in color. It was written by Robert Cahn and was entitled, *Hollywood's 1951 Model Blonde*. Published on September 8, 1951, it was Marilyn's first significant national-magazine biography. (*Look*, in its issue of June 20, 1950, had printed a photograph of Jean Hagen and Marilyn— Miss Hagen, who later became Danny Thomas's television "wife," had also been in *The Asphalt Jungle*—with the caption: "The Girls in *The Asphalt Jungle*—Two New Stars?")

Cahn made two interesting observations. "Marilyn Monroe," he wrote, "is not a girl anyone quickly forgets. While Hollywood blondes are generally considered the industry's most expendable item, Miss Monroe's value during the past year has risen faster than the cost of living." She had created a value for herself although she had not appeared in any film for nine months. It didn't matter, because Marilyn now represented the quintessence of a certain style of womanly loveliness. Her image was still more important than her cinematic work.

Cahn also wrote, "Off the screen, Marilyn Monroe has managed to maintain an almost Garbo-like reticence about her private life." Skolsky, writing in 1953, made a similar comparison to the great Swedish actress: "Whether by design or merely because of her native shyness, Marilyn was pulling a Greta Garbo without anyone's being aware of it." There is a paradox here. Marilyn gave the impression that she was a withdrawn personality. Yet she was unlike Garbo. She was willing to pose for publicity pictures and do anything bizarre to attract attention. She enjoyed being the center of attention. She enjoyed being interviewed. She was always a charming, clever, and altogether delightful subject for writers. Far from shunning publicity like Garbo, far from making herself inaccessible to the press, Marilyn was available in those years.

Garbo had said that she wanted to be alone, and she never deviated from this solitary behavior. Marilyn never wanted to be alone. Adulation was important to her, and she never pretended it wasn't.

But if she was not like Garbo, she was not like other stars either, and perhaps it was this curious difference that led Cahn and Skolsky to compare Marilyn to Garbo. Marilyn did not want to play the Hollywood game. She loathed *premières*. For instance, although pressure had been put on her, both by Mankiewicz and Zanuck, she had refused to attend the world *première* of *All About Eve*. You didn't see her at the fashionable cafés and restaurants. She shunned parties.

Marilyn was dumped into *As Young as You Feel* in the role of a stenographer to Monty Woolley. In this justifiably forgotten comedy, Woolley played the main character of the story, an aged hand-press operator who impersonates the absentee president of a large manufacturing firm. In a Hollywood comedy, the stenographers usually are office playgirls incapable of writing shorthand or typing anything more complicated than the word "cat." Marilyn's part was in the great tradition of movie stenographers. The film was released in August, 1951. Or rather, as an old Hollywood joke runs, "the picture wasn't released, it escaped." It was usually played as the second half of a double bill. It was what *Variety* calls a "dualer."

In her next film, *Love Nest*, Marilyn again played an insignificant role but was given more film footage. *Love Nest* was also a "dualer." It was also a light comedy—a very light comedy, so light in fact that it was practically weightless. June Haver and William

120

Lundigan co-starred in this picture. Miss Haver played the wife of Lundigan. While her husband was in the Army overseas, she had bought an old New York brownstone and converted it into an apartment house. She dreamed of becoming rich by charging high rents. Her dreams of wealth were shattered when Lundigan returned and invited old friends from the service to live rent free in the house. Among the old Army friends was Marilyn Monroe, a former WAC.

During the shooting everyone on the 20th Century-Fox lot who could make an excuse to leave his desk wandered on to the sound stage to watch Marilyn working. One day, when she was doing a scene in which she wore a rather sparse red-and-white polka-dot bikini with, as somebody cracked, "hardly enough room for the dots," the sound stage was so overwhelmed with studio employees that director Joseph Newman finally had to bar the set to all visitors. Marilyn had seized the imagination of the jaded technicians and the office personnel.

Even Zanuck finally condescended, after he had seen some of the daily rushes, to issue a grudging acknowledgment of her quality. He said, "Miss Monroe is the most exciting new personality in Hollywood in a long time." This may *sound* like a warm compliment, but in the land of superlatives that is the movie business, it was comparable to saying, "She's not bad."

In one scene of *Love Nest*, Marilyn was to enter her room and remove her clothes before taking a shower. Unknown to her, Lundigan, who had had a fight with his wife, was asleep on the couch in Marilyn's room. His wife was to enter and find them in a compromising situation. The scene had been explained to Lundigan and Monroe. Marilyn, at the word "action," opened a door, walked across a room to her closet, and kicked off her shoes. On the couch, meanwhile, Lundigan was fast asleep. He was to remain fast asleep until his wife broke in. Marilyn had stripped off her stockings and her dress and had got down to her lingerie when Newman shouted, "Cut."

Marilyn looked at him guiltily. "Did I do anything wrong?" she asked.

"No," he said, "you were fine—but Lundigan was peeking!"

Aside from its place in the Monroe canon, the only other historical significance of *Love Nest* is that it marked Jack Paar's first appearance in the movies. It was also his last, although he was, variously, under contract to RKO and 20th Century-Fox for about four doleful years. Recalling his brief contact with Marilyn, Paar wrote: "Looking back, I guess I should have been excited, but I found her pretty tiresome. She used to carry around books by Marcel Proust with their titles facing out, but I never saw her read one. She was always holding up shooting by talking on the phone. Judging from what's happened, though, I guess she had the right number."

Reviewing the movie, *Variety* said, "Jack Paar strolls aimlessly in and out of the plot." Marilyn also strolled aimlessly in and out of the plot. She strolled aimlessly in and out of the plot of the next movie in which she worked, *Let's Make It Legal,* another "dualer" that "escaped." This one co-starred Claudette Colbert and Macdonald Carey as a divorced couple. After the divorce Carey decides he is in love with his ex-wife and returns to the old homestead to pay court to Miss Colbert, who is also being courted by Zachary Scott. In *Let's Make It Legal,* however, Marilyn's aimless strollings were enhanced by a variety of interesting costumes. She appeared in two different bathing suits, in tennis shorts, in low-cut evening dresses, and in low-cut morning and afternoon dresses.

To her public she was a sight for sore eyes, but Zanuck's eyes were not at all sore. He did not see her as anything more valuable than something with which to garnish a movie, to impart a touch of sexual titillation.

At RKO, co-producers Jerry Wald and Norman Krasna were preparing the movie version of Clifford Odets' *Clash by Night.* It had been a failure on Broadway when Tallulah Bankhead starred in it in 1941. It was in writing of this play, which struck New York as rather lukewarm Odets, that a critic asked, "Odets, where is thy sting?"

Wald and Krasna changed the locale of the script from Staten Island to southern California and made the characters cannery workers. The role of Peggy, which Marilyn played, was not in the original playscript. Wald told me, "Norman and I were looking for somebody to put in this picture to attract the teen-agers in the audience; somebody with a new kind of sex appeal. I didn't think of Marilyn at first."

By 1950, television was making inroads on the movie audience. More and more, the majority of the audience was composed of boys and girls between fourteen and twenty. Subsequently the quality of movie audiences changed again, and more adults went to pictures because the movie industry, to compete with free television, turned to wide-screen spectacles and themes of adultery.

Barbara Stanwyck, Paul Douglas, and Robert Ryan had already been signed as stars of *Clash by Night*.

One day Skolsky dropped into Wald's office. Wald happened to remark that he was having a great deal of difficulty in finding a sexy blonde to play Peggy in *Clash by Night*. Did Skolsky have any ideas? It so happened that Skolsky had a very definite idea.

"Marilyn Monroe."

Wald shook his head. "She can't have anything," he said.

"She's good," Skolsky said.

"If she's so good, why did Metro release her after *Asphalt Jungle*?"

"She's great," Skolsky said. "She's another Jean Harlow. She's got a real Jean Harlow quality."

"Yeah?" Wald said. "So why doesn't Twentieth do something with her?"

"I don't want to argue with you, Jerry," Skolsky said.

"There must be something wrong with her."

"Tell you what I'll do," Skolsky said. "I'll set up a date for you to meet Marilyn. Make up your own mind."

Two days later, Wald and Skolsky lunched at Lucey's, on Melrose Avenue. Marilyn was late. She had taken a good deal of trouble to dress herself in the role of Peggy. As a captain escorted her to Wald's table, Wald saw a luscious peach of a girl—she was over twenty-five but she looked sixteen—whose progress across the room was one long *double-entendre*. She was wearing a low-cut white blouse, tight plaid pedal pushers, and loafers. No stockings. In the cleavage of her blouse she had placed a large red rose. Skolsky introduced her to Wald, and then he departed. Wald saw that here was an actress with a good-humored animal sexuality. He envisioned her in the amorous wrestling scene she was to play with Keith Andes.

That afternoon he telephoned Lew Schreiber, one of the executives at 20th, and asked for Miss Monroe. When Schreiber demanded merely $3,000 for six weeks of her time, Wald was suspicious. There must be something wrong with Monroe or she wouldn't be going so cheaply.

Wald and Krasna planned to give Marilyn equal billing with Miss

Stanwyck, Douglas, and Ryan. Would they resent it? Wald timorously introduced Marilyn to his stars one by one.

Marilyn could be humble when she needed to be. She was deferential when she met Miss Stanwyck, a strong personality. Marilyn's hands actually sweated with what seemed to Wald and Miss Stanwyck to be fear. After the meeting, Miss Stanwyck said, "She's a cute number." Paul Douglas described her as a "nice cookie," and she struck Ryan as a "scared rabbit."

When Wald had previously brought up her name all three had been furious and asked, "Who the hell is *she*?" Now their resentment had turned into protective affection.

All during the shooting, Marilyn continued to be the "scared rabbit." She was skating on thin ice because her co-stars soon resented Marilyn's getting more publicity than they. They complained to Wald and Krasna. They observed that when photographers came to the set—the film was shot on location—they only wanted stills of Marilyn. "It became damn embarrassing," Wald said. One night, after a day's work, when Miss Stanwyck was having dinner with Douglas and Ryan, Douglas became very bitter.

"Why the hell don't these goddam photographers ever take any pictures of us?" he bellowed. "It's only that goddam blonde bitch."

"It's this way, Paul," Miss Stanwyck said sadly, "she's younger and more beautiful than any of us."

Ryan's impression of Marilyn: "I got the feeling she was a frightened lonely little girl who was trying awfully hard. She always seemed to be so mournful-looking around the set, and I'd always try to cheer her up. She never went out with the rest of us socially after work. I remember, after we finished the picture, she sent me a box of candy. I don't know why."

It was during the shooting of *Clash by Night* that Natasha Lytess first appeared on the set of any Monroe film. Up till then, Lytess had remained in the background. After every take, Marilyn would look over to Lytess and Lytess would signal to her by nodding her head or shaking it. If she shook it, Marilyn asked to have the scene reshot, even though Fritz Lang, the director, was satisfied and had given the curt command, "Print it." Marilyn now began to go retake crazy. She demanded, and still demands, more retakes than any other star in movies.

Lang said he would not put up with Marilyn's coach. A director with an international reputation, Lang expected to be in complete control. He did not accept insubordination from anybody—not even a star. He went to Wald and said, "I do not want anybody directing behind my back. I want this Lytess woman kept off my set. I am giving orders not to allow her on the set."

Now Marilyn bared her fangs. If Lytess was not allowed on the set, then Marilyn could not work. For two days, Lang shot around Marilyn until Wald resolved the conflict. Miss Lytess would be permitted on the set, but she must not signal or contradict any of Lang's orders.

Clash by Night was previewed at the Crown Theatre in Pasadena in December, 1951, and Marilyn Monroe stole the picture, small as her part was. "She got terrific applause," Wald said, "and the preview cards raved about her." The film was scheduled for release in May, 1952. *Variety,* reviewing it, said, "While Marilyn Monroe is reduced to what is tantamount to a bit role, despite her star billing, she does manage to get over her blonde sexiness in one or two scenes, and the film could have used more of her."

Time observed, "Also on hand, in a minor role: shapely Marilyn Monroe as a fish-cannery employee who bounces around in a succession of slacks, bathing suits, and sweaters."

But John McCarten, movie critic of *The New Yorker,* who was, over the years, to maintain consistent doubt of Miss Monroe's miming talents, began the first in a long line of adverse critiques of Marilyn. "*Clash by Night* also gives us a glimpse of Marilyn Monroe and Keith Andes, who play a pair of lovers. Both are quite handsome, but neither can act."

Kate Cameron in the New York *Daily News* called Marilyn "the new blonde bombshell of Hollywood," and Irene Thirer in the New York *Post* cruelly noted that "Miss Stanwyck looks remarkably youthful—though not when she's face to face with Miss Monroe, a real charmer." As for her acting ability, Alton Cook, of the *World Telegram & Sun,* disagreed with McCarten. Cook wrote: "Before going further with a report on *Clash,* perhaps we should mention the first full-length glimpse the picture gives us of Marilyn Monroe as an actress. The verdict is gratifyingly good. . . . This girl has a refreshing exuberance, an abundance of girlish high spirits. She is a forceful actress, too, when crisis comes along. She has definitely stamped herself as a gifted new star, worthy of all that fantastic press agentry. Her role is not very big, but she makes it dominant."

History has sided with Cook rather than McCarten.

15 Some Ghosts Return

Marilyn came back to her studio as a star, at least theoretically. She had not achieved stardom by the quality of her work. Stardom had been thrust upon her by the masses and two independent producers who capitalized on her publicity to sell a movie in which she actually played a minor role. But such are the curious habits of the motion-picture industry that now this woman, after four years of failure in pictures and after she had demonstrated her ineptitude in the art of miming, had to be given roles of star calibre and granted billing above the picture title—that emblem of honor for which all actresses yearn. But Marilyn was still not a star, truly. She was hardly an actress. She had only begun to learn how to act; only in brief moments in *The Asphalt Jungle* and *All About Eve* had she suggested the possibility that she could indeed create a valid character.

20th Century-Fox selected *Don't Bother to Knock* as her first important vehicle. The screenplay was based on the suspense novel *Mischief*, by Charlotte Armstrong. Daniel Taradash had made a tightly wrought treatment of the story which reflected life with a high degree of psychological truth. Marilyn played a psychopathic nursemaid working in a New York hotel. While baby-sitting for guests of the hotel, Marilyn's sense of reality begins deteriorating. Richard Widmark is an airline pilot who is in the midst of an unhappy love affair with a night-club singer. Marilyn identifies him with a man she once loved. Across the airshaft Marilyn flirts with

Widmark, who is in a room opposite, and they get an intrigue under way. Before the film is over, Marilyn almost murders the baby, her uncle, and a hotel bellman whom she has schizophrenically identified with her father.

Incidentally, the girl who played the night-club singer was a failure in this and other movies. After many years of frustration in Hollywood, she went to Broadway and became a success. Her name is Anne Bancroft, the Gittel Mosca of *Two for the Seesaw* in 1957 and the Anne Sullivan of *The Miracle Worker* in 1959.

The English director Ray Baker attempted two interesting things. He shot and edited *Don't Bother to Knock* in what is known to film workers as "time for time": that is, the elapsed time of the dramatic action equaled the running time of the film, both being 90 minutes exactly. Secondly, in order to make the film on a low budget, Baker rehearsed the actors for two weeks and then shot the movie in continuity—that is, he photographed the scenes in the same sequence in which they occurred. He printed the first take of every scene. As incredible as this may seem to those who are familiar with Marilyn's propensity for retakes, there was not one retake during the shooting!

On the morning of March 10, 1952, just as Marilyn had finished a scene for *Don't Bother to Knock,* the assistant director gave her a message to telephone one of the executive producers as soon as she was free. While the next scene was being lighted, she went to her dressing room and put through the call.

The executive's voice was frantic.

"Something terrible has happened," he said. "We're all going to be ruined if it's true."

"What is it?" she asked.

"You're in trouble," he said. "I just hope it's not true. God knows what we'll do if it is. They're talking already about not releasing *Don't Bother to Knock.* They're talking about canceling your contract on the morals clause."

The tension got to Marilyn. "Wh-what d-did I do moral, I mean not moral?" she asked, her stammering recurring.

"Now, let's not lose our heads," he shrilled. "There may not be anything in this at all. It's just that Harry Brand got a call from Aline Mosby of the United Press and maybe the whole thing is a lie. So be calm. Did you ever pose for dirty pictures?"

"Wh-what do you mean dirty pictures?"

"You know what I mean. Nudes. Nude pictures. They got one on a calendar, the nineteen fifty-two calendar, it came out in January, and somebody tipped off Mosby the girl ôn the calendar is you and we'll have every religious group on our necks if it gets out. We tried to kill the story. We can't. Is it true?"

In December, 1950, Tom Kelley had called to say that *Golden Dreams* was going to be one of the featured items in the 1951 line of John Baumgarth calendars. The number had been so popular with art lovers that it was reproduced again for 1952. A few weeks before *Clash by Night* was scheduled for release—June 18, 1952, was the national release date—Wald began receiving a series of threatening phone calls from a man who said he had evidence that Marilyn Monroe had posed for a nude calendar that was being distributed nationally and that unless he was paid $10,000 he would reveal the information to the newspapers. The bad publicity, he said, would wreck the success of *Clash by Night*. At first, Wald didn't take the blackmail threats seriously, but when they kept recurring, he became worried. He stalled, but on May 9 the blackmailer gave him an ultimatum. Like all studio executives, Wald lived in fear of offending one of the influential religious groups or the columnists who watch over morality in the movie colony.

Finally, he sent out for a copy of the calendar. The face on the calendar was compared with the face of Marilyn. It was *Monroe Desnuda,* without a doubt. At first, Wald believed RKO should ignore the threat in the hope that the blackmailer would be silent. Krasna suggested, however, that the exposé would be a publicity coup. It would enhance the public's desire to see *Clash by Night*. After all, it wasn't illegal to pose for nude calendars, and the calendar was being sponsored by various commercial firms catering to the bar-and-grill mystique. Krasna said that not only should they *not* conceal the truth, they should help expose it!

Perry Lieber, publicity head of RKO, was called in. The three men debated the problem. Lieber finally sided with Krasna, and Wald was won over. It was Lieber who had phoned the tip to Aline Mosby. Aline Mosby had called Brand, demanding an interview with Marilyn. She said she had studied the calendar, and the face on it bore a startling resemblance to that of the girl who had suddenly become an important "property" to 20th Century-Fox.

Brand said one could never be sure in such cases, since all naked-girl pictures tended to look more or less alike, and Miss Mosby said that some naked-girl pictures might look more or less alike but not when Marilyn Monroe was the girl.

This was how Marilyn came to be explaining herself to the studio executive.

She finally admitted that she had posed for the photograph.

"Is there anything wrong with that? So they found out it's me. So what?"

"What kind of a woman are you?" he yelled. "What do you mean they found out? What do you mean, so what? Look, I'm going down to the set to talk to you. Don't say anything to anybody, and don't mention the subject to anybody, and don't give any interviews to anybody."

Later he came down to her dressing room. He was wringing his hands, and moaning, over and over again, how could she do such a terrible thing? Didn't she know how offensive it was to public morality? This could ruin her entire career in pictures if it came out. She could be blackballed by every studio.

"There's only one thing to do," he said, finally. "Deny it—deny everything. You didn't pose for the picture. It's just a case of mistaken identity."

"Well," she said, beginning to cry, "I didn't think I ever *would* be identified. I mean I thought the lighting the photographer used would disguise me."

"Get this straight. You never posed for any naked calendars. You don't know anything about it. Just stick to that story and we may be out of the woods."

He slammed the door on his way out. Marilyn sat on the cot in her dressing room, and panic swept over her. She was going to be destroyed, unless she could lie her way out. She telephoned Skolsky. She told him that the secret—which he had known about for a year —was about to be exposed unless she denied it and made the denial stick.

"What shall I do, Sidney?"

He replied, "First tell me this. How do you really feel about posing in the nude for the calendar?"

"I don't know," she said. "I'm so scared, Sidney. I'm so mixed up and scared. I don't really feel ashamed. I didn't do anything so bad, did I? I wouldn't have done it if it was bad. I needed the money for the rent. They're trying to make me feel ashamed, but I'm not. Should I tell the truth? I know I wouldn't condemn anyone who told me such a thing."

"You've solved the problem," he said. "Just tell everybody what you just told me."

At lunch that afternoon, she did tell Mosby the truth—but it was not exactly the whole truth. Her claim that she was behind in her rent at the Studio Club and had to pose in the nude so as not to be thrown out in the streets was inaccurate. She was still repeating the same story as late as 1956, when she told Pete Martin that at the Studio Club a tenant was only allowed to get one week behind in the rent and that she was three weeks behind and had gotten several warnings. Actually, she moved out of the Studio Club on March 13, 1949. She posed for Tom Kelley, two months later, on May 27, 1949. She needed the money to meet a payment on her new convertible. But she suspected that few persons would feel sorry for a girl whose problem was how to pay for a $2,500 convertible.

Miss Mosby's story broke on March 13, 1952, and was picked up by almost every newspaper in the United States. The story, in part, ran as follows:

"A photograph of a beautiful nude blonde in a 1952 calendar is hanging in garages and barbershops all over the nation today.

"Marilyn Monroe admitted today that the beauty is she.

"She posed, stretched out on crumpled red velvet, for the artistic photo three years ago because 'I was broke and needed the money.'

" 'Oh, the calendar's hanging in garages all over town,' said Marilyn. 'Why deny it?'

" 'Besides, I'm not ashamed of it. I've done nothing wrong.'

"The beautiful blonde now gets a fat paycheck every week from an excited 20th Century-Fox Studio. She's rated the most sensational sweater girl since Lana Turner. . . . She lives in an expensive hotel room. . . . She dines at Romanoff's. . . .

"But in 1949 she was just another scared young blonde, struggling to find fame in the magic city and all alone. . . .

"After an unsuccessful marriage, she moved into Hollywood's famed Studio Club, home of hopeful actresses.

" 'I was a week behind in my rent,' she explained. 'I had to have the money. A photographer, Tom Kelley, had asked me before to pose, but I'd never done it. This time I called him and I said I would as soon as possible, to get it over with.

" 'His wife was there. They're both very nice. . . .'

"Marilyn speaks in a breathless, soft voice, and she's always very serious about every word she says.

" 'Tom didn't think anyone would recognize me,' she said. 'My hair was long then. But when the picture came out, everybody knew me. I'd never have done it if I'd known things would happen so fast for me.' "

No organizations, either pious or aesthetic, denounced the *Monroe Desnuda*. And there was no reason why they should have. It is a lovely photograph of a lovely girl.

The nude calendar established Marilyn firmly as the epitome of the desirable woman of her time, and from then on, no matter how fully dressed she was on the screen, the audience would see, beneath the cinematic image, the naked Venus. Krasna's intuition about the public was vindicated. Audiences flocked to *Clash by Night* to see the naked Venus. In many theatres her name received the most prominent billing on the marquee. In smaller theatres with smaller marquees her name was the only one spelled out in electric bulbs or neon cylinders.

When the calendar story broke, newspapermen came to Craft, knowing he was Marilyn's press attaché, and asked him for copies of the *Monroe Desnuda*. "Well," Craft says, "the publicity department didn't have any. Finally I heard about a guy on the lot, a movie extra, small-time actor, and he had a connection through whom he was able to get a supply of these calendars for nothing, and he was selling them for a dollar each. I went to Brand and I got a requisition for a hundred dollars, and I bought a hundred of these calendars and gave them out to the press."

Two months after the naked calendar revelation, another skeleton rattled out of Marilyn's closet. For years, she had informed the press that she was an orphan. As she became more successful, the studio was plagued by persons who claimed to be her mother or her father, or by persons who asserted they had documentary evidence to prove that one or both of her parents were alive. Once, a Hollywood mortician telephoned Zanuck's office and stated that he was holding the corpse of Marilyn Monroe's father, who had recently passed away; he wished to know Marilyn's plans for the funeral. Zanuck told his secretary, "Tell the man he'll have to write us a letter. This is the second Marilyn Monroe father we've had this week!"

Incidentally, my hypothesis as to the identity of Edward Mortenson will be challenged. There is a widespread belief that Marilyn's father is still living and that he is today a prominent personality in the motion-picture industry. I have never seen any evidence to sustain this theory. Recently two persons—one a friend of Marilyn's and the other an associate of hers—assured me that her father is living, that his real name is not Mortenson, and that he is a well-known citizen of Los Angeles.

And Marilyn, herself, frequently received letters and phone calls from persons claiming to be her father, or purporting to know the whereabouts of the mysterious "Edward Mortenson." These informants were usually con-game operators preying on a movie actress for money. Yet she investigated every rumor about her father's existence. Something in her did not want to believe that he was dead. She wanted him to be alive and to receive her into his loving arms. Invariably the rumors, when traced, were false or outright frauds. Once, though, in 1950, she was given the name and telephone number of a dairy farmer living 150 miles south of Los Angeles. The informant supplied several convincing details which persuaded Marilyn, who wanted so badly to be persuaded, that this time the truth was out. She would go to see this man. She would confront him. She would not warn him in advance. He would be so overcome by her sudden appearance that he would accept her at once.

She and Natasha Lytess set out early one morning. But a few miles from their destination, her resolution weakened. To confront him so suddenly would be a shock, perhaps. She pulled into a gas station. She asked Natasha to ring up her "father" and gently break the news. Natasha did so. Upon hearing that he had a daughter, the well-known Marilyn Monroe, who was anxious to commence a filial relationship with him if he was indeed her authentic father, the man lost his temper. He shouted that he was a respectable married man with children and he wanted to have no truck with his illegitimate daughter—if he actually had an illegitimate daughter. "The man was common and cheap," Miss Lytess reported to her protégée. Marilyn went to the phone. She pleaded that he grant her an interview to set her mind at rest. He was rude to Marilyn. She then gave him her Los

Angeles number and begged him to ring her if he ever came to Los Angeles. She did not ever speak to him again. Who was this man and how trustworthy was the information that had led her to him? Was it her mother who revealed the name of the real father? Had he not died in an automobile accident? Was "Edward Mortenson" a name invented to fill a space in a birth certificate? We do not know the final answers to these questions. Gladys Monroe Baker, because of her unstable condition, cannot be a reliable source. A cloud hung over it all. The uncertainty has plagued Marilyn all of her life.

Now, in 1952, in a state hospital for the mentally ill, there was a patient who boasted that she was Marilyn Monroe's mother. She was a little lady with white hair, lacking any faded fragments of a former beauty that might have made the story believable. Nobody at the hospital paid any attention to the tattered newspaper clippings she displayed. The doctors and the nurses at the hospital were not impressed. This was, after all, a California sanitarium; there were numerous elderly female patients who boasted that they were the mothers of Clark Gable, Ava Gardner, Lana Turner, Gary Cooper, Elizabeth Taylor, Cary Grant, and other luminaries. For once, however, a mental patient was not lying. The little old white-haired lady was, indeed, Gladys Monroe Baker. One day, a woman visiting a sick friend in the sanitarium, overheard Mrs. Baker babbling about her famous daughter. The visitor thought she was hearing the ravings of a maniac, but she repeated them. Soon the rumors came to the ears of Erskine Johnson, Hollywood correspondent of the Newspaper Enterprise Association (NEA). Johnson put the heat on the studio, and the studio put the heat on Marilyn and she gave Johnson an exclusive story. It broke on May 3, 1952:

"Marilyn Monroe—Hollywood's confessin' glamour doll who made recent headlines with the admission that she was a nude calendar cutie—confessed again today.

"Highly publicized by Hollywood press agents as an orphan waif who never knew her parents, Marilyn admitted she's the daughter of a one-time RKO studio film cutter, Gladys Baker, and said, 'I am helping her and want to continue to help her when she needs me.'

"Said Hollywood's new glamour queen: 'My close friends know that my mother is alive. Unbeknown to me as a child, my mother spent many years as an invalid in a state hospital. . . . I haven't known my mother intimately, but since I have become grown and able to help her, I have contacted her. I am helping her and want to continue to help her when she needs me.'

"The news that Marilyn's mother is alive and in Hollywood came as an eyebrow-lifting surprise because of extensive studio publicity that Marilyn had never known her mother or her father."

Despite her direct experience with the schizophrenic personality, Marilyn could not make the character of Nell in *Don't Bother to Knock* true and moving. She had an opportunity to create as unusual a cameo as Robert Montgomery did as the smiling murderer in *Night Must Fall*. She didn't. Marilyn's psychopathic killer was a cold almost non-human person. She played her with glazed eyes and a stiff body. Her scenes of passion with Widmark were ridiculously overplayed. Her voice was almost inaudible at times and unpleasantly shrill at others. She didn't even look physically attractive. She had worked hard on this role. She had moved out of the Beverly Carlton and into the small apartment of Natasha Lytess on Harper Avenue so that she would have more time for analysis of the role.

Miss Lytess says that Marilyn did not work hard enough. Marilyn's friend Skolsky believes that the reason for her failure was that she was miscast. Marilyn believes that the director, Ray Baker, did not understand her and did not give her space and time to move around in and slowly feel herself into the role. She felt that he was rushing her all the time. He did not sympathize with her anxiety. He did not explore the motivations of the character or discuss the emotional coloration of each scene.

But aside from all this, Marilyn was not ready to play a role of this dimension. Even now, a decade later, one wonders if she could bring off such a somber role.

Except in the trade press, Marilyn's attempt to emote seriously was ridiculed. However, reviewing the movie in *Motion Picture Herald*, Vincent Conley wrote, "It . . . proves conclusively that she is the kind of big new star for which exhibitors are always asking." Exhibitors weren't interested in art. They sought weapons against television. New performers, whom everybody longed for, were potent weapons. Marilyn Monroe was one of these, and the public paid to see her in anything, even *Don't Bother to Knock*.

Marilyn's failure to deliver a satisfactory performance in her first starring role for 20th caused anxiety in the front office. Was Zanuck right after all? Yet the studio had to do something with her. But what? She was the most intriguing new personality in Hollywood, and they didn't know what to do with her. If she actually had been miscast in *Don't Bother to Knock,* if she really couldn't play a strong dramatic role and they continued to put her in dramas, she could be destroyed in a year. On the other hand there was no evidence that she could play light comedy like Claudette Colbert and Ginger Rogers, or that she could sing and dance like Betty Grable. They did not dare to put her in a Cinemascope, Technicolor filmusical that cost a minimum of $2,000,000.

On the other hand, the studio was unable to make experimental films with Marilyn until they had discovered her peculiar forte. Making movies in Hollywood is too expensive. Every producer was urged to rack his brains and suggest vehicles for her. When the top producers met with the front-office executives, the question of the nature of Marilyn's quality was endlessly kicked about and just as endlessly unresolved.

While waiting for a solution to crystallize, the studio put her in two episodic films, *Full House* and *We're Not Married.* The "sequence film" is an old formula to keep stars employed while you are looking for a good story for them. Occasionally, as in the case of *If I Had a Million* and *Tales of Manhattan,* the project turns out to be an entertainment. A well-done sequence film is like a well-routined bill of vaudeville, even if several of the sequences or acts are mediocre, the others may turn out to be good, and the audience has a sense of hopeful expectation awaiting the next episode. *If I Had a Million* was lifted to a superb height with the sequences of W. C. Fields and Alison Skipworth, Charles Laughton, Mary Boland and Charlie Ruggles. In *Tales of Manhattan* there was a marvelous Laughton sequence as well as ones by Henry Fonda and Ginger Rogers, Edward G. Robinson, Paul Robeson and Ethel Waters.

Full House was based on five O. Henry short stories. This movie was close to Zanuck's heart. He was fond of O. Henry's fiction; in fact, O. Henry was his favorite writer, and he read an O. Henry story each night before retiring. Five separate directors were hired to do each of the sequences. Fred Allen and Oscar Levant were in *The Ransom of Red Chief,* Farley Granger and Jeanne Crain in *The Gift of the Magi,* Anne Baxter in *The Last Leaf,* and Richard Widmark in *The Clarion Call*. Marilyn Monroe appeared in *The Cop and the Anthem*, the one about a bum who feels the autumn chill and attempts to commit some small crime so he can be sent to the workhouse for 90 days and have a warm place to live during the winter. In the original narrative there was one bum. In the movie version there were two bums. (To paraphrase the pigs in George Orwell's *Animal Farm*, Zanuck's motto was, One bum good—two bums better.) The bums were played with amusing raffishness by Charles Laughton and David Wayne. Marilyn played a good-natured streetwalker who was staring into the window of a store as the bums were planning to hurl a rock into it. She engaged in some banter with Laughton, the point of which was that they weren't the sort of toffs she was in search of.

On the theory that perhaps what Marilyn needed was a director who was known as a "woman's director"—that is, a man with angelic qualities of patience and gentleness to soothe the presumed changeable and unpredictable moods of the female—producer Andre Hakim assigned Henry Koster to direct the Monroe sequence. Koster had been successful in making a star out of Deanna Durbin at Universal. Marilyn had so little to do in her scene and there were so few problems, aside from her 1890 costume, coiffure, and make-up, that whatever charms his genius might have deployed to thaw her out did not have a chance to operate. *Full House*, in its entirety, was not a good sequence film, and it was recut and re-edited under Zanuck's personal supervision even after it had been completed. One of the sequences—the Allen-Levant episode—was omitted when it was released.

We're Not Married was more successful—in fact it was one of the more delightful comedies of 1952. Produced and written by Nunnally Johnson, whose hand is genuinely light, it was directed by Edmund Goulding. Goulding was even more celebrated as a "woman's director" than Koster. A virtuoso during the silent movie era, he had directed Gloria Swanson, Nancy Carroll, Garbo, and Bette Davis. He was experienced at putting an actress into a state of serenity and drawing emotions out of her. He had never been noted for his comic skill, but, working closely with Johnson, he brought off a fine sequence comedy. The film glittered with Ginger Rogers, Fred Allen, Victor Moore, David Wayne, Paul Douglas, and Eve Arden. The twist of the plot—or "the weenie" as they say in Hollywood story conferences—was this: Victor Moore, playing a Justice of the Peace, learns that he has performed five marriages before the date on which his appointment became official and that therefore five couples who think they're married are not. Among the couples are Marilyn and David Wayne. As the sequence opens, Marilyn is about to enter a Mrs. America contest. Like Jim Dougherty, Wayne wants his wife to be at home and finds her ambition disturbing. When informed by Victor Moore that he and Marilyn are not legally married, Wayne is delighted. Now she will not be able to pursue her silly desire to be Mrs. America, since she is no longer a Mrs. He goes to the auditorium where the judging of the contestants has already gotten under way, routs Marilyn out of the contest, and breaks the news to her. He expects that she will now come to her senses. But Marilyn is elated. She promptly enters the Miss America contest.

We're Not Married was an amusing example of cinematic fun and games, but Marilyn's contribution to it was not remarkable. All that the movie proved was that she was beautiful. But everybody had known that before. Her flesh had the same impact it had had before. But she still seemed to be a victim of emotional anemia before a camera. The performances that Huston and Mankiewicz had got out of her seemed like miracles. John McCarten somewhat acidly summed up the general critical opinion when he wrote, "As for Mr. Wayne, he lives through the unlikelihood of being married to Miss Monroe as well as anybody could expect."

Nevertheless, when the theatres played these pictures, the marquees read "Marilyn Monroe in *Full House*" and "Marilyn Monroe in *We're Not Married*." The other stars didn't count. The exhibitors were plaguing Spyros Skouras with demands for more Marilyn Monroe pictures, and Skouras, in turn, plagued Zanuck.

Now every producer on the lot was anxious to find a place for her in any script that was ready to go into production, and if there wasn't a place for her they hastened to make it. The most successful producers on the lot—including Nunnally Johnson, Charles Brackett, and Sol C. Siegel—were frantically combing the studio archives and the newly bought literary properties, belaboring their favorite writers to invent a vehicle in which Marilyn's qualities— about which everyone was still uncertain—could be displayed to advantage. At this time, it was estimated that Marilyn's name on a movie increased the gross by at least $500,000. From the wallflower,

Marilyn had suddenly become the belle of the ball. Everybody wanted the next dance with her.

Sol Siegel was the first one to manage it, mainly because he had a story all ready to shoot, *Monkey Business,* a concoction of farce and fantasy in which the front office felt that Marilyn Monroe could not do herself any harm even if she again failed to project herself with authority. The story had been conceived and written by two veterans of farce, Ben Hecht and Charles Lederer. I. A. L. Diamond, who had written the scenario of *Love Nest* and was to collaborate on the wildly farcical script of *Some Like It Hot,* added jokes and several of the far-out sequences that were his specialty. Cary Grant, Ginger Rogers, and Charles Coburn were starred with Marilyn, and Howard Hawks directed.

Grant was a biochemist in a large chemical factory owned by Coburn. Miss Rogers played Grant's wife. Marilyn played Coburn's secretary. The role portrayed her as a voluptuous creature with an intelligence quotient of about 69. She was unable to spell, punctuate, take dictation, or type. In one scene, Grant and Coburn are in conference, and Marilyn enters to deliver a message. As she saunters out of the office, her *derrière* undulating like a well-oiled machine, the camera catches Grant and Coburn staring raptly at the vision; then we see them looking at each other, mutely sharing the experience. After several beats, Coburn sighs and remarks, "Well, *any* stenographer can *spell!*"

In the scenes that required her to speak lines and perform simple pieces of dramatic action, Marilyn was an amateur. Her voice was small and ridiculous and her body was stiff. There was only one sequence in which her miraculous cinematic power came through. Grant, who has been experimenting with an elixir of youth, accidentally drinks some water in which a lab monkey has poured a potpourri of drugs. The mixture invigorates Grant, and, with Marilyn, he goes on a fling. In the course of his spree, he purchases an MG sports car. He speeds recklessly in and out of traffic. Hawks got marvelous close-ups of Marilyn—her hair blown back by the wind, her eyes wide with excitement, her body relaxed, her face reflecting feelings of adoration for Cary Grant. Except for these moments, her contribution to the film was anatomical. In one scene, she showed her beautifully curved leg while demonstrating a new synthetic hosiery material invented by Grant. Her costumes and how she wore them were more significant than her lamentable attempts at dramatic interpretation.

Bill Travilla, 20th's stylist, designed, for the laboratory scenes, a turtle-necked wool-jersey number that clung to her like a wet bathing suit. For the exterior sequences, she wore a slate-blue dress with a stand-up white collar and a plunging neckline. This also clung to her like a wet bathing suit. Travilla even designed a wet bathing suit for her. Midway through the shooting, Hawks inserted a swimming-pool sequence in which Cary and Marilyn rent bathing suits. Marilyn's suit was a "plain" black satin one-piece suit with the rental number on the bodice.

"But on Marilyn," remarked Travilla, "nothing looks plain. We cheated a bit. It isn't really a typical rented bathing suit. It's cut way, way down—that is, in the back."

Monkey Business demonstrated that Marilyn's upper back was beautiful and that her lower back was marvelously callipygous. She need not take a back seat to anybody. Paul V. Beckley, reviewing *Monkey Business* in the New York *Herald Tribune,* said, "Not having seen Miss Monroe before, I know now what that's all about, and I've no dissenting opinions to offer. She disproves more than adequately the efficacy of the old stage rule about not turning one's back to the audience."

Marilyn now had her favorite hairdresser and her favorite make-up man: Gladys Rasmussen and "Whitey" Snyder. They were to remain with her through almost every 20th Century-Fox film she made. Over the years, the color of her hair went through many permutations. She was ash blonde in *Asphalt Jungle,* golden blonde in *All About Eve,* silver blonde in *Young as You Feel,* amber blonde in *Let's Make It Legal,* smoky blonde in *Love Nest,* honey blonde for her sequence in *Full House,* topaz blonde in *We're Not Married,* her natural unbleached dark blonde in *Don't Bother to Knock.* In *Monkey Business* she finally became a platinum blonde.

Miss Rasmussen once explained to me: "There are several problems in doing Marilyn's hair. Her hair is very fine and therefore hard to manage. It gets very oily if it isn't shampooed every day. And her hair is so curly naturally that to build a coiffure for her I have to first give her a straight permanent. She doesn't prefer any one style of coiffure. She can wear anything—a pony tail, a poodle cut, Italian style, elegant pompadour, shoulder length. When she has an important social date, I will do her hair for this. She never likes to wear her hair the same way twice. The way we get her shade of platinum is with my own secret blend of sparkling silver bleach plus twenty-volume peroxide and a secret formula of silver platinum to take the yellow out. I have to do her hair every three, four days, when she's working in a picture."

"Whitey" Snyder, her cosmetician, said it takes an hour and a half to make her up. It takes as long to make her up for an important social evening as it does for a scene in a movie. But if she's just relaxing with friends or husbands, she doesn't wear any make-up at all, "not even powder on her nose." When her face is *au naturel,* she rubs on a solid film of some oily substance—lanolin or olive oil—to protect her skin from the sun and wind. Snyder said: "Marilyn has make-up tricks that nobody else has and nobody knows. Some of them she won't even tell me. She has discovered them herself. She has certain ways of lining and shadowing her eyes that no other actress can do. She puts on a special kind of lipstick; it's a secret blend of three different shades. I get that moist look on her lips for when she's going to do a sexy scene by first putting on the lipstick and then putting a gloss over the lipstick. The gloss is a secret formula of vaseline and wax. You see, when I have the lipstick on, which may take almost an hour, then I'll say, 'Kiss me, honey,' and when she puckers up her lips I put on the gloss. Interesting thing about Marilyn is she's one of the few gals you can photograph full face and she'll look good, the most of them you take it three quarters or side view. Her left profile is great and she's great in three quarters. Her right profile is bad, for some reason. She's got a bad jawline on that side. If she has to work a scene with her right profile to the screen, we have to do a lot of work on the right jawline."

Incidentally, it is not true that 20th Century-Fox has a standing prize of $100 for any person who can submit a photograph of Marilyn with closed lips. The rumor sprang up about five years ago, and each month the studio gets dozens of Monroe closed-lips pictures from persons who need money. Earl Theisen once told me, "Everything she does for a camera has been studied carefully. She knows exactly what she's doing. You can watch her, as you're focusing your camera on her, getting ready to turn it on. She knows exactly how far she wants to open her mouth, how much to raise her upper lip."

Pete Martin reports her saying, "As for my mouth being open all the time, I even sleep with it open. I know, because it's open when I wake up. I never consciously think of my mouth, but I do consciously think about what I'm thinking about."

When Marilyn Monroe walked out on her studio because she refused to play in a comedy, *How to Be Very Very Popular*, producer Nunnally Johnson hired platinum-blonde Sheree North as a substitute. "She will not use the Monroe technique, however," Johnson cracked. "She will play the entire role with her mouth closed." There *are* some closed-mouth pictures of Marilyn. One of the few was taken outside an English country home in which she was living while playing an American chorus girl in *The Prince and the Showgirl*, opposite Sir Laurence Olivier. The rare picture shows her with Olivier, Vivien Leigh, and Arthur Miller. Marilyn's lips are quite sealed.

16 A Rendezvous with Joe Di Maggio

After she had finished *Don't Bother to Knock,* Marilyn fell into a sustained melancholy. Although she had forced herself to face up to them, the revelations about the calendar and her mother's condition humiliated her in her own mind. Lying about her mother and posing naked were two actions that conflicted with her moral ideals. They may not have been ideals to which she adhered, but usually, if she fell short of maintaining them, she concealed the lapses by some unconscious, but nonetheless effective, rationalization. This enabled her both to do what she wanted to do and to live up to that small-town morality which her series of foster parents had impressed upon her. Among the formulas she employed to make peace between her conscience and her desires, the most useful to her own psychological well-being was that of the lonely orphan.

The miseries of her childhood justified, by an obscure operation of her unconscious, various sorts of adult behavior that her conscience wished to outlaw. These and other devices were only secondarily for the world; primarily, they enabled her to function in the competitive and hostile environment of Hollywood without suffering anxiety. Any event that shattered her illusion of herself, that brought her face to face with an obvious disparity between the way she thought she ought to behave and the way she actually behaved, brought on the blues because then the old self-deceptions wouldn't work. In these moods, she tended to withdraw into herself.

Marilyn had gotten to know a talkative, good-natured chap, David March, who tried to persuade her to let Leslie and Tyson, a firm of business managers with which he was connected, handle her finances. Marilyn didn't become his client, but she found his Broadway banter a distraction. March found her a small frame house at 1121 Hilldale Avenue, which she rented early in 1952. But living alone didn't help.

She felt bored. She was tired all the time. She felt as if "all the colors had run out of the world." When she was with Skolsky of an evening, she was withdrawn. She had no women friends of her own age with whom to share her moods. The only man she enjoyed seeing was March, but his interest in her was purely professional.

"I never made a pass at her," March said. "All I wanted was her business." She once gave him a copy of the nude calendar and on it wrote, "To David—do you still want my business?"

She was not being courted. She didn't even want to be courted. The memory of Arthur Miller was now as faded as a dead flower pressed between the pages of a book. At the studio, she was sullen and uncommunicative. Word of her despondency got to Zanuck, and he, for the first time, invited her to his office and rolled out the red carpet. He turned on all his charm, for now she was a star, in a manner of speaking. "Always keep the star happy" is an axiom in show business. Zanuck wanted to make her feel wanted. In her present mood it seemed to her only that "he looked at me briefly and mumbled a few words of advice. I should trust him and he would do everything for the best to make me become a big star." She was quite sure he still hated her.

This was not so, of course. Zanuck had been studying the box-office returns on *Clash by Night,* and he knew, at last, that his studio possessed the most precious asset a studio can have—one of the great screen stars of a generation. He was as desperately anxious as Marilyn to launch her in the pictures that would fulfill all the promise that he now saw in her personality.

Marilyn's "dark night of the soul" lasted for months. In her restlessness, she moved again, this time to an elegant modern apartment in a new building on Doheny Drive in Beverly Hills. That didn't suit her either, and she took an expensive suite at the Bel-Air Hotel. She paid $750 a month for the suite, which had a gardened terrace and overlooked the hotel pool.

Sometimes she invited March over and they dined on the terrace. Then, when the chill evening air of Los Angeles drove them indoors, he lighted a fire in the fireplace. They sat and talked for hours. She would often sigh and say, "Life—what is it all about?" Not being a philosopher, March could not explain the inscrutable mysteries of existence. He often told her that what she needed was a man whom she could love and who would love her. But her experiences in the movie colony had made her withdraw from relations with actors, movie writers, directors, or producers.

"Nobody's ever going to dictate my life," she once said to March. "I'm not going to date any jerks the studio tells me to date. There isn't a decent man in Hollywood. They're all out for one thing. They don't even bother romancing you. Some of them are good-looking and they think that's enough. The hell with that. I don't care for a man who's good-looking. To make me happy, a man has to have some character. I want a man who's honest, intelligent, and not afraid to say what he thinks. I'd rather be lonely by myself than lonely with a man who has nothing to offer."

Hollywood is full of lonely beautiful women, and Marilyn was one of the loneliest. She often walked, alone and unrecognized, down Sunset Boulevard, looking in the windows, watching the passers-by, brooding on life and the human condition.

Monkey Business went into production on February 26, 1952. Four days later, Marilyn woke up hot, weak, and feverish. She lay in bed all day hoping the sick feeling would go away. It got worse. She called Dr. Eliot Corday, her personal physician. He found she was running a high fever. She complained of severe pains in her abdomen. It looked like appendicitis. Dr. Corday summoned an ambulance to take her to Cedars of Lebanon Hospital.

The movie proceeded, with Hawks shooting scenes in which she did not appear. At the hospital, she was given massive injections of penicillin, which brought down the inflammation. On March 5, she was X-rayed, and it was decided that the operation could be postponed until she finished the movie. Her appendix was frozen.

On her last day at the hospital, she had wardrobe fittings. Travilla came to her room with sketches and fabrics and tape measures and two aides, Marilyn's wardrobe girl, Sue Shannon, and the studio's head fitter, Zoya Nedsvetzky.

One of the columnists informed Marilyn's worried public that a "nurse will stand by to see that Marilyn has plenty of rest intervals between the fittings."

Not long after Marilyn had begun tempting Cary Grant in *Monkey Business*, David March called her and said an old friend of his, whom he knew from the old Broadway days at Toots Shor's, was anxious to meet her.

"He's a nice guy," March said.

"Are there any nice guys left?" Marilyn inquired cynically.

"You meet him and you'll see for yourself."

"What's his name?"

"Di Maggio," March said, expecting her to be delighted.

"What's that?"

"Di Maggio, Joe Di Maggio," he said.

"Who's he?"

"You mean to tell me you never heard of Joe Di Maggio, Marilyn?"

"I think he's a baseball player or a football player or something like that, isn't he?"

"He's the greatest baseball player since Babe Ruth."

"Who is Babe Ruth?" Marilyn inquired.

"He was the greatest ballplayer before Di Maggio came along."

"Well, I don't know," Marilyn said.

"Oh, come on, what have you got to lose?"

After some more persiflage, Marilyn finally consented. They were to meet at six-thirty the following Saturday at the Villa Nova, an Italian restaurant on the Sunset Strip. March said he would bring a date, a young actress, Peggy Rabe. Joe and Marilyn were to arrive separately. Di Maggio had told March that Marilyn Monroe was the girl he wanted to meet most in the whole world. He had been dreaming of her since the spring of 1951, when he had seen a photograph of her in a newspaper. On one of the publicity jaunts on which Craft had conducted her, she had gone to a Pasadena ballfield where the Chicago White Sox were in training. She had posed holding a bat at home plate while Gus Zernial stood beside her, presumably giving her technical advice. Marilyn was clad in tight white shorts, a tight jersey blouse, and a ballplayer's cap. She batted left-handed.

"I didn't know Marilyn Monroe liked ballplayers," Joe said wistfully to March. He didn't know that she had never seen a ball game, and had no desire to see one. Like most people, Di Maggio believed what he read in the papers, and the fact that he had seen a picture of Marilyn with two ballplayers was convincing proof that she must be a devotee of the national pastime. "I sure wish I could meet Marilyn Monroe," he sighed.

At the Villa Nova the lights are low, the music is sentimental, the booths are *intime,* Chianti bottles in raffia dangle from the ceiling, and oil paintings of Italian landscapes adorn the walls. The excellent food is conducive to the amorous mood.

When Miss Rabe and March arrived at the café, Joe was already sitting in a booth, the last booth on the lefthand side as you enter by the entrance near the parking area. (I had dinner in this very booth once with March to experience vicariously that historic moment.) Joe was nervous. He was sipping a sweet vermouth on-the-rocks. He had folded the large menu into quarters and was now engaged in folding it into eighths. The time was six-forty. Miss Rabe and March ordered dry Martinis. They all settled down to wait. At seven, Joe morosely remarked, "I don't think she's coming."

"She's always a little late," March said.

"I don't think she's a friend of yours," said Joe.

"Peggy, do I know Marilyn?" March asked plaintively.

"He certainly does, Joe," she said.

"And if she says she'll be here, she'll be here, Joe. She's very anxious to meet you," March said, laying it on a bit.

"I don't believe it," Joe said.

It turned out to be a long wait, and Di Maggio became increasingly uneasy as the next hour went by. Finally, at half past eight, Marilyn swept in, done up to the nines and wearing a blue tailored suit and a low-cut white Shantung silk blouse. Exhaling deeply, Marilyn sat down and turned her blue-gray eyes on Joe. Di Maggio's auricles and ventricles were beating. March made the formal introductions.

"I'm glad to meet you," Di Maggio said wittily. These were about the last words he spoke to Marilyn during dinner—he is not a voluble man. But he did not take his eyes off her. He was profoundly smitten.

Marilyn was also smitten—though not quite as strongly. She had expected that her blind date would be a brash, illiterate, fast-talking man in a loud checked suit. She had apparently gotten her conception of ballplayers from old Joe E. Brown movies. She found herself beside a quiet, handsome gentleman, with genteel manners and a soft voice. He was conservatively dressed in a gray flannel suit and a blue polka-dot tie. She said later that if she hadn't known he was a ballplayer she would have taken him for "either a steel magnate or a Congressman."

Marilyn, who is not exactly garrulous either, spoke only one sentence to Di Maggio during dinner. She said, "There's a blue polka dot exactly in the middle of your tie knot. Did it take you long to fix it like that?"

Di Maggio, who is obviously not one of the great conversationalists of our time, shook his head.

They had both run out of topics of conversation, and now March took the center of the stage and regaled them with humorous stories about Hollywood producers, which is what one always does at dinner parties in Hollywood when the going gets dull. Marilyn and Joe laughed dutifully, and March felt they were beginning to melt. For dinner they had anchovies on pimento, spaghetti *al dente* with garlic and olive oil, a scallopini of veal with a light wine sauce, and *caffè espresso*.

Just as a *rapport* was building up, an unfortunate thing happened. Mickey Rooney, who was dining with a girl at an adjacent table, strolled over. He started talking baseball to Joe.

"Rooney wouldn't go away," March says. "I tried signaling him, but he wouldn't take the hint. He just kept hanging around, talking baseball averages and earned runs and asking questions about the coming season. After Rooney joined the party, Joe and Marilyn couldn't get a word in edgewise."

The group disbanded at ten. Miss Monroe offered to drive her blind date home. On the way, she apologized for not knowing anything about baseball and for not having known who he was when March had telephoned her. He didn't feel humiliated by her ignorance. He was amused by her naïveté about baseball and by her honesty in admitting it. He later said that she was a refreshing change from the phonies and the back-slappers whom he was with so much of the time.

He liked beautiful girls. He especially liked beautiful actresses. He had been married to one some years before, Dorothy Arnold. He found Marilyn different from the other beautiful girls he had dated since his divorce. Marilyn listened to him when he talked. She gave him the impression that she was "really interested in the conversation." This was an unfortunate impression for her to leave, and perhaps if Joe had known that Marilyn was not less but more of a narcissist than any woman he had ever known, he would never have seen her again. Perhaps Di Maggio wanted what all men in the United States dream of—the woman who is both mistress and wife. Marilyn—sexual but sweet, voluptuous but subdued—seemed like the not-impossible she.

She parked her car outside the Hollywood-Knickerbocker Hotel, in the Hollywood area. Joe asked her to come up to his room and see his baseball trophies. She said that it was too late. She had to be at the studio at seven-thirty for make-up. Joe embraced her suddenly and kissed her. She drew away coldly and said, "Good night."

"I'll call you tomorrow," he said, trying to smile.

She didn't answer.

March rang up Marilyn the next morning.

"Where'd you and Joe go after you left us?" March asked hopefully.

"I drove him home," Marilyn said in tones of world weariness, "and then I went home and I read a book." She didn't say what book.

"How did you like Joe?" he asked.

"He struck out," Marilyn said.

Di Maggio telephoned her the next day. She was quite reserved. No, she didn't have any time this week. He called every day, and she refused him. After two weeks, Di Maggio gave up. When he stopped calling her, Marilyn found herself beginning to think of him with affection. She says she has always been able to figure out what it was that drew her to a man, but in the case of Joe she couldn't determine the source of his attraction. This may be because their interests and temperaments were so different. It is possible that between their first and second meetings, she created a romantic character for Joe. If she mentioned Di Maggio to the electricians, carpenters, and grips on the set, their eyes lit up. She began to realize that Joe was a hero. So Marilyn overcame her pride and telephoned Joe for a date. They had dinner in an obscure Italian restaurant where they would have privacy and not be disturbed either by movie fans or by baseball fans. After dinner, he said, "What would you like to do?"

She shrugged. "I don't know. What would *you* like to do?" He had been well-behaved during dinner, and his hands had been discreet. He was really a nice man, and the fact that he had seemed forward on their first date could be forgiven.

"Well," he said, "I don't know if you'd like this, but I'd like to just, well, just take a drive and talk, I mean really talk."

"I'd love it," she said, "it's a lovely night for a drive." It was warmer than usual, and there was a huge romantic moon in the deep-purple sky. She headed west to her favorite highway, the Pacific Coast Highway, and they drove at scene-blurring speed past Malibu, past Escondido Beach. They drove for three hours that night. They stopped for hamburgers and coffee at a drive-in. Di Maggio had not made any physical overtures. He had talked and she had talked. He said that he had had a good time. He said that he usually didn't have a good time on the second date with a girl, and rarely had a third one.

"There's a friend of mine, George Solotaire, and he pries these girls loose when I get tired of them."

Marilyn asked whether Solotaire was in Hollywood. He was. He had come with Joe from New York.

"I hope I won't be too hard for Mr. Solotaire to pry loose," she said.

"I won't have any use for George this trip," Joe said.

Then there was a long silence between them. In fact, the proportion of silences to speech during this and subsequent meetings was about two to one, and the proportion increased in favor of silence as time went on.

On the next date, he got up enough courage to tell her he had seen her picture last year.

"Which one was it?" she said eagerly, hoping to get a favorable critique of one of her performances.

"The one," he replied, "where you were with Gus."

"Gus who?"

"You know, Zernial, Gus Zernial, that ballplayer."

"Oh you mean that picture!" she said, rather let down. "What's so interesting about that? You must have posed with celebrities for lots of publicity pictures when you were in baseball."

"The best I ever got was Ethel Barrymore and General Mac-Arthur." He smiled. "You're much prettier." Marilyn wrote, "This admission"—that she was prettier than Douglas MacArthur or Ethel Barrymore—"had an odd effect on me. I had read reams and reams of writing about my good looks, and scores of men had told me I was beautiful. But this was the first time my heart had jumped to hear it."

She decided she was falling in love. She didn't think the feeling would last, however. These affairs were always "nice" when they began, but "they always ended up in dullness." But she found herself feeling comfortable with Joe and then needing him. She listened with fascination as Joe told her how he had become a ballplayer.

He was born in 1915 in San Francisco. He was the eighth of nine children, six of whom were boys. His father was a fisherman who made a poor living working out of his own small boat, fishing for salmon, herring, smelt, and crabs. Marilyn warmed to his stories of the exuberant Italian family life of the Di Maggios in the old stucco house near Fishermen's Wharf. Joe idolized his mother, who had died in 1949. He once said that his mother, Marilyn, and his only son were the "three great influences in my life." Like any other orphan, Marilyn became misty-eyed when she heard about large families. She often said that when she married again she would have a large family—five or six children. She loved children.

Joe had gone from sandlot to semi-pro baseball. From there he went with the San Francisco Seals; his heavy hitting and fielding brought him an offer from the New York Yankees, whom he joined in 1936. In his first year in baseball he hit .323 and 29 home runs, and for 15 years he was the greatest attraction in baseball. In 1941, he set a record when he hit in 56 consecutive games. He played in ten world's series. He was earning a salary of $100,000 a year when he retired from baseball in September, 1951, because of foot and shoulder injuries.

The days of Joe's glory were behind him when he began courting Marilyn. Her glory was only beginning. He was not entirely inactive. He did a 15-minute commentary before and after each Yankee game and was the star of a weekly filmed television show for boys in which he gave helpful hints on how to become a heavy hitter. Di Maggio had no idea, when he began falling in love, that Marilyn was on the verge of great success.

Marilyn saw her first baseball game on March 17, 1952. The Hollywood Stars, a professional minor-league ball team, were playing a pickup team, the Major League All Stars, at Gilmore Field, for the benefit of the Kiwanis Club's children's fund. It was the only time Marilyn ever saw Joe play ball. He had an errorless night on the field and got two hits out of four times at bat, a single and a home run.

By now, items were beginning to appear in all the gossip columns that something was afoot between the All-American Baseball Hero and the All-American Sex Heroine. Asked by one sportswriter, "How does it figure that a guy who's been trying to dodge the spotlight all his life is dating the most famous girl in the world?" Di Maggio replied, "It's like a good double-play combination. It's just a matter of two people meeting and something clicks."

The legmen for the columnists and the fan-magazine writers haunted the *Monkey Business* set every day. Romance was the commodity their customers were most avid for, and this was a storybook romance. Marilyn was badgered every day for news of her engagement. She said she wasn't engaged. She said she and Joe were "friends."

She was asked whether, in the event that she got married, she would give up her career. She replied, "A career is wonderful, but you can't curl up with it on a cold night." She was also to find, as many another frustrated wife has found, that sometimes you can't curl up with a husband on a cold night, either. However, to paraphrase A. E. Housman, she was six-and-twenty, no use to talk to her. And Di Maggio was seven-and-thirty, and there was no use to talk to him, either. There really is no logic to *any* love affair or any marriage, for that matter.

She was asked if she was interested in baseball, and she said, "Not yet—but I hope to be. We've been discussing baseball."

"Haven't you been discussing love?" was the next question.

"Love isn't something you discuss," she said.

Joe came to the studio one day and watched her do several sequences with Cary Grant. At Roy Craft's request, he docilely posed with Marilyn and Grant. When the pictures appeared in newspapers throughout the country the next day, Grant's face had been cropped from the photograph. When Marilyn and Joe went out, they were afraid to be seen in any public place because hordes of romance-hungry movie fans immediately pounced upon them. They usually spent their evenings with Vic Masi and his wife, who lived in Ensenada, in the valley. Masi was an old San Francisco friend of Di Maggio's.

They had a home-cooked meal with the Masis and watched television. Other nights, they spent in Marilyn's suite at the Bel-Air Hotel, eating hotel-cooked meals and watching television. Had she but known it, the future of her marriage was writ large on the 21-inch screen of this monster. For Di Maggio had an incurable craving for television, comparable to the addiction some men have for alcohol. He would have his dinner while watching the seven-o'clock news, and then he would go straight through an evening watching all the Western and crime programs and even the Late Show and the Late Late Show.

In those days, Marilyn thought this a pleasant way to pass an evening, for they occasionally talked and exchanged observations on the programs they watched. But for a student of Stanislavsky and an admirer of Proust, Thomas Wolfe, Dostoevski, Chekhov, and Shakespeare, it must have been rather tedious watching Hopalong Cassidy, Boston Blackie, Gangbusters, and other dramatic masterpieces of that era. She did not complain. Perhaps she hoped, as many women who marry alcoholics hope, that through the power of her devotion she would reform Joe.

In April, Joe, together with Solotaire, who had observed the flowering romance with bewilderment, flew back to New York. Joe had to get his own television program under way. A week later, Marilyn went into the hospital for an appendectomy. The first gift to arrive was a bouquet of two dozen roses that Di Maggio had wired from New York.

"In addition," said a studio bulletin, "to flowers from studio executives and from practically every agency in town, the most unique arrangement was sent by Dan Dailey. Dan's cheery get-well gift was a tree arrangement of tulips, with toy canaries on every limb. The canaries sing when wound up."

When she had recovered from the operation, Marilyn returned to work and did her last sequence with Grant. This comprised the swimming scene, a roller-skating episode in a rink, and the wild ride in the MG, which ended in a smash-up.

The publicity department, which now was under orders to trumpet the name of Marilyn Monroe with every instrument in the brass section, arranged for her to make a personal appearance before 10,000 marines at Camp Pendleton. She got a screaming ovation. She sang "Somebody Loves You" and "Do It Again." She was still no Ella Fitzgerald or Mary Martin, but she was adequate if given enough volume by the sound engineer.

There was method in her madness. The studio had bought for $500,000 the Broadway musical version of *Gentlemen Prefer Blondes*. It had been announced as a vehicle for Betty Grable. Marilyn was conducting a quiet campaign to get the role of Lorelei Lee assigned to her. From the volume of fan mail, the front office knew that Miss Grable's popularity had declined as much as Marilyn's had increased. But could Marilyn sing and dance? She proved, at Pendleton, that she could sing and had enough acting ability to delude an audience into believing that she was an accomplished dancer. The marines, that day, would not let her go. They stamped and shrieked and whistled for her to come back again and again.

She looked out at the vast audience—the largest flesh-and-blood audience she had ever appeared before—and said, a smile on her face, "I don't know why you boys are always getting so excited about sweater girls. Take away their sweaters and what have they got?"

On June 1, she celebrated her twenty-sixth birthday alone in her suite at the Bel-Air Hotel. She had steak and a bottle of champagne. Joe telephoned from New York and spoke to her for a long time. Her rooms were running over with telegrams of congratulations, baskets of flowers, and expensive presents from 20th Century-Fox executives, producers at her own and other studios, and a great number of prominent actors and actresses.

Sitting in solitary splendor, preparing to leave for Niagara Falls, New York, where she was to shoot several weeks of location sequences for her next film, *Niagara*, Marilyn was filled with a sense of triumph. That day, word had come to her, through an intermediary, that she had gotten the Lorelei Lee part in *Gentlemen Prefer Blondes* and the picture would go into production as soon as she completed *Niagara*. So the juiciest plum on the lot had fallen into her lap. A famous hero was in love with her. She had everything. She could walk to a French window and see, from her terrace, the quiet luxury of the Bel-Air Hotel, which is more like a country club in a tropical paradise than a hotel, with oleanders and honeysuckle climbing up the walls, palm trees and orange trees and lemon trees outside.

Yet beneath the elation there was a niggling uneasiness about herself. In 12 months she had progressed with a dizzying speed. She had become the acknowledged queen, not only of her own studio, but of the motion-picture industry. But she continued to feel she was losing herself. One of her favorite quotations from the New Testament is: "What shall it profit a man, if he gain the whole world and lose his own soul?" She was gaining a world she had long been ambitious to conquer. And it wasn't so much that she was losing her soul as that her soul was not developing. Or maybe this was how you lost it. That overpowering feeling of fatigue, of ennui, which had taken all the colors out of living earlier in the year, had been dissipated in the excitement of her romance with Di Maggio and in the prospect of playing important roles in *Niagara* and *Gentlemen Prefer Blondes*. But now that she had it, was this what she really wanted, after all?

Life, she often thought, what's it all about? But she did not sit down with herself long enough to formulate any replies.

17 A Shooting in Niagara Falls; a *Première* in Atlantic City

The producer of *Niagara* was Charles Brackett, a distinguished novelist of the 1920's and the first movie critic of *The New Yorker*. In 1950, he found himself obsessed with the idea of doing a film against the background of Niagara Falls. He had no story and he tried to rid himself of the obsession, but the *idée fixe* became stronger. One evening, at a dinner party, he confided to the hostess that he was sorely troubled by his Niagara Falls obsession and, for the life of him, couldn't imagine why the idea had suddenly sprung into his mind. She laughed. "I can, Charlie," she said. "The next time you go down stairs to the lavatory, you know, the one you gentlemen use, take a good look around."

He did. On one of the lavatory walls, affixed to the most suitable location, was a dramatic Currier and Ives print of the cascading waters of Niagara Falls. (After the film was done, the woman presented the print to Brackett, and it now hangs in his office.)

Brackett roughed out a plot for a suspense murder story. Walter Reisch and Richard Breen collaborated with him on the screenplay. It was finished and approved for production just before Marilyn started shooting *Monkey Business*. Henry Hathaway, a director outstanding for his ability to combine documentary realism with mystery narration, was to direct. Hathaway had directed such excellent films as *Kiss of Death, Call Northside 777, The House on 92nd Street*.

Brackett describes the heroine of *Niagara* as "a beautiful young

155

thing with the clear eyes and the untroubled expression of a girl with no moral restraints whatever."

Brackett was sure that he and Hathaway would get a performance of some scope out of Marilyn if they made her feel secure. Therefore, even before work on the film began, both men often met with Marilyn to discuss problems of the script and casting. To play Marilyn's lover, a good-looking young actor had been suggested. He was tested with Marilyn. The following morning, Brackett got a call from her.

"I don't think he's right for the part," she said.

"Why?"

She seemed embarrassed. "Well," she said in her soft, uncertain voice, "it's just I don't think he'll do the love scenes right, Mr. Brackett."

"He looked rather good in the scene we tried, Marilyn."

"He's not masculine enough."

"What do you mean?"

"Well," she said, "what I mean is, well, he's a pansy."

Brackett said he was sure she was mistaken. However, when he made inquiries in certain circles, he learned that Marilyn's intuition was correct. "Obviously," Brackett once told me, "her glandular secretions are in excellent working order."

Brackett promised that Natasha Lytess would be welcome on the set. Marilyn could have as many retakes as she needed. He even agreed to consider Marilyn's opinion on editing the daily rushes. She would not, of course, have the final approval of which one of several takes of a scene would be used in the completed version of *Niagara;* this is the prerogative of the director. Only the producer and the executive producer can overrule the director's decisions. As a matter of fact, Marilyn, in the end, found herself in close agreement with Brackett and Hathaway. Zanuck, however, insisted on cutting out several of Marilyn's most important scenes. "I think," Brackett recently remarked, "some of her best scenes were cut." Brackett and Zanuck had many violent arguments about the scenes. But Zanuck had his way.

Marilyn flew to New York to be with Di Maggio. He took her to his favorite saloon, the old Toots Shor's on West 51st Street, known to an intimate circle as "the store," and he showed her off to his sporting and show-business friends. Then she flew to Buffalo.

Marilyn played a young wife married to a psychotic war veteran. The wife is a bit on the psychopathic side herself. But the early sequences give the audience the impression that Joseph Cotten—who played the husband—is suffering from delusions of infidelity and plans to murder his wife without reason. Actually, Marilyn has a lover and is planning to kill her husband. The film counterpoints, in a rhythm of mounting tension, these two murderers, each hoping to kill his partner before he could be murdered himself.

At this stage of her acting development, Marilyn was no Garbo, nor even a Bette Davis. Yet she did achieve a degree of believability in *Niagara*. Her voice rang out with some authority. The photography—of Marilyn's exquisite loveliness, of the falls, of the cliffs and mist-sprayed walks around the Falls, the vulgar neon-lighted motels and bars and cabarets and souvenir shops, and the chase sequences up and down the narrow wooden staircases on the cliffs—was magnificent. Under Hathaway's direction, the camera explored Marilyn's mysterious beauty more successfully than ever before. She had always been beautiful on film, but in *Niagara* she was ethereally beautiful.

The opening sequence established the mood of the film: a panoramic shot of Niagara Falls and then, coming into the foreground, Cotten, seen as a lonely insane figure, watching the Falls at dawn from the balcony of a motel. After the exterior sequence, the action cuts to the darkened bedroom. Cotten is seen shaving in the bathroom. There is a sense of the ominous in every movement he makes, in the grimness on his face. In the bed, we see Marilyn asleep—or pretending to be asleep. The camera catches her in a wild beauty of disordered hair, disordered pillow and bedclothes, her mouth open, bare shoulders suggesting she is naked under the covers. She actually *was* naked. She told Hathaway that she couldn't project the mood unless she played without any clothes.

It was in *Niagara* that Hathaway trained a camera on an actress for the longest walk in cinema history. The view was from the rear. Marilyn's posterior, in tight red satin, dominated the scene as she sauntered across a cobblestoned avenue to an iron bridge overlooking the Niagara River. The 116 feet of film took 16 seconds on the screen.

Somebody once said that Marilyn Monroe was the only actress who makes her greatest entrance when she exits!

Harmon Jones, who directed her in *Young as You Feel,* observed, "She can squeeze more meaning out of a few steps than most actresses can get out of six pages of dialogue." Marilyn has been called the actress with the horizontal walk. She professes to be puzzled by this: "I don't get what they mean by horizontal walk. Naturally I know what walking means. Anybody knows that. And horizontal means not vertical. So what?"

She told Pete Martin: "I've never deliberately done anything about the way I walk. People say I walk all wiggly and wobbly, but I don't know what they mean. I just walk. I've never wiggled deliberately in my life, but all my life I've had trouble with people who say I do. In high school, the other girls asked me, 'Why do you walk down the hall that way?' I guess the boys must have been watching me and it made the other girls jealous or something, but I said, 'I learned to walk when I was ten months old and I've been walking this way ever since.'"

Yet, in 1951, when she was on the threshold of greatness, she confided to a unit-man of the 20th Century-Fox publicity department who had been assigned to cover a film she was shooting that she was making a study of actresses and their styles of walking and that she thought French actresses were best at this art. "They just don't plod down the street like so many horses," she explained. "They jiggle, they bounce, they weave, they undulate—they come to life." In private, Marilyn is quite capable of moving across a room without undulating. The movie walk is contrived and therefore an aspect of her artistic ingenuity, though she denies this. By denying it, she enhances the mystery. Explanations of her peculiar walk are rife in Hollywood. I have been told it was the result of a swimming accident. Emaline Snively told me, "She's double-jointed in the knees. When she walks, her knees lock. So she can't relax, and that's why her hips seem to sway when she walks into a room."

Skolsky writes: "It's all the result of an accident when she was ten. She had dawdled after school one day and suddenly remembering the chores she had at home, she broke into a run, fell, and broke her ankle. When she was finally allowed to walk she tried to walk so as to avoid pressure on the weak ankle. In all probability, the bone never set properly, for it is still weak and the walk has become a habit."

When I put the matter to her once, she shook her head in bewilderment at the human race. "I don't know where they get all these things," she said. "I never had a swimming accident. I've never been double-jointed. My knees don't lock. There is nothing wrong with my ankles. They were never fractured. I walk the way I have always walked. *I have walked this way since I was eleven or twelve.*" My impression is that this last statement—which contradicts her other remembrances of things past—is in the area of truth. For it was between the ages of twelve and thirteen that she consciously set out to intrigue the male sex.

Joseph Cotten was the first of many veteran actors to discover that this blonde had real and awesome talent. "Everything that girl does is sexy," he said. "She can't even light a cigarette without being sexy. A lot of people—the ones who haven't met Marilyn—will tell you it's all publicity. That's malarkey. They've tried to give a hundred other girls the same publicity build-up. It didn't take with them. This girl's really got it."

After *Niagara* the critics began to take notice of Marilyn. In the New York *Times,* A. H. Weiler wrote: "Seen from any angle, the Falls and Miss Monroe leave little to be desired by any reasonably attentive audience. . . . Perhaps Miss Monroe is not the perfect actress at this point. But neither the director nor the gentleman * who handled the camera appeared to be concerned with this. They have caught every possible curve both in the intimacy of the boudoir and in equally revealing tight dresses. And they have illustrated pretty concretely that she can be seductive even when she walks."

In the New York *Herald Tribune,* Otis Guernsey, Jr., wrote: "Miss Monroe plays the kind of wife whose dress, in the words of the script, 'is cut so low you can see her knees.' The dress is red. The actress has very pretty knees, and under Hathaway's direction she gives the kind of serpentine performance that makes the audience hate her while admiring her."

Time said that "what lifts the film above the commonplace is its star, Marilyn Monroe." It quoted director Hathaway as saying, "She can make any move, any gesture, almost insufferably suggestive."

McCarten remained her steadfast dissenter, however. Oscar Wilde, on first seeing Niagara Falls, remarked of it, "The second great disappointment of the American bride." MM was the second great dis-

* Joe Macdonald, ASC (American Society of Cinematographers).

appointment of the *New Yorker* critic. He wrote: "Marilyn Monroe, whom Hollywood has been ballyhooing as a new-day Lillian Russell, takes a fling at big-league melodrama in *Niagara* and demonstrates a wide assortment of curves and a tendency to read her lines as if they were in a tongue she is not entirely familiar with. . . . However admirably constructed Miss Monroe may be, she is hardly up to competing with one of the wonders of this continent."

But the public didn't care about her diction. *Niagara* cost $1,250,-000 and it grossed $6,000,000.

The location work on *Niagara* was completed on June 25. The cast was now to move to the Coast to complete shooting. Meanwhile, *Monkey Business* was ready to be released. The sales and publicity departments suggested that the studio tie Marilyn into the Miss America contest at Atlantic City. The promoters had agreed to make Marilyn the Grand Marshal of the big parade preceding the judging of the beauties. Why not hold the world *première*—or *preemeer* as they say in Hollywood—in Atlantic City?

Marilyn said no, a loud, firm, definite no to the plan.

She was weary of interviewers and photographers, of crowds cheering, of autograph hunters. A place in the sun, which seems so wonderful when you're in the shade, is a hot and open place, and the sun of public adulation beats fiercely. She longed for privacy, but she had lost her privacy forever. She wanted time for herself, time to be with Joe in New York. If there was a week of freedom between Niagara Falls and Hollywood, she wanted to go to New York. The studio struck a bargain with her. In return for her co-operation on the Atlantic City hoop-la, they would give her several days in New York.

The interlude in Manhattan was flat. She and Joe were never alone. They were followed by reporters and fans. At Shor's, Joe's friends sat with them and talked about the 1952 pennant races. She was bored. She wanted to see the new plays. She wanted to go to the Metropolitan Museum and to visit the hot jazz spots, like Eddie Condon's. Joe didn't care for theatre, music, art. His world was the world of sports, his cronies were sports-loving men like George Solotaire, men who lived in a closed-in masculine world of gin rummy, sports, betting, money talk, inside jokes.

She felt removed from Joe's world. He already seemed to be taking her for granted. He was proud of her—but pride in her was not what she wanted. She didn't want to feel like a desirable object a man had captured so his friends would envy him.

And the publicity demands on her never let up. The phone in the hotel didn't stop ringing. Newspapers wanting stories. Can she meet Winchell at the Stork? Leonard Lyons at Sardi's? Earl Wilson wants to do a column on her. Wilson, who had made a reputation among breast fetishists with his articles, asked Marilyn, "True or falsie?" She replied, "Everything I have is mine."

About her swirled a hurricane, and she was its eye. It seemed as if every newspaper and magazine in the country wanted an exclusive interview with her. The engagements piled up, and she was late to all of them. Punctuality had never been one of her virtues, but now the mounting pressures, colliding with her fear of human contact, resulted in a tardiness that grew and grew until it became monumental. For now her power enabled her to flout other people's convenience at her sweet will. She is almost never on time. She may be from one to four hours late for an appointment. Once, en route to be the guest of honor at a festival in Long Beach, California, she stopped on the highway to fix her make-up. She emerged from the ladies' washroom an hour and 40 minutes later! She was two hours late for her appendectomy. Innumerable times, she has missed trains, planes, and boats. After 1952, she got into the habit of being late even at the studio. Billy Wilder, who was to direct two of her best films, once told me what her lateness means on the set: "She's never on time. It is a terrible thing for an acting company, the director, the cameraman. You sit there and wait. You can't start without her. Thousands of dollars you see going into the hole. You can always figure a Monroe picture is going to run an extra few hundred thousand dollars because she's coming late. It demoralizes the whole company. It's like trench warfare. You sit and sit, waiting for something to happen. Of course, I have an Aunt Ida in Vienna who is always on time to the second, but I wouldn't put her in a movie. I don't think Marilyn is late on purpose. Her idea of time is different, that's all. I think maybe there's a little watchmaker in Zurich, Switzerland, he makes a living producing special watches only for Marilyn Monroe."

Once, when she was an hour and three minutes late to a press conference, syndicated columnist Phyllis Battelle asked her, "Why were you late?"

"I was detained," Marilyn said mysteriously.

Sometimes she gives one of a number of excuses. She lost an important article of apparel. She lost her wristwatch. She forgot to set her alarm clock. The door of her bathroom jammed. The battery in her car died. Her ignition key disappeared. Once, she told a producer that she'd run out of gas on her way to the studio and couldn't get a lift. The idea of nobody's being willing to pick up Marilyn was preposterous, but a studio car was sent out for her.

She once rationalized her tardiness by explaining, "It's not really me that's late. It's the others who are in such a hurry."

What is Marilyn up to during these moments and hours when others are waiting for her? She is communing with her body, that's what. She may fall into a reverie while looking at her face in a mirror. She may be brushing, brushing, brushing her hair. She may decide to wash her hair several times in succession. Many women are indecisive about what to wear, but Marilyn's indecisiveness is almost a religion. She may change her mind about what to wear ten times, twenty times, a hundred times. As her wardrobe increased, so did her indecisiveness. But most of all, she will bathe, she will lave herself in hot perfumed waters for hours on end, with almost the neurotic compulsiveness of Blanche Dubois in *A Streetcar Named Desire*. In a rare burst of perspicacious self-analysis, Marilyn once wrote: "When I have to be somewhere for dinner at eight o'clock, I will lie in the bathtub for an hour or longer.

"Eight o'clock will come and go and I still remain in the tub. I keep pouring perfumes into the water and letting the water run out and refilling the tub with fresh water. I forget about eight o'clock and my dinner date. I keep thinking and feeling far away.

"Sometimes I know the truth of what I'm doing. It isn't Marilyn Monroe in the tub but Norma Jean. I'm giving Norma Jean a treat.

"She used to have to bathe in water used by six or eight other people. Now she can bathe in water as clean and transparent as a pane of glass. And it seems that Norma Jean can't get enough of fresh bath water that smells of real perfume.

". . . After I get out of the tub I spend a long time rubbing creams into my skin. I love to do this. Sometimes another hour will pass, happily.

"When I finally start putting my clothes on I move as slowly as I

162

can. I begin to feel a little guilty because there seems to be an impulse in me to be as late as possible for my dinner date. It makes something in me happy—to be late. People are waiting for me. People are eager to see me. And I remember the years I was unwanted. All the hundreds of times nobody wanted to see the little servant girl, Norma Jean—not even her mother.

"I feel a queer satisfaction in punishing the people who are wanting me now. But it's not them I'm really punishing. It's the long-ago people who didn't want Norma Jean.

"It isn't only that, either. I get thrilled as if I were Norma Jean going to a party and not Miss Monroe. The later I am, the happier Norma Jean grows."

While the business of Norma Jean, the unwanted "little servant girl," is a bit thick for me to swallow—it is verbal magic by means of which Marilyn justifies to her conscience her anti-social behavior —I believe that in her awareness of the hostility underlying her act she has seen into the core of her delaying actions. She is punishing. And she is not just spitefully paying off old scores; she is paying off present ones as well. The open expression of resentment in direct, unmistakable words and deeds is so difficult for Marilyn that she relies on various devices, including lateness, as a means of venting hostility. And the persons so treated feel her hostility and take it for what it is—punishment. In the activity preceding her lateness, however, there are other implications. The prepossession with one's appearance is a characteristic of all movie actresses. No matter how lovely they are, to them this beauty is imperfect and unconvincing. Inwardly they feel unattractive. They take infinite pains at the dressing table and are, like Marilyn, rarely punctual, although nobody in Hollywood is as chronically late as she. Two actresses whom I personally know to be from an hour to two hours late to engagements are Jennifer Jones and Elizabeth Taylor.

The compulsive character of Marilyn's ablutions certainly indicates a trace of the well-known "washing compulsion." As explained by the psychiatric profession, this is a means of alleviating anxiety. One substitutes the idea of being physically unclean for more disturbing sensations or thoughts. In washing away non-existent dirt, one ritually washes out the disturbing elements from one's field of awareness.

But "after such knowledge, what forgiveness"? It doesn't make the lot of those waiting for her any pleasanter.

In the plane to Atlantic City, Marilyn put on the red dress she had worn in *Niagara,* the one "cut down to the knees."

A sheriff and a motorcycle escort met her at the airport. Sirens screaming, they took her to the railroad station, arriving only a few seconds after the train pulled in, the train on which she was supposed to arrive and which she had missed. The Mayor, looking slightly confused, welcomed her, kissed her, gave her a large bouquet of roses, and pinned the Grand Marshal's badge on her—it took a good deal of exploring to find enough silk on which to pin a badge.

Later some people in Atlantic City berated her for the indecency of her clothes. To these prudes Marilyn replied, "I wasn't aware of any objectionable décolletage on my part. I'd noticed people looking at me all day, but I thought they were looking at my Grand Marshal's badge."

Mounted on the folded-down top of a convertible, Marilyn triumphantly motored through the solidly packed streets of the city, throwing roses to admirers. Her automobile cruised up the boardwalk itself.

After the usual frantic cocktail-party interviews and photographing, Marilyn hurriedly showered and dressed and went to the theatre for the *première.* She did not eat any dinner. She did not have any appetite. She came out on the stage and said a few words about *Monkey Business.* Just clichés.

"Row upon row, two thousand jaws hung agape at the vision before them," recalls Ben Ross, a photographer who was present. "Nobody stirred. Nobody laughed at the corny routines.

"It was mass paralysis."

A great force of nature, Marilyn Monroe had become a victim of her own struggle to build herself up. Her time was not hers. Her personality was not hers. She had no privacy. She had murdered privacy, as Macbeth had murdered sleep. She had sought out the formless mass of the public and made it love her. She had co-operated with the propaganda machine, and now she was a victim of it. She had no way of knowing what was genuine in what was printed about her. Had the troops in the Aleutians really voted her "the girl most likely to thaw out Alaska"? Had an entire battalion in Korea volunteered to marry her? Had the 7th Division Medical Corps chosen her "the girl we would most like to examine"?

In Atlantic City, shifts of contestants were brought to her. She posed with each of the 48 girls. Then the pictures were shipped to the home-state papers. It was all part of a high-powered program, and the reward was a caption mentioning two words, *Monkey Business*, and an increase in Marilyn's fame.

Somebody in Army public relations asked Marilyn to pose with a WAC, a WAVE, a SPAR, and a WAF. She did. It was a routine picture, uninterestingly photographed. The United Press sent it out. Feature editors just filed it away. Then a horrified Army officer saw the print. He was horrified at the cleavage Monroe was showing while standing side by side with four uniformed women officers. This was a disgrace to the service! He ordered the picture killed. The UP sent out a teletype to all its papers ordering the picture killed. Naturally the editors who got the "kill" order resurrected the picture the Army had tried to "censor." Suddenly, it became an amusing news story. A stuffed shirt, an Army bureaucrat, had made a fool of himself. Hundreds of newspapers printed the photograph, and many of them put it on the front page.

Marilyn said she didn't know why the picture aroused such a furor. "You would think all other women kept their bodies in vaults," she said.

She was beginning to suspect people were laughing at her. She didn't like being pictured as a dumb fool or a dumb slut or a good-looking featherbrain without any acting talent. And Joe didn't like the picture. He told her she shouldn't let the studio make her pose for "naked" pictures. It wasn't proper. It wasn't the sort of thing a nice girl does, you know. Joe got the uneasy feeling that his friends were snickering at him behind his back. She had to promise to behave herself and be respectable.

Marilyn didn't like Joe's domineering tone. They weren't married and he was pushing her around. He wanted to get married. She wasn't in a hurry. She kept postponing the date. They were still deluding each other that they were in love. But why, said she, be in a hurry to get married? Wait until she finished *Niagara*. He said he couldn't stand living 3,000 miles away from her. But it was the very distance that lent enchantment to their feelings for each other.

Upon returning to Hollywood in July, 1952, to complete *Niagara*,

Marilyn was troubled by a sense of artistic stagnation and personal alienation. She seemed to be a piece on a chessboard, the queen it is true, the sex queen, but yet a piece shifted about by all-powerful figures whose decisions were final. Somehow she had to assert her independence. She began studying with Michael Chekhov. A nephew of the Russian playwright, Chekhov had acted in the Moscow Art Theatre before the revolution. In recent years, he had been writing and teaching. He took few pupils. Marilyn startled him with her raw acting talent. At the Actors' Lab, she had already sampled Stanislavsky's technique of converting personal experiences into states of dramatic emotion during the playing of scenes. She was intellectually stimulated by her hours with Chekhov. Natasha Lytess, still her faithful counselor, was jealous of any other influence over Marilyn. She argued against the Stanislavsky approach. She said Chekhov's teaching would be harmful to Marilyn's character. It would encourage her to be less disciplined than she already was, to rely on her instincts instead of training herself consciously to meet any acting challenge. Marilyn, she said, needed to develop a strong control over her emotions. She needed to train her voice, body, heart, to obey the commands of her mind. Marilyn, while using Natasha as a friend and as a critical super-ego, disdained her theories of acting. Her instincts told her that the "warm heart and the cold mind" technique, the way of the English and French actors, was not her way. It was too late for that. She was too old. Only a non-disciplinary orientation promised hope for her. Her personality was organized around a pattern of disorganization. She could not become the controlled disciplined actress that a Lynn Fontanne is. Marilyn would have had to undergo a total change of personality to discipline her emotions artistically. She had to find her way to artistic fulfillment through an intuitive, romantic method. Eventually, by means of the teaching and encouragement of Lee Strasberg, Marilyn fulfilled herself.

Michael Chekhov believed that Marilyn was, potentially, a sublime talent. Twice a week, she went to his house for two-hour lessons.

Once they were doing a scene from *The Cherry Orchard*. When they finished, he asked her if she had been deliberately projecting sexuality. She said no because she knew sex was not called for in the scene. Chekhov laughed uproariously, slapped his thigh, pounded on the floor. He suddenly understood her problem. No matter how she tried to play a scene she could not help emanating powerful animal vibrations. Just now, the air had been filled with them.

"The whole world is already responding to your wibrations, Mahrahleen," he said. "What do the owners of the studio care if you're an actress or if you're not an actress? With your wibrations, you only have to stand in front the camera, and you're wibrating, and for them you make a million dollars."

"I don't want that," she said grimly. "I want to be an artist, not a freak."

Each day she phoned Zanuck's office. She says that neither he nor any other top-ranking executives would see her. She recalls, "They said, 'Just be on the set when you're notified.' "

It was the same desire to prove herself a serious artist, not a studio appendage, that prompted her to go to the Roy Goldenburg auction galleries one Saturday in December, 1952. She intended to bid on a collection of 178 play and movie typescripts which had been annotated by Max Reinhardt. Natasha had told her about the collection. Attending the auction that day were representatives of libraries and important private collectors. The scripts had no market value, and those who were interested in them expected to buy them for several hundred dollars, at the most. But Marilyn kept jumping the bids. When the bidding reached $1,000, everybody dropped out of the action except Marilyn and a man from the University of Southern California. USC had a fairly complete collection of Reinhardt's books and manuscripts, lacking only these 178. The bidding went higher and higher. At $1,335 it stopped. Marilyn bought the collection.

But she gained no respect by this *coup*. The gossip columnists and newspapers ridiculed her pretensions. Some papers printed the story with a *décolleté* picture of her and the caption "Is Marilyn Going in for Culture?" Feature writers impaled her with thrusts like "her closest link to the classics is in the form of a classic sort of art calendar." Meanwhile, representatives of USC, UCLA, Harvard's Houghton Library, Yale, Princeton, and Columbia, were asking for the collection as a gift. Marilyn was sorry she had ever gotten involved in the affair. Gottfried Reinhardt, Max's son, said he wanted to buy the collection. She said he could have it for what she had paid for it. Reinhardt made the deal. Cynical observers of the Monroe phenomenon took the attitude that it had all been part of a calculated scheme to saturate the newspapers with Marilyn Monroe publicity. You couldn't have bought for a hundred thousand dollars the advertising space in newspapers that Marilyn got with the Reinhardt collection. Smart angle—the intellectual pitch. Nobody would believe that she seriously wanted a collection of Max Reinhardt scripts. So much of the texture of Hollywood is make-believe that one comes to look for the dishonest motive in any human action.

18 *Gentlemen Prefer Blondes—* but Joan Crawford Didn't

For the present, Marilyn resigned herself to accepting that station in life to which God or Darryl Zanuck—and on the 20th Century-Fox lot the two were synonymous—had assigned her.

On May 11, 1953, she reached the $1,500 a week contractual ceiling. And the contract still had five years to run! How bitter was the knowledge that other actors without her box-office draw were earning $5,000, even $10,000, a week. She nagged at the Morris Agency to get her out of the contract. They said it could not be done. They would try to get her more money, but if the front office didn't want to give her more money there was nothing she could do about it. She said it wasn't just the money. She wanted to be taken seriously as a human being, and in Hollywood and other capitalistic centers one's valuation as a human being is fixed in monetary terms.

In this crisis, Marilyn did what a movie actress usually does. She blamed it on her agents. She left the Morris Agency. For a period of several months she was without representation. This resulted in a deluge of invitations from other agencies to luncheons and dinner parties. Fresh flowers came from them each day. She was being "romanced," as they say in the picture business, by every important agency executive. It was Charles K. Feldman, head of the Famous Artists Agency, who captured her. But Feldman was not able to budge Zanuck, who believed that a contract was a contract and that Marilyn had an obligation to live up to hers.

Since the coming of sound in 1928, the lavish film musical has been a basic Hollywood commodity. By the 1950's, film musicals cost from $2,000,000 to $5,000,000 to produce. Sometimes these concoctions turned out to be delightful entertainments like the Ginger Rogers-Fred Astaire musicals that RKO produced during the 1930's; Arthur Freed's color musicals for MGM: *Singin' in the Rain, Seven Brides for Seven Brothers, Funny Face;* or the Hope-Crosby "Road" musicals for Paramount.

Gentlemen Prefer Blondes was Marilyn's second venture into the genre. Howard Hawks, a veteran director noted for his flair for creating vivid compositions that displayed groups in movement, was to direct. Hawks had done good outdoor action films like *Red River* as well as high comedies like *Bringing Up Baby.* Jack Cole, famed for highly sensual dance sequences, was the choreographer. Hal Schaefer was Marilyn's new vocal coach. In addition to the Julie Styne-Leo Robin score, which had been featured in the Broadway musical, Hoagy Carmichael was to write four new songs. Charles Coburn, the expert of the fastidious leer, was to portray Sir Francis Beekman, a genial roué.

Miss Monroe, it was announced, would sing, really and truly sing, the same songs that Carol Channing had sung in the Broadway production, including "Diamonds Are a Girl's Best Friend." When Zanuck saw the early rushes he refused to believe Marilyn was really singing. He thought someone else's voice had been dubbed in. She had to sing privately for him to prove she could sing. Later, when a recording of "Diamonds Are a Girl's Best Friend" was released to disc jockeys, the studio sent with it a statement signed by Zanuck and validated by a notary public that the voice was the voice of Marilyn Monroe and not that of a professional vocalist.

After seeing the first week's rushes, Zanuck rushed out a bulletin: "If anyone has ever had any doubts as to the future of Marilyn Monroe, *Gentlemen Prefer Blondes* is the answer. Just as a top star can never turn a bad story into a box-office success, so will *Blondes* prove that the best talents in story telling and star appearances are still a combination that can't be beaten." Marilyn felt that nobody but Zanuck himself had ever had any doubts as to the future of Marilyn Monroe. She would simply not face the fact that aside from Chekhov, Lytess, and a handful of others, everybody who knew Marilyn Monroe thought her a dumb sexy blonde. Zanuck was her *bête noire.* She had no respect for his judgment, though he had won three Irving Thalberg awards and produced such excellent films as *Wilson, Pinky, Gentlemen's Agreement, No Way Out, Viva Zapata, All About Eve, Man in the Gray Flannel Suit.* She felt about Zanuck the way Cato felt about Carthage. Zanuck was the embodiment of all that she hated in Hollywood.

The studio had paid Howard Hughes an immense amount of money for the loan of Jane Russell to play the brunette in *Gentlemen Prefer Blondes.* Jane Russell is a woman as amply endowed with the necessities of feminine life as MM. Jane got top billing— over Marilyn. The columnists anticipated temperamental explosions. Earl Wilson described it as "The Battle of the Bulges." Skolsky said the co-stars were two contenders fighting "a fast nine-reel bout for the glamour championship of the world."

During the first days on the set, the contenders murmured polite hello's and good-bye's. It was Marilyn who broke the ice. She fell back on her never-failing psychological device. She was poor, helpless, confused, bewildered. She needed advice. The technicians on the set were soon astonished to see Jane and Marilyn in amiable conversation.

They talked about love and marriage. Jane had been happily married for some years to Bob Westerfield, a famous professional-football player.

One afternoon, Jane returned from the commissary bringing, in a paper bag, two hamburgers and a carton of milk for Marilyn. Marilyn often got so absorbed in her reveries that she forgot to eat. Marilyn said she would eat afterward but now she wanted to read some lines to Jane from Kahlil Gibran's *The Prophet.* " 'Give your hearts, but not into each other's keeping. For only the hand of life can contain your hearts. And stand together, yet not too near together. For the pillars of the temple stand apart, and the oak tree and the cypress grow not in each other's shadow.' "

"That's a beautiful thought," Jane said.

"Is it true? I mean do you *have* to keep yourself apart?" Marilyn asked.

Miss Russell is a mystic herself. "In what way do you mean 'apart'? Apart from God?"

"Well, no," Marilyn said. "I mean if a woman loves a man, does she have to give up her own individuality? Do you have to give your own identity up?"

Marilyn did not state explicitly that she was the cypress to Di Maggio's oak, or that they were separated temple pillars.

Jane said confidently that if a woman loved a man and a man loved a woman, they could be happy in marriage without surrendering their identities.

On another occasion, Marilyn asked Miss Russell how she found time to manage both a career in acting and a home and children. "It seems impossible to me," she said.

"When I go home at night," Jane explained, "I put the studio completely out of my mind. You've got to have a good housekeeper to run the house for you, and a cook. Then when you come home, you have plenty of time to concentrate on your family. I know lots of women in Hollywood who are doing it, Marilyn."

Marilyn asked Jane if she thought one could have an interesting married life with a man whose interests were not one's own.

But of course, Miss Russell maintained. "You see," she argued, "when a husband and wife are different, each gives something exciting to the other. Nobody gets a chance to be bored that way."

Di Maggio returned to Los Angeles in September. Marilyn moved out of the Bel-Air Hotel and rented a house in a secluded area of Brentwood. She told Jane Russell that she cooked spaghetti whenever Joe came for dinner. She didn't cook carrots-and-peas however. Men didn't care for carrots-and-peas, she had come to realize. She confided an interesting fact to Jane, which was that she, Marilyn, loathed spaghetti.

But housekeeping became a bore, and Marilyn moved into the Beverly Hills Hotel. She failed to find the "good housekeeper" or a cook who would remain. The prosaic confounds Marilyn. There are persons who are able to perform the most complicated tasks, and yet cannot plan three meals a day or operate a vacuum cleaner. Marilyn falls into dreamlike states in which she lives in a world of her own. Marilyn has always had a fondness for unreality. Miss Lytess once told me, "Marilyn is a moonwalker. When she used to live in my house, I often felt like she was a somnambulist walking around."

Nunnally Johnson is candid in his distaste for somnambulism as a way of life. He said to me on one occasion: "You can't talk to her. Talking to her is like talking to somebody ten feet under water. Between you and her there is a wall of thick cotton. You can't get through to her. She reminds me of a sloth. You stick a pin in a sloth's belly and eight days later it says 'Ouch.' She lives in her own world. I remember once I'd left my office and I was walking down the hall. She suddenly ran up to me. I don't know what she was doing in the Administration Building. She was all breathless and she said, 'Which way is the men's room?' I still haven't figured out what she meant by that question. I told her where it was and she went the other way and went down the stairs and out of the building."

Marilyn's relation to other people's reality is rather tenuous. Once she asked a girl friend to her apartment on Doheny Drive for dinner. Marilyn promised broiled lamb chops. When the girls looked in the refrigerator and the cupboards, they found both almost bare. There was a bottle of milk. That was all. No meat, no butter, no bread, no vegetables, no canned foods, no salt, no pepper. Marilyn didn't seem at all embarrassed. She served milk for dinner.

Jane Russell says: "Marilyn is a dreamy girl. She's the kind who's liable to show up with one red shoe and one black shoe. We had to be on the set for hair and make-up by seven-thirty, and sometimes I'd find out when we took a break at eleven, that she hadn't had any breakfast and forgot she was hungry until I reminded her. She can't manage little things like answering letters or phone calls, and she's impressed with anybody who is efficient. She once got her life so balled up that the studio hired a full-time secretary-maid for her. So Marilyn soon got the secretary as balled up as she was, and she ended up waiting on the secretary instead of vice versa."

Marilyn can't keep track of addresses, phone numbers, messages. In her dressing room and at home, she scrawls them on the backs of envelopes or pieces of Kleenex and then loses them. She has been given address books, memo pads, and desk calendars. She loses them. She loses her driver's license constantly. She once gave Billy Wilder a lift in her black Cadillac convertible. He says: "I didn't realize what a disorganized person this is until I see in the back of the car. It is like she throws everything in helter skelter because there's a foreign invasion and the enemy armies are already in Pasadena. There's blouses laying there and slacks, dresses, girdles, old shoes, old plane tickets, old lovers for all I knew, you never saw such a filthy mess in your life. On top of the mess is a whole bunch of traffic tickets.

I ask her about this. Tickets for parking. Tickets for speeding. Tickets for passing lights, who knows what. Is she worried about this? Am I worried about the sun rising tomorrow?"

On Christmas Eve, 1952, Marilyn went to the studio party. Overcome by *Weltschmerz* and eggnog, she returned home feeling her loneliness. Joe didn't care for her. He had gone to San Francisco the previous week to spend Christmas and New Year's with old friends and his family. At the desk, she got her key and glanced at her mail pigeonhole. Empty. She rode the elevator upstairs. She trudged down the corridor to her room at the end of the hall. She opened the door. She switched on the lights. In a corner, to her surprise, she saw a Christmas tree. The tree was hung with tinsel and lights. It was crowned with an angel. She ran to the tree. Propped against its base was a large unsigned card: MERRY CHRISTMAS.

She heard the noise of a door opening. Out of the closet emerged Joe Di Maggio. He was smiling at her, his bashful smile. "Merry Christmas," he said.

"You didn't forget me, Joe," she murmured. She was crying. "That's the sweetest thing anybody has ever done for me in my life, Joe, in my whole life, Joe, the sweetest thing."

One day, it was bruited about that Joe was to look in on the set of *Gentlemen Prefer Blondes*. A photographer asked Marilyn, "Would you pose with Joe?"

She frowned thoughtfully. "I don't know," she said. "Maybe you better ask him." The question of her publicity pictures was a sore point. Joe arrived on the sound stage after lunch. The photographer asked, "Can I take some pictures of you and Miss Monroe this afternoon, Mr. Di Maggio?"

"What's it for?"

"Newspapers. Just an informal shot of you and Marilyn."

"Oh, I guess I have to," he said, sighing. "Well—come around four o'clock."

He watched Marilyn do the "I'm Just a Little Girl from Little Rock" number. He autographed baseballs for the gaffers and the grips. And he waited. It is the fate of all married men to be kept waiting by their wives. It is the fate of men married to movie stars to be kept waiting ten times as long. At four, the photographer arranged a bank of lights in a corner of the stage. He told Joe he was ready. Marilyn sequestered herself in her dressing room. She was going to change from her sequin costume into a street dress. Joe waited some more. The photographer and he had run out of small talk. They both waited. Suddenly Joe said, "Ah, the hell with it." He strode away, and over his shoulder called out, "No pictures today, pal."

Joe went to Marilyn's dressing room. He entered it without knocking. He slammed the door. Their voices were raised in an argument. When they walked out, his face was expressionless. She was white. A columnist's legman smilingly loped alongside them as they headed for the iron door. He asked if the lovers were dining together tonight. And where were they going after dinner?

"I don't know," Marilyn said. "I'll have to ask Joe about our plans."

"How about it, Mr. Di Maggio?" asked the legman.

"None of your damn business," Joe said.

He stomped away. She trotted after him, apologetically.

He came to the set no more.

During the making of this film, Marilyn's capacity for work impressed her colleagues. At dance rehearsals, she continued working when Miss Russell and the chorus were exhausted. Jane once told me she had never seen any actress with such a drive to rehearse and rehearse. It seemed to Jane as if Marilyn perpetually gritted her teeth. She did not allow herself to get tired. She didn't allow herself to be satisfied easily. She always wanted to do a scene or rehearse a song "just once more." Her compulsion to work caused choreographer Jack Cole and musician Hal Schaefer to give her more and more of their time and attention. She came to be a good friend of both men. Joe Di Maggio didn't like this. He was jealous of any man who was attentive to Marilyn. It takes a heroic man to live happily with a celebrated beauty. There is practical philosophy in the calypso ballad which advises a man to marry a woman uglier than himself.

There was friction between Marilyn and the director, Howard Hawks. Marilyn's lateness was now chronic. Shooting was frequently held up for as long as two hours. Disputes over lines in the script—which had been written by Charles Lederer from the musical-comedy libretto by Anita Loos and Joseph Fields—took place constantly. Bickerings over scenes and Marilyn's interpretation of scenes were daily, even hourly, occurrences. Natasha Lytess was a fixture on the set.

After the shooting of the "Bye Bye Baby" sequence, Hawks approved the first take. Marilyn looked over to Lytess, and Natasha swung her head slowly from side to side in a distinct negative. Marilyn asked to do the scene over. They did nine more takes. None of them were as good as the first take. Hawks became properly enraged. He cried, "When I say 'cut,' I want you to look at me, not at Natasha!"

Yet it was difficult to quarrel with Marilyn and resolve differences of opinion. She didn't bring issues to a head. If events took a turn she didn't like, she looked blank and *distrait* if you spoke to her. She retired to her dressing room and locked the door. She sobbed. She got sick headaches and vomiting spells. Nobody was sure whether these attacks were genuine or deliberately staged.

Producer Siegel, now head of production at Metro-Goldwyn-Mayer, was the diplomatic go-between in the daily crises that involved Marilyn, Lytess, and Hawks.

But no solution was possible. Marilyn did not trust Hawks. Did Marilyn's distrust unconsciously creep into her work in dramatic scenes? Did she sparkle more in her dancing and singing sequences when she was working with Cole and Schaefer?

In the *Saturday Review*, Hollis Alpert commented, "It [*Gentlemen Prefer Blondes*] is an empty and graceless remake of a fair to middling musical that only comes alive when Marilyn Monroe and Jane Russell stop talking and start wiggling."

Did La Monroe really have a talent for the musical film? Was she another Ginger Rogers, another Rita Hayworth? Alpert said that her beauty was so blinding that it got in the way of an objective critical appraisal. "I made an honest attempt to evaluate her dancing, singing, and acting ability, but I couldn't keep my mind on the problem."

Bosley Crowther found the "sight gags" tenuous, the jokes grim, the direction tediously boring. "And yet," he wrote, "there is that about Miss Russell and Miss Monroe that keeps you looking at them even when they have little or nothing to do. Call it inherent magnetism, call it luxurious coquetry. Call it whatever you fancy. It's what makes this a, well, a buoyant show."

Otis Guernsey, Jr., found Marilyn looking as though "she would glow in the dark, and her version of the baby-faced blonde whose eyes open for diamonds and close for kisses is always as amusing as alluring. . . ."

John McCarten was still implacably opposed to MM, and he wasn't exactly bowled over by Jane Russell, either: "The pneumatic aspects of Marilyn Monroe and Jane Russell are examined extensively in *Gentlemen Prefer Blondes,* and while it is plain that both ladies are most pleasantly configured, it is also apparent that neither of them have more than a glancing acquaintance with the business of acting. . . ."

Critics were unable to give a dispassionate analysis of Marilyn's performance. In France and Italy, they saw it more clearly and more favorably. But American critics could not separate the Monroe of publicity from the Monroe on the screen. They could not free themselves of the "dumb sexy blonde" stereotype. Marilyn was platinum blonde, her body was voluptuous, her naked calendar had become the icon of hordes of American males—consequently she herself must be stupid and she could not act. She was playing herself when she played Lorelei Lee.

Actually, as we have seen, there was less of Lorelei Lee in Marilyn's nature than any other of the conventional feminine types. She did not esteem money or the things money bought, especially things with diamonds in them. Her nature drew her to things of the spirit— to poetry and love. There are, of course, innumerable other aspects to her personality, but one thing she had never done was to use her beauty to allure a rich old man. Far from exploiting men, it was she who bought her first love an expensive gift instead of the other way around!

So what Marilyn did and said in *Gentlemen Prefer Blondes* was acting. A sort of comical naïveté, into which she had timorously ventured in several of the scenes in *Monkey Business,* she developed into a genuine style of her own in *Gentlemen Prefer Blondes.* As a matter of fact, *Gentlemen Prefer Blondes,* far from being the ephemeral piece critics judged it, is a well-realized example of the cinema musical that has held its interest for audiences when most other films of that year have long ago palled on everybody, including critics. *Gentlemen Prefer Blondes* is one of the most revived films of the 1950's. During the summer of 1959, I saw it for the third time. It was playing on a double bill with Marlon Brando's *Viva Zapata* in a Greenwich Village movie house, which caters to the sophisticated *jeunes*. Though I saw it on a weekday evening, the orchestra and balcony were completely filled. The audience responded to the effervescent pace and gaiety of the film, and it was apparent, from the manner in which the laughter came at the right moments, that they appreciated Marilyn's comic artistry. Whatever temperamental squabbles Hawks had had with Marilyn, every part of the film, the dialogue scenes as well as the musical scenes, was excellent and of a piece. It was an integral piece of cinema craftsmanship. In her characterization of Lorelei Lee, Marilyn put together a sympathetic portrait of a girl who mingles tenderness of heart with a greed for status symbols. Although it may seem so to the critic, it is not easy to do this. Nor is it easy to pretend to be naïve and make an audience laugh at your ignorance—and yet not lose the audience's sympathy in doing so.

The film opens boldly with the jazz sounds of "We're Just Two Little Girls from Little Rock" and the splendid images, full length, of Marilyn and Jane Russell, singing and dancing together, their bodies swaying. They are still singing as the opening titles are rapidly superimposed over their images, and so, without any tiresome preliminaries, we meet the girls and it is established that they are singing in a New York cabaret. At a table is Tommy Noonan, a shy Harold Lloyd type. He is in love with Marilyn. His father is immensely rich and opposes his marriage to Marilyn on the grounds that Marilyn is a gold-digging adventuress. (Shades of *Ladies of the Chorus!*) In her dressing room after the show, Noonan gives her an engagement ring. It seems a little tight as he slips it on her finger. He asks her whether it is big enough. Marilyn, fluttering her eyebrows at the enormous diamond, speaks in the baby-talk voice she used for the character: "Oh, they never can be *big* enough."

She and Russell go to Paris on the *Ile de France*. Marilyn's beau is to meet her in Paris and marry her. Noonan sees Marilyn off. In her cabin, he hands her an envelope and informs her that it contains a letter of credit. She says that the boat hasn't even sailed yet and he's writing her letters already. He is so sweet, she says. Then he explains that a letter of credit is something that enables you to get money, and she says, "Write me a lot."

On the boat she encounters Charles Coburn, who plays an international diamond merchant. Coburn makes love to Marilyn under cover of showing her what a python does to a goat in India, Marilyn playing the goat to Coburn's python. One doesn't see a sequence as delicious as this two times a year nowadays. Since Coburn's wife is on board, Coburn bribes Marilyn into discretion with a diamond tiara. She tries to pin it on her dress; Coburn explains that a tiara goes on one's head. Marilyn is simply breathless with excitement.

"Oooh," she says, "I love finding new places to wear diamonds!"

The United States Olympics team is also on the boat, and naturally every member is making a play for Marilyn and Jane. When Marilyn spurns one athlete, he says, "But I'm the only four-letter man on the team." She looks at him with withering disdain and remarks, "Well, I should think you'd be ashamed to admit it."

There is no need to trace in detail the plot intrigues, but two sections of the film are worthy of mention. One is the "Diamonds Are a Girl's Best Friend" sequence, which was a dance number to a very fast rhythm. Marilyn danced with an ensemble of boys. She danced with grace and abandon and a kinetic surrender to the music and the design of Cole's movements. The sequence ran four minutes and established her as an actress who could dance superbly in a musical sequence, which is not as common as non-dancers may suppose.

Toward the end of the film, Noonan's father comes to Paris. He offers Marilyn a large sum of money if she will give up his son. And here there is a scene between the father and Marilyn—shades of Act II of *La Traviata*—in which Marilyn, for the first time, begins to show us she can act out a thoughtful speech. She has a long block speech to deliver, a solid mass of dialogue, in which she explains that she loves Noonan—but also loves his money, just as a man wants the girl he marries to be beautiful, though her beauty is not all he is marrying her for. As you watch this scene, you see that, for all the awkwardness of her body, Marilyn's face and voice are now expressive of the emotions she is conveying as an actress. Her eyes are filled with gentleness, her voice with honesty, her speech with conviction.

Twenty years from now, no doubt, the critics of the art-film quarterlies will discover that *Gentlemen Prefer Blondes* was one of the excellent works of its time, for it was completely true to its genre. It crystallized a viewpoint, a style, and a character in her time and her place. It will be shown at the Museum of Modern Art auditorium and studied by scholars in the archives of the Eastman Film Library at Rochester.

Joe and Marilyn compromised on her publicity. She had often complained, when he criticized her revealing garments, "What do you want me to do—hide in a basement?" Finally, it was agreed that while she would, of course, wear whatever costumes she had to in a movie or for publicity, she would wear simple things with high necklines in private life.

She took another fling at domesticity. She moved out of the Beverly Hills Hotel into a modern three-room flat in a new apartment building at 882 N. Doheny Drive.

Jane Russell was pleased with Marilyn's decision. Jane said, "It will give you a nice feeling of security to be in your own home, with your own furniture and things. You've got to get used to managing your own home now, before you get married. Every woman should have her own home. Hotel life is no kind of life for a woman." Jane recommended her own interior decorator, Thomas Lane. Marilyn employed Lane and had the apartment painted and fitted out according to his suggestions. She took out of storage the old piano her mother had bought 20 years ago. She had it painted oyster white and placed in the living room. Her books, paintings, and photographs adorned the cocoa-brown walls. A huge photograph of Abraham Lincoln was hung over her bed. She slept on a low-slung davenport covered with a quilted velvet throw in an outré orange-copper shade. "It sounds horrible," she said, "but it's dreamy."

In the evenings, Marilyn cooked spaghetti and other things and she and Joe ate together. Skolsky wrote of these evenings: "After dinner, Joe would stretch out on the couch and watch a Western movie on television. Marilyn would study her lines for the next day or confer with friends on the telephone. Joe didn't try to guide her career or offer advice on the interpretation of a role. Occasionally he would make a sage remark drawn from his own glorious history. 'Never mind the publicity, baby,' he would say. 'Get the money.' "

Increasing success did not diminish her sense of alienation from herself. "I feel as though it's all happening to someone right next to me," she'd say. "I'm close, I can feel it, I can hear it, but it isn't really me."

In the reception room of the Administration Building her gold-framed photograph hung alongside the other 20th Century-Fox luminaries: Betty Grable, Dan Dailey, Susan Hayward, Tyrone Power, Clifton Webb, Robert Wagner, Jean Peters, and Victor Mature.

Her feet and hands achieved immortality in the forecourt of Grauman's Chinese Theatre on Hollywood Boulevard. In July, 1953, Jane and Marilyn lay side by side and pressed their hands into wet plaster as newsreel and television cameras recorded the event. Then they squashed their bare feet into the plaster. Marilyn had suggested that instead of the traditional hands and feet, she and Jane register the imprint of their breasts and buttocks for the benefit of future generations.

Yet the woman who suggested this idea was the same woman who had begun fighting for "serious" roles in "serious" films with "serious" directors.

"A biography is considered complete if it merely accounts for six or seven selves, whereas a person may well have as many as one thousand," Virginia Woolf wrote. Two of Marilyn's thousand selves were in flagrant contradiction: the self wishing to flaunt its nakedness to the world and the self seeking to pursue a high artistic goal.

The ambivalence created tension, for each tendency was strong. If she stayed home and delved into Freud, the movie actress in her said she ought to be exhibiting herself. If she participated in a publicity stunt at Grauman's Chinese, the artist in her sneered that she was betraying her aspirations.

But had not the aspirations changed? Now she had all she had dreamed of getting when she was a child and her mother and Aunt Grace had taken her walking on Hollywood Boulevard and indoctrinated her with the Mary Pickford fantasy. The child in her was pleased by the symbols of success. But this child was threatened by the woman she was slowly becoming. As a woman, she was unable to come to terms with her life, with the motion-picture industry, with her friends and colleagues, and with her lover.

For she was ambivalent about Joe. What did the aesthetic Monroe have to do with the curious, muscular man who sprawled on her davenport and immersed himself in cowboy programs?

She was also ambivalent in her feelings toward Hollywood and its values. In *The Second Sex,* Simone de Beauvoir observed: "The subjection of Hollywood stars is well known. Their bodies are not their own; the producer decides on the color of their hair, their weight, their figure, their type; to change the curve of a cheek, their teeth may be pulled. Dieting, gymnastics, fittings, constitute a daily burden. Going out to parties and flirting are expected under the head of 'personal appearances'; private life is no more than an aspect of public life . . . a shrewd and clever woman knows what her 'publicity' demands of her. The star who refuses to be pliant to these requirements will experience a brutal or a slow but inevitable dethronement."

While the Hollywood producer is neither so all-powerful nor the star so compliant as Mlle. de Beauvoir suggests, it is accurate to say that a certain depersonalization occurs in a movie star's life. In time, many women, especially those who rise into the highest rank, begin enjoying their synthesized selves. They acquire an appetite for luxury and a taste for power.

Marilyn found the pressure of Hollywood a strain. But it became harder to avoid her social obligations. She was a national institution. Even serious observers of the social scene like James T. Farrell were taking note of her. With the stylistic gracelessness for which he is justly famous, Farrell had written, "The story of her rise should make Horatio Alger regretful in his grave."

There were public festivities to which she had to lend her presence.

March is the season for the movie colony's most important ritualistic ceremonies: the awards dinners. The *Look* awards, the *Redbook* and *Photoplay* awards, the awards given by the foreign press, the Los Angeles press, the women's division of the Los Angeles press. The series of awards dinners is climaxed by the Academy Awards affair—the presentation of the Oscars of the Academy of Motion Picture Arts and Sciences.

Photoplay Magazine, one of the oldest and most influential of the fan magazines, had selected Marilyn Monroe as the best new star of 1953. She was to be given an award at their annual dinner. Her way of making an appearance at the *Photoplay* banquet was to play the sex symbol to the hilt. She had Bill Travilla run up the most revealing evening gown the mind of man could imagine, a scintillating one-piece affair, a size too small, in gold lamé. She literally had to be sewn into the gown by the ladies of 20th's wardrobe department!

Di Maggio refused to escort her to the gala. Skolsky did the honors. During this year it was Skolsky who escorted her to the important receptions and dinners. Skolsky liked pinch-hitting for Joe and Marilyn. "Mickey Mantle," he said, "can take Joe's place with the Yankees. I much prefer to take his place with The Monroe."

Skolsky was nervously pacing about the lobby of the Beverly Hills Hotel when Marilyn hove into view—two hours late. She pressed his hands gratefully. He took her arm and they went into the grand ballroom. Because the hemline of her dress was tight around her knees, she walked with mincing steps which emphasized the rotations of her hips. Her curves shimmered in the golden dress. Slowly she walked down the room to the head table. Dining was suspended. Breaths were drawn in. Gasps of horror, and admiration, filled the room. For a long moment, conversation halted. Then she sat down. The conversation resumed, in a lower key, and the topic was Marilyn Monroe. Jerry Lewis, who was master of ceremonies, pretended to be carried away by mad passion and leaped on the table and whinnied like a lust-crazed stallion. Since everybody who was anybody was at the dinner, Marilyn, with one fell swoop, antagonized nearly every movie actress in Hollywood by her brazen display.

From this moment on, nobody in Hollywood could take Marilyn Monroe seriously. She could chatter about Dostoevski and Stanislavsky until she was blue in the face, but she had established herself in the colony's mind as a sexpot who reveled in vulgarity.

Joan Crawford expressed the common wrath when she issued a *denunciamiento* to the Hollywood correspondent Bob Thomas. Thomas began his story with a summary of some recent public outcries by women's clubs against Marilyn's salacious publicity. He also reported that there were rumors that her last two films had done badly—which proved that vulgarity did not pay. (This was true at the time that Thomas wrote, but by year's end, when the figures on *Niagara, Gentlemen Prefer Blondes,* and *How to Marry a Millionaire* were in, Marilyn's pictures had grossed over $25,000,000, without counting foreign earnings; they were being described as "blockbusters," and *Time* estimated she had made more money for her studio than any other movie personality in 1953.)

Well, what had Miss Crawford thought of La Monroe at the dinner? "It was like a burlesque show," she said. "The audience yelled and shouted, and Jerry Lewis got up on the table and whistled. But those of us in the industry just shuddered. . . . Sex plays a tremendously important part in every person's life. People are interested in it, intrigued with it. But they don't like to see it flaunted in their faces. Kids don't like her. Sex plays a growingly important part in their lives, too; and they don't like to see it exploited. And don't forget the women. They're the ones who pick out the movie entertainment for the family. They won't pick out anything that won't be suitable for their husbands and children. The publicity has gone too far. She is making the mistake of believing her publicity. Someone should make her see the light. She should be told that the public likes provocative feminine personalities; but it also likes to know that underneath it all, the actresses are ladies."

Marilyn was crushed by the Crawford attack, with which everybody—including her lover—agreed. She was so embarrassed that she did not go outside her apartment for a fortnight. She decided that Joan Crawford, like all women, was jealous of her because she was beautiful and had a fatal attraction for men. Skolsky told her she was wrong to suppose all women hated her.

Louella Parsons certainly didn't. She had met Marilyn several times and had taken a motherly liking to the blonde. She opened her vitally important column so Marilyn could express her agony.

"I think," Marilyn told Miss Parsons, "the thing that hit me the hardest about Miss Crawford's story is that it came from her. I've always admired her for being such a wonderful mother—for taking four children and giving them a fine home. Who, better than I, know what it means to homeless little ones?"

When in danger, Marilyn always fell back on the strategy of the "orphaned child." Her "orphaned" past was to her what the flag and patriotism are to a demagogue.

"Although I don't know Miss Crawford very well," Marilyn went on, "she was a symbol to me of kindness and understanding to those who need help.

"At first all I could think of was Why should she select me to blast? She's a great star. I'm just starting. And then, when the first hurt began to die down, I told myself she must have spoken to Mr. Thomas impulsively, without thinking. . . ."

It didn't occur to Marilyn that perhaps she herself had showed bad taste in attending a formal dinner in such a costume. She was a "homeless little one" and Miss Crawford was good to "homeless little ones" and therefore, logically, Miss Crawford should be on her side.

The studio publicity department didn't retreat under fire. They sent out a story saying that Marilyn Monroe did not have to wear tight dresses to look sexy. She would look sexy in a potato sack. To prove this, they secured a potato sack—an Idaho potato sack, by the way. They slit open the bottom, cut armholes in it, and slipped it over Marilyn's head. She looked fine in a potato sack.

19 *How to Marry a Millionaire—* but Marilyn Didn't

There were two important gentlemen in the studio, producer-writer Nunnally Johnson and director Jean Negulesco, who, unlike the critics, were aware that Marilyn Monroe had successfully extended her acting range and was on the point of developing a style. In *Gentlemen Prefer Blondes* they had seen that she could suggest sentiment, provoke laughter, and project sensuality with a charming unself-consciousness. A beautiful woman able to play farce and still be sexually alluring is as rare in the cinema or the theatre as it is in life. Yet, during its history, Hollywood had found four amorous *farceuses*: Gloria Swanson, Ginger Rogers, Carole Lombard, and Claudette Colbert. As the special type of comedienne that such an actress becomes—as contrasted with the Zasu Pittses and Martha Rayes—one can say that Marilyn was following in the Swanson-Rogers-Lombard-Colbert tradition. Yet one difference set Marilyn apart from the tradition. This was the innocence she imparted to her characterizations. Her predecessors—in the way they wore their clothes, in their attitudes, their moods, their fleeting facial expressions, their awareness of all that is subtle about men and love—were sophisticated. The characterization Marilyn was exploring was naïve.

The studio had paid Doris Lilly, a society authoress, $50,000 for the movie rights to a work of non-fiction, *How to Marry a Millionaire*. Assigned to do something about this expensive property, Johnson set to work employing bits and pieces of characters and plot from two Broadway plays, *The Greeks Had a Word for It* (by Zoë Atkins) and *Loco* (by Katherine and Dale Eunson). Johnson spiced it all with his own sardonic wit. The result was a flashing comedy of modern manners that retained only the title of Miss Lilly's *vade mecum*. The story was about three fortune huntresses, Pola, Loco, and Shatzi, who come to New York on a millionaire safari. They lease a furnished penthouse terrace apartment. They sell the grand piano and other valuables and with the money give parties to entrap rich men. Johnson wanted Marilyn for Pola, a nearsighted and disoriented blonde dish who doesn't wear her spectacles when men are about and is consequently even more confused about reality than usual. Betty Grable was set for Loco, the amiable sexpot, and Lauren Bacall for Shatzi, a sultry brunette. Rory Calhoun would be Grable's catch, Cameron Mitchell would be Bacall's, and Marilyn would get David Wayne, a millionaire traveling incognito because of income-tax problems.

Negulesco assured Zanuck he would get a performance out of Marilyn. By now, everybody in the front office knew that Marilyn had "something." The problem was how to get a performance out of her. Negulesco would be her friend and confidant. She would come to trust him. Negulesco, who had helped Jane Wyman give a fine dramatic performance as the deaf mute in *Johnny Belinda,* had a reputation as a "woman's director." A Roumanian émigré, Negulesco was good-looking, urbane, and sensitive. He had been a painter originally, and he still painted for his own pleasure.

Marilyn read the screenplay. She recoiled at the idea of portraying myopia. She would look ghastly in horn-rimmed spectacles. How dared they! Now Loco she would be interested in. Why hadn't they given her the part of Loco? Why was the front office always favoring Grable over her?

Johnson turned on his Georgia charm, but she was unmoved. She liked Johnson. She likes tall thin men, replicas of the Abraham Lincoln physique. Nunnally Johnson was lanky enough. He didn't understand anything she was saying, and she didn't understand anything he was saying, but she enjoyed her meetings with him. She didn't appreciate his dry sense of humor. It was sarcastic wit—the wit of the 1920's, of the Algonquin Round Table. Johnson was no respecter of Hollywood mores. He poked fun at the established institutions. If Marilyn could have understood the drift of his barbed remarks, she would have agreed with them. But the Hollywood prose style—a mixture of self-hatred, boastfulness, unconvincing deprecation, snobbism, and caustic hostility—put her off. She was always on guard against Hollywood conversation, never being sure that she wasn't being ridiculed. She was afraid to reply because her remarks were often twisted—she thought—and then she was made fun of in Mike Connolly's column in the *Hollywood Reporter*.

Negulesco leaped into the breach and swathed her in Roumanian *politesse*. I once asked him how he had won her over.

"Well," he replied, "I have much sympathy for her and she feels this. I say to her that no matter what you do in a picture, if you pick up a glass of water and drink it, right away it's censorable. You cannot help being the essence of *sax*. To the whole world you stand for sax. So you don't have to sell this goddam *sax* all the time. In this story, I say, you look just as saxy with your glasses on, and then think, I say to her, think of how utterly charming you become to the audience when you take off the glasses and the world is a blur and you are bumping into walls and doors and hitting yourself on furniture. This is good for you, I say. This is a whole new dimension of *saxiness* for you."

He got through to her, and she consented to play Pola. For two weeks before shooting started, Negulesco saw her many times for conversations and spaghetti-less dinners. Sometimes they talked about the screenplay and sometimes they talked about art.

"This girl," Negulesco says, "has a hunger for knowledge. She's slow to absorb, but she absorbs. It is difficult to come close to her. She becomes vague. She puts up a curtain between herself and people." He painted her portrait in oil on canvas and explained the technique he was using. He spoke to her of the post-impressionist painters. She was fascinated. He says her questions were sensible. He told her about Matisse, Chagall, Derain, Pascin, Braque, Gauguin, Picasso, and Buffet.

Once she sighed and said, "I can't seem to understand these modern paintings."

Negulesco said, "Art is like sax. Art is not to understand but to feel."

They conversed about literature. She asked him to lend her some books he had mentioned which she had not read. He remembers lending her Hemingway's *Old Man and the Sea*, W. H. Hudson's

Green Mansions, and Irving Stone's biography of Van Gogh, *Lust for Life.* They talked about the books after she read them. He was the first director since Huston who had got *en rapport* with her.

Negulesco believes that her sexuality is the mysterious secretion of some unknown chemical inside her. It does not emanate from her eyes or her body.

"She represents to man something we all want in our unfulfilled dreams," he told me. "She's the girl you'd like to double-cross your wife with. A man, he's got to be dead not to be excited by her. Yet what a terrible problem she has. Conceive for yourself. How can one be a normal human being and do normal human acts, like for instance eat mashed potatoes, if one knows 150,000,000 men all over the world want to go to bed with one?"

On the first day of shooting, for which she was on time, he was impressed by the fact that she didn't worry about dressing-room protocol. Usually when there are several stars in a film, which one will be the last out of the dressing room becomes a great psychological issue. Marilyn didn't mind being the first one out. Soon, though, she began coming late. In the early weeks of shooting, Negulesco took her to task for her lateness. He said she had had a nine o'clock call and had come in at ten minutes past eleven.

"But *mentally* I was with you at nine," she explained.

He didn't say that the camera couldn't photograph mentality. He smiled bravely and resigned himself. He moved her calls back to 7:00 A.M., on the assumption she would arrive at eight-thirty and be ready to work by ten.

Her obsession with work delighted him. She could drive herself— when she finally got on the sound stage—for ten, twelve hours at a time. While working, her mind was concentrated on the script. "You say hello to her or it's a nice day today, and she answers with a line from the script," Negulesco says. "She forgets everything but the work."

Once, Marilyn and Miss Grable were "running lines" off camera. Marilyn seemed so absorbed in her lines that Miss Grable, in response to a line of Marilyn's that went, "I don't think so," and to which Grable had to reply, "I do," ad libbed instead, "Sonny Tufts?" (The phrase "Sonny Tufts," spoken with a rising, questioning inflection has been a standard Hollywood nonsense joke ever since a movie star, emceeing a variety program on radio, read off the list of next week's guest stars and came to the name of Sonny Tufts. He first said "Sonny Tufts" declaratively and then repeated it as an incredulous question.) Well, Marilyn didn't react to the "Sonny Tufts" joke. She went right on reading her lines, oblivious of Miss Grable's change.

Another time, the dialogue director read Miss Grable's lines during a rehearsal with Marilyn. At the end of it, Marilyn raised her eyes from the script and said, "Betty, I think I've got it right now." Then she saw it was a man with whom she had been rehearsing, and she did a double-take.

"Ooh, *you're* not Betty Grable," she said.

"I didn't think I was," he replied.

She loved rehearsing. "She rehearses forever," Negulesco says. "But there is a reason for this. She thinks slowly and carefully. She is not one of your quick types like a Bacall. She has a slow tempo. You have to adjust to her tempo. You have to do much rehearsing with her. And when she has learned a scene finally, memorized the lines, and you have to make a change—ah, this is murder. She hates to change it. But if a director is willing to take the trouble to feel out her tempo and go at her pace, she will give you a superb performance."

Miss Grable's first meeting with the woman who was supplanting her as 20th's leading blonde did not prove as tense as had been expected. Marilyn was humble. Miss Grable accepted the situation graciously. As they shook hands, Miss Grable whispered, "Honey, I've had it. Go get yours. It's your turn now."

Marilyn was anxious to propitiate Miss Grable. Once, the action of the story called for her to push Betty slightly. She pushed so hard that Betty lost her balance and fell. Marilyn knelt and helped her get up. "I'm so sorry," Marilyn said. "I feel terrible. Are you all right?"

Betty smiled. "It wasn't your fault, really. I was standing on one foot."

Later, Marilyn stepped on her feet. Betty winced. Marilyn apologized. "I know *this* was my fault. I'm very sorry. I didn't do it on purpose."

"It's nothing."

"Oooh, I smeared your shoe."

190

Norma Jean Baker
at eight months (1927).

At four years (1930).

At eight years (1934).

Norma Jean, at sixteen, when she became the bride of James Dougherty (1942).

Norma Jean Dougherty on her honeymoon at Lake Sherwood, California. Pinned to her shirt is a fishing license; James Dougherty was the first husband to try to interest her in sports (1942).

James Dougherty, in 1953, standing in front of the bungalow he and Norma Jean occupied a decade earlier in Van Nuys, California.

Just a pretty girl. Norma Jean, in ringlets, poses with five other employees of the Radio Plane Parts Company at Burbank, California, where she worked during World War II (1944).

The transformation of Marilyn Monroe begins. The portrait of Norma Jean Dougherty, model, that was submitted to photographers and advertising agencies (1945).

Norma Jean and four other models after a fashion show at the Ambassador Hotel in Hollywood (1946).

She poses for a magazine-cover shot at Santa Monica (1946).

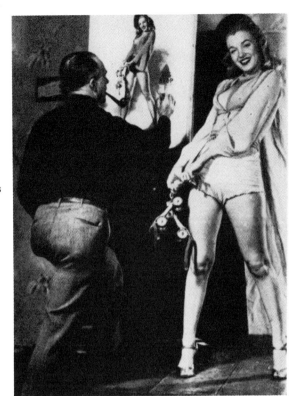

Norma Jean poses for Earle Moran, magazine illustrator; she became his favorite model. The words "bus stop" were to play a part in her life again (1946).

Fred Karger was the good and kind friend of the young Marilyn Monroe, and she was devoted to him. This photograph, taken in 1952, shows him with his wife, Jane Wyman.

Marilyn's agent and friend Johnny Hyde, who wanted to marry her, escorts her to Betty Hutton's party for Louis Sobol and his bride at the Crystal Room of the Beverly Hills Hotel. The evening began as a Viennese waltz party by candlelight, but wound up with a Charleston contest (1950).

Sidney Skolsky, the columnist, also befriended Marilyn. Here they are shown at the wedding reception of Sheilah Graham (1953).

Marilyn and Jane Russell engrave their handprints, footprints, and autographs in wet cement in the forecourt of Graumann's Chinese Theatre on Hollywood Boulevard (1953).

The Second Marriage. Marilyn and Joe Di Maggio on their wedding day in the chambers of Judge Charles S. Peery. Marilyn's suit is high-necked, as Di Maggio preferred (1954).

On suspension from her studio, an exuberant and defiant Marilyn arrives in Japan on a trip with her husband. At this press conference in Tokyo, Marilyn remarked that the stole draped on the chair was "fox—not the 20th Century kind" (1954).

Marilyn changing into costume in an improvised dressing room near the front lines in Korea (1954).

The day the marriage stopped. Marilyn drives away on the morning of her separation from Di Maggio (1954).

Di Maggio did not want to make their parting final. Here, nine months after the divorce, he escorts Marilyn to the world première of *The Seven Year Itch* in New York (1955).

At the start of her exile from Hollywood in 1955, Marilyn sequestered herself in the home of Milton H. Greene, the photographer who became her partner. This photograph, taken from the C.B.S. telecast "Person to Person," shows them with Mr. Greene's wife, Amy.

Monroe shows great aplomb at press conferences. Here, meeting reporters at the Plaza Hotel in New York, she continues to answer questions and pose for pictures after her dress strap has broken (1956).

Sir Laurence Olivier and Monroe just after they had agreed to co-star in *The Prince and the Showgirl*. He was calling her "Sweetie" and she was calling him "Larry"; they used less affectionate terms before the filming was over (1956).

Monroe is presented to Queen Elizabeth at the Royal Film Performance in London (1956).

The Third Marriage. Monroe and Arthur Miller after their marriage at the home of his agent in South Salem, New York (1956).

Marilyn, in one of her ironic moods, posed in the notorious gold lamé gown which had so upset Joan Crawford at the Photoplay Awards banquet. La Belle Monroe is satirizing the oversexed blond bimbo she was supposed to be (1954).

Monroe never received an Oscar, but she has not gone unrecognized. Here she receives the Gold Medal Award of *Photoplay* magazine as the best new star of 1953. Her dress aroused some harsh comment (1954).

At another Photoplay Awards banquet, two years later, she poses with Alan Ladd. I have always felt this picture gives us a glimpse of the kind of person she was when she was with other persons. Notice how she is aware of Ladd, how she seems to be in communication with him (1956).

Georges Auric, distinguished French composer, presents to Monroe the Crystal Star, annual award of the French Film Institute for the best feminine interpretation in films. The prize was given for her performance in *The Prince and the Showgirl* (1958).

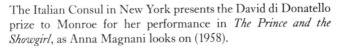

The Italian Consul in New York presents the David di Donatello prize to Monroe for her performance in *The Prince and the Showgirl*, as Anna Magnani looks on (1958).

The Face of the Star: Manfred Kreiner's photograph of Monrõe arriving in Chicago for the première of *Some Like It Hot* (1959).

Mentors of Marilyn. Monroe and Natasha Lytess, her acting coach from 1948 to 1954, go over a script.

The ebullient Billy Wilder, under whose direction Monroe did two sparkling comedies, frames a composition on the set of *The Seven Year Itch* (1954).

Paula Strasberg, Monroe's coach and confidante since 1955, on the set of *Bus Stop*, with Monroe and the noted stage-and-screen director Joshua Logan (1956).

Monroe at a cocktail party at the 20th Century-Fox Film Studios in January, 1960 with *(left to right)* her husband, Arthur Miller; Simone Signoret (Mrs. Yves Montand); Yves Montand; and Frankie Vaughan. Montand, the leading French actor-singer, and Vaughan starred with Monroe in *Let's Make Love*.

"Ah, forget it, honey. The shoe doesn't show in the shot. Besides, the shoe belongs to wardrobe, not me. It's all right."

With Lauren Bacall, Marilyn had only the most nodding of acquaintances. Miss Bacall, a sophisticated woman, had no liking for what she imagined was a package of spurious mannerisms. The two were coldly polite to each other.

Unlike Negulesco, Nunnally Johnson found Monroe a disturbing experience. "I used to be sympathetic with actresses and their problems," he once told me. "Marilyn made me lose all sympathy for actresses. She doesn't take the trouble to do her homework. In most of her takes she was either fluffing lines or freezing. She doesn't bother to learn her lines. If it hadn't been for Natasha Lytess, she wouldn't have been able to learn *any* lines. Personally I was glad we had Natasha on the set. I had to run to Natasha and get her to explain the simplest thing to Marilyn. And her diction—well it's so phony. Somebody taught her elocution. She tries to be genteel with you, and it's ridiculous. She's met my wife several times, and whenever I see her, she says, 'And how's your chawming wife?' as if she's in an English drawing-room comedy." He didn't know about the English actors with whom Marilyn had lived as a child.

At that time, Johnson didn't think Marilyn had any genuine talent. "I don't think she can act her way out of a paper script. She's got no charm, delicacy, or taste. Nobody will ever call *her* America's Sweetheart. She's just an arrogant little tailswitcher. She's learned how to throw sex in your face.

"No matter how many times you've been introduced or how often you've been with her, you're never sure she knows who you are. She walks right by you with those glassy eyes, like she's in some hypnotic trance. She gave me the idea for the heroine of *How to Be Very Very Popular*. It was about a girl who gets hypnotized. I had Monroe in mind to play the girl.

"Marilyn's a phenomenon of nature, like Niagara Falls or the Grand Canyon. You can't talk to it. It can't talk to you. All you can do is stand back and be awed by it."

In the part of Pola, Marilyn built a real character who was sympathetic, awkwardly lovable, voluptuous, and comical. As Otis Guernsey, Jr., remarked in the New York *Herald Tribune,* "She plays with a limpid guile that nearly melts the screen."

In quantity, Marilyn's role was no larger than Miss Grable's or Miss Bacall's. But Marilyn received top billing. Before the film was released, Miss Grable saw the handwriting on the option. By mutual agreement, she parted with 20th Century-Fox. She didn't attend the world *première*. Marilyn was awarded permanent possession of dressing room M—which had belonged to Betty Grable for ten shining years.

Nineteen fifty-three, the year in which Marilyn Monroe emerged into stardom, was the time of a technical revolution in movie making—the wide screen. The year before, America had been fascinated by the 3-D process in which a multiple image was flashed on the screen, and the audience, watching the movie through Polaroid lenses, had the illusion of depth, as well as height and width. In autumn, 1952, Fred Waller's Cinerama process was a sensation on Broadway. In January, 1953, Spyros Skouras announced that 20th Century-Fox had bought the American rights to the French "anamorphic" lens, which photographed film so that it could be projected on a wide screen, in this case a screen about 50 feet long and 20 feet high. The process was Cinemascope. Twentieth advertised Cinemascope as "the modern miracle you see without special glasses." *How to Marry a Millionaire* was the second Cinemascope production. The first was the $5,000,000 Biblical spectacle *The Robe*.

The success, technically and commercially, of *How to Marry a Millionaire,* was important in the recent history of cinema. The Cinerama travelogues and *The Robe* had proved that the enormous screen could realistically project scenes of natural grandeur, the sweep of great masses of actors, the epic. Would a light intimate comedy be viable in Cinemascope? *How to Marry a Millionaire* showed that it was. There were still problems to be solved—problems of tight close-ups, of montage, of quick cutting—but *How to Marry a Millionaire* proved that the Cinemascopic screen and the multi-stereophonic sound track could be employed to tell any kind of story. Cinemascope was not just a novelty to lure people away from television. *How to Marry a Millionaire* cost $2,500,000 to make, and it grossed $12,000,000.

The world *première* was held at Fox's Wilshire Theatre, a 5,000-seat house on Wilshire Boulevard and La Cienega Avenue, in southeastern Hollywood.

Di Maggio refused to escort Marilyn to the *première*. He criticized her own eagerness to go, pointing out that she was always talking about being a serious actress and about the false values of Hollywood. What could be more phony than a world *preemeer*?

But Marilyn does not suffer from the foolish sort of consistency that, Emerson tells us, is the hobgoblin of little minds. She could say one day, and with sincerity, that she despised Hollywood and its fakery, and the next day, with equal sincerity, she could drink the distillation of Hollywood's soul, a world *première*. Did she contradict herself? Very well. So she contradicted herself. She contained multitudes, as Walt Whitman wrote of himself. Whitman was her favorite poet. She kept *Leaves of Grass* on her night table and often found solace in its barbaric yawps.

Joe flew to New York. It was officially announced that the separation was due to "business reasons." The ubiquitous Mr. Skolsky was for once unable to be her cavalier; he had made other arrangements for the evening. She would go alone.

On the morning of the great night, Wednesday, November 4, 1953, Marilyn awakened feeling sick. There was the customary nausea. Her nerves shook. She swallowed a painkiller. She retched and threw it up. She squeezed a glass of orange juice for herself and stirred a packet of gelatine powder into it. She couldn't keep solid food down. She prayed the juice would stay down. It did. Then she took two more painkilling capsules. She took a long perfumed bath and put on a pair of nylon panties, a Hawaiian print shirt, beige slacks, and loafers. Then she took two more pills. She went down to the parking area behind the apartment house and got into her black Cadillac convertible. Yes, she had recently acquired a Cadillac, which every Hollywood star must have, unless she is driving a Jaguar, a Rolls-Royce, a Mercedes Benz, a Lincoln Continental, or a Dual Ghia. She had not bought it. She had received the Cadillac with the compliments of Jack Benny when she had been a guest star on his television program in October.

Marilyn drove two miles down Pico Boulevard to the studio and parked in front of the Stars Building. In dressing room M, hairdresser Gladys Rasmussen and make-up man Alan Snyder were awaiting Her Highness. It was five minutes of one. Kendis Rochlen, who writes the Candid Kendis column for the Los Angeles *Mirror-News,* was allowed to watch the transformation. Miss Rochlen reported on the experience.

" 'I want to be all platinum and white tonight,' Marilyn explained to me, as anxious as a girl getting ready for her first prom. . . . 'How will I feel when I get out there and look at all the people looking at me?' "

Gladys gave Marilyn a straight permanent. Then she bleached and tinted her hair and set it. Marilyn was wearing it long that night, shoulder length. Gladys painted her fingernails and toenails with platinum polish. Her slippers, her evening dress, her long white gloves arrived from wardrobe, together with two wardrobe women. A messenger boy delivered a box with diamond earrings. Her furs had come that morning. The furs were her own. The first furs she had ever owned. Except for the white fox fur stole and muff, and her panties, everything she wore belonged to the studio. The hair, the nails, a good deal of the face were also the studio's. They were hers and they were not hers, just as the woman on the screen was she and not she.

Roy Craft dashed in to kiss her on the cheek and wish her luck and say that the town of Monroe, New York, had changed its name for one day to Marilyn Monroe, New York. Telegrams arrived. Phone calls from friends, demi-friends, pseudo-friends. Joe finally called from New York. He said he missed her. He said he loved her. He hoped she understood. He was praying for her. His heart was with her. He was sorry they weren't together. She said bitterly, "Give my regards to Georgie Solotaire."

"Whitey" Snyder began changing her face, powdering her shoulders, pencilling lines around her eyes, putting the high gloss on her lips. The wardrobe women helped her into the strapless evening gown.

Unchastened by Joan Crawford's pronouncements, Marilyn had chosen a dress made of white lace lined with flesh-colored crepe de Chine and embroidered with thousands of sequins. It had a high waist, and it curved under her breasts revealingly. A long white velvet train trailed from a gold belt. The long gloves were drawn up the length of her arms. The stole was placed around her shoulders. She put her right hand into the muff and with her left she carried the train as she walked outside to a waiting studio limousine.

The time was seven-fifteen. It had taken six hours and 20 minutes to get her into a disguise for the festivities.

Miss Rochlen drove with her to the Nunnally Johnsons'. Doris

Johnson was giving a dinner party for Marilyn, Lauren Bacall, and Lauren's husband, Humphrey Bogart.

"Marilyn sat on the edge of the seat as we drove," wrote Miss Rochlen.

" 'I guess I'm pretty nervous,' she said.

" 'Are you happy?' I asked.

"She looked out the window, then smiled at me. 'I guess this is just about the happiest night of my life,' she answered. 'Somehow it's like when I was a little girl and pretended wonderful things were happening to me. Now they are.' "

Even now, she wasn't going to let anybody forget that she was Norma Jeane Mortenson, the poor little orphan girl.

In its lurid extravagance, the scene outside the Fox-Wilshire Theatre was typical of movie *premières*. For five blocks on each side of the theatre, traffic was being rerouted. Without an invitation, no car could get past the police barriers. Huge searchlights, mounted on trucks, circled about, playing radiantly on the theatre entrance, piercing the sky with shafts of light as if seeking for enemy aircraft. On each side of the theatre and across the way, bleachers had been hurriedly erected, and several thousand persons were seated on the wooden planks. Those who had come too late for seats were tightly pressed against the wooden sawhorses. The limousines were arriving. The mob roared, commenting on the appearance, the clothes, and the most recent film of each celebrity. It was coronation day in a monarchy. And finally the queen arrived at ten minutes after nine. The mob cry rose to a screaming pitch. *Marilyn . . . Marilyn . . .*

There she is.

That's her. It's really her.

Marilyn Monroe. Marilyn. Marilyn. Marilyn.

Her name didn't belong to her either.

She felt the strange ecstasy that comes from the sweat and mass love of the mob. It is a sensation of dizziness that is pleasurably painful, that takes you utterly out of yourself. This, in the end, was what you worked for, intrigued for, lied for, prostituted yourself for, got sick at your stomach for, drilled yourself relentlessly for. This curious mass hysteria engulfed her as she walked under the marquee and into the lobby. The flashbulbs of photographers exploded during her progress as if her feet had tripped wires. Reporters clung to her, asking questions. Microphones were thrust into her hand. Television cameras focused on her. But the queen had no prince consort.

She had been invited to several supper parties after the *première,* but she was tired. The studio limousine returned her to the studio—now almost deserted. A wardrobe woman waited in dressing room M. It was almost midnight and time to end the masquerade. Off went the gloves, the earrings, the shoes, the gown. Off went the false face, erased by cold cream and paper tissues. Now she looked like a girl again, her beauty awkward and unfinished, a girl barely out of her teens. She looked smaller and less imposing out of high heels and the long dress. She looked like a human being. She got into the slacks and the sport shirt and the loafers. She placed the muff and the stole in their boxes, carried the boxes to her car, and dumped them in the back seat. She felt fatigued but not sleepy. A restlessness pervaded her. She drove out by the sea, cruising along the highway for a long time. When she got home, she drank a glass of orange juice mixed with gelatine and took three Seconals. Gradually, the restlessness blurred away into a drugged sleep.

That night she was the most famous woman in Hollywood.

Between the completion of *How to Marry a Millionaire* and the *première* just described, a period of about four months intervened. It was during this time that Marilyn co-starred with Robert Mitchum in *River of No Return,* a film which was not released until May, 1954, and which, if our heroine had had her way, would never have been released at all. Students of the Monroe canon generally agree that this is her worst film. Some may quibble with this judgment, arguing that for amateurishness and slow pace *Don't Bother to Knock* is superior, or that for banality and lapses of good taste, *No Business Like Show Business* excels, but the detached observer must give the palm to *River of No Return.* This one not only abounded in unconvincing acting, clichés of character and plot, and bad taste, but it was relentlessly boring. Marilyn herself has described it as a "Z cowboy movie, in which the acting finishes third to the scenery and Cinemascope." Those who saw her self-conscious posturing would be inclined to say it was a good thing, too.

River of No Return was made during the transition period between the old small screen and Cinemascope. Audiences had shown an eagerness to pay good money for what were nothing but extended travelogues like *This Is Cinerama* and *Cinerama Holiday*. They had also shown an eagerness to pay money to see Marilyn Monroe in anything. Without waiting for a good story and the right director, the studio rushed her into this "bomb." It was laid in the Northwest and displayed vistas of the Rocky Mountains, primeval forests, and dangerous rivers.

Marilyn played a bad girl who is reformed by a good man. Despite the fact that she had proved several times that she could not portray a *femme fatale*, she was cast as Kay Weston, a dance-hall girl who sings *double-entendre* songs and makes bedroom eyes at strangers in bars. The mystique of Theda Bara, Jean Harlow, and Marlene Dietrich haunts the front office of all movie studios.

The situation was not improved by Marilyn's feelings about the director, Otto Preminger. She and Preminger took an instant dislike to each other, and it got stronger as the shooting progressed. Preminger is an autocratic director, as are most of the great directors in films, because the film is a director's medium, not a writer's or an actor's medium. But other directors, like George Stevens, John Ford, and Billy Wilder, disguise their autocracy under a mask of gentleness.

More sure of herself than ever before—she had already seen a rough cut of *How to Marry a Millionaire* and knew that she was, as they say in Hollywood, slightly colossal—Marilyn was in no mood to be "pushed around" by anybody. And she now defined even the slightest criticism as pushing around. While Nunnally Johnson and Negulesco had seen Natasha Lytess as an ally, Preminger did not like Miss Lytess on the set. He didn't want allies. He just wanted an actress to obey his directions promptly. Marilyn functions badly in such a situation.

Between takes, she sulked in her dressing room, more like Achilles than Venus, confiding her bitterness to Natasha, Gladys, or "Whitey" Snyder. She exchanged a few kind words with Robert Mitchum, a good-natured, sociable chap, but otherwise she shunned the rest of the company and remained alone with her clique.

Snyder tells of her diverting herself with simple pastimes: "She'd come out of her room mornings, like before breakfast, see me, and yell, 'Whitey, I'll race you to the telephone pole.' It's about three blocks from where we are, see? Between takes, she'd sit by the river, Athabasca River, skimming stones on the water. Like a kid, see? I remember one time two boys came by on bicycles. Didn't know who she was. She asked if she could get the loan of a bicycle. Sure. She gets on one and was gone for an hour."

Tormenting Preminger in subtle ways also seemed to give her pleasure. One day, Preminger had been setting up all afternoon for a scene to be photographed at the "magic hour." The magic hour is a cinematographer's term for a period in the late afternoon that lasts about five minutes. It takes place when the sun is setting but there is still enough light to show distance and to suggest night in an unearthly and poetic way. A reading on a light meter registers the approach of the magic hour. During the early afternoon, Preminger had been coaching Marilyn and Robert Mitchum in their actions. Finally the electricians, grips, and carpenters had finished setting up. It takes two to three hours to set up a scene. Marilyn and Mitchum were in their places. The assistant director barked, "Quiet please, this is a take." Silence fell. Preminger told the cameraman to start rolling, and then as the enormous burning sun went down, he called, "Action."

At this crucial moment, Marilyn broke away from Mitchum's embrace. She tripped over to Preminger. He glared at her.

"What is it, Marilyn?" he said trying to keep his voice under control.

"Well, Mr. Preminger," she said, "you'll have to excuse me. I have to go to the bathroom."

Preminger, a man noted for his explosions on the set, was, for once, shocked into dumbness.

On another occasion, Marilyn kept fluffing her lines, take after take. After the thirty-second take, Preminger decided to try a little tenderness. He called a ten-minute break. He went over to Marilyn. "Just relax," he said to Marilyn. "It'll be all right. Don't worry."

She looked up, blinking her eyelids naïvely. "Why? Is anything the matter?"

In January, 1960, Otto Preminger appeared on a television-panel discussion of the movies. He was asked by David Susskind how he had liked directing Marilyn Monroe. Preminger groaned. He stated that he would never again make a movie with Monroe, no, not for a million dollars—not even for a million *tax-free* dollars!

While the company was on location in Banff, Canada, Marilyn

was playing in a scene in which she and Mitchum are boarding a raft to escape from a tribe of hostile Indians. Marilyn slipped from the raft and fell into the river. She struck a hidden rock and hurt her foot. She was limping badly. The registered nurse—all companies on location include a studio nurse—felt her ankle and ordered her to bed. At the hotel, a local doctor examined her. He said she had torn a ligament. He warned her that if she did not stay off her foot for 30 days she would be permanently disabled.

That night Joe phoned from San Francisco. He sensed her anxiety.

"What's the matter?"

"Nothing."

"There's something wrong."

"Oh, no," she said.

"What happened? I know something happened."

"I hurt my foot this morning," she burst out. "I might be crippled for life. Why did I come here? The picture is terrible. Mr. Preminger is mean to me." She began weeping.

"I'm taking the next train up."

"There's nothing you can—"

"I've got to be with you. I'm bringing a doctor with me."

He arrived the next morning. Again his tenderness melted her doubts. Oh, she did love him, and he did love her.

The California doctor gave a more optimistic prognosis. The ligament was torn but not badly. And she would be able to continue working. He put her foot in a plaster cast. Mitchum dropped in to say a few encouraging words and sign the plaster. Mitchum cracked, "Well, Marilyn, you can't say you haven't got a good supporting cast."

That was about all she did have. Otis Guernsey, Jr., expressed the common critical reaction when he wrote, "This stint is something of a disappointment after her recent sparkling comedy performances and the edges of her peacock feathers are to be seen peeping out from the game-bird disguise."

On the way back to Hollywood, to shoot the interior scenes and retakes of the close-ups for *River of No Return*, Joe and Marilyn stopped over in San Francisco. During a storm in the bay, one of Joe's brothers had drowned in a fishing accident. His body was found floating in Bodega Bay. In his grief Joe turned to Marilyn, and for the first time she sensed his vulnerability. She felt pity for him and with it an emotion she thought was love. She said she would marry him as soon as she finished *River of No Return*.

In July, Roy Craft told her that *Look* Magazine wished to put her on the cover and also publish a layout of color photographs. He asked her to keep a Saturday open. The magazine had assigned a new man from New York to do the job. He wanted to photograph her in the magazine's studio. She went to the studio, and so met Milton H. Greene, who was to figure significantly in her career. Greene is a slim, youngish chap, of modest height. He was puffing on a pipe as he spoke to her. He was thirty-two years old then, but he looked callow. Marilyn did not trouble to conceal her disappointment.

"Why," she said, "you're just a boy!"

"And you're just a girl," Greene answered.

They smiled and were friends.

"We liked each other at once," Greene recalls. "In an hour we were old friends."

The photographs he took delighted her. They even found favor in Di Maggio's eyes. A selection from her first sitting with Greene appeared in *Look* for November 17, 1953. One page showed 12 small shots of her. She was in a bulky over-sized gray knit sweater and was plucking a mandolin. Another photograph, a full page, was shot against a black background. She wore a black dress and only her legs, hands, and head were exposed.

About a year later, Greene returned to the Coast on another assignment. He now had many sittings with her.

"I captured certain sides of her in pictures nobody captured before," Greene said. "I got the idea of doing a book, a big book, about Marilyn, pictures of her, all her different moods, a whole book of my pictures about Marilyn. We talked about the idea, and I shot a lot of pictures with the book in mind."

Marilyn was proud of the pictures. She showed them to Negulesco for a painter's reaction.

Negulesco once explained to me: "Well, this Greene, he had some kind of hypnotic power over her, because he did get her to pose in certain ways she had never posed before. I think there was a certain way Marilyn had always thought about herself, but no photographer saw it in her. To an actress, how she looks is important to her. Greene saw something virginal in her, something sweet, pure, and he caught it with the camera. This was how she wanted to see herself, so maybe that's why she thought he was a movie genius. There was no other reason for her to come under his influence."

But who really came under whose influence?

And now we flash back to November, 1953. Joe and Marilyn had set a date for the marriage—New Year's Day, 1954.

And what did Marilyn Monroe do during the six weeks between the moment she had set the date and the day she expected to be married? Did her girl friends give her a shower? Did she shop for linens and flat silver? Did she take counsel with interior decorators about color schemes? Was she planning the wedding details? Was she in a gay whirl of luncheons and parties before the climax?

No, she did not take part in any of the usual pre-marital activities of the American bride. Even movie stars, when they are brides, do all the things other brides do. But not Marilyn. For a woman must have girl friends to be involved in the whirl before marriage, a whirl stirred up by women who love marriages. Marilyn had no girl friends. Her life has been characterized by an inability to form permanent friendships with other women. She has had fairly durable relations with her dramatic coaches: Natasha Lytess and then Paula Strasberg. She has had casual friendships during the making of a film with colleagues such as Jane Russell and Eileen Heckart. But nothing deeper.

In the period before her marriage, Marilyn was embroiled in a serious row with her studio. Without informing her, the studio announced that her next vehicle would be *The Girl in Pink Tights,* shooting to start on December 15. Frank Sinatra had been signed at $5,000 a week to play opposite her. Marilyn, having floated up to her contractual ceiling, was to be paid a paltry $1,500 a week, although she was to receive top billing.

Marilyn struck a pose of hurt indignation. She said the very title made her nervous. All she knew about the story was that it was a musical version of an old Betty Grable epic. "I was working," she wrote, "with all my might, trying to become a real actress. I felt that the studio might cash in by exhibiting me in pink tights in a crude movie, but that I wouldn't."

She said she must read the script before she would agree to play in it. The front office refused to show it to her.

Marilyn said that her latest assignment was a deliberate act of Zanuck hostility, because "I kept him waiting for an hour at an Academy Award presentation."

But her quarrel with the studio, she said, went beyond her vendetta with Zanuck or her feeling that she deserved better than the coolie wages she was getting. "The trouble was about something deeper. I wanted to be treated as a human being who had earned a few rights since her orphanage days."

Her "orphanage days" were now about 15 years behind her, and Zanuck had not put her in the orphanage anyway. But in any crisis, she waved the flag of that orphan before society, demanding compensation for the past.

Marilyn became a "hold-out." She informed her agent, Charles Feldman, she wouldn't be on the lot until she had read the script and approved it. Then she disappeared. Nobody could get her on the phone, not even her agents or Inez Melson, her new business manager. She wasn't seen in any of her usual haunts. Her Cadillac was gone from its parking place. Even Skolsky and Lytess didn't know where she was.

The studio announced her suspension. She was off salary. December 15 came. No Marilyn. It was costing the studio about $25,000 a day as Sinatra and the others waited for Monroe, a pastime as frustrating as waiting for Godot.

Then Marilyn telephoned from San Francisco, where she had been holing up secretly. The studio sent her the script and announced that she was off suspension. She read the scenario, which was about a virtuous schoolteacher at the turn of the century who becomes a "hoochie coochie" dancer in a low-class Bowery joint.

Marilyn described the heroine as a "dreary cliché-spouting bore, who was the cheapest character I had ever read in a script." She said that she "blushed to the toes" whenever she thought of playing a "rear-waggling schoolteacher doing a cheap dance."

One cannot blame Zanuck for being perplexed by this sudden spasm of morality, considering that she hadn't caviled at waggling her rear in *Niagara, Gentlemen Prefer Blondes, How to Marry a Millionaire,* and *River of No Return.* Nor had her inhibitions been evident at such public functions as the notorious *Photoplay* affair. Perhaps Zanuck had never read Emerson on inconsistency.

The studio announced that Marilyn was again suspended.

Now, there is that about foregoing $1,500 a week which is disturbing to the mind in a bourgeois society. One must be a dedicated ascetic to spurn $1,500 a week. Marilyn, although her recent statements indicated a devotion to female chastity, was not quite *that* ascetic. She chafed in San Francisco. Yet she had been told by Di Maggio that the scenario was terrible. She had been told by Natasha Lytess that it was unworthy of her great talent, that she must free herself from undignified films and rise to serious dramatic heights. Choreographer Jack Cole had told her she would make a marvelous Nana. She had read Zola's novel and tried to get George Cukor, a famous "women's director," to film her as the celebrated courtesan. Cukor didn't like the idea. Her agents had hoped that if she put her back up, the studio might write a new contract. Well, now it looked as if they weren't going to write a new contract. She was quaking. Maybe she ought to change her mind and play the hoochie coochie dancer.

Nonsense, said Joe. Now was an ideal time to get married. He had to go to Japan in February with Lefty O'Doul, to play exhibition baseball and coach two Tokyo ball teams. He and Marilyn would have a quiet honeymoon in Japan. But, suggested Marilyn, why couldn't they go to Japan without getting married? Why marry *now*? Shouldn't they wait? After all, movie actresses were different. Rita Hayworth had traveled around Europe first with Aly Kahn and then with Dick Haymes before marrying either. Lana Turner and Lex Barker, Ava Gardner and Frank Sinatra—they too made the grand tour without benefit of clergy. One ought not to rush recklessly into matrimony.

Di Maggio didn't relish the danger of scandal. When he'd gone up to Banff to comfort her, he had not stayed at her hotel, the Banff Springs, but had put up at an inn in Lake Louise, 40 miles away. No. They must get married before leaving.

She surrendered on Thursday morning, January 14, 1954. The decision was almost impromptu. Reno Barsocchini, manager of Di Maggio's restaurant on Fishermen's Wharf, telephoned Municipal Court Justice Charles S. Peery. Peery was at a Bar Association luncheon. Barsocchini asked the Judge to please get over to his chambers quickly, as he had been chosen to perform the wedding ceremony of the year. Judge Peery did not stay to finish his meal. He hustled over to City Hall and was ready for the couple at 1:00

P.M. Joe and Marilyn, accompanied by Mr. and Mrs. Reno Barsocchini and Mr. and Mrs. Lefty O'Doul, arrived at 1:25. By now, the news had been whispered about, and there were hundreds outside City Hall. The wedding party had to push its way to the elevator. When they got to the third floor, Joe was so excited he took a wrong turn and he and the wedding party raced down the corridor to arrive at a dead end. Ominous omen for a wedding day. They reversed themselves and ran as rapidly in the opposite direction.

The bride was wearing a tailored blue broadcloth suit with a white ermine collar and a corsage of white orchids. On the marriage license, Marilyn gave her age as twenty-five, a slight understatement, since she had been twenty-seven the previous June. The groom was 12 years older but in fine fettle. The reporters circled around and threw questions.

"I'm terribly excited," Marilyn said. "I just couldn't be happier." She said she would be in movies for only two or three years more. Then she looked forward to becoming a "full time housewife and mother."

"Yeah," boomed Di Maggio, "we're going to have a large family."

His Honor signaled Di Maggio to get on with it. Di Maggio, as one reporter put it, "leaped up with the enthusiastic spirit of a rookie second baseman and said, 'Okay, let's get this marriage going.'" His impatience was understandable. He had been waiting a long, long time. Barsocchini stood up for Joe. The O'Douls were witnesses. The knot was tied at precisely 1:48. Joe was in a cordial mood as he posed for pictures with Marilyn. Judge Peery did not exercise the jurist's usual prerogative of kissing the bride.

"It was my first meeting with her and I didn't want to be too forward," he sadly explained later.

The couple quickly said good-bye and strode away.

"We've got to put a lot of miles behind us," Joe said, grinning.

Just before going to City Hall, Marilyn had phoned Harry Brand at the studio.

"Harry," she said, "this is Marilyn Monroe. I'm in a big hurry. I'm on my way to City Hall to marry Joe. I promised I'd let you know first if I ever did it, so I'm letting you know. Bye."

She hung up.

20 Mrs. Joe Di Maggio

For a wedding present, the studio lifted her suspension. It was a nice present—worth about $15,000. During the next two weeks, the newlyweds dropped from sight completely. Without make-up and fine clothes, Marilyn Monroe did not look like Marilyn Monroe. Nobody recognized either Marilyn or Joe during the honeymoon. The bridal night was spent at a motel in Pasa Robles. Before registering, Joe wanted to know if there was a television set in the unit. There was.

We do not know what television programs Joe enjoyed that night.

(Two days later, the motel-keeper saw a photograph of Joe and Marilyn. He experienced the shock of recognition. To mark the historical site, he placed a brass plaque outside their unit: JOE AND MARILYN SLEPT HERE.)

The following morning they were on the highway early. Nobody identified them in any of the restaurants at which they stopped during the long day's drive. Marilyn wore slacks, a blouse, and a beige wrap-around polo coat. Dark glasses hid her eyes, and a kerchief covered her platinum hair. Their destination was a mountain retreat near Idyllwild, about 50 miles from Palm Springs. Lloyd Wright, her attorney, lent them his lodge there. They had two weeks alone. The earth was covered with snow, and they walked in the snow for hours. Marilyn confided, "There wasn't a television set in the cabin. Joe and I talked a lot. We really got to know each other. And we played billiards. There was a billiard table there, and Joe taught me how to play."

They returned to Los Angeles quietly. Joe flew to New York on business. Marilyn skulked about the city incognito. She did not communicate with the studio or go near her apartment. And still nobody recognized her. She was holed up in a motel in Westwood under the name of Norma Baker. The word leaked out that Marilyn was secluding herself somewhere in the city. But she departed as surreptitiously as she had arrived. Joe returned, and in San Francisco, she and Joe boarded a Pan American Clipper for Honolulu. At the Hawaiian airport a mob surrounded the passenger lounge, which was finally closed off. As the Clipper's wheels bumped to a stop, thousands of Hawaiians ran out onto the field. Four policemen encircled Marilyn and Di Maggio. Slowly they pressed through the crowd.

Hands reached out to clutch at her. Her spun-gold hair fascinated the citizenry.

"They keep grabbing at my hair," she murmured anxiously. "Do you see what they're doing, Joe? They keep grabbing at my hair."

It was frightening. Strands of her hair were actually torn away. More police came. They formed a cordon and the newlyweds were able to enter the airport lounge. There they sipped glasses of freshly squeezed pineapple juice. Marilyn wanted to go back home. But she was assured that in Japan she would find the serenity for which the Orient is noted. She would have a quiet respite in the land of the tea ceremony, flower arranging, hokku verse, and Zen.

They embarked on the flight to Tokyo.

As the plane was preparing to land at the Tokyo airport, a General Christenberry introduced himself to Mr. and Mrs. Di Maggio.

"How would you like to entertain our men in Korea, Miss Monroe?" he asked. "It would give them a great lift."

Marilyn remembered that not long ago Mrs. Anna Rosenberg, assistant secretary of defense, had toured Army bases in Korea. She had reported, "What the soldiers want most is Marilyn Monroe for Christmas."

Marilyn looked questioningly at Joe. "It's your honeymoon," he said, shrugging. "Go ahead if you want to."

She did. She agreed to make a three-day tour of the front.

At Tokyo's Haneda International Airport, swarms of Japanese movie fans covered the field. The word "fan," an abbreviation of fanatic, is usually misused, but now it applied. Ten thousand fans were in hysteria.

The stairs were pushed to the four-engined plane. The passenger door was opened. Marilyn took one look at the stampede below her and withdrew, flinching. The door was shut. Police tried to persuade the fanatics to go home, but nobody did. A scheme was now put into action. The door was again opened. Other passengers descended. While the mob waited for Marilyn, she was crawling out through the baggage hatchway and racing across the field to the Immigration Office. It took an hour to spirit Marilyn—who is affectionately known in Japan as *mon-chan* or "sweet little girl"—out of Immigration and into a long black convertible. The top was down, and she received one of the most spectacular ovations any movie star has ever gotten. She was driven eight miles into downtown Tokyo. The stretch was lined with Japanese, screaming *mon-chan, mon-chan, mon-chan,* or, *Malyn, Malyn, Malyn Monloe.*

The Imperial Hotel, where she and Joe had reservations, was surrounded by tight-packed multitudes. Knowing that the Imperial has ten different entrances, the fans had divided into squads that blocked each entrance. Two hundred policemen tried to keep order to protect Miss *Monloe* from serious injury or the loss of the rest of her hair. When she finally squeezed into the sanctuary of the lobby, police closed the huge plate-glass doors behind her and held them closed. But the Japanese fanatics would not be stayed. They hurled themselves against the plate glass, which shattered. Amid screams of pain and streams of blood, the fanatics gushed into the lobby. By now *Malyn* was in her suite upstairs.

The next morning, Mr. and Mrs. Di Maggio were interviewed by the Japanese press. Yoko Hazama, a Japanese movie fan and a loyal reader of *Modern Screen* magazine, insinuated himself into the conference and made notes of the repartee, which he set down in a letter to the editor of *Modern Screen.* He apologized because "my English is limited." Here is Hazama's transcription of the interview in Limited English:

"Q. What is your opinion about your famous Monroe Walk?

"A. I had been walking since I was six months old and couldn't stopped yet. It naturally come to me.

"Q. Is it true you didn't wear any underwear clothes, whether or not?

"A. I'm planning to buy a Japanese kimono and I'm wearing underclothes like this lace slip.

"Q. What is your first impression of Japan?

"A. I hardly to tell that answer because I just arrived here only yesterday but I heard about Japan from my husband. I really never expected before such cameramens waited here.

"Q. Who is your closest best friend.

"A. Miss Jane Russell and Miss Betty Grable.

"Q. Who is your respectable people who are engaged in motion-picture field?

"A. Ingrid Bergman, Charles Laughton, Humphrey Bogart, Marlon Brando.

"Q. You think your husband is a millionaire?

"A. No, I don't think so. I guess he is empty."

She was asked if she slept in the nude. She refused to answer.

"When you go to Korea you wear ermine bathing suit like Terry Moore?" (Miss Moore had gone to Korea to give our battle-weary soldiers something for Christmas. The ensuing scandal had practically set off a Congressional investigation.)

"No," Marilyn said, "I'll wear a plain cocktail dress."

"Do you agree with Kinsey Report, Miss Monloe?"

"Yes, maybe," she said.

"You plan give up career?"

"No. But my marriage comes before my career."

"Is it true you want six children?"

Joe interrupted to say, "You should ask *me* that question."

But hardly anybody was asking Joe questions.

Between interviews and mob scenes and visits to military hospitals, Marilyn had little time to go sight-seeing. "My travels have always been the same," she wrote. "No matter where I've gone or why I've gone there, it always ends up that I never see anything." She did manage to get in an afternoon of shopping in the Ginza and a visit to the Kabuki Theatre. Mornings she went out to the stadium to watch Di Maggio coach. Sometimes at night, she watched Di Maggio and O'Doul play snooker in the game room at the hotel.

On February 10, the Special Services branch of the armed forces completed arrangements with Marilyn to join a USO troupe of variety acts which was in Okinawa at the moment and would arrive in Seoul on February 16. Pfc. Albert Guestafeste, of Uniondale,

N.J., was given the honor of being her pianist. They rehearsed four numbers: "Diamonds Are a Girl's Best Friend," "Bye Bye Baby," "Somebody Loves Me," "Do It Again."

Early on Tuesday morning, February 16, Marilyn flew to Seoul. When she alighted, cold winter blasts hit her. She had brought no warm clothes. The Army fitted her out with combat boots, pants, Army shirts, and a leather jacket lined with sheepskin, and she was flown by helicopter to an airstrip on the western front, within shooting distance of the Communist armies. There was no time for the elaborate preparations she went through before a public appearance. A platform had been constructed, and, behind it, burlap curtains were strung on four poles. Marilyn changed in this makeshift dressing room. It was late in the afternoon. The sky was gray, the air cold and damp, her skin prickled with chilliness. She had begun to get the sniffles. She got into the low-cut cocktail dress, smeared some lip rouge hurriedly on her lips, clipped golden circle earrings on her ear lobes, and snapped a pearl bracelet around her wrist. She could hear a tap dancer ending his number. A captain called to her. "You're on next, Miss Monroe."

He didn't have to be explicit. The air told her. The roar of thousands of voices.

"Hey, Marilyn!"

"We want Marilyn!"

Thousands of men were clapping their hands in rhythm.

"We   Want   Marilyn!"

Her larynx was scratchy. Her chest hurt. She was coming down with a cold, a bad cold. She sounded hoarse. Her voice was drying up. But for once she wasn't scared. She felt grateful to the men out there. It was these soldiers, sailors, marines, Air Force heroes who had fallen in love with her picture. It was they who had forced the studio to make her a star. She belonged to them in a way she could perhaps never belong to any individual man.

The captain helped her up the steps to the platform. Then she was alone, and all heaven broke loose in a passionate cry of desire from the 13,000 throats of 13,000 marines of the First Marine Division and men of the 3rd and 7th Army divisions. And it was all for her, or really for all the women that she represented, being in herself the embodiment of all women. She had not yet become, first inured to, then bored by, and lastly contemptuous of the mob's adulation. It was still a new experience to her—this strange drunken rapture.

Before the next performance, the Special Services officer told her that she would have to refrain from singing "Do It Again," as the lyric was "too suggestive." She took refuge in wide-eyed innocence. Something suggestive about that aria? Why it was a romantic ballad!

"I sing it as a straight wistful love song," she said.

She bowed to the military, however. During the next two days— in all, she gave ten shows to an estimated 100,000 men at various points along the front—she did not urge them to do "it" again.

At Taegu, her laryngitis developed into a bad grippe. She was running a high fever by the time she was back in Tokyo. But the memory of the reception was exhilarating. "It was so wonderful, Joe," she said. "You never heard such cheering."

"Yes, I have," he said. "Don't let it go to your head. Just miss the ball once. You'll see they can boo as loud as they can cheer."

If it be true, as Negulesco has remarked, that it is difficult to be Marilyn Monroe and perform a simple everyday act like eating mashed potatoes, how much more difficult it must be to be Marilyn Monroe and put on an apron, go into the kitchen, peel the potatoes, boil the potatoes, and mash them. The only force that keeps many bored housewives mashing potatoes is the lack of alternatives. Yet the dream of being a normal woman obsesses every movie actress to whom I have ever talked, just as the dream of becoming a movie actress obsesses almost every American woman. The actress invents a fantasy of the happy home in which she prepares meals for a grateful husband and healthy, red-cheeked children. After the competitive pressure of movie-making, the role of wife and mother seems heavenly. But an actress, because of the very qualities that make her an actress, is usually incapable of underplaying her ego, as a housewife so often must do, unable to place herself now and then in a position secondary to her children and her husband. Marilyn Monroe had become the center of her own universe. Everything had to revolve around her.

When she returned to San Francisco, in April, 1954, she was filled with exaltation at the prospect of having her own home and children. She and Joe would live in San Francisco most of the time. They would go to Los Angeles only when she had to appear in a film.

Di Maggio owned a two-story house in the Marinas district of San Francisco. His widowed sister, Marie, was to be the housekeeper. Joe was a prosperous businessman, with extensive holdings in real estate and stocks and a successful sea-food restaurant, "Joe Di Maggio's," on Fishermen's Wharf. He also had his baseball programs on radio and television. He intended to stay out of Marilyn's business affairs, but he expected her to submerge her career and become Mrs. Di Maggio. She tried. She tried very hard. She tried for several months to be a dutiful companion and helpmeet. The trouble was that even when she wanted to submerge the public personality of "Marilyn Monroe," the rest of the world would not let her do it. If, so to speak, she wanted to mash potatoes, her sister-in-law would not let her demean herself. The Di Maggio family all took to Marilyn. They found her unpretentious. She played with their children. She listened with admiration to their banter. She even learned how to fish. She'd get up at dawn, put on dungarees and an old sweater, and go out for a day's fishing on Joe's trawler. She got seasick all the time, but she stuck it. She played golf with Joe. She went on picnics with Joe. She watched television with Joe. In the evening she went to the restaurant as the dutiful wife of any restaurant-keeper might do. When he was in San Francisco, Joe was at his restaurant every night, acting as host. Marilyn would come there at six, have dinner, and then sit alone in a booth in the back of the restaurant. Her presence brought customers flocking to the place. Like the cable cars, Chinatown, and the Golden Gate Bridge, she became one of the leading tourist attractions in San Francisco. The public ogled. They asked for autographs. They asked embarrassing questions. It was true that in a cosmopolitan city like San Francisco she was able to recede into the landscape more easily than in Los Angeles. But she was never able to forget that she was Marilyn Monroe, not Mrs. Joseph Paul Di Maggio.

In May, she went to Los Angeles to discuss her future activities at the studio. Her next vehicle was to be *No Business Like Show Business,* one of those hackneyed backstage musicals in which she was to play a cabaret singer who falls in love with Donald O'Connor. It was one of the most implausible combinations the mind of Hollywood ever conceived. The role was a ratty one—as ratty as *The Girl in Pink Tights.* Marilyn accepted it because the studio said that in return they would give her the comedy acting plum of the year—the starring role opposite Tom Ewell in the movie version of *Seven Year Itch. Seven Year Itch* was to be directed by Billy Wilder. Marilyn regarded Wilder as one of the best directors in Hollywood. Even if the role was not exactly Dostoevskian, she thought that playing in an important Broadway vehicle would lend prestige to her reputation. Wilder had several talks with Marilyn, whom he admired as a classic cinematic beauty.

Louella Parsons interviewed Marilyn on the radio during this trip. She told Louella that she wanted to make a success of her marriage.

"I wish," wrote Miss Parsons, "that Marilyn could be as happy always as she was when she came home from her honeymoon. Although she was still suffering from a heavy cold and had just gotten over pneumonia, she was happier than I have ever seen her. I believe their marriage is stable, and although I could be wrong, I think they will both do everything within their power to keep it successful if only the rumor hounds will let them alone."

No Business Like Show Business was to roll in June. In May, the Di Maggios leased an English-provincial cottage on N. Palm Drive in Beverly Hills for six months at $750 a month. In the rear was a large area with a patio, a swimming pool, fruit trees, and rose bushes. Overlooking the patio was a comfortable sun porch with garden furniture and a built-in barbecue. As she went through the house, Marilyn saw herself as the ideal housewife. She and Joe would spend their evenings here, broiling steaks or hamburgers, drinking beer, watching television—yes, she would put the television set here, on the sun porch, opposite the couch, and Joe and his friends could sit and watch television and she and Natasha Lytess could sit in the living room and work out cinematic problems. But in her dream of the future that would not happen very often. If Joe was immersed in a television program, she would not interrupt him. After her day at the studio she would quietly go to the kitchen and prepare dinner and bring it to him. She would get a folding table and place the dinner on the table so he wouldn't even have to miss a commercial. She would wait on him hand and foot. "He won't have to move a muscle," she vowed. "I'll treat him like a king." She would see that his suits were cleaned and pressed and his shoes shined; and she herself would wash and iron his shirts. She liked to look at Joe when he was wearing a shirt she had ironed. She thought she ironed men's shirts, especially the collars, better than any woman alive. And a budget! Oh, yes, she would put herself on a budget and run the whole house. Plan the meals, do the marketing—so much for food, so much for entertainment, so much for clothes, so much for maid; by the way, she had better hire a maid, a capable, responsible, hardworking maid, as Jane Russell had advised her. And then in the early evening sometimes, she would go into the garden—oh, yes, she would learn how to grow flowers—and she would cut fresh flowers, for sometimes there would be romantic evenings when he wouldn't watch television and they would have dinner in the dining room, just the two of them, flowers in a centerpiece. She would have to learn flower arranging—oh, there were so many wonderful things she would have to learn in this new life. And candles, yes, she would have candles in lovely antique candlesticks, and the glasses of wine would reflect the glow of candlelight as they sat opposite each other, consumed with mutual affection. She wasn't ashamed of being romantic. Just because people were married was no reason to stop being romantic. She and Joe would court each other forever. These are the dreams of every woman when she begins married life, but when an actress dreams she dreams with greater intensity. She would be the ideal stepmother for Joe, Jr., the son by Joe's first marriage. He would have a bedroom with masculine wallpaper and rugged furniture and pennants on the walls and crossed foils. And there would be a nursery and a child of her own, a little girl she hoped, by the end of the year. She didn't like the double bed in the master bedroom. It wasn't large enough. She believed in double beds, but they had to be enormous. A bed, she maintained, should be large enough so husband and wife had "their own sleeping independence." While separate bedrooms were popular in many Hollywood *ménages,* Marilyn didn't like the idea.

"I don't believe in that," she confided to Skolsky once. "Often in bed you think of something you want to say, or something you've forgotten. You're not going to get out of bed and chase down the hall to another room. I don't buy it. This separate bedroom deal is not in the American tradition. In the pioneer days, did you ever hear of a man and his wife sleeping in separate covered wagons?"

Marilyn had recently bought a beautiful full-length, black natural-mink coat for $12,500. There were other non-pioneer aspects in her pattern of living—swimming pool, convertible, television, a maid, dining by candlelight, vintage French wine.

The romantic dream began disintegrating in the acids of daily living. Had Marilyn not been working in a film, had she been able to concentrate entirely on shirt ironing, potato mashing, and bed making, it is possible that her strong will and her strong desire for a real home to compensate for the kind of homes she had had as a child would have driven her to make the dream come true, at least to some degree. But a film demands such concentration of thought and energy that very little remains for the mundane job of operating a house, which is itself a complicated one—not only technically, but emotionally, because a housewife must deal with human beings as well as candles and shirts. Anyway, Marilyn's deepest traits ran counter to housekeeping. She had no head for figures except the 38-26-37 of her own. She couldn't add, subtract, divide, or multiply. After a week of domesticity, the budget was so confused that Di Maggio took it over. A succession of maids, cooks, and housekeepers tried to cope wtih Marilyn's vagueness. They failed. The shirts were sent to a laundry. She usually came home too late to prepare dinner, and so she and Joe went out to restaurants. There wasn't a single candlelighted dinner at N. Palm Drive.

From the beginning, her work went badly in the film. She had been away from the discipline of movie-making for eight months. On her first day back at the studio she said she felt as she had "when I was going to a new foster home and had to go to a new school and try to make friends again." She was playing with such seasoned experts at musical comedy as Donald O'Connor, Dan Dailey, and, above all, Ethel Merman. Their *expertise,* their speed in grasping director Walter Lang's commands and carrying them out, frightened her. She felt incompetent as a dancer and hopeless as a singer. She got into a series of rows with choreographer Robert Alton, one of the great dance directors of Broadway and Hollywood, and said she could not perform unless Jack Cole were brought on the set. Over Alton's objections, Cole was brought in to stage Marilyn's big solo number, the "Heat Wave" number. Competing with the lung power, the phrasing, the verve, and the self-confidence of Ethel Merman, Marilyn felt defeated. She doubled her private coaching sessions with Schaefer. She drove herself relentlessly, working with him four hours a day, practicing breathing and phrasing. When she saw the early sequences in the projection room, she was dismayed at how horrible she looked opposite O'Connor. She looked old enough to be his mother. The casting was absurd. Their chemistries did not combine. She had to play her scenes with him in stocking feet because in high heels she was six inches taller than he. Her friends had never seen her so nervous before. She blew up constantly and became compulsive about retakes. Three times during the shooting she collapsed on the set and had to be given several days off. She became a constant item in Harrison Carroll's "medical" column of movie gossip in the Los Angeles *Herald-Express*. Carroll loves to report sickness, fractured bones, accidents on location, bouts in the hospital. He reports them in morbid, almost clinical detail, lingering lovingly over the more macabre diseases and injuries. Marilyn Monroe figured regularly in his column.

Irving Berlin, 34 of whose songs were featured in *No Business Like Show Business,* was pleased with her rendition of the three she sang. He said that her way of handling "After You Get What You Want, You Don't Want It" was exciting. "This is the way it should be sung," he said. "If it had been sung that way in nineteen twenty when I wrote it, it would have been a hit song. But I saw it as a slow ballad. It took Marilyn's interpretation to make me see how sexy it was. Even I didn't know how sexy it was."

The rumor hounds of Hollywood were spreading the news that there was dissension between the Di Maggios. Louella Parsons reported encountering Marilyn Monroe at a "party of celebrities. Marilyn, wearing long black gloves and looking very pretty despite the unbecoming gown selected for her by the studio, whispered in my ear: 'Joe is going to pick me up after the party. There are too many people here. You know he doesn't like all this publicity and he won't get dressed up even for me.'"

Leon Shamroy, who was the cinematographer of *No Business Like Show Business,* told me he once happened to be dining at Bruce Wong's, a fashionable Chinese restaurant on La Cienega Boulevard. He watched Joe and Marilyn, at another table, for two hours. He says they did not exchange a single word and there seemed to be looks of coldness on both faces.

To offset the rumors, Joe finally consented to pay a visit to the set. He refused, however, to pose with his wife. He posed only with Irving Berlin. He told somebody that the reason he had come was to hear Ethel Merman sing. The "Merm," as she was known around Toots Shor's, was a great favorite with Di Maggio and his Broadway cronies. Joe said Ethel Merman was his favorite star. The news quickly got back to Marilyn, and the couple had the first of many violent rows over his "interest" in other women. He was, of course, even more violent about her "interest" in other men. There were arguments, small in the beginning, over everything. It was Marilyn's acting, of course, that Joe hated, but he did not dare to say so. He criticized her for her slovenly habits, for leaving her clothes lying around on chairs or the floor, toothpaste tubes open, electric lights on when she left a room, the water tap running. He complained of her late hours. "You come home nine, ten o'clock," he said, "and you're too tired to do anything but go to sleep. I could just as well have stayed a bachelor. You're married to the goddam movie studio. You complain about my watching television. What the hell else have I got to do, Marilyn? It's worse than being a bachelor. I'm rattling around in this big house with nothing to do, nobody to talk to."

At first she would say she was sorry, and he would say he was sorry, but when the arguments ceased there were silences, long silences, between them. Once he did not speak to her for ten days in a row. He seemed cold and indifferent to her, his face was a glacial mask. But under the mask he needed her love. He loved her and he wanted her love, but he was too proud to beg for it. He suffered inside. An old duodenal ulcer, quiescent for years, began bleeding again. He was bleeding inside when she thought he was cold and indifferent.

None of her colleagues—she had no personal friends—was allowed to come to the house. She said that Joe's attitude to her "actually affected my health. I was under the care of a doctor most of the time I was living with Joe."

She began drinking heavily. She was a secret drinker; she hid a bottle in a drawer of her vanity table. He was downstairs on the sun porch watching television. She was upstairs drinking herself into forgetfulness.

She still tried to keep up appearances, though. She told everyone, even old friends like Skolsky, that the marriage was fine. Of course, they had their little disagreements, like any married couple—human nature was human nature. But they always worked their little differences out amicably. Kendis Rochlen, encountering Marilyn on the set one day, asked her why Joe never came to the studio.

"He likes golf better," Marilyn explained. "He's always out playing it. Me? I've tried it out. I've got all the clubs and everything, but I've found it's just not for me."

Miss Rochlen asked if Di Maggio was ever going to lift his ban against letting photographers take pictures of the Di Maggios in their love nest on North Palm Drive. "They're panting to show you as the happy bride cooking at the stove and what not," she said.

Marilyn laughed, reported Miss Rochlen. "I'm afraid Joe doesn't like that kind of publicity," Marilyn said.

Marilyn could not face the probability that her marriage was on the rocks. To her, a good marriage was the noblest consummation of a woman's life. She could not be a woman if she could not be a wife, if she could not be a mother. She could not make it work. Week by week, she and Joe grew farther apart. In an effort to stave off the collapse of the marriage, Marilyn began seeing an analyst. She had attempted psychotherapy before; this time she continued faithfully in treatment for about six months. But the insights she gained tended to make her feel more hopeless about the marriage. She became convinced that her problems lay in her emotional immaturity. She must find her own identity and her own form of self-expression. She was losing her soul in the Hollywood miasma. She was dying as a woman in the boredom and indifference of her marriage. Inwardly, in her intellect and her emotions, she was developing as a woman—a late development perhaps, but one that was quite real. In her living habits she still followed self-destructive patterns.

It was in the last stages of *No Business Like Show Business* that Marilyn was first introduced to Paula Strasberg. Mrs. Strasberg, who was in Los Angeles visiting her actress daughter, Susan Strasberg, was invited to the 20th Century-Fox lot by Marlon Brando, an alumnus of the Actors' Studio. Brando was playing Napoleon Bonaparte in the Movie *Desiree*. As the two Strasberg ladies were watching Brando, Sidney Skolsky introduced himself. He asked them if they were interested in meeting Marilyn, who was working on a nearby sound stage. They were. Skolsky brought them to Marilyn. Marilyn professed some interest in the Actors' Studio. She seemed excited at meeting Paula and Susan Strasberg. She said that Elia Kazan had told her that Lee Strasberg was an inspiring teacher. She said she hoped someday she would be able to live in New York and study with him.

21 *The Seven Year Itch* and the Nine-Month Marriage

The final shooting weeks of *No Business Like Show Business* were hell. Marilyn was before the camera seven days a week to catch up with the time lost because of her illnesses. *The Seven Year Itch* was to start on August 10. At night she studied scenes of *Itch* after the day's shooting of *No Business*. A low-grade virus infection sapped her energies. Joe and she had ceased speaking to each other. She needed his understanding, but he had come to that point where he believed that the marriage could not endure while her life was consecrated to motion pictures. He did not stop loving her. He stopped expressing his love. He hoped that a miracle would happen, that maybe she would become pregnant, that maybe they would move to San Francisco and live peacefully. Several times she said that she would be examined by her gynecologist, Dr. Leon Krohn, and that she would have an operation so she could have children, but he distrusted her promises now. He found that she said whatever she thought would please him in a certain mood and then when her mood changed forgot the promises. He had taken, more and more, to staying out nights with his friends, playing poker or billiards or talking about football and baseball. In the daytime, he played golf at the Riverside Country Club or went fishing. He had nothing to say to her that he had not said to her before. She could say nothing to him. She had to change her life. She had to live the way he wanted her to live or leave him.

Without even a day of rest, she went directly from *No Business* to the set of *Itch*. And Natasha Lytess went with her. "Without Natasha," Wilder told me, "there would be nothing. Natasha stays up with her all night and gives her some conception of the scene. They discuss the scene and characters and the meaning of the scene. To me, Natasha is an ally—not an enemy."

Wilder, a trim, muscular energetic gentleman, is one of the great creative personalities in films today. A former screenwriter himself, he still actively collaborates on every screenplay he directs. He has a sympathetic, though strong, personality which brings out the best in actors. He has a powerful sense of the camera and what it can do. He has a genius for sophisticated comedy. His work scintillates with wit, subtle touches of characterization, and, above all, a rapidity of timing and a dexterity in cutting that make his motion pictures really move. As a person, he is worldly, even cynical, and nothing has been known to upset his equilibrium. He is famous for working "under the gun," for being only a page of script ahead of the shooting. He works best in crises. He was the ideal director for Marilyn at this juncture of her career. He spoke serenely to her as if he didn't have a worry in his head, and his air of serenity gave her comfort.

"That was nice the way you did it, Marilyn," he'd say, after a take, "but I think you can do it better. Shall we try it again?"

She was being the frightened little bird, and he accepted her as that and held her in the palm of his hand and treated her as if she might break in two if he were not careful. Aware of his competence, she trusted him completely. He didn't find fault with her or rant at her. He didn't want to know why she came late. Or why she couldn't remember lines. Wilder said, "She can't remember a line. She never hits the groove the first time. I've directed many pictures, and when you say 'Action' an actor will do something—anything—even if it's the wrong thing, it's instinctive with an actor to do this. Not Marilyn. It takes her twenty seconds to say a line or make a move. Maybe it's a psychological hurdle. I've noticed that if she gets past the first two or three lines, sometimes, she can go on and on, even if it's a long speech. She doesn't seem to get tired. She'll do take after take. She poops out the other actors. But Marilyn blooms as the day goes on, and she's at her best in the late afternoon when the other actors are dropping like flies."

Wilder had decided to shoot the exterior shots of *Seven Year Itch* on location in Manhattan. Marilyn was scheduled to take a sleeper plane to New York on September 9. She wasn't surprised when Di Maggio said he wasn't going with her if Natasha Lytess was going.

"Either she goes or I go," he said.

He didn't go.

She arrived at Idlewild at a quarter after eight in the morning. Even at this ungodly hour, hordes of her fans were there to welcome her. All flights at the airport were disrupted for an hour because every mechanic crowded up for a close look at her. Whatever emotional burdens she may have been bearing, she had never looked more ravishing than she did that morning in a beige-colored knit wool dress that clung to her curves and a white fox stole draped around her shoulders. She beheld the swarms of admirers who had broken through the barrier and surrounded the plane. She gaped at the numerous newspaper and newsreel photographers.

She batted her eyelashes. She looked naïvely out of her large blue-gray eyes. She acted as if it were all a big surprise to her. "I just can't understand what all the fuss is about," she said. "I just can't understand why so many people are here so early in the morning." She wasn't wearing stockings. "I hardly ever wear stockings," she said, "but I meant to put on some this morning. We got here so early I didn't have time."

Although nobody knew this at the time, not even her husband, she had come to New York not only to do the location sequences for *Seven Year Itch*. She had become convinced that she would not be able to work out her salvation as long as she lived in Beverly Hills. She was going to sever her connections with her studio. She was going to cut herself off from Hollywood and the Hollywood colony. She was going to live in New York from now on. During the six days that she was in New York, she had several secret conferences with Milton Greene and his lawyer, Frank Delaney. Greene, who had planned nothing more earth-shaking than a book of photographs of Marilyn with appropriate captions, was overwhelmed with pleasure when she told him that she was prepared to break from Hollywood and go into partnership with him. He would be the producer of her films from now on. She trusted his judgment. She admired his conceptions. He was a genius. But at the moment she was a little strapped for cash. Did he think he could—well—finance her during the interim period? Did he? Visions of fame and riches danced in his head. Yes, he would resign from his $50,000-a-year position at *Look* Magazine. He would pledge his life, his fortune, his sacred honor to the greater glory of Marilyn Monroe. Delaney suggested that a corporation be formed, Marilyn Monroe Productions Incorporated, and that Marilyn sign a contract with Marilyn Monroe Productions. The studio would have to negotiate with Monroe Productions if they wanted the services of Monroe. Delaney believed she had two valid grounds for breaking the old contract. During the period when the studio had been pleading with Marilyn to return to work and to play in *No Business Like Show Business,* one of the executives had written her a letter—this was at a time when she could not be reached on the telephone—and had made a vague promise that if she came back to work they would negotiate a new contract with her. All this was couched in insubstantial terms, but Delaney believed it gave Marilyn a reason to claim legally that the studio had, in effect, abandoned the old contract.

Delaney also suggested, after a long study of the old contract, that it was morally and legally untenable, that it was in effect a "slave contract," because it compelled her to work in any movie that the studio chose to put her in. They had proposed, as her next vehicle, *The Revolt of Mamie Stover,* in which she was to play a prostitute in Honolulu during World War II. Another script for her was *The Girl in the Red Velvet Swing,* in which she was to play Evelyn Nesbit, the mistress of Stanford White and the bride of Harry Thaw. These were degrading roles to play, Delaney said. "Human beings should not be compelled to do things that lower their dignity as human beings," he told Marilyn. "Every person has a basic right to stay decent."

It was agreed that Delaney would begin drawing up the corporation papers of Marilyn Monroe Productions, Inc., but that no formal steps would be taken until after the completion of *Seven Year Itch.*

During the day, she did the exterior sequences, in one of which she was seen looking out of a window of a brownstone house in the East 60's. She had a new stand-in, a luscious blonde, Gloria Mosolino, who had a figure and a face not unlike Marilyn's. Miss Mosolino reported that Marilyn was very considerate of her at all times and even said she would try to do her scenes faster so that Gloria wouldn't have to tire herself out holding certain monotonous positions. Miss Mosolino has since gone on to higher things. She married the novelist James Jones.

In one sequence of *Seven Year Itch* Tom Ewell is strolling up Lexington Avenue with Marilyn. They have just seen the movie *Creature from the Black Lagoon*. It is a hot August night. To cool herself, Marilyn stands over a subway grating. A blast of wind from below sends her skirts flying high. Wilder shot the scene in front of the Trans-Lux Theatre on Lexington Avenue at 2:30 A.M., when the street is normally deserted. But the news leaked out, and a mob of 4,000 was milling around. At one point during the shooting, a fire broke out down the street, and the fire engines, trying to get through, added the scream of their sirens to the general pandemonium. A large electric fan was placed under the grating to provide the wind. Marilyn worked four hours on this scene of the flying skirts, and the crowd roared every time she did another retake. Joe Di Maggio was in the crowd. He had come to New York the day before. He had been sitting with Walter Winchell in Toots Shor's and Winchell said why didn't they walk over and watch the scene. Now Joe stood on the outskirts of the crowd looking grim and tight-lipped. For him this was the extremest humiliation of his marriage. "I shall never forget the look of death on Joe's face," Wilder says. A reporter asked Joe what he thought of all this.

He curtly snapped, "No comment."

An editorial in the Catholic weekly *America,* headed "New York's Disgrace," commented on the episode: "It is hypocrisy for the secular press to deplore adolescent sex crimes and still publish such pictures. It is also hypocrisy for the American public to deplore adolescent sex crimes and still want to see such pictures published. There is more than one way to subvert free society. Even the *Daily Worker* doesn't publish sexy pictures which help erode the moral basis of American democracy. . . . As for Miss Monroe's husband, Joe di Maggio, who married her outside the church, it was pitiful to have the former Yankee clipper among the ogling onlookers. . . . Let's hope they cut it [the skirt scene] before the film appears. Otherwise they are looking for trouble."

Subversion and immorality—and hypocrisy—were rampant in the New York City press during the ten days Marilyn was shooting. No such amount of space had ever been given so continuously to any actress in the history of local journalism. Four-column photographs, long feature articles, news stories, interviews, items in the gossip columns were published in the nation's most sophisticated newspapers day after day. New York City had become as excited as a small town which had never before been visited by a movie star. Marilyn set the town on its ear in a way it had never been set on its ear before. The New York *Herald Tribune,* a hitherto respectable bulwark of conservative philosophy and the Republican party, the organ of Walter Lippmann and David Lawrence, gave her a front-page story with photographs every day for five consecutive days! Outside the Hampshire House, where she and Joe were staying, dozens of photographers waited patiently until she emerged. Her every move was dogged by hordes of crazed movie fans, bug-eyed young men and women who came from the outlying boroughs, from the suburbs, from New Jersey and Connecticut. Some of them had hitchhiked hundreds of miles. It was not easy to elude them for the surreptitious conferences with Greene and Delaney.

She was endlessly queried about the rumors that her marriage was breaking up. Was it true, for instance, that Joe was often away from home playing poker with his cronies? "Joe does all his poker playing at home," she retorted. "He has no gypsy in him that would cause him to stay away nights. It's difficult enough to get him out of the house. He likes to putter around, take an occasional dip in the pool, and just lounge in a big easy chair."

She continued to believe that Joe would go along with her plans, would accept her destiny as an actress, would make her the focal point of his life, would accept a subservient position in the marriage because he was so wildly in love with her. They went out on the town in the evenings, and they looked to observers like a loving couple. There is a photograph of them in the Stork Club, Marilyn smiling, and Joe also smiling, a little more forced and strained, but smiling all the same. Almost up to the very day of their final rupture, she persisted in telling everybody that there was no trouble between them. She told it to her most trusted confidants among the columnists, to Earl Wilson, to Sidney Skolsky, to Louella Parsons. Miss Parsons was shocked at Marilyn's perfidy when the separation occurred. Never before had she been so blandly deceived by a seemingly naïve motion-picture personality, for there was no woman in Hollywood who was as clever and all-knowing as Louella, no woman who knew where so many bodies were buried and the exact locations of all the closets containing skeletons. It was almost enough to shake Louella Parsons' self-assurance.

"I must admit," she wrote, "that this comes as a complete surprise to me, because three weeks ago Marilyn said that all the rumors that she and Joe were battling were untrue. I wrote a story and quoted her on this. Then, when she and Joe were in New York while she made *Seven Year Itch*, they appeared together at El Morocco, the Stork Club, and other night clubs and were apparently very much in love. This, of course, could have been a cover-up." Louella discovered, as many persons had discovered before her and after her, that the brain of Marilyn Monroe is a beautifully engineered instrument of self-preservation.

She was supposed to take a plane back to Los Angeles on September 12. She was delayed two days by storms and a hurricane, and finally left on September 15. Natasha Lytess returned by another plane. This time Marilyn's companion on the flight was her husband. She slept during most of the trip. She liked sleeping on planes.

Back home she continued to work in the studio by day and to try to come to an agreement with Joe at night. She could not sleep. Neighbors saw her walking the streets, alone, at one in the morning, distraught and weeping. She had made her decision and chosen her way of life, and it was a way of life into which Joe told her he could not fit. She would have to decide whether she wanted to be Mrs. Di Maggio or Marilyn Monroe. She couldn't have it both ways, he told her. She lived inside of a perpetual tornado of publicity, and he couldn't stand it any longer. He knew she wasn't being unfaithful to him with other men. He knew that her singing coach, Hal Schaefer, for instance, was not a womanizer. But people suspected things. People made fun of Joe, and he didn't like it. When Schaefer had gotten sick in July and had been taken to the West Los Angeles Hospital after a breakdown at the studio, Marilyn had gone to see him every day. Sure—Joe knew it was friendship, but the world didn't. And he didn't want to live that way for the rest of his life.

Marilyn decided there was no truth in the well-known song "Happiness Is Just a Thing Called Joe."

On Friday, October 1, 1954, Joe had to go to New York to cover a world-series game for a newspaper syndicate. Before he left, they came to the decision—divorce. She called Jerry Giesler, Hollywood's famous lawyer, and asked him to draw up the papers. On Monday morning she telephoned Billy Wilder, at 8:00 A.M. She was sobbing and hysterical.

"I—Mr. Wilder—I can't come to work today," she said.

"What is it, Marilyn?" he asked. "Are you all right?"

"Joe and I have—Joe and I—J-J-Joe and I are going—" Then she broke down completely.

"I can't hear you," Wilder said.

"J-Joe and I are going to get a d-d-divorce, Mr. Wilder," she said.

Wilder communicated with Harry Brand. Brand got in touch with Giesler. Giesler confirmed the news. Brand gave the word to the columnists and the wire services. The studio said that the reason for the divorce was "incompatibility resulting from the conflicting demands of their careers." The Associated Press reported "the news hit Hollywood like an A bomb." Oscar Levant said it proved no man could be a success in two national pastimes. Giesler and Brand rushed over to the love nest at 508 N. Palm Drive. By ten o'clock a mass of reporters and photographers were trying to storm the house. Nobody was allowed to enter. Mary Karger, the sister of Marilyn's former friend Fred Karger, was comforting Marilyn upstairs in the big double bed. Joe was living downstairs, sleeping on the couch on the sun porch with the folding table and the television set. "The battling lovebirds," cracked a Hollywood wit, "were cooped up in the same little cage." Other cynics wondered why Marilyn had to employ the movie colony's famous criminal lawyer to handle a simple divorce case. Giesler was usually hired by movie stars when they were accused of murder, statutory rape, unmarried paternity, and marihuana smoking. He rarely handled anything so prosaic as a divorce. Did Marilyn know that Giesler made headlines and did she always deliberately play for headlines? At half past two that Monday, Brand and Giesler finally emerged from the love nest, looking considerably shaken. They were immediately set upon by the reporters. Brand said, "Marilyn Monroe will hold a press conference on Wednesday at eleven in Mr. Giesler's office."

But they wanted to interview her right now.

"She can't see anybody today," Giesler said. "She is sick. She is in bed right now. She is very sick. Joe has nothing to say. Yes, he is in the house. Miss Monroe is not talking to anybody. She is very sick. We're going to file a divorce complaint in Santa Monica, Superior Court, tomorrow. Mental cruelty. I have spoken with both parties and come to the conclusion that they can't get together. They have talked it over and have reached a friendly understanding. We are definitely going ahead with the divorce. It doesn't look to me like there is any chance of a reconciliation. She will not sue for alimony. There will be no property settlement."

On Tuesday, Helen Kirkpatrick, Giesler's secretary, came to the house, bearing the complaint. *The defendant caused her grievous mental suffering and anguish, all of which acts and conduct were without fault of the plaintiff. . . .* The secretary went up to the master bedroom. There, under several layers of quilts, lay Marilyn, wan, ravaged by a severe cold, physical exhaustion, and emotional trauma. Miss Kirkpatrick handed her the paper. She signed it. Then Miss Kirkpatrick took it downstairs to Joe. He signed it.

The Wednesday press conference was canceled, but that morning a scene took place as dramatic as any that was ever invented for the most sentimental of motion pictures. In front of the house, scores of reporters and photographers milled about, pacing the sidewalk, trampling the lawn and the flowers, waiting for Marilyn to come out so that they could take an action shot of her. Some of the newspapermen circled the house to make sure their quarry wouldn't escape from the rear. Photographers were shooting pictures of the two black Cadillacs of Mr. and Mrs. Di Maggio, exterior views of the house, the windows of the bedroom, the sun porch, the front of the house. At ten-twenty, a man emerged, carrying two leather suitcases and a bag of gold-handled golf clubs. He told the reporters his name was Reno Barsocchini. He unlocked the trunk compartment of Joe's car and put the suitcases and clubs in it. A few minutes later Joe Di Maggio appeared, his forehead creased with frowns, his eyes bloodshot, his jaw clenched. He said "Hi ya," to the reporters.

"Where are you going?" one of them asked.

"I'm driving to San Francisco."

"Is that going to be your home?"

"That is my home and always has been."

"Are you coming back?"

He turned around and looked at the house.

"No," he said, "I'll never be back."

An hour later, the front door opened and Giesler came out with Marilyn on his arm. Giesler's face was puffy. Marilyn looked as if she were going to a funeral and she was, in fact—attending the death of a dream. She was all in black—black wool-jersey dress and black wool coat. Her eyes were red from crying. She tried to control herself.

The reporters sprang.

"Did Joe say good-bye?"

"I'm sorry," she said, her voice almost inaudible.

"What about Hal Schaefer?"

"I'm sorry," she said again.

Giesler took her by the arm and conducted her to her Cadillac. He told the reporters, "Can't you see she's upset? She and Joe couldn't get along. That's all there is to it! Any other facts will be brought out at the proper time and the proper place."

In the car, she could hold back no longer. Her body was racked with sobs. Tears flowed down her cheeks. Giesler drove her to the studio. Wilder sent her home.

Wilder told the reporters, "She couldn't work today. She has a comedy part. She couldn't see any comedy in life today."

Three weeks later, Marilyn Monroe appeared before Superior Court Judge Orlando H. Rhodes. She looked considerably more chic than she had two weeks before. She was dressed in a black silk cocktail dress with a low-cut scoop collar. But she began to cry when she took the stand to testify under the guidance of attorney Giesler. She said: "I hoped to have out of my marriage love, warmth, affection, and understanding. But the relationship turned out to be one of coldness and indifference. . . ." Fifteen minutes later she was granted an interlocutory divorce on the grounds of mental cruelty.

About six months later, during an interview with Marilyn, I asked her why she really divorced Di Maggio.

She replied: "For the reasons I gave in court. I know a lot of women, when they're getting a divorce they put out reasons which are not the true reasons. But I said the truth. He didn't talk to me. He was cold. He was indifferent to me as a human being and an artist. He didn't want me to have friends of my own. He didn't want me to do my work. He really watched television instead of talking to me. So what I said in my testimony was really so."

22 The Crisis

Between October and December, 1954, Marilyn Monroe went through a personal crisis so threatening and so incapable of solution by any conventional means that she found it necessary to wrench herself out, by the very roots as it were, from the hothouse garden in which she was blooming so luxuriantly. She transplanted herself into a different earth. She cultivated that earth and nourished herself in a completely new style. Now, other actresses had faced great crises in their lives and careers—the crisis, after all, is a constant in the lives of all who live by the emotional gun—but in the annals of Hollywood no actress ever confronted a crisis with a response at once so violent, so rash, and so revolutionary. Her response was a trial at reconstructing all—root, branch, leaves, flower.

Since her childhood there had been in her a war between her impulses and those standards of behavior she had been taught were proper. The contradictions between the two sharpened with her notoriety as the *Monroe Desnuda* and her establishment as the great sexual symbol. Her efforts—those rationalizations that one's ego makes to placate one's conscience—to bridge this gap between her desires and her moral code became more urgent and failed more conspicuously.

It was true she had become a motion-picture star, but she was, alas, not the motion-picture star of the Mary Pickford fantasy. She was a "great sinner"—even as a movie star. Most of her foster mothers had reared her in the traditional Christian precepts. She had been taught to revere the home, marriage, and motherhood. Several of her moral guides had firmly implanted in her the idea that pleasure is evil and man is by nature a vile sinner. The concepts of Christian Science, to which she was exposed later, while encouraging her to express herself, also intensified her sense of guilt. Was she not constantly suffering from "beliefs" in nausea, vomiting, laryngitis, virus infections, hives, and sick headaches? Did not this prove she was full of error and sin, for otherwise she would not have "believed" she was sick when she was not sick?

These were the attitudes to which her conscience and her consciousness paid respect. But her dark impulses opposed these attitudes. The other Monroe was a hot-blooded animal. She wanted to injure others for the injuries the world had done to her during her early years, beginning with her illegitimacy. This Monroe gloried in her appetites. She despised people. She wanted to flaunt her naked body and march victoriously over "prostrate forms." "I used to dream," she once wrote, "I was standing up in church without any clothes on, and all the people there were lying at my feet on the floor of the church and I walked naked with a sense of freedom over their prostrate forms, being careful not to step on anyone."

She had formerly achieved a working adjustment with the discrepancy between her impulses and her values by developing the image of herself as the abused orphan waif, the hungry innocent victim of society. She had posed for the naked calendar because she had been hungry and homeless. She had exploited her secondary sexual appurtenances because Zanuck made her do it for publicity and the box office. And how could that Special Services officer be so insensitive as not to realize that "Do It Again" was a sentimental ballad?

But this time, in the twenty-eighth year of her age, the clash could not be resolved with the familiar verbal legerdemain. She had failed, and failed conspicuously and publicly, to live up to her moral standards. The vulgarity of *River of No Return* and *No Business Like Show Business* was written large for all to see. Her skirt-blowing exhibition on New York's sidewalks had disgusted the right-thinking members of the community.

The reviews of *No Business Like Show Business* were disastrous. Marilyn was criticized for cheapness and bad taste. Hedda Hopper and Ed Sullivan wrote bitter columns lashing out at her. "Miss Monroe," wrote Sullivan, "has just about worn the welcome off this observer's mat. . . . One of them [her numbers], 'Heat Wave,' frankly is dirty, particularly unpleasant in a script which features a young priest. . . . 'Heat Wave' is easily one of the most flagrant violations of good taste this observer has ever witnessed."

And now the fan mail was turning against her.

"You're a disgrace to your own sex."

"Marilyn Monroe sickens me and even my children. She was never more offensive than in *No Business Like Show Business*. Why did they put her in it?"

"Why did you let Monroe do those sexy wrigglings? It spoiled the picture. Are you producers crazy?"

"I and all the members of my family will never see another Marilyn Monroe picture after seeing her disgusting exhibition in *No Business Like Show Business*."

Marilyn craved the approval of the "good people" more than that of the New York critics—although the New York critics also had deplored her mediocre performance in this film. But it was the "respectables" she really cared about, for they represented Grace Goddard and Ana Lower; they were the decent small-town souls of her Los Angeles upbringing.

This time she couldn't blame her troubles on Zanuck or the Los Angeles Orphans Home. It was she who had insisted that Jack Cole be brought in to choreograph her "Heat Wave" routine. It was she who had been delighted to be photographed with skirt high on Lexington Avenue. As an actress, she could tell herself that *Seven Year Itch* was, while not the epitome of sound Christian philosophy, at least in a nobler category of immorality than *River of No Return*, since it was conceived and photographed with artistry and wit. But the person she was had existed in her long before the actress. Oscar Wilde's theories of the essential amorality of all art hardly suited the small-town morality of America's heartland.

Now, it is possible that Marilyn could have rooted out her morality and become a hedonist, relishing her status as a sex symbol, tasting material luxuries, basking in the mob's adulation, changing husbands, enjoying clandestine romances. Or, she could have forsaken it all for the simple life of Mrs. Di Maggio. Or, she could have dedicated herself to the acting art, becoming a votary of experimental cinema and the avant-garde theatre.

But she wanted everything. She wanted to be righteous and she wanted to be a sex symbol. She wanted to be admired for her nakedness and respected for her seriousness. She wanted to be a successful movie star and she wanted to be a good wife. She still believed in the importance of being married. The breakup of her second marriage had been a severe blow to her self-esteem. She could blame the first marriage on her ignorance, but she couldn't pardon the second failure.

Norma Jean Baker had failed to become the woman that Ana Lower would have respected.

How could she devise a *modus vivendi* by means of which she could remain the idealist, explain her movie failures, justify her divorce, satisfy her dark impulses, punish her Hollywood enemies, and make a noise in the world? For all of us must come to terms with ourselves before we can live with others.

Let us now return to October 7, 1954, and follow Marilyn's devious twists and turns as she seeks a way out of her dilemma. The day after the dramatic separation from Joe, she went back to work. She arrived at the studio at 7:00 A.M., with a punctuality that stunned Wilder. He was also struck by her quick recovery. Her voice was clear, her eyes were calm, her work proceeded with professional alacrity. She was ready for the first take by nine-forty. Wilder was shooting the second encounter of Marilyn and Tom Ewell. Ewell has been sitting out on his garden terrace drinking raspberry soda on a hot night. A heavy iron pot from above falls near his head. He looks upward. There is Marilyn, peering over a row of plants. It was she who had knocked over a tomato plant. Ewell invites her down to his air-conditioned flat for a drink.

She knew her lines cold. She grasped Wilder's suggestions and followed them flawlessly. Each segment of the sequence was printed on the first or second take, instead of the usual dozen or more it required to get a good performance from Marilyn.

Natasha Lytess beamed. Natasha had not had any more use for Joe Di Maggio than the outfielder had had for her. Natasha believed that Marilyn's difficulties on the set were caused by the outrageous demands of her husband. Imagine a man wanting his wife home for dinner or wanting to spend the evening with her or wanting to go to bed with her at a reasonable hour! Miss Lytess said, "Now she does everything better. She concentrates better. She remembers lines better. She's much easier to work with. She knows what I'm talking about. Sometimes now with one word, I will make her know what Mr. Wilder wants from her."

Seven Year Itch finished shooting on Friday, November 5. It had taken three weeks longer to complete than had originally been estimated. It ran $150,000 over the budget. But the executives at 20th and co-producer Charles Feldman knew it was a superb comedy. Marilyn Monroe projected every nuance of her unique blend of naïveté and sexuality. Unlike even her best work in such previous films as *How to Marry a Millionaire,* her characterization in *Seven Year Itch* was not flawed by inconsistencies and lapses from character. Her work in *Seven Year Itch* was delicate, fine-spun, amusing, and consistently in harmony with the part she, Wilder, and writer George Axelrod had conceived. By means of his patience and his *Mittel*-European charm, Wilder had teased a fabulous performance out of her.

How she looked on the screen! Wilder thought. Who else could give you such pleasure as she, just by sitting in an armchair with her legs up on an air conditioner? Who could look at an actor the way Marilyn looked at Ewell? She walked right off the screen and into the spectator's mind, and the spectator couldn't get her out.

For her part, Marilyn was so delighted by Wilder's consideration and finesse, especially in the last weeks of shooting, that she suddenly lost interest in her own production company. Her phone talks with Greene became ambiguous and cold. She would set a date for her return to New York. Then she would postpone the flight. Was she contemplating the possibility of continuing her career with 20th Century-Fox?

And why shouldn't she remain in Hollywood? On November 1, she rented an expensive duplex apartment, with a large bedroom on the upstairs level, in a modern building at De Longpre and Harper avenues, near the Sunset Strip. Here she moved her books and records, *objets d'art,* her hair dryer and her 26 bottles of Chanel #5, her old white grand piano and her large low bed, her photographs of Eleanora Duse and Abraham Lincoln.

Yes, she would settle down here forever. Hollywood wasn't really a chamber of horrors. Why, everybody was so nice to her. It was a real nice friendly town. Lew Schreiber was dancing attendance on her and telling her all about the nice friendly new contract the studio was drawing up for her, even though they didn't *have* to do it by law. She'd get a lot of money, like $50,000 a picture, maybe more. And Hugh French, her agent from Famous Artists Agency, told her she was the greatest of all time in *Seven Year Itch,* and Charlie Feldman, also of her agency, besides being her co-producer, was crazy about her. And Nunnally Johnson, such a nice friendly producer he was, was writing a screenplay just for her, a vehicle. Although a comedy, it would be a very refined and high-class picture. It would be called *How to Be Very Very Popular.* Oh, everything was coming into focus now. Yes, Natasha had been so right. It *had* been Di Maggio who was to blame after all. A crude chap, really, no feeling for her fine-grained sensibility.

Ah, one felt so free now, strolling again on Sunset Boulevard in the early evenings, dropping into the Schwabadero, dipping into the fan books, having a malted at the fountain, gossiping with Sidney Skolsky. How absurd to leave her dear friends and appreciative colleagues for a stranger, this man Greene, with his wild ideas about producing plays and television shows and movies and buying novels! No, this was where she belonged, in Hollywood. And why shouldn't she come out of her shell and have a good time now that she was free. She would play the gay divorcee. How exciting. . . .

On Saturday night, the day after *Seven Year Itch* was completed, Feldman played host to a soiree in honor of Marilyn Monroe at Romanoff's. A late supper, steak Chateaubriand, champagne, a band for dancing—and look who had come to pay tribute to La Monroe: a roster of the leading personalities in the film colony, powerful producers like Jack Warner, Sam Goldwyn, Leland Hayward and— could it really be he?—Darryl Francis Zanuck. Yes it was indeed Zanuck paying homage to little Norma Jean Baker. Well, who knows, maybe he was a decent chap after all, Mr. Zanuck. Why did she ever let those embittered old European failures, Michael Chekhov and Natasha Lytess, talk her into disliking Darryl Zanuck? And movie stars had come to *her* party—Jimmy Stewart, Claudette Colbert, Gary Cooper, Doris Day, William Holden, Susan Hayward, Humphrey Bogart, and the actor who was known, even to other actors, as "the king"—the incomparable Clark Gable. Oh, Marilyn was in fine fettle that night. Gone, for the moment, was the shy, stammering, socially insecure Marilyn that movie people had seen holding up the wall at other parties. She was dressed in good taste in a subtle black tulle gown. Her breasts were not bared, and her *derrière* was on its good behavior. Even Joan Crawford would have been proud of her that night, but Miss Crawford hadn't been invited.

Marilyn that evening actually made small talk with ease and wit. When George Axelrod came over and complimented her on the magical quality of her performance, she said, "Oh, it's due to Billy Wilder. He's a wonderful director. I want him to direct me again. But he's doing the Lindbergh story next. And he won't let me play Lindbergh."

And she danced with Gable! They danced two dances, holding each other close and seemingly absorbed in conversation. The columnists had them falling madly in love. Actually the conversation went something like this.

"I've always admired you and wanted to be in a picture with you," Marilyn said.

And Gable replied, "I screened *Gentlemen Prefer Blondes* six months ago. First time I ever saw you. You sure have the magic. I'd like to do a picture with you."

"I'd like to do a picture with you, Mr. Gable."

"Call me Clark."

"Well, I would, really I would, Clark."

"Who would we get to direct? Oh, I'm sorry—I didn't mean to step on your feet, Marilyn."

"How about Billy Wilder? It didn't hurt in the least little bit, Clark."

"He's all tied up, Marilyn. He's doing the Lindbergh picture."

"Oh, I remember now. I was just telling George that—"

"George who?"

"Axelrod, you know. George Axelrod. The writer. Don't you find writers are interesting people, Mr. Gable, I mean Clark?"

"Yeah, they're all right if you like writers."

"That's true."

"You were saying, Marilyn?"

"Was I?"

"Well anyway it would be a nice idea, I mean if we found the right story."

"That's true."

The following day, Sunday, Marilyn posed with Tom Ewell for publicity stills. In the afternoon Joe Di Maggio, who, according to her statements in Superior Court not three weeks earlier, had visited great mental cruelty upon her, picked her up at the studio and drove her to Cedars of Lebanon Hospital. On Monday morning, she was to undergo a "gynecological operation of a minor corrective nature." It was hoped the operation would alleviate her agonizing menstrual pains and make it possible for her to have children. Marilyn told a "friend" who told someone else who told Louella Parsons who told her readers that "she's glad the divorce won't be final for a year because it leaves the door wide open should she change her mind about a reconciliation." Marilyn's indecision lasted a long time, even after Arthur Miller began his courtship. For some seven months, she kept Di Maggio dangling between hope and despair.

The operation was successful.

She remained in the hospital until Friday. Joe paced the hospital corridors all day. By Saturday, she had rallied and was her gay self again. She dined with Joe and Dominic Di Maggio at the Villa Capri. Joe was kind and attentive, and Marilyn wondered if she hadn't been an impulsive fool.

Meanwhile, back in New York, Milton Greene got the uneasy feeling that she was slipping away. His lawyers, Frank Delaney and Irving Stein, told him that if he didn't get to Marilyn and get to her fast, she might succumb to the studio pressure and her agents' blandishments. Lest Marilyn Monroe Productions go up in smoke, Greene hurried to Los Angeles on November 16. He checked into the Beverly Hills Hotel and rang up Marilyn right away. She told him to come on over to her new apartment. She was in lounging pajamas. She looked awfully pale. Her maid served coffee and cookies. Greene flipped open his attaché case and spread out the imposing papers on a table.

Aside from being a gifted camera artist, Greene has a large imagination, courage, and a sound sense of business. He had believed the things Marilyn told him about her artistic yearnings. He believed in her great talents. He now began explaining, in specific detail, the advantages to her of the corporation. Capital gains. Millions of dollars in profit. The power to choose her own stories, her own directors, her own supporting casts.

As he spoke, her mood swerved sharply. Suddenly, the dramatic possibilities became vivid all over again. She visualized herself as another President Monroe—wasn't she his descendant, after all?

She saw herself barking orders to directors and screenwriters. Signing checks. Making Zanuck grovel in the dust before her. Making everybody in the movie colony bow respectfully to her. Making all those who, over the years, had sneered at her, eat their scorn. She would show them all she was another Garbo. She would go to New York and study hard. With Lee Strasberg. She would revolt against this shabby business of making sordid sexy movies for dirty dollars. She would worship Art. In Marilyn's philosophy, everything is felt in terms of superlatives. Reality is too dull. Even the loveliest of calla lilies can stand a slight gilding. Would not freedom and her own company settle the conflict between her high morals and her "sinful" desires? She would be the underdog fighting for independence against a heartless corporation which wanted to strangle her artistically. By means of the magical verbal formula of Artistic Consecration and Proletarian Rebellion, she would reconcile the anxiety-provoking discrepancy between her ideals and her actions.

How could she subsist? "But, Milton," she said, "s'pose Twentieth is right. S'pose we can't break the contract."

"We're not breaking a contract, Marilyn. They broke it when they wrote you that letter. Don't you remember what Delaney said? Even if they didn't write you that letter, they can't hold you to a slave contract."

"Maybe he's wrong. Then I won't work. For years."

"Why not?"

"The studio won't let me, not until the contract is used up."

Greene brandished his pipe in the air. "All right, Marilyn, let's assume the studio is right. Let's go on the basis the worst comes to the worst. Let's say you don't work for three and a half years."

"I'll starve to death. They'll throw me out of my room."

"Like hell they will," he said. He arose and came to her. "I will take care of you for three and a half years. I will support you. I will pay all your bills. I will put it in writing in our agreement. You will live better than you are living now. I will pay for everything. You won't have to worry. I'll buy your clothes. I'll put you up in the best hotel. Don't worry. I'll pay your beauty bills, your psychoanalyst's bills—"

"I stopped going, Milton."

"Well, you should start. We'll get you the best analyst in New York. You can't separate yourself as an artist from yourself as a human being. The happier you are as a person, the finer you will be as an artist."

Greene portrayed a fine future for Marilyn Monroe Productions. He planned to invite other movie stars into the corporation. He dreamed of a combination of creative personalities, like the original set-up of United Artists, which had been formed by Mary Pickford, Douglas Fairbanks, Charles Chaplin, and D. W. Griffith in 1919.

Greene was anxious to return to New York with his president and start firing the opening guns of the battle of Monroe against 20th Century-Fox. It is possible that, at this stage, Marilyn was still playing with the idea as a fantasy for "kicks." She didn't expect it to lead to a reorganization of her personality and her mode of living. No human being, no matter how wretched, likes basic changes in his life pattern. But Marilyn's troubles were deeply rooted, and the roots spread out into many areas of her personality. Besides the moral dilemma just described, there was a genuine resentment against the way she had been exploited. She wanted to be her own woman. Not the studio's woman. She wanted, or at least some part of her wanted, what Simone de Beauvoir calls her "autonomy" as a human being.

And let us not entirely discount her artistic drive. Beneath her affectations was a real instinct for dramatic expression. Originally, acting had been a weapon of power. But she had grown. She was open to ideas. Through her wide reading and the influences of Actors' Lab and Chekhov, she now saw movies as not merely the opium of the people. Cinema was one of the great art forms capable of portraying the human condition through mobile images. She wanted to be an artist as well as a sexpot. And she wanted to be a great many things as well as an artist. Her soul was a tumult of innumerable desires, swaying her at the same time.

She didn't rush headlong to New York with Greene. She delayed, postponed, procrastinated, as she always did when a crucial decision had to be made. To pass the time of procrastination pleasantly, she continued the Hollywood gaiety. Greene was pressed into service as her escort when she did the town. Columnists printed romantic innuendos about the "handsome Milton Green." (Hollywood didn't even know the correct spelling of his name.) Marilyn went dancing at Ciro's and the Mocambo. She danced at the Crescendo with

Jacques Sernas. Sernas, a Baltic Slav, who had become a French citizen, was Hollywood's latest import. He was being groomed for stardom at Warner's. He was known as the "libidinous Lithuanian." Sernas never got very far either with Marilyn or with Warner's. Marilyn was linked with Mel Torme, Marlon Brando, and Sammy Davis, Jr. She was linked with every unmarried Hollywood actor, including a homosexual or two. The real news—that she was secretly planning one of the most spectacular revolts in the history of movies—was a well-kept secret.

Greene recalls taking Marilyn to a party given by Clifton Webb. Zanuck was among the guests. Instead of the ogre he'd expected to meet from Marilyn's description, Greene found Zanuck a friendly, intelligent, amiable person. Zanuck expressed admiration for Greene's photography and wanted to know if he were available to do some special art work for 20th.

"I felt bad," Greene says. "He was being nice to me, not realizing I was going into partnership with his biggest star. I couldn't say anything to him. We hadn't signed the papers yet. Later, some of the people at the party got up and sang and entertained, and somebody asked Marilyn to sing, and she sang some Irving Berlin numbers. She was great. She knocked everybody at the party out. Marilyn can do everything. Sing, dance, play comedy, play drama. People were whispering it was a 'New Marilyn.' I was told it was the first time she had ever sung at a party. They didn't know why suddenly she had so much confidence. I knew why, of course. She wasn't afraid of them any more."

What finally propelled Marilyn into making the break was the nationwide release of *No Business Like Show Business* on December 15. The public obloquy precipitated the severest emotional crisis in her life. Again the whirligig turned. She was plunged into remorse and self-hatred. Marilyn rarely conceives of experience in any but the most extreme dimensions. Now she was the all-time failure. She was a sinful slut, the great sinner. Desperate measures had to be taken.

Greene picked her up late one night and they drove to the International Airport.

"You don't think anybody will recognize me?" she whispered to Greene.

"No," he said.

She was in a black wig, dark glasses, and a plain dress.

"I'm going under the name Zelda Zonk," she said, seriously. She was now playing the heroine in a self-invented cloak-and-dagger Cinemascope movie.

Miss Zonk and Mr. Greene arrived in New York unheralded. Mrs. Greene met them at Idlewild. Mrs. Greene, a pert young woman with a turned-up nose and a pony tail, looks even younger than her young-looking husband. A descendant of an old Spanish family, she had been a model. She is a vivacious person, and she and Marilyn took to each other at once.

"We became close and intimate, like two girls rooming together in a dormitory at college," Mrs. Greene says. "We shared girl secrets. We giggled together over crazy things. I thought of her as a friend, a real friend, and she told me I was the only friend she had ever had in her whole life, her best friend, which was rather flattering, I must say. All the time she'd say how she idolized Milton and how good I should feel to be married to him. How he saved her life. And so on. She'd say, 'You and Milton and Josh' "—Josh was the Greenes' seventeen-month-old son—" 'are the only real family I have ever known.' " (Marilyn had made similar declarations to Di Maggio's brothers and sisters.)

For some three weeks, Marilyn vanished from public view. Only the Greenes and the lawyers knew where she was sequestered. She was living *chez* Greene in a tiny guest room on the ground floor. It is known to the Greenes as the "purple room" because it is decorated with purple wallpaper and there is a purple spread on the small cot. Marilyn told Amy Greene that she loved purple, it was her favorite color and also the most restful color. Actually, her favorite colors are white and black. The Greenes live in a charmingly remodeled barn, high on a rise of ground on Fanton Hill Road, near Weston, Connecticut. Not even friends of the Greenes realized that a famous woman was staying with them. On weekends, when friends visited the Greenes, Marilyn was out of sight, secreted either in one of the upstairs bedrooms or in a locked study behind the garage.

Marilyn usually awakened at seven, did her exercises for a half hour, and then dressed in an hour and a half. She got her own breakfast. In fact, she insisted on being as little trouble as possible and helped with the cooking, the cleaning, the baby sitting, for the Greenes had only one servant. During the day, she played with the dachshund, took long solitary hikes in the woods, and read books on acting and plays. She dined with the Greenes at seven, and then they all listened to classical music on the high-fidelity phonograph. Marilyn, of course, had told Amy the sad story of her childhood and enlisted Amy's emotions in her behalf. On New Year's Eve, when the Greenes went out to a party, Marilyn sat alone and minded little Josh. During the period of her admiration for Greene, I happened to ask Marilyn her opinion of this man, who was regarded as a mystery figure by persons in Hollywood.

"Milton Greene and I have a lot in common," she said. "We have parallel aims and ideas. I think he's very capable and very talented and very artistic, and a lot of other people will know it someday. You'll see. I feel deeply about him. I'm sincere about his genius. He's a genius. He knows more about color and lighting effects and getting things out of you with a camera in his little finger than nine tenths of those Hollywood people. He's not using me, and I'm not using him. No, I didn't manage to save any money on my salary at Twentieth Century-Fox. I have a lot of expenses people don't know about. How am I living now? That's my business, how I'm living and how I'm supporting myself."

The corporation papers were finally drawn up and signed. Attorney Frank Delaney held a cocktail party and press conference at his home at East 64th Street. Delaney promised the press that a "new Marilyn Monroe" would be unveiled, and that she would make a world-shaking announcement. Almost 100 journalists came to report the news.

As far as her sense of time was concerned, she was still the old Marilyn. She was an hour late. And the "New Marilyn" when she arrived didn't look as if she were a candidate for a convent or even for the role of one of Chekhov's three sisters. She swished into the salon in a tight white satin gown which revealed 40 per cent of her bosom. She was made up to the nines—hair in a new shade of "subdued" platinum and lips carmined to extravagance. Delaney said it gave him great pleasure to announce the formation of Marilyn Monroe Productions, Incorporated. Fifty-one per cent of the 100 shares issued were held by Marilyn, and 49 per cent were held by Greene.

"I formed my own corporation," Marilyn explained, "so I can

play the better kind of roles I want to play. I didn't like a lot of my pictures. I'm tired of sex roles. I don't want to play sex roles any more."

"What makes you think you can play serious roles?"

"Some people have more scope than other people think they have, rahlly they do," Marilyn chirped, in what was almost an Old Vic accent.

"Do you want to play *The Brothers Karamazov*?"

"I don't want to play the brothers. I want to play Grushenka. She's a girl."

Delaney announced that Marilyn Monroe had been elected president of the corporation and that Milton Greene had been elected vice-president.

Upon hearing this news, Nunnally Johnson said, "Well, it will be the first time in history that a vice-president didn't want the president assassinated."

The following week Marilyn returned to the West Coast to play in several new scenes that had been added to *Seven Year Itch*. As she walked onto the set, Wilder greeted her, "Hello, Marilyn. How are you?"

"Ooh," she cooed, "I feel wonderful. I'm incorporated!"

Louella Parsons received a strange telephone call from Marilyn that evening. In it Marilyn denied some of the things she had said in her New York press conference: "I've never said I won't make pictures for 20th Century-Fox. I think *Seven Year Itch* is the best picture I've ever made. I love working with Billy Wilder, and I learned a lot from him. I need somebody to help me, and he gave me great help. Of course, I still want to make musicals, and good comedies and dramas—but not heavy dramas as everyone says."

But mercury is stable compared to Marilyn. Two days later, she announced, on the set, "This is my last picture for Twentieth."

Zanuck riposted, "This will be her last picture for anyone but Twentieth Century-Fox for three years and four months. She's under contract to this studio and she'll fulfill it." Zanuck's childlike faith in the sanctity of contracts was to be shaken before the year was out.

Conferences between her lawyers and 20th's lawyers were going on. They continued to offer her compromises during the year. A hundred thousand dollars a picture. The right to make one independent production a year. But Marilyn insisted on approval of screenplay and director. These rights the studio was not ready to surrender.

In February, she returned to New York. She had crossed the great divide. She was going to have to live up to her words or eat them. With the infallible machinery of self-preservation that never failed her, Marilyn did everything right during the ten months of warfare with her studio.

23 She Declares Her Independence; a New Life in New York

Temporarily, Marilyn returned to the little purple guest room in Greene's country house. In March, Edward R. Murrow trained his smirk, his cigarette, and his camera on Marilyn Monroe and Mr. and Mrs. Greene. During the preparations for the 15-minute interview on "Person to Person," Greene took over the production, ordering engineers and cameramen about and compelling CBS to change its elaborate set-up of lighting at a cost of several thousand dollars. He wanted to "protect" Marilyn Monroe. Greene said the CBS technicians were using "flat" lighting, which gave a harsh effect to Marilyn's skin. He insisted on a softer "bounce" lighting, so that Marilyn would emerge bathed in an aureole of Renoir-like illumination. Greene knew what he wanted, and he fought ruthlessly for Marilyn, making enemies and courting criticism. He had already severed Marilyn's connection with Charles Feldman's agency and persuaded her to sign a management contract with MCA (Music Corporation of America).

During the actual "Person to Person" telecast, Marilyn was overcome with shyness. She spoke in monosyllables. Amy Greene answered for her. Mrs. Greene looked so beguiling that people in Hollywood suggested Darryl Zanuck forget about Marilyn Monroe and sign a contract with Amy Greene.

Now that Marilyn had made an open break with Hollywood, she didn't have to live incognito. She was the guest of honor at many parties.

A woman I know was at one of these parties, and she reports her impression that Mrs. Greene treated the fabulous blonde in a curious manner of sarcastic disdain.

"I got the feeling," she says, "that Amy looked down on Marilyn Monroe as a stupid little bitch. Amy was better dressed, more chic, more sophisticated, and much cleverer than Marilyn. She even looked better. In fact, you couldn't believe that this queer little duck you saw sitting around the Greenes' was really Marilyn Monroe. I remember we played charades, the girls against the men. We went into a bedroom to select the sentences. We had some quotations from poetry and things like that, and then somebody said how about the title of a book, and Amy looked over at Marilyn and said, 'Come on, Marilyn, give us a book title, will you? You're always reading all those books.' I got the feeling that Amy was implying that Marilyn was a phony about being intellectual and didn't read any of the books she pretended to read and that Marilyn knew Amy had this low opinion of her mind. Or maybe it was that Amy resented all the gossip going around that Milton was having an affair with Marilyn and she wanted to show us that she was in command of the situation.

"What happened later convinced me of this. About half past twelve we all got hungry—oh, there were about ten of us—and Amy turned to Marilyn and ordered her—she didn't ask her, she ordered her, the way you would a servant—'Marilyn,' she said, 'Marilyn, go in the kitchen and make sandwiches.' And Marilyn obeyed her. She went into the kitchen and made sandwiches and coffee and served them to us."

In April, Marilyn subleased a three-room apartment in the Waldorf Astoria Towers. The apartment belonged to the actress Leonora Corbett. Supporting Marilyn in style cost $1,000 a week! The money to support her came entirely from Greene. There were no other investors in Monroe Productions. He mortgaged his home and property to the hilt, cashed in bonds and securities, and borrowed to the limit of his credit. Among her regular expenses were $100 a week for her mother's care in a sanitarium; $125 a week for five visits to a psychoanalyst; and $500 a week for beautification.

I once expressed surprise to Greene that any woman could spend such a vast sum, every week, on improving her appearance. Had she gone to exclusive beauty salons? Used expensive imported estrogenic skin creams and rare unguents?

"She didn't go to any beauty salons," Greene explained. "She turned her apartment into a beauty salon. She had her own personal hairdresser on salary, a hundred twenty-five dollars a week, and he came three, four times a week. She had manicurists, podiatrists, masseuses, specialists in this, that and the other thing, make-up people—I've got the bills to prove it. And she'd use perfume like it was water. Maybe fifty dollars a week on perfume alone, some weeks even more. It costs a lot of money to look like Marilyn Monroe. You don't just wake up in the morning and wash your face and comb your hair and go out in the street and look like Marilyn Monroe. She knows every trick of the beauty trade. She knows what has to be done to make her look the way she wants to look. Besides the money she needed to live, the corporation, in other words Milton Herman Greene, was also paying for a private secretary and an expensive publicity man, Arthur Jacobs. You see, it was essential to keep Marilyn living in the Waldorf, looking her best. I spent three thousand dollars on new clothes for her in two months that spring, and she thought it was a present from me personally until I explained that the corporation was investing it in her. It was also essential to hire a press agent to keep her name alive in the press. We had to create the impression at the studio and among the stockholders of 20th Century-Fox that Marilyn was well-heeled and prepared to hold out forever if her terms were not met."

Greene was convinced that 20th would eventually give in. It was true that he was spending $50,000 a year. But it was also true that every film that was made without Marilyn earned at least $1,000,000 less because her name was not on the marquee.

Greene explains his strategic reasoning: "As soon as the bills started coming in, I knew it would cost me about fifty thousand dollars a year for the three years that remained on the Twentieth contract. All right—so I'd be out a hundred and fifty thousand dollars if they refused to meet our conditions. But, assuming that, at the very minimum, they would lose a million dollars a year without Marilyn, then it was their three million dollars against my hundred and fifty thousand. I figured the odds were favorable and that the stockholders would start screaming by nineteen fifty-six. Actually, they started screaming right away, and they screamed all during nineteen fifty-five, because Lew Schreiber kept coming to us with new and better propositions all the time. Marilyn was their hottest box-office attraction, but more than that she was the most spectacular personality in the whole industry. And her popularity was worldwide—she was big in France, big in Italy, big all over. They had to come to us."

In March, Marilyn had been to a dinner party. Opposite her sat Cheryl Crawford, the Broadway producer and one of the co-founders of the Actors' Studio. Miss Crawford had never met Marilyn before. During dinner, she began to draw Marilyn out about her future plans, and Marilyn said she was serious about developing herself as an actress.

"If you are," Miss Crawford said, "then you belong in the Actors' Studio. But first you should meet Lee Strasberg. If he thinks he can help you, he may take you on for private lessons."

The Studio is a group of some 250 professional actors and actresses who meet on Tuesdays and Fridays, between eleven and one. The members perform several scenes, of about ten minutes' duration each, and then they critically discuss the performances. Strasberg, who is the high priest of the Method, analyzes the performances and speaks about the principles of acting interpretation and the emotional laws of the actor's personality. Membership in the Studio, which is a non-profit corporation, is free to those actors who qualify by experience and by passing an audition. Strasberg also gives private lessons to groups of about 30 students.

Strasberg is the most articulate of the popularizers of the Stanislavsky Method. He and other Method teachers like Stella Adler, Sanford Meisner, Mira Rostova, Tamara Dayarkhanova, and Method directors like Elia Kazan, Robert Lewis, Daniel Mann, Harold Clurman, Arthur Penn, have developed a style of performing that stresses psychological realism and subjective truth. The style has influenced the movies, television drama, and the Broadway theatre, in such pieces as *Death of a Salesman, Marty, A Streetcar Named Desire, East of Eden, Tea and Sympathy, On the Waterfront, Middle of the Night, Patterns, A Hatful of Rain, Baby Doll, The Miracle Worker, The Dark at the Top of the Stairs, Sweet Bird of Youth.* Among those who had been—or still were—members of the Studio were Marlon Brando, Jimmy Dean, Kim Stanley, Shelley

Winters, Rod Steiger, Eli Wallach, David Wayne, Geraldine Page, Paul Newman, Viveca Lindfors, Montgomery Clift, Maureen Stapleton, Tom Ewell, Julie Harris, Anthony Franciosa, and Eva Marie Saint.

Marilyn went to Miss Crawford's office the afternoon following the dinner party. "She was only thirty minutes late," Miss Crawford recalls. "I gather that's very prompt for Marilyn." Miss Crawford had already booked an engagement with Maestro Strasberg, and the two ladies boarded a taxi and headed uptown, where the Strasbergs then lived in a high-ceilinged, old-fashioned, eight-room apartment on Broadway and 86th Street. They were shown into a large den that had bookshelves up to the ceiling on every wall. The books—in French, German, and Italian as well as English—overflowed onto tables, sofas, and the floor. A high-fidelity turntable and amplifier stood naked. Marilyn felt a sense of awe at these visible signs of learning and culture, and a sense of fear that she would not be good enough to be taken under *il gran maestro's* wing. He bustled in suddenly, unexpectedly, not smiling, nodding to Miss Crawford, nodding to her, scrutinizing her with small black eyes that bored into her through his thick eyeglasses.

Could this be the famous Lee Strasberg? He was on the small side and he looked undistinguished. His cheeks had the dark stubble of men who always look unshaven. He was wearing a dark-blue shirt and no tie and a badly fitting rumpled suit. He looked like a harassed small businessman, a drugstore owner maybe, or a delicatessen store owner who was on the verge of bankruptcy.

But when he began to talk, he became transfigured. Strasberg is a great teacher, in the sense that he knows his subject, loves his subject, and can communicate both his love and his knowledge to other persons. But beyond that, he is a sage, a master in the Oriental sense. I have attended many meetings of the Actors' Studio—a certain number of non-members in the theatre arts, including those who write about actors or criticize plays, are permitted to attend, although they are not allowed to participate in the group discussions —and I have always come away feeling inspired.

After twenty minutes of conversation, during which he asked her seemingly prosaic questions, Strasberg agreed to give Marilyn private lessons.

For Strasberg, even at their first meeting, Marilyn threw off gleams of greatness. As he got to know her better and began to work on technical and psychological problems with her, he came to believe that she possessed unusual talent.

As a rule, Strasberg does not like to give private lessons because "actors have to work with other actors, not alone." But in the case of an actress who had already established such a reputation and was "grooved" to a working pattern, he wished to study her problems and her possibilities before "subjecting her to the terrific pressure of class work." He had seen several of her films; she had made little impression on him. But at the first interview, "I saw that what she looked was not what she really was, and what was going on inside was not what was going on outside, and that always means there may be something there to work with. In Marilyn's case, the reactions were phenomenal. It was almost as if she had been waiting for a button to be pushed, and when it was pushed a door opened and you saw a treasure of gold and jewels. It is unusual to find the underlying personality so close to the surface and so anxious to break out and therefore so quick to respond." In her private work, according to Strasberg, there was an intense quickness to respond, which, he says, is "typical of great actors." The class exercises are intended to stimulate and test these responses. After three months of private lessons, Marilyn entered a class and also attended meetings at the Actors' Studio.

I asked Strasberg whether her stammering, which she had never conquered, showed itself in class.

"No, it didn't," he said. "But it was one of the fears we treated in private lessons. I explained to her that her stammering came from the fact that she grew up in an environment where she was expected to say certain things and these things were not at all what she felt or what she thought. When she had tried to explain what she felt or thought, she had been slapped or laughed at. As a result when she had to speak but did not dare say what she wanted to say, she'd stammer. When she says what is on her mind, she doesn't stammer. Stammering in her almost always indicates a divided reaction. But in doing scenes in class or in speaking memorized lines, she never stammered."

Myself, I have heard her stammer on just two occasions. Once, during an interview with her, the phone rang. It was Eli Wallach calling to say his wife had just given birth. Marilyn began expressing her joy at the event; suddenly she couldn't get the words out and was stammering badly. On the theory of the "divided reaction," one assumes that she was ambivalent—happy for her friends, the Wallachs, but also jealous because she had no baby herself. The second instance occurred during the movie *Bus Stop*. Marilyn has to lie to the hero, to tell him that she is going to meet him later when actually she is planning to run away from him. When Marilyn began to lie, though it was in the script, she stammered quite perceptibly. It is the only time her disability ever manifested itself in a movie.

Of her acting capability, Strasberg says: "She can call up emotionally whatever is required in a scene. Her range is infinite, and it is almost wicked that she has not used more of her range or that the films she has been in so far have not required more of her. She is highly nervous. She is more nervous than any other actress I have ever known. But nervousness, for an actress, is not a handicap. It is a sign of sensitivity. Marilyn had to learn how to channel her nervousness, this wild flow of energy, into her work. For too long, she had been living for the newspapers, for that publicity. She had to live for herself and her work. As a movie star, she combines the qualities of Pauline Lord and Jeanne Eagels. Her quality when photographed is almost of a supernatural beauty."

Once Paula Strasberg asked her husband what would have happened to Marilyn Monroe if she had been born before the invention of cinematography.

He thought for a second and then replied, "It would have made no difference. The world would still have had a great artist. She would have fulfilled herself in ballet, in opera, in the theatre, in one of the performing arts."

Under the goad of his teaching, Marilyn now embarked on her most serious attempt to explore her resources as a woman and to use them in her acting. In her psychoanalysis, she was also exploring herself. The major goal of her psychotherapy was to help her break the crust of self-absorption she had formed in early life to protect herself from a destructive environment.

Of immediate importance was the problem of her acute sense of sin. The shallowness of many of her rigid moral standards became apparent to her. Her own intrinsic value as a person came to the surface. Gradually she came to know that the impulses in her that she had been made to feel damned her to eternity—her hostility, for instance—were normal components of every human being.

With Strasberg, she had a two-hour lesson twice a week. During one lesson she did exercises, during the other she did scenes from contemporary or classic plays. The exercises might be as simple as singing a popular song without moving the body, so that she used the inner nervousness subjectively instead of leaking it out through random, unconscious bodily tics and jerks. Strasberg employs several singing exercises to decrease self-consciousness in his pupils and to induce relaxation. Another one was jumping up and down while singing. There were exercises to cultivate "sense memory." For example, Marilyn would be asked to close her eyes and recapture a childhood experience in all its sensory immediacy, by saying what had happened and trying to relive the old experience emotionally. The ability to summon up past emotions and convert them to the needs of the fictional character one is playing is one of the principles of the Stanislavsky Method.

There were exercises in improvisation; Marilyn might be given three words, "sky," "bird," "automobile," and asked to improvise a monologue, with action, using these words. The purpose of this exercise was to train her in spontaneous expression.

She was taught such principles of the Method as *justification, mood, adjustment, plasticity, objectification, public solitude, concentration, contact.*

Later, during the making of *Bus Stop,* in which Marilyn played a night-club singer who speaks in an Ozark drawl, she spoke in a Southern accent all the time. Don Murray asked her once why she talked in the accent after working hours. She replied, "Cain't you-all see ah'm makin' contact with mah character?"

When Billy Wilder was directing her in *Some Like It Hot,* she was reading a speech too slowly. He asked why she was taking it so languidly.

"I'm trying to make contact with Sugar Kane," Marilyn said, frowning.

"Go ahead and make contact with Sugar Kane," Wilder said. "But for God's sake, could you contact her a little faster please?"

Justification requires the Method actor to find some emotional, logical, or factual reason for every action he performs. *Objectifica-*

tion is relating oneself to the physical objects, the props, in a scene. *Concentration* is the immersion of oneself in the story to such an extent that one achieves a trance-like state, existing entirely in terms of the make-believe world. When concentration occurs, it leads to what Stanislavsky called "public solitude," which is the ideal of the Method actor. We shall see Marilyn putting some of these principles into practice in her later work.

24 *The Seven Year Itch*

The world *première* of *The Seven Year Itch* was to take place at Loew's State Theatre, New York, on June 1, 1955. The date was no accident. It was Marilyn's twenty-ninth birthday. The studio, for legal reasons, did not invite her directly. They sent a pair of tickets, marked "Actors' Studio," to Sam Shaw, a magazine photographer who had been employed to do an interesting set of still pictures of Marilyn in connection with the publicity. Subsequently Shaw had become one of her companions. They sometimes went out socially in Manhattan, although by now she had begun warming up the embers of her love for Arthur Miller. And Joe Di Maggio wasn't out of her romantic program either. The Yankee Clipper was in New York. He hoped to glue together the pieces of the broken marriage. They spoke to each other on the telephone and occasionally dined together. To get himself back into Marilyn's good graces, Joe agreed to escort her to the *première*. He also tendered a supper party in her honor at Toots Shor's.

As was to be expected, Marilyn came late. But, according to Walter Winchell, this time there was method in her lateness.

"Tom Ewell," reported Winchell, "who received rave reports from the critics for his role in *Seven Year Itch* is on the screen nearly all the time. . . . But at the *première* at Lowe's State, that other gifted performer, Marilyn Monroe, managed a subtle bit of scene thefting in a thoroughly original way. . . . Feminine, calculated, and exquisitely effective. . . . She delayed her arrival until about 20 minutes after the film began. . . . At this point in the movie, Mr. Ewell is engaged in a long soliloquy. . . . And there is a patch of about five minutes during which Marilyn doesn't appear at all. . . . During this lull, she made her appearance with Mr. Di Maggio. The flashbulbs popped in sequence after her as she swept glamorously down the aisle. . . . Nobody bothered to watch Mr. Ewell's soliloquy—as the eyes were on the doll giving one of her most virtuoso performances. . . ."

During the birthday party, Joe and Marilyn got into an argument. They exchanged hard words and cold looks. Marilyn suddenly got up and stalked away. She asked Shaw to take her home. From now on, Di Maggio knew it was hopeless to pursue his ex-wife.

The reviews of *Seven Year Itch* illustrate the dilemma in which critics find themselves in evaluating a Monroe performance. Her beauty tends to blind them to her artistic work. In the New York *Times,* Bosley Crowther wrote: "From the moment she steps into the picture, in a garment that drapes her shapely form as though she had been skillfully poured into it, the famous screen star with the silver-blonde tresses and the ingenuously wide-eyed stare emanates one suggestion. . . . Mr. Wilder has permitted Miss Monroe, in her skinfitting dresses and her frank gyrations to overpower Mr. Ewell. She, without any real dimensions, is the focus of attention in the film. . . . Thus the undisguised performance of Miss Monroe, while it may lack depth, gives the show a caloric content that may not lose her any faithful fans. We merely commend her diligence when we say it leaves much—very much—to be desired."

The *Time* reviewer was one of the few who detected a gleam of artistry in her acting: "Marilyn Monroe's eye-catching gait is more tortile and wambling than ever. She also displays a nice comedy touch, reminiscent of a baby-talk Judy Holliday."

The *New Yorker's* John McCarten was still an implacable foe of the Monroe doctrine. He said *Seven Year Itch* "offered stimulating views of Marilyn Monroe as a substitute for the comedy George Axelrod got into the original version of this trifle. There are occasions when Tom Ewell evokes a laugh or two, but when Miss Monroe turns up as a young lady too substantial for dreams, the picture is reduced to the level of a burlesque show."

It is a biological fact that no heterosexual male film critic, no matter how conscientious, can isolate the acting subtleties of a

Monroe performance on a first viewing. I have seen Marilyn's best films many times over, and I find that only by the third viewing have I been able to grasp the artistry of, say, The Girl Upstairs in *Seven Year Itch*. Reviewing the film in *The New Republic*, the poet Delmore Schwartz was completely carried away by her beauty.

"She can be understood," he wrote, "only from one point of view, that of beauty, which is its own excuse for being, a truth which, as Emerson was but one among the first to recognize, must be pointed out to the American public time and again. Nothing that Miss Monroe says in any role can be quite as meaningful as the ways in which she sways: her poise and carriage have a true innocence: have a spontaneity, an unself-consciousness which are the extreme antithesis to the calculated sex of the strip tease and other forms of the propagation of prurience."

Billy Wilder once told me: "Every movie star has a certain voltage. It is as if one were to hold up a light meter to the screen and certain stars will register more than others. Well, Marilyn has the highest voltage. The moment that face comes on the screen, people drop the popcorn bags, believe me. She never flattens out on the screen. In any scene she is in, there is never what I call a hole in the screen. She never gets lost up there. You can't take your eyes away from her. You can't watch any other performer when she's playing a scene with somebody else."

Paradoxically enough, you can't even see Marilyn's artistry in her portraits of Lorelei Lee, Pola Debevoise, The Girl, Cherie, Elsie Marina, Sugar Kane. It looks so natural and she plays as if she were playing herself. But it is no accidental triumph that The Girl Upstairs, to quote William Zinsser, "is so wide-eyed and naïve that she rarely knows what she is talking about."

All her gestures and her speeches are directed to an end. In the dramatic version, The Girl was an abstraction, figuring in the fantasies of the hero, Richard Sherman. In fact, the play was almost a long monologue by Ewell.

In the film, the character of The Girl is enlarged because of the thinking and the feeling that Marilyn put into the characterization and realized before the camera.

Over the last three years, she had perfected her own individual style of comedy. "Marilyn knows comedy," Wilder says. "Her sense of timing is precise. She knows how to stress the best word in the gag to get the laugh when she is playing for a laugh. And, over all, she projects such a quality of humor about herself. This can be seen whenever she makes her first entrance in any picture, as in *Some Like It Hot,* when she comes undulating down the station platform. She comes on with her two balconies sticking out, and you know she's killing everybody with her looks, but she always seems surprised that her body is kicking up such an excitement. Now this is a real comic attitude. It's not anything I, as a director, showed her. It's instinctive. Of course, she helps it along by never wearing a girdle or a brassière in a scene. Never. That's why she looks fat around the tummy. People think she's pregnant. She puts fat on around the tummy and because she doesn't wear a girdle it looks like that. I, for one, say more power to her without a girdle. Who can get enough of Marilyn Monroe? So we're back to the women of Rubens! Is that bad?"

Such moments in *Seven Year Itch* as when she indolently dabbles a fragment of potato chip in Ewell's champagne and the later episode of the four-handed version of Chopsticks exemplify her skillful comic touches. Ewell has dreamed of an erotic meeting in which he will play a Rachmaninoff Piano Concerto as Marilyn, garbed in a long red evening dress, sits beside him. He will peer at her intently and then kiss her very hard. What really happens is that he plays Chopsticks and she joins him. He embraces her and plants an awkward kiss on her face. They lose their balance and tumble off the piano bench. Ewell is flustered and guilty.

He says contritely, "This never happened to me before."

"Oh," says Marilyn, "it happens to me all the time." She doesn't struggle with him. She isn't outraged. She rather likes the shy little man.

And this is the point of her interpretation of the role. It comes through after one shakes loose from the spell of her beauty. She likes this unhandsome, nervous, inferior chap. She is aware at the first meeting that Ewell is gazing at her lustfully. She knows he will be too cowardly to act. She feels no risk of involvement with him, and yet she wishes he would do something. As the story progresses, she becomes grateful to him, and at the end she likes him very much —there is even a fleeting suggestion that she feels love for him stirring in her. She would certainly have been delighted to go to bed with him, but not because she is the great sex symbol, Marilyn Monroe, but because she is a woman whose heart is affectionate.

For instance, she makes this statement, and not with words, during the first scene. She has lost the key to her flat. She rings, by chance, Ewell's bell so she can get into the house. Ewell pushes the buzzer, then opens his door to see who it is. He sees this transcendent beauty at the foot of the stairs, holding a bagful of groceries in one arm and an electric fan in the other. She wears a red polka-dot halter dress. She has paused for a moment and now she starts up. Then she asks him to sound his buzzer again.

"My fan is caught in the door," she says, her tone playing slightly on the implied pun.

Ewell's poached eyes float along her body, her rear, her legs, follow the electric cord stretched taut across her flank. The cord is freed from the door. She explains that she has leased the apartment above and it is so hot she bought a fan. Meanwhile Ewell is going limp against the banister. She knows quite well that she is arousing him. And she has also told us—though not poor Ewell—that she rather likes him.

In the next scene, after Ewell has invited her for a drink, his fancy soars into a seduction scene, in which she enters as a *femme fatale,* in a sequin gown, smoking a cigarette in a long holder.

Then the bell sounds. The reality appears—a fairly sweet, if voluptuous, creature in pink lounging pajamas. He looks thunderstruck. Who can this be?

"Don't you remember me?" she asks, the slightest of smiles hovering over her lips. "You know—the tomato from upstairs?" Her phrasing of the *double-entendre,* the momentary delay between "know" and "tomato," is masterly. She knows what "tomato" means in slang—but you never can be absolutely sure she knows.

And so the evening proceeds. Ewell mixes her a Martini—"a long cool Martini"—and then she remembers she has a bottle of champagne upstairs and goes for it. She returns, having changed into a stunning white dress, since this is now a party. Besides the champagne she brings a bag of potato chips. Ewell fumbles about in pathetic attempts to make love, and she tries to encourage him, but he can't bring it off.

The next night they have dinner and see a movie. On the way

home, she finally takes the initiative and kisses him. But he still doesn't respond. He still can't believe that this beautiful girl would have an affair with him. He invites her to spend the night in his flat —so she can enjoy the comfort of sleeping in an air-conditioned bedroom. She does. He gives her the bedroom. He sleeps on the couch. In the morning, they have orange juice, cinnamon toast, coffee. Ewell has decided to cease struggling with his inhibitions. He will return to his wife and son in Maine. He hurriedly packs his things. He is saying good-bye to The Girl. It is during this farewell scene that one sees how carefully Marilyn has worked toward the crystallization of the character. She tells him how nice he is. She tells him that girls aren't taken in by the big tall men in the fancy clothes who strut about at a party, thinking they can make any girl fall flat on her face.

THE GIRL: Well, she doesn't fall on her face. . . . But there's another guy in the room . . . way over in the corner . . . maybe he's kind of nervous and shy and perspiring a little. . . . First you look past him, but then you sort of sense that he is gentle and kind and worried and that he'll be tender with you and nice and sweet and that's what's really exciting! If I were your wife, I'd be jealous of you . . . I'd be very very jealous!
She kisses him. A real kiss. Then—
THE GIRL: I think you're just elegant.
RICHARD (*with a little smile*): Thank you.

In the look of her eyes, in the quality of her kiss, her tenderness and pity for him overflow. She has known him two days—and yet she has known him a lifetime. She has sensed his fear of women and, because she likes him, she is going to make him feel wanted, make him know you don't have to look like Gregory Peck to be attractive to a beautiful girl. As Wilder puts it, "She gives this poor *schloomp* a sense of his own value as a man."

Now all these things are there on the screen, and they are not put there by the jutting of bosoms but by acting.

Despite the puzzled tone of the reviews, *Seven Year Itch* was a box-office success. Its production cost was $1,800,000, and it has so far grossed $8,000,000. (I say so far, because Monroe pictures are constantly being revived and play to good business. During a six-week period recently in New York, local theatres were showing *Monkey Business, Don't Bother to Knock, Gentlemen Prefer Blondes, How to Marry a Millionaire,* and *Bus Stop*.) As the gate receipts of *Seven Year Itch* mounted, the stockholder pressure on the 20th Century-Fox executives to come to terms with Marilyn increased.

25 I Interview Marilyn

My first interview of any length with Marilyn took place in July, 1955, although I had previously been introduced to her at a dinner in honor of Walter Winchell given by the Los Angeles Press Club in 1953. I saw her then under her heavy coat of make-up and in a tight, low-cut gown of green sequins. Though fantastically beautiful, she did not seem quite real. The *mystère* fascinated me. At that time, she did not wish to divulge any biographical information. But in 1955, anxious for publicity to keep her reputation alive in the press, she gave interviews to several writers, including myself. I had three sittings with her in July, lasting a total of about nine hours. She had been a hold-out for seven months. Her fan mail was decreasing. From an average of 8,000 fan letters a month in 1954 she was now down to 5,400.

I arrived at her apartment at the Waldorf Towers at the appointed time, 9:30 A.M. Frank Goodman, her New York publicity man, was there. We waited. She was "getting ready," Goodman told me. We waited. At ten past ten, she emerged. Goodman went away, and her secretary, Peter Leonardi, was sent out to do some errands.

Marilyn, judging by the flush on her skin—and I was able to see a good deal of her skin—had recently bathed. The aroma of Chanel #5 pervaded the small living room. She wore a white terry-cloth robe with nothing underneath. No stockings and no slippers. Her legs were slim and finely tapered, and sometimes, when she flowed into a change of position in the armchair in which she was curled, I glimpsed a vista of white thighs. Her thighs were also beautifully tapered. I was struck by the fact that her toenails were painted platinum-white, to harmonize with the shade of her hair. Her hair was unkempt. I assumed she had not had time to brush and comb it. Later I found out she doesn't like kempt hair. She wore no cosmetics on her lips, cheeks, or eyelashes. I wasn't sure about her eyebrows. She might have had eyebrow pencil on her eyebrows. She appeared sweet and guileless, though the mole on her left cheek imparted an eighteenth-century Mme. Du Barry touch, a dramatic contrast to her angelic features.

She was clear about her goal. She said: "I want good stories and good directors and just not to be thrown into any old thing. I am a serious actress. I want to prove it. I know the body is good. But I have feelings and ideas—and I want these to be part of my work. New York is my home now. I love it here. I'll never live in Hollywood any more. I want to work there but not live. I expect to make pictures there. And I am hoping to play in stage plays and . . ."

I had interrupted her to ask, "How would you make the eight-forty curtain?"

"What—what do you mean?" she asked, genuinely taken aback. She leaned forward to grasp the meaning of my question.

"People say you can't be on time."

"Oh, that," she said. She shrugged the problem away and the robe fell away from her shoulders together with the problem. "Don't believe all the things people say about me, that's all. Just take it with a grain of salt, whatever they say about me."

"So you definitely expect to live in Manhattan?"

"No, Brooklyn. I've fallen in love with Brooklyn. I'm going to buy a little house in Brooklyn and live there. I'll go to the Coast only when I have to make a picture."

"Do you feel the studio was underpaying you?"

"My fight with the studio is not about money. It is about human rights. I am tired of being known as the girl with the shape. I am going to show them I am capable of deeper acting."

Had she changed in any way since living in New York?

"Oh, yes," she said. "I have found freedom and independence, and I don't intend to give them up."

A small gray kitten skittered out of the bedroom. Marilyn threw it a rolled-up woolen sock, and the kitten played cat-and-mouse with

260

the sock. A handsome gearshift English bicycle rested against a window by the kitchen. Marilyn told me she often bicycled in Central Park and on Ocean Parkway in Brooklyn. At eleven-forty-five, she concocted milk punch for us. Chocolate syrup, milk, and a slug of Marsala—a heavy-bodied Italian sweet wine, rather like sherry. She said she had developed a taste for Marsala during her relationship with Di Maggio.

Among the books on an end table were Joyce's *Ulysses; How Stanislavsky Directs,* by Michael Gorchakov; the letters of George Sand; Edith Hamilton's *Greek Mythology;* and Emerson's essays. I asked her if she had been reading *Ulysses.*

"Here and there," she said.

"You mean you started it in Los Angeles and finished it in New York? How long did it take you to read it? Did you have trouble reading it?"

"I mean I read it here and there partly."

"What part?"

"Oh, any part that looked interesting."

"The last chapter?"

"Oh," she said, her gray-blue eyes darting a shared look of literary immorality, "the one with the words."

"Lovers of the modern novel think of it as the Molly Bloom soliloquy."

"Like Hamlet's?" She peered at me more keenly. She had a fresh interest on her face. She had not realized I cared about Joyce or that I had some knowledge of modern fiction.

"It's not really a soliloquy," I said, proud of displaying a little erudition. "Not in the sense of a Shakespearean soliloquy or one of Browning's monologues, let's say. It's really using the stream-of-consciousness. As you do during psychoanalysis."

"You been analyzed?"

"Yes," I said.

"Seems like everybody I know is."

"Have you?"

"I don't want to go into that," she said. "No comment."

"Well, what is your opinion of Joyce?"

"He's an interesting writer," she said.

"I see," I said. "What do you think of Molly Bloom?"

"She certainly has sex on her mind constantly." She accented the word in a way that seemed to imply Mrs. Bloom had been the Marilyn Monroe of Dublin. "It's interesting that a man, I mean like Mr. Joyce, would go into a woman's mind."

I said that Arnold Bennett had once remarked that the Molly Bloom soliloquy was the finest study of a woman's psychology in literature.

"Did he say that?"

"Yes."

"Who is he and how would he know anyway?"

"He was a novelist. He may have asked his wife's opinion, although I don't remember whether Bennett was married."

"I think he's crazy. Both of them. Women don't have sex on their mind *that* much."

"Do you?"

"Of course not," she replied.

The following week I returned, in the late afternoon of a heavy, humid day, for our second tête-à-tête. There was no answer when I rang the bell. I waited outside the door for a long time. I decided to go away. . . . Then the elevator door opened and Marilyn stepped out. She had just come from an art store where she had purchased a reproduction of the bust of Queen Nefertiti.

"Somebody told me," she explained in the hallway, "that I look like her."

I regarded the statue.

"Do you think so?" She fumbled for the key in her purse. She opened the door and we went inside.

"I don't think so," I said.

"No?"

"I think Nefertiti's face is longer than yours. She's thinner. Her cheekbones are higher."

"That's interesting. Look, it's so hot, why don't we have this talk in the bedroom? It's air conditioned."

A huge print of Lincoln hung above the bed. Marilyn was clad in black velvet toreador trousers and a white jersey blouse. She uncoiled herself prone across the bed, her head peering up at me. I was sitting in a chair opposite her. The air conditioner was an excellent machine, and the room, at first, was chill. But as I had to look at her, I found the room—or rather myself—growing unbearably hot. The jersey blouse was cut loosely, or perhaps it was my mind that was cut loosely that day, but the blouse did hang down alarmingly, and one got disquieting glimpses of her breasts. In a way, it was like the situation in *Seven Year Itch,* except that it was Miss Monroe's apartment that had the air conditioner. A combination of literary curiosity and lust sorely tempted me to fling myself on the bed and make love to her. What would have been her reaction? And how inspired was she as an *amoriste*? Well, I didn't have any more gallantry or nerve than Tom Ewell, so the world will never know what might have happened.

However, we did not, I am sorry to say, analyze these intriguing problems. We returned to literature. She told me of her interest in writing. She said she often wrote free verse. Recently, she had written a poem about Manhattan. Its title was *The Towers.* I wrote down the opening lines:

> "So many lights in the darkness
> Making skeletons of the buildings. . . ."

She then recited a longer poem about taxi drivers, which concluded:

> "Impatient taxi drivers, driving hot dusty New York streets,
> So they can save for a vacation driving hot dusty
> Highways all across the country to see
> Her relatives."

("Her" refers to the taxi driver's wife.)

In Hollywood, the opinion was that La Monroe was a naïve innocent, being taken for a sucker by Milton Greene and Lee Strasberg. Marilyn's helpless air convinced everyone that she was a pawn. And she had no talent, they said. She was a photogenic freak. What would she be without a studio behind her? Nothing. In a year, she'd be forgotten by the public.

Later in that summer of 1955, I had a conversation with Billy Wilder, who was in New York for a few days. He thought Marilyn was being misled by people who were exploiting her for prestige or money.

"Here you have this poor girl," he cried, "and all of a sudden she becomes a famous star. So now these people tell her she has to be a great actress. It is like a man writes a stupid jingle, 'Doggie in the

Window,' and it becomes a hit, and he's forced to write symphonies for Toscanini to play. They're trying to elevate Marilyn to a level where she can't exist. She will lose her audience. She is a calendar girl with warmth, charm, great charm—and she's being compared to Duse. Duse! They tell her she's a deep emotional actress. I don't know who's to blame. Kazan? Strasberg? Milton Greene? Who is Milton Greene anyway? It's like herring à la mode. Put the chocolate ice cream on the herring and you spoil the ice cream, and the herring is no damn good either.

"I don't say Lee Strasberg is a bad teacher. But if she must go to a school, why doesn't she go to Patek Phillipe in Switzerland and learn to run on time? Marilyn's whole success is she *can't* act. She's going through a bad evolution. If she takes it seriously, it is the end of Monroe. She is being taught acting by the kind of people who don't believe in under-arm deodorants. They believe in sitting on the floor even if there are six comfortable chairs in the room. They'll make her into another Julie Harris. She'll lose everything of her own. She'll make herself ugly. The crowd in the bleachers will hate her."

Wilder's prophecies of doom were based on a misunderstanding of Marilyn. Self-preservation is the first law of her nature. She had developed a style of living almost impervious to failure because she was able to redefine success. Her rebellious speeches and her new philosophy did not mean she intended to lose what she had already. At times, it may have seemed that she was losing ground, trying a hazardous attack, a foolish skirmish, but she always won her wars in the end.

26 Re-enter Mr. Miller

No event in Marilyn Monroe's life has provoked as much speculation as her love affair with Arthur Miller. A good deal of the published commentary on Marilyn since 1956 touches on the "incongruity" of the liaison between the "intellectual" and the "naked Venus." In a description of "Marilyn's Marriage," magazine writer Robert Levin remarked, "The marriage of the pin-up girl of the age and the nation's foremost intellectual playwright seemed preposterous." A series of articles in the New York *Post*, entitled "Inside Story of a Romance: Marilyn's Man," referred to the strange connection between "America's foremost representatives of the body and the mind."

At the source of such tortured speculations lies the error of equating a public image with a private reality. A woman who portrays sexually desirable women must herself be highly oversexed. One assumes that a Pulitzer Prize-winning playwright must be a dispassionate intellectual.

There are, it is true, actresses such as Ava Gardner who lead lives of erotic splendor as dramatic as those of the heroines they play. And there are playwrights—Giraudoux, Anouilh, Shaw—who are men of reason, though most playwrights are not, for the theatre is the most emotional of literary arts.

Marilyn is no more a lustful little animal than Miller is a servant of pure reason. As a young man, Miller played baseball and football. He still loves sports and fishing and hunting.

He was so little the intellectual that he was still signing up for popular-front causes during the late 1940's when most American writers had long ago seen that the Communist party was a sell and the Soviet Union an illusion. Most of the writers and intellectuals—Edmund Wilson, Ernest Hemingway, Sidney Hook, Dwight Macdonald, James T. Farrell, Ignazio Silone, Richard Wright, John Dos Passos—who had been attracted by the Communist program during the 1930's turned away from it by 1939 when Stalin and Hitler jointly attacked Poland and when the Soviets invaded Finland a year later. But it is in 1939 that we find Miller joining a Marxist study course in Brooklyn, and in 1940 he signed an application for Communist party membership!

Whatever fragments of influence the Communist party still exerted over American writers fairly well vanished after World War II when the Soviet *coup* in Czechoslovakia disabused them of their faith in Soviet promises of workers' democracy. But in 1947, 1948, 1949, we still find Miller sponsoring a World Youth Festival in Prague, a World Congress for Peace in Paris, a Peace Conference at the Waldorf-Astoria in New York, and a ragbag of other fronts. (It was the Waldorf conference, which was attacked by liberal and leftist intellectuals like Mary McCarthy, Dwight Macdonald, Robert Lowell, and Norman Mailer, that really did the fellow travelers in.) Miller drifted out of the front organizations after 1950. But he remained a silent apostate. As late as 1955, Howard Fast was writing an article in the *Daily Worker* entitled, "I Propose Arthur Miller as the American Dramatist of the Day." Fast eventually packed it in after the Khrushchev speech attacking Stalin, and he wrote a book about his disillusionment. Miller had had it some time before, but in all of his non-dramatic writing, there is no *intellectual* analysis of Marxism, Leninism, Stalinism, the nature of bureaucracy in the Soviet Union, the anti-Semitism there, the anti-cosmopolitanism, the cultural terror. He seems to have had no awareness of the critical writing on the Soviet Union, the Moscow purge trials, and the Spanish Civil War that had been done by André Gide, Max Eastman, Victor Serge, George Orwell, Hemingway, James Farrell, Sidney Hook, Edmund Wilson.

Miller was essentially what we used to call, in the 1930's, an "innocent." Now, there is nothing terribly sinister about his getting mixed up with a pack of frowzy fronts in the late 1940's. But it indicates either mental apathy about, or a studied lack of interest in, the history of one's time and its chief intellectual crises. It was not until 1957 when the USSR invited Miller to write an essay for a Dostoevski centenary in Moscow that he finally attacked Soviet censorship and the politicalization of the arts. But this was, for "America's foremost representative of the mind," rather late in the game.

By temperament, Miller is naturally athletic and muscular, as were Marilyn's first two husbands. Like Dougherty and Di Maggio, Miller has sought to interest Marilyn in fishing and the outdoor life.

For Marilyn, *au contraire*, the reading of books of philosophy, mysticism, and poetry has been a lifelong habit. She has a vast hunger for knowledge. She would rather browse in Martindale's bookshop in Beverly Hills than in I. Magnin's.

As I have said, what she does on the screen—Wilder notwithstanding—is conscious artifice. It is based on a study of female anatomy and masculine instinct. It is as much a formally patterned expression of art as Garbo's Camille or Guiletta Masina's Cabiria. Her Lorelei Lee, Girl Upstairs, and Cherie may appear spontaneous—but isn't that, after all, one of the signs of a great artist, that she makes us feel her feats are done without strain and sweat, that it is life itself, not a performance?

Instead of regarding the match between Miller and Monroe as peculiar, one might say that it was almost inevitable. What was more logical than for Marilyn to fall in love with the country's leading unhappily married non-homosexual playwright? After all, actress and playwright make as compatible a coupling as any other combination. Eugene O'Neill, Sidney Howard, Charles MacArthur, Clifford Odets, William Saroyan, Maxwell Anderson, Hartley Manners, Robert E. Sherwood, Elmer Rice, George S. Kaufman, Moss Hart, are among those who have been or are married to actresses.

Devious psychological explanations are plentiful to justify Miller's love for Marilyn. One theory asserts that he was drawn to the "All-American sex symbol" to restore himself in the eyes of the American people after the humiliations he had suffered from investigating committees and red-baiting groups. A satirist in *Punch*, identified only as B.A.Y., celebrated the Miller-Monroe nuptials with a poem called *Epithalamic Blues*:

"Arthur was a writer, he had Left Wing traits;
He wrote *Death of a Salesman* and wowed them in the States.
So then he wrote another piece, obliquely named *The Crucible,*
And, politically speaking, it was almost unproducible.
Arthur sought a passport from his Uncle Sam,
And when he couldn't get it, he sure was in a jam—
But he knew
What to do
And so
He hauled off and married
Marilyn Monroe.
Yeah, he hauled off and married Marilyn Monroe!
Her fans stayed as faithful as before, or more so,
But turned their attention to her head from her torso,
While in every milk-bar and sports arcade
The hepcats sang this serenade:

"I'm just crazy over Mrs. Arthur Miller!
Mrs. Arthur Miller's my number one thriller.
With her new-style dumb-intellectual blend
She can show you how Timon is a girl's best friend. . . .

"If her countrymen forget her real talent when she's dead
You can wager they'll remember her for something else instead
For she's made a public hero of a one-time Red—
Mrs. Miller, the queen of them all!"

Another theory holds that, to Miller, La Monroe is a status symbol. It satisfied his male ego to have legal possession of Marilyn.

Both theories are absurd. What drew him was her incandescence. I remember once talking to Frank Delaney, the suave lawyer who had guided Marilyn through the complicated legalities during her war with the studio. When I spoke to him he had been ousted as an officer of Marilyn Monroe Productions. (And he predicted to me that when it suited her interests she would find a method of casting Milton Greene overboard.) Anyway, Delaney smiled nostalgically and said that the year he had worked for Marilyn had been a year of great excitement for him. "When anybody gets involved with Miss Monroe," he said, thoughtfully, "things start to happen. You get a sense of quickening. Everything becomes dramatic. She's different from other human beings. She's larger than life. When you're involved with her, things start to happen to you."

It was this vitality that drew Miller. Brief though their knowledge of each other had been in 1951, the separation left him with an emptiness. His wife, Mary Grace Slattery Miller, was political, literary, intense in the style of the 1930's, and she was an intellectual—it was she who was the family intellectual. She had been Miller's intellectual stimulus, his creative inspiration, his economic support. She had worked as a waitress and later as an editor at Harper & Brothers to support him while he established himself as a writer. From the experiences of her father—an insurance salesman—he drew the mood and the hero of *Death of a Salesman.*

Two children were born of the union—Joan Ellen, now sixteen, and Robert, now twelve. Mary Slattery was a Roman Catholic, and the children were raised without any sense of being half-Jewish. One of the difficulties in the marriage was the distance between Mary Miller and Arthur's mother. (We shall see that Marilyn handled the mother-in-law problem with her usual exquisite strategy.) One gets some sense of Miller's reverence for his mother in the idealized portraits of the mothers in *All My Sons* and *Death of a Salesman.*

In the two plays that Miller wrote after his contact with Marilyn in 1949, that is, *The Crucible* and *View from the Bridge,* there are significant overtones of his personal crisis. At the time of its *première, The Crucible* was regarded by critics and audiences alike as employing the frame of the seventeenth-century Salem witch hunts to enclose a picture of modern Congressional investigating committees. It was not until 1957 when he came to write the introduction to the collected edition of his plays—which, by the way, is dedicated "To Marilyn"—that Miller himself saw the underlying sexual motif in both plays. (In the November, 1955, issue of *Theatre Arts* Magazine, I undertook to analyze the sexual themes of *View from the Bridge* and *The Crucible.* I pointed out that if one looked beyond the obvious political message of *The Crucible,* it was a triangle play and a very fine triangle play. As time goes on and the "messages" are forgotten, I believe that *View from the Bridge* and *The Crucible* will be highly regarded works of dramatic art.)

In the two plays which Miller wrote after his meeting with Marilyn, there are themes he has never touched before. One theme is the love of an older man for a young girl. The second is the effect of unfaithfulness on an American marriage.

The triangle in *The Crucible* consists of John Proctor; his wife, Elizabeth; and Abigail Williams, a young servant girl, once a maid in the Proctor house and now an accuser of many persons, including Mrs. Proctor. She accuses Mrs. Proctor of being a witch. She does not accuse Proctor. The play concerns guilt, the guilt of a married man who has betrayed his wife.

The triangle in *View from the Bridge* consists of Eddie Carbone; his wife, Beatrice; and their ward, Catherine.

Miller's emotion about Marilyn Monroe, recollected in artistic disquietude, went into the characterization of Abigail and Catherine, I believe. Both plays reflect an acute personal crisis which the author underwent between 1950 and 1956.

When, even before its production on Broadway, Clifford Odets read *The Crucible* in script, he remarked to a friend that Miller and his wife would be divorced within a few years. "No man," he surmised, "would write this play unless his marriage is going to pieces." I do not think Miller himself realized until sometime in 1955 that it was going to be impossible to keep his marriage together. He had put more of his psychological state on paper than he himself had been fully conscious of. Miller has written "that the less capable a man is of walking away from the central conflict of the play, the closer he approaches a tragic existence." He had tried to avoid tragedy for five years by "walking away" from the other woman, by evading a choice, by cutting off every contact with Marilyn. Because he could not walk away from it, in the end, his was a personal tragedy.

On the level of conscious creative intention his play was meant to examine a community in the grip of irrational fears. Yet *The Crucible* became a play about marital infidelity, and its tragedy is that of a man tormented by shame and guilt. The dark rituals in the forest practiced by Abigail and her young friends, who dance naked around fires, are the rituals of eroticism. Witchcraft, if you like, for is it not a sort of magic that can turn a serious man from his family ties and his occupation with the important social forces of his time and enslave him to a young girl's beauty and vivacity? Both *The Crucible* and *View from the Bridge* are concerned, wrote Miller in 1957, with "the awesomeness of a passion which, despite its contradicting the self-interest of the individual it inhabits, despite every kind of warning, despite even the destruction of the moral beliefs of the individual, proceeds to magnify its power over him until it destroys him." Looking back on *The Crucible* he could now see that "the central impulse for writing it at all was not the social but the interior psychological question, which was the question of the guilt residing in Salem which the hysteria merely unleashed but did not create. Consequently, the structure reflects that understanding, and it centers in John, Elizabeth, and Abigail."

In this play, John has tried to abide by his "moral beliefs" at all costs. He has sent the girl Abigail from the house. He touches her no longer. He does not even see her. If he dreams of her in unexpected moments, he does not act on his desires. But John's wife, who has believed that she and her husband had been sealed to each other until death, cannot condone even the single transgression with Abigail. It has shattered her pride. It has dispelled her illusion of an abiding love. She cannot forgive him. She punishes him with silences and coldness, with frowns and bitter allusions. In Act II, John says to her: "Spare me! You forget nothin' and forgive nothin'. Learn charity, woman. I have gone tiptoe in this house all seven months since she is gone. I have not moved from here to there without I think to please you, and still an everlasting funeral marches round your heart."

And what of Eddie Carbone?

In 1957, Miller suddenly identifies himself with Eddie Carbone! Between the New York and London productions of *View from the Bridge*, he divorced his wife and married Marilyn. He rewrote the play for its London engagement. Now he no longer sees Eddie Carbone as an anti-social "squealer," a namer of names, a betrayer to government agencies, whose sex perversion is but a symbol of his social perversion. Now he sees that the play "was expressing a very personal preoccupation and that it was not at all apart from my own psychological life. . . . Therefore many decisive alterations, small in themselves but nonetheless great in over-all consequences, began to flow into the conception of the play. Perhaps the two most important were an altered attitude toward Eddie Carbone, the hero, and toward the two women in his life. I had originally conceived Eddie as a phenomenon, a rather awesome fact of existence, and I had kept a certain distance from involvement in his self-justifications. Consequently, he had appeared as a kind of biological sport, and to a degree a repelling figure not quite admissible into the human family. In revising the play it became possible to accept for myself the implication I had sought to make clear in the original version, which was that however one might dislike this man, who does all sorts of frightful things, he possesses or exemplifies the wondrous and humane fact that he too can be driven to what in the last analysis is a sacrifice of himself for his conception, however misguided, of right, dignity and justice. In revising it I found it possible to move beyond contemplation of the man as a phenomenon into an acceptance for dramatic purposes of his aims themselves. Once this occurred the autonomous viewpoints of his wife and niece could be expressed more fully and, instead of remaining muted counterpoints to the march of Eddie's career, became involved forces pressing him forward or holding him back and eventually forming, in part, the nature of his disaster. The discovery of my own involvement in what I had written modified its original friezelike character, and the play moved closer toward realism and called up the emphatic response of its audience."

What in a sense Arthur Miller had done in the revision of *View from the Bridge* was to compose, in dramatic form, an *apologia pro amore sua*. He went through hellish agonies of guilt, and of struggles with his guilt and his desires, before he made his decision.

Marilyn knew nothing of these "interior psychological" conflicts that were raging in the man she idolized. She had decided that he did not love her. She perhaps believed that a man like Miller could not really admire her.

After 1952, according to the testimony of their friends as well as the internal evidence of his later plays, the Millers became incompatible. He still lived at home. He had no alternative, it seemed to him, because of the children. But when he met Marilyn again, in 1955, his feelings were stirred again.

One can find unworthy motives for Marilyn, as well as Arthur, in explaining their union. One might say that Arthur Miller was a badge of triumph she could wear to discomfit her Hollywood enemies. Well, she had captured America's great "intellectual" playwright, hadn't she? In Hollywood, Miller's name was part of a

272

mystique of "integrity" and "nobility." He was looked up to for his uncompromising courage, especially by those who had compromised their ideals for money.

Or one could argue that she schemed a marriage with him so he would write serious dramatic vehicles for her, just as Laurette Taylor had set her husband, Hartley Manners, to the writing of vehicles for her.

Perhaps these motives were present, but the primary fact is that Miller and Marilyn fell deeply in love with each other.

I once asked Marilyn how she defined love. She said love was trust; if you loved another person, you trusted him completely. I agreed with her, for this came close to my own definition of love. And Marilyn trusted Miller. She respected his strength, his sense of balance about money, his simplicity of living, his well-disciplined work habits.

On the basis of the internal evidence of his later plays, we can deduce that Miller's relationship with his first wife had been poisoned by guilt. He owed her too large a debt for her sacrifices to his career. To Marilyn he owed nothing. He could be himself. He could please her by pleasing himself. Indeed, he could do more for Marilyn than she could do for him. What if his own work suffered because of his love for her? Now it was he who made the sacrifices!

Their first encounter, after the long separation, took place sometime around May, 1955. Marilyn was attending parties given by actors and theatre people. Miller, whose social life was carried on apart from his wife, was also coming out of his shell. A withdrawn, shy person—in fact, not unlike Di Maggio in this respect—Miller had previously not been part of the theatre's gay whirl. He had lived a hermit's life. He had only three close friends outside his family: Elia Kazan; the poet and playwright Norman Rosten; and the publicist James Proctor. Kazan and Miller parted company in 1953 after Kazan had been a friendly witness before the House Committee on Un-American Activities.

At a party, Miller saw Marilyn, her back to the wall, looking serene and lovely in a simple white dress. She was sipping a vodka-and-orange juice. He went over to her. Immediately, she felt her skin warming. But she would be more careful this time about showing her feelings. They spoke in a casual way about the Actors' Studio and about Lee Strasberg. She asked him about his next play, and he told her something of the story of *View from the Bridge*. He did not take her home. She had come with the actor Eli Wallach and Mrs. Wallach (professionally known as Anne Jackson). Wallach, one of the charter members of the Studio, had become one of her dear friends. She once said to him, "Eli, you're like my big brother."

He looked at her and grinned. "Yeah, Marilyn, but what happens if I go for you?"

"Well," she said airily, "there's always incense."

Although she has dated directors, producers, writers, musicians, and cinematographers, Marilyn has never allowed herself to be romantically interested in actors. "Actors," she once wrote, "are wonderful people—but I couldn't love an actor. It would be like loving a brother with the same face and family traits as my own."

The Wallachs took her home that night. She didn't say anything about Miller, but they recall that she looked "dreamy" and seemed absorbed in happy thoughts. Miller had not asked for her telephone number.

About two weeks later, he telephoned Paula Strasberg to ask for Marilyn's unlisted number. Scenting romance, Mrs. Strasberg was delighted to supply the information. She thought that Arthur would be "good" for Marilyn, and Marilyn would be "good" for Arthur. Miller telephoned Marilyn and asked her to meet him at the home of Hedda and Norman Rosten. And here, during most of the next seven months, until their liaison officially leaked out, is where they held most of their trysts. Friends of Miller say he wanted to keep his love a secret to avoid embarrassing his wife.

He could have separated from Mary, of course, and set up his own apartment. But that was expensive. Foes of Miller describe him as a frugal gentleman who does not throw his money about with wild abandon. He has rarely been known to pick up a check in a restaurant. He wears chain-store suits and cheap shoes. He never takes taxis. Why, argue Miller's detractors, would he throw away money renting an apartment? Why spend money taking his girl to high-class restaurants?

The few persons who knew the secret kept it well. That summer, Arthur and Marilyn saw much of each other, at the Greenes' in Weston, Connecticut, at the Rosten summer place in Port Jefferson, Long Island, or at the Strasberg cottage on Fire Island.

Marilyn began drawing that summer. One day, on the beach, all the Strasbergs were sitting about, busy at water colors, charcoal sketches, oil painting. Finally, Mrs. Strasberg gave Marilyn a sketching pad and a stick of charcoal and told her to draw something. Her first drawing was remarkably good. With a few quick curving lines she drew a tall, elegantly dressed woman holding a glass of champagne. Marilyn titled it, "Oh, what the hell!" It hangs on a wall of the present Strasberg apartment on Central Park West.

That fall, Miller's new play went into rehearsal. Now he began seeing Marilyn more frequently, either at the Rostens' or at her apartment. She had moved out of the Waldorf and was now living at 2 Sutton Place.

Not a hint of the romance appeared in the columns. Eli Wallach covered for Miller by escorting her whenever she had to be taken to a party to which Miller was also going. They came separately and they left separately. Winchell later described Wallach as the "beard" of this intriguing affair. A "beard" is a term used by gamblers to describe a man who places big bets with bookmakers on behalf of other persons, usually well-known gamblers who don't want their names revealed.

A columnist who had gotten a reliable tip asked Marilyn directly whether she and Miller were having a love affair.

"How can they say we're having a romance?" she replied, her eyes wide with gray-blue innocence, her lips drawn in hurt sadness. "Why, he's a married man."

In September, Earl Wilson asked her, "Do you have any love interests now?"

"No serious interests," she replied, "but I'm always interested."

"There are rumors about your attractions driving this or that famous man, sometimes married, to distraction. What do you say to those tales?"

"Oh, first of all, it just isn't so. I like men, and I guess my friendship for some is sometimes misunderstood. Some of my best friends are men."

"In view of today's changing morals, do you think it's all right for a single girl to encourage the attentions of married men?"

Marilyn shrugged her shoulders. "I think everybody ought to do what they feel. Who am I to make any kind of rules?"

Her psychoanalysis was relieving Marilyn of a few of the moral inhibitions that had hobbled her spontaneity since childhood.

As the year drew to an end, Monroe Productions was in financial turmoil. By November, there were $20,000 in unpaid bills. Milton Greene had exhausted his cash and credit. He could not find any investors. He tried to sell part of his stock. Nobody wanted it. Miller did not put up any money. If 20th Century-Fox had held its ground longer, Marilyn would have surrendered.

Miller discreetly stayed out of her business affairs. At this time, he believed, with Karl Marx, that the cash nexus between man and woman was an unhealthy nexus. Miller's lack of interest during this time of troubles increased Greene's bitterness later when Miller turned against him.

At the studio, there had been a revolution. Darryl Zanuck had resigned as production head to set up his independent producing organization. Buddy Adler was the new head. He was determined to conciliate Marilyn and bring her back into the fold. The studio had paid $500,000 for the movie rights to *Bus Stop*, and Marilyn was ideal for the leading role.

In December, suddenly, negotiations were speeded up, and in the days before Christmas, Delaney worked around the clock to write a contract between 20th and Monroe Productions satisfactory to both parties.

On December 31, 1955, Marilyn signed the new contract. The date was crucial to her because income she received before the year's end would be taxed in a low-income year, in fact in a no-income year. Upon signing, Marilyn received a check for $142,500. This payment represented a special compensation, because Charles K. Feldman, co-producer of *Seven Year Itch*, had also been Marilyn's agent, and he had represented her in her negotiations with himself without having got a release of her fiduciary rights. The studio paid Monroe Productions $200,000 more for the rights to a screenplay based on the novel *Horns for the Devil*. This was a capital-gains deal. Monroe Productions used the capital to purchase *The Sleeping Prince*, Terence Rattigan's comedy, for which Greene had been bidding. Marilyn agreed to the purchase without reading the play.

The contract is a fascinating 85-page document. It gave Marilyn rights no movie star had ever secured before. She agreed to do four films for the studio, at a salary of $100,000 a film, during a period of seven years. She was permitted to make at least one film a year independently and to appear on six television shows a year. (She has refused offers of $500,000 to appear on a single television show.) While working in any 20th film, she was to receive $500 a week for expenses and a maid.

All her films must be "feature-length class A pictures." Although approval of screenplay was not spelled out in the deal, the "Class A" phrase was ambiguous enough for her to claim that any story she didn't like was not "Class A." Clause 4 gave her the right of approval of director. The contract listed 16 directors acceptable to her: George Stevens, Fred Zinneman, Billy Wilder, William Wyler, Alfred Hitchcock, Vittorio de Sica, Joseph Mankiewicz, George Cukor, Elia Kazan, Carol Reed, David Lean, John Huston, Joshua Logan, Lee Strasberg, John Ford, and Vincent Minelli (for musicals only).

Marilyn also got the right to name her own cinematographer. Among those listed in her contract as acceptable were Harry Stradling, Hal Rossen, James Wong Howe, and Milton Krasner.

Clause 11 of the contract begins: "Artist's services herein contracted for are of a special, unique, unusual, extaordinary and intellectual character and of great and peculiar value to Fox, and Artist's talent and services cannot be replaced by Fox. . . ."

Such a sentence, or one like it, appears in every contract, for it lays the groundwork for a damage claim if an actor defaults on his promises.

The sentence, though highly flattering, is legal mumbo-jumbo with little relation to the real status of an actor. Almost anybody can be replaced.

Not Marilyn Monroe.

The studio had tried to live without her for a year. It couldn't.

She was indeed "special," "unique," "unusual," "extraordinary," and of very great and very peculiar value to 20th Century-Fox.

27 Joshua Logan and *Bus Stop*

At a press conference in New York on February 9, 1956, President Monroe announced her forthcoming collaboration with Sir Laurence Olivier in *The Sleeping Prince*, a play by Terence Rattigan. "It has long been my hope and dream to act with Sir Laurence," she said. It was at this meeting that she encountered press antagonism in a naked form. She didn't know why it was happening. She didn't know how to meet it. Her old tricks of working on public sympathy by playing the orphan waif or the lush blonde wit no longer worked now that she was a $100,000-a-picture movie queen and the president of a big company besides. She was also called upon—as if she were a defendant being cross-examined by a prosecutor—to justify her proclamations of her devotion to art. Words to an actress can often mean only words and yet be very real. But the world expects words to have a connection with deeds. Except for the religious moralizers, the press had always been favorable to Monroe. When she desperately needed publicity during the hold-out, her press agents had courted and flattered the press.

But now she became increasingly aloof. Her public-relations minister, Arthur Jacobs, was a Hollywood image-merchant. He and Monroe would decide when, how, and where she would speak. Like a statesman, she preferred to communicate her thoughts at press conferences. Magazine and newspaper men seeking exclusive interviews or photographs, experienced what they described as a "runaround" from Monroe.

She had broken one of the unwritten rules of the American game. She was acting as if she were better than the masses. She was. She had become an aristocrat. But in a democracy it doesn't do to act like one, even if you are. One has to adopt the mucker pose, the spurious humility, the smile, and the handshake. Or, if you are going to stand above the common people, then you had better be consistent and eschew publicity altogether, as Garbo had done. But Monroe had gorged herself so long on a rich diet of publicity that she could not abstain from it.

At the press conference, Monroe, Sir Laurence, Rattigan, and Vice-President Greene posed for photographs. Monroe looked sleek in an elegantly styled bouffant coiffure. She wore a low-cut black velvet sheath dress with string straps. One of the straps broke during the conference. Judith Crist, of the New York *Herald Tribune,* provided her with a safety pin and helped pin her up.

Monroe was relentlessly grilled about her love of the theatre, the rumors of her friendship with Miller, the Actors' Studio, Vivien Leigh, Dostoevski. She insisted she was serious about playing Grushenka.

"How do you spell Grushenka?" somebody sneered.

She paused, looking for the source of the pain, like a bear being baited by dogs it couldn't see. "I think it begins with a G," she replied, uneasily.

How did Vivien Leigh feel about her husband's playing opposite Monroe, considering that Miss Leigh had played the role during the London run?

"My wife never wanted to—" Sir Laurence began.

But Marilyn's innocence dropped. She cut in. "I own it. I mean— my corporation owns *The Sleeping Prince.*"

Asked to define her quality as an actress, Olivier improvised an acute summation of her cinematic quality: "In my opinion, Miss Monroe has an extremely extraordinary gift of being able to suggest one moment that she is the naughtiest little thing and the next that she's perfectly innocent. The audience leaves the theatre gently titillated into a state of excitement by not knowing which she is and thoroughly enjoying it."

But most of the questions were directed at her. She was taken aback by their skeptical asperity.

A photographer asked, "Hey, Marilyn, how did it feel when the strap broke?" His tone indicated he thought the accident had been prearranged. Her temper broke through the façade. She glared at him, her lips working soundlessly for several seconds. Then she replied, almost violently, "How would you feel if something of yours broke in front of a whole room full of a lot of strangers?"

She turned on her stiletto-heeled evening shoes and strode out of the conference, with Greene trotting after her. She felt sick. She felt that once again she had to fight a hostile world. But why were they against her now? She did not realize that the hostility vented on the failure is as nothing to the hostility vented on the success. In a competitive society, being a success is a dangerous affair.

There was no turning back. She would prove herself all over again. At the Actors' Studio she had sat quietly for a year without speaking one word. Then one morning she and Maureen Stapleton did the opening scene of *Anna Christie*. Some time later she did the famous park-bench lovers' scene from *Golden Boy*. Both times, the professional actors who watched her described her work as "amazing," "wonderful," "real," "truly felt." The day before she was to do the scene for which she had been privately rehearsing with Miss Stapleton, she telephoned her and said, "Maureen, I don't think we should rehearse tomorrow. I hear somebody is going to do a very interesting scene at the Studio tomorrow morning, and I don't want to miss it."

"Marilyn," Miss Stapleton said, "the important scene is from *Anna Christie*. It's our scene."

"Tomorrow's the day—we—we do the scene? God, I thought it was next Friday!"

In February, also, she plunged into discussions with Joshua Logan about her conceptions of Cherie in *Bus Stop*. Encouraged by Greene, Monroe had asked Adler for Logan as her director.

Logan, who had already done an exciting Cinemascope version of *Picnic,* was the ideal director for this film and for Monroe. For one thing, he was close to the thinking of Stanislavsky; he was a good friend of Lee Strasberg; he had a good opinion of the Studio. Logan is the only American stage director who studied with Stanislavsky. In 1931, Logan, then twenty-three, lived in Moscow for a year. He watched Stanislavsky directing a production of *Coq d'Or*. He often went to the master's home for informal lectures on the dramatic art. From Stanislavsky, Logan learned infinite patience (Stanislavsky would rehearse a play at least six months). He learned to trust the instincts and the emotions of the actor and to wait until the actor's emotions crystallized in the moment of truth. It is not that Logan is against external discipline and professional control. No serious Method director—Robert Lewis, Kazan, Harold Clurman, Danny Mann—believes in uncontrolled spontaneity. It was rather that Logan's orientation gave him a favorable inclination to the disorderly means through which Monroe made characters. Olivier, on the other hand, like all English actors, had schooled himself to keep his emotions under control, making them the servants of his conscious artistic intentions, and he could not get along with Monroe. Olivier, after his experiences with her, described her as a "professional amateur."

To Logan, Monroe is "as near a genius as any actress I ever knew. She is an artist beyond artistry. She has the unfathomable mysteriousness of a Garbo." He once spoke to me in high praise of her creative work in *Bus Stop*.

"Marilyn herself," he told me, "conceived the basic approach to Cherie. What I did, well, I helped her get it on film. It wasn't just Cherie—but her feeling about the whole story put us all in the right key emotionally. She stimulated every one of us. George Axelrod, for instance, would come away from a meeting and say he wanted to rewrite a scene to get in some phrases Marilyn had happened to use in commenting on a part of the movie, or I'd get an idea for a good piece of action from something she did spontaneously.

"From the start, she visualized playing Cherie in a tender area that lies between comedy and tragedy. This is the most difficult thing for an actor to do well. Very few motion-picture stars can do it. Chaplin achieves it. Garbo, too, at times, in *Camille* and *Ninotchka*. And you know, I believe Marilyn has something of each of them in her. She is the most completely realized and authentic film actress since Garbo. Monroe is pure cinema. Watch her work. In any film. How rarely she has to use words. How much she does with her eyes, her lips, with slight, almost accidental, gestures. Of course, the basic theme of the illiterate girl with the hillbilly accent who thinks she's going to make it big in Hollywood, well, it was in Bill Inge's original play and it was in Kim Stanley's interpretation on the stage. But Marilyn put her own flesh on the character, and made the tawdriness, the pathos, the honesty of the girl so believable. Maybe it was because *Bus Stop* emotionally was the story of her life, but I can tell you this—she inspired all of us to do our jobs better."

Before his first meeting with Monroe, Logan decided he had better be briefed by Lee Strasberg. He was flabbergasted by the near rapture of Strasberg, knowing him to be a man not led astray by acting trickery. Could Monroe be as great an artist as Lee said? Strasberg told him to forget any preconceptions he had formed about her from her publicity.

"She is an actress," he told Logan. "She is a great actress. The two outstanding talents in the Actors' Studio were Marlon Brando and Monroe. You'll have problems, Josh. She's a frightened human being. She's insecure. But the problems don't matter because what she can give you is so beautiful."

Logan could understand fear because he had had to fight fear inside of him all his life and sometimes he had lost and had had to be hospitalized. "Anybody who is any good in the theatre is insecure and afraid," Logan says. He felt empathy for Monroe and she, sensing this affinity, trusted him completely.

Because of this empathy and also because the cinema medium was fairly new to him, Logan departed from well-established techniques of shooting. He made an experiment with her that proved of immense value in tapping her reservoir of feeling. He allowed her actress's imagination to run wild, ignoring time and expensive film grinding away, and the result was an uncanny texture of psychological realism Monroe had never achieved so perfectly in any film.

She was determined to prove she had been right about her talent. Never before had she worked with as much seriousness.

For 15 months she had not faced a camera. And she was getting older. She had become painfully aware of her age as she drew close to that symbolic boundary line in a woman's life, the age of thirty, the age at which a woman feels she is entering upon her middle age. It is a difficult time for any woman. For an actress, above all a Hollywood movie actress, it is a horror. She exists in a sub-culture which places an absurdly high value upon youth. She is competing with twenty-year-old starlets, fresh, firm-fleshed, healthy, vibrating with ambition.

Yet Monroe didn't look her years. Her face was rounder and more interesting than it had been. But she did not look twenty-nine on the screen, and she did not look twenty-nine off the screen. Except during periods of great fatigue or severe illness, when her face suddenly crumpled into maturity, she preserved the flesh and the innocence of adolescence.

Monroe's obsession about growing old was revealed during her discussions with Greene and Logan over the casting of Bo Decker, the primitive cowhand who tries to win the girl as if he were roping a calf. They went over a long list of available actors.

"There isn't a man you can't think of whom we didn't try to see if he was right for the part," Logan recalls. Most of the names were rejected by Monroe. "He's too young." "He's too short." "He'll never do, that one—I'll look like his mother." "This one's too sweet." "Oh, he's sooo like a baby." The trauma of playing opposite Donald O'Connor had not been forgotten. She wouldn't make the same mistake again.

At one of the early meetings, Greene suggested Rock Hudson. Could they get him on loan from Universal-International? Would he be able to cope with the accent? Did he have a sense of comedy? Monroe strongly believed Rock Hudson was an actor, and not merely a strong silent physique. Logan became enthusiastic. Greene began negotiations with Henry Willson, Hudson's agent.

"I must have spent over five hundred dollars in phone calls to the Coast," Greene says.

Then Monroe wavered. What if Hudson overshadowed her? She must be careful. Paula Strasberg, who had become Monroe's coach, repeatedly said, "Albert Salmi's the only one to play Bo as he should be played." Salmi, a member of the Studio, had given a vigorous reading of the reckless Bo in the stage version. He had got all of Bo's crudeness without making him unsympathetic. Monroe hovered between being sure Hudson was perfect and Salmi was perfect. By the time Hudson had been persuaded to play Bo, however, Monroe decided to think it over. She left for Los Angeles, in March, with Bo still uncast.

Monroe's arrival at the International Airport was a triumph. "Hollywood turned out to meet her as few women have been met," reported *Time*. The press coverage was fantastic, and thousands of admirers were milling around. The absence of 15 months had only made their hearts grow fonder. She had not been forgotten. The ovation was tremendous, like that in Korea. It took her two hours to get free of the mob.

The Greenes had rented a small Colonial house on Beverly Glen Boulevard. Monroe stayed with them. She was afraid to live in a hotel. She was deathly afraid of Natasha Lytess. She was afraid Miss Lytess would do something to her. Miss Lytess had made no threats, but Monroe was terrified—terrified, perhaps, of the projection of her own guilt. For she had cut herself off from her old friend and teacher without an explanation. She had not spoken to her or written to her, and she had not replied to Natasha's letters. Until *Bus Stop* went into production, Natasha believed she would continue at Monroe's side. Then she received a lawyer's letter notifying her that her services would not be required any longer. The studio took her off the payroll. It must be a mistake! Natasha tried to get Monroe on the phone, but Monroe was never there when she called. Natasha made no secret of her bitterness. "I did more for her than a daughter," she said. "With just a motion of her fingers, she could have told them she wanted me to stay at the studio even if she didn't want me herself on this picture. So this is my reward for sitting with her until midnight and two A.M., night after night, trying to teach her to become an actress."

Monroe was changing in many ways. The studio tendered a cocktail party to introduce what they called the "new Marilyn" to the movie colony and the movie writers. They saw a different person. She was dressed with more style, for one thing, for Mrs. Greene, who had been a high-fashion model, was now assisting her with her personal wardrobe. Monroe looked chic, she looked sophisticated. She didn't look like a little girl dolled up in a fancy dress costume who had wandered by mistake into a party of grown-ups. Dorothy Manning, a fan magazine writer, was struck by the difference: "Gone was the shy, tense, little girl voice, the slow groping for just the right word, the hesitation in answering a question. . . . In its place was a poised woman who could take command of a party. Gay, relaxed, less self-conscious, she came up in a few minutes with sprightlier conversation than most stars can manage in hours."

She felt her own power now. Always a self-absorbed person, she'd been compelled, while struggling upward, to conceal her nature under a mask of humility. Now it wasn't necessary. She was the queen of her studio. The drastic change in her attitude to other people is indicated by her new behavior on the set. During the making of her next three films, she ignored almost everybody on the set, including, at times, the three directors. She did not condescend to make any of the conventional democratic gestures of friendliness to the grips and electricians. Her conduct to most of her fellow actors and actresses ranged from airy superiority to downright rudeness.

Inhabiting a universe of one, oblivious to the rest of humanity, she now could revel in her obliviousness. Formerly her hostile impulses had been expressed indirectly by withdrawing or in the form of psychosomatic illnesses. Now she frequently lost her temper. She would say cruel things. She belittled and upset her leading men— Don Murray in *Bus Stop,* Olivier in *The Sleeping Prince,* Tony Curtis in *Some Like It Hot.* On some days, Monroe literally drove Olivier to drink. Curtis became so enraged by her "vicious arrogance" and her "vindictive selfishness" that during the shooting of one scene he slapped a glass of water out of her hands. Her behavior to Murray was so insulting on one occasion that he went to Logan and said that he refused to work with her any longer unless she apologized. In the first encounter between Murray and Monroe in the Blue Dragon Café, the action called for Monroe to escape Murray's advances by running off the cabaret floor; Murray clutches at her gown to hold her; he manages to rip off her long train. Monroe read her line, "Give me back my tail," and then she snatched the heavy sequined train and whipped Murray across the face so violently that he was cut in several places.

Logan took up the matter with Monroe. She agreed to make the *amende honorable.* She planned a gracious speech, but when she started saying it, she burst into tears and yelled, "Damn it, damn it, damn it—I won't apologize to you, no, no."

One of the dubious advantages of psychoanalysis is that by freeing the neurotic from his inhibitions, it also reveals, in a naked form, his anti-social tendencies. It is, of course, healthier for the patient to vent hostility openly than to repress it. As for the health of those who have these hostilities vented upon them, well, that, as the psychoanalysts like to say, is *"their* problem."

The casting of Don Murray, an unknown actor of twenty-seven who had never before appeared in films, was a last-minute decision. By the time Logan had persuaded Monroe to accept Rock Hudson,

Rock's pride had been wounded. He turned down the role. 20th Century-Fox would not give Salmi the role unless he signed a three-picture deal. Salmi refused. Logan then suggested Murray, whom he had seen in the ANTA revival of *Skin of Our Teeth*. Murray was hurriedly screen-tested and hired.

For two weeks before *Bus Stop* began shooting, there were daily conferences in an office set aside for Logan on the lot. Present at the meetings were Logan, Monroe, Don Murray, Greene, Mrs. Strasberg, Axelrod, and Buddy Adler. Adler was as deferential to Monroe as his predecessor had been distant.

Monroe made her newly acquired power felt not only in the matter of casting, but in make-up and costumes. The costume department at 20th had submitted sketches for the clothes she was to wear. Monroe said they were too glamorous.

"Let's not have my clothes made to order," she said to Logan. "Let's go find them in wardrobe." She and Greene rummaged about the racks until they found tawdry-looking blouses, skirts, kimonos, dresses that Monroe felt suited the character of the ratty girl who had never had money for good clothes, who was strictly a small-time cabaret B girl without any big talent. She liked Travilla's design for the long gown to wear during her ballad number at the café. But after it was made, she insisted on tearing it in many places and having the rents repaired; she pulled off spangles here and there, and let it get soiled. The net stockings she used in the scene in which she sings "That Old Black Magic" were ripped and then darned with crude stitching. Monroe knew how it had been with her when she had only one pair of nylons and one dress.

Her desire to be true to life, down to the torn hose, delighted Logan, though it horrified the front office. What if, in her desire to be so realistic, she dispelled her glamour? Suppose Cherie looked like a tramp? But Monroe would not be deflected. Greene, having pondered the lighting and make-up of Monroe as if it were the sole purpose of his existence, had conceived a chalky-white make-up. "Almost a clown make-up," Logan says.

The customary color tests were made. The front office was aghast. "Every day," Logan says, "we got a message from Buddy Adler or somebody else, telling us to change the chalk make-up. I kept saying, 'Trust her. Trust me. We are doing this with a purpose.' "

286

A disciple of Strasberg, Monroe looked for the dominant quality of the character's appearance. It lay, she decided, in Cherie's weariness. Cherie is never out in the sunlight. She sings in the café until 4:00 A.M. She sleeps around after that. She doesn't get much rest or sunshine. She is a pale, dead white. Her fatigue contrasts vividly with Bo's vitality.

Monroe saw Cherie's central motivation, as well as the sum of the movie, in this sentence: Will this girl who wants respect ever get it? (Stanislavsky urged actors and directors to sum up the plot of a play in one key sentence. His celebrated summary of *Hamlet* was: "To catch a murderer.")

"To me," Logan says, "Marilyn's attitude toward her make-up and costume was courageous. Incredible, really. Here you have a well-established star. She was willing to risk her position with a make-up many stars would have considered ugly. She wasn't afraid. She believed she was right in her analysis of the character, and she had the courage to commit herself to it completely."

On March 12, the entire company was scheduled to fly from Los Angeles to Phoenix, Arizona, where an actual rodeo was to begin on March 15. The location sequences—on the street, at the parade, at the rodeo—were to be shot first. Monroe missed the plane by 20 minutes.

Aware that he was dealing with a highly nervous woman, and considerably upset by the irresponsibility she had shown by missing the plane, Logan expected that the location sequences would go badly. The first day's shooting was done during the actual opening parade and ceremonies of the rodeo. Logan had to integrate long shots of the real paraders and onlookers with medium shots of Arthur O'Connell (playing Virgil, Bo's friend) marching as a cowboy and with shots of Marilyn and Don Murray. The shots were not faked. Those of Monroe, balancing unsteadily on Murray's shoulder as he raced out whooping, were taken amid the exuberant Phoenix citizens. A crowd of 25,000 persons flooded the streets.

Before the parade started, Logan had rehearsed the action with Monroe, Murray, and O'Connell. He noticed a rather alarming fact. The Phoenicians, especially the masculine ones, instead of acting naturally were staring at Monroe. If they did this during the shooting, the footage would be useless. And if Monroe fluffed her lines the first time, the sequence would be ruined. There would be no chance for retakes, and Josh had already heard rumors that Monroe never did a scene right the first time.

Logan is a big man—6 feet 2 inches tall, with the face of a Roman emperor and a commanding bulk. His personality is likewise commanding. Through a public-address system rigged up on the main street, he bellowed to the crowd: "Ladies and gentlemen, I just want to say a few words before we start the cameras rolling. I know you all want to see yourselves in the movies. Now, if you want to see yourself in pictures you'll have to do what I tell you. Don't look at the cameras. Don't look at Don Murray. And above all don't look at Marilyn Monroe!" (Whistles, cheers, and laughter.) "I know this is going to be hard—but you'll have to do it."

Logan used three cameras—one for the parade and the crowd, one for O'Connell, and the third for Monroe and Murray. The crowd comported itself like Hollywood extras, and the scenes of the parade went marvelously. What delighted Logan even more was that Monroe didn't blow a line. Surely all those rumors about her retakes were just spiteful gossip. He expected he'd be getting every shot on the first or second take. He'd bring the film in ahead of schedule and way under the budget. It's harder for movie actors to work on location than in the studio. Not Monroe. Playing *al fresco* before a crowd of strangers encourages her to give a good reading on the first take. Everything went smoothly: the scenes of Marilyn and her confidante, the waitress (played by Eileen Heckart), watching the rodeo from the stands; Monroe trying to escape from Bo, racing across the arena.

Only once did Monroe display her legendary temperament (there were to be more displays when they returned to Pico Boulevard for the interiors). This was during a scene at the bus depot. Cherie has stolen out of a rear window at the Blue Dragon Café. She's still wearing her sleazy cabaret costume, over which she has flung an old coat. She is carrying her suitcase. We next cut to her running down the street to the bus depot. It is about ten at night.

Logan and cinematographer Milton Krasner wanted to shoot this scene at the "magic hour." On this evening, it would fall at about twenty minutes after six, calculated Krasner. When the scene was on film, however, the viewer would have the illusion that it was late at night.

In order to get set for the scene, the company and the technicians had left the stadium (where some medium shots for the rodeo sequence had been taken that morning) and arrived at the bus depot at two. Monroe was settled in a nearby hotel room which had been converted into her dressing room.

"It was a marvelous exterior," Logan says. "You could see the mountains in the background. The bus station looked right. The street had a lot of neon-lighted pizza parlors and taverns. Just the gaudy quality we wanted to get into the scene."

At about two-thirty, Monroe had retired to have her hair fixed. She was wearing a poodle cut of Greene's design in this film; instead of the usual platinum sheen, her hair was a reddish-blonde shade. Her make-up man then began working on her face. The hours drifted by. At five-forty-five, Monroe's stand-in made the trial run, down the street and into the depot. The positions were marked. Krasner had his camera operator alerted to follow the action. At five minutes after six, there being no sign of Monroe, Logan sent his assistant director to the hotel. The a.d. did not return.

The minutes ticked on. Logan got tenser. "Where's Marilyn?" he inquired of nobody in particular. "Where's Marilyn?" Krasner was squinting at the sky, watching the formidable streaks of orange and turquoise in the heavens.

Logan dispatched the script girl to remind the a.d. of his mission. Still no Monroe.

Krasner cursed. "We'll miss it," he said, and called down imprecations upon Monroe's reddish-blonde head. "We have four minutes left, Josh, that's all, four minutes."

Logan groaned. "Even though my name is Joshua, I can't make the sun stand still," he said. With roughly three minutes left, he suddenly broke into a sprint. He ran into Monroe's hotel room like an enraged bull. There she sat, bemused at her reflection in a mirror.

"Come on," he panted. "Run!"

He grasped her hand. He yanked her down the stairs, and when they got within camera range he pushed her violently and told her to run and keep on running, goddamit, until she got into that goddam depot, and to Krasner he screamed, "Action. Roll it, roll it."

If Monroe looked flustered, breathless, frightened in the scene, it was not because of Bo Decker, but because of Josh Logan.

The only member of the company with whom Monroe was on a companionable basis was Eileen Heckart. Miss Heckart (Mrs. Jack Yankee in private life) had brought her children, Mark, six, and Peter, four, with her. Monroe became friends of the boys and played with them when she wasn't otherwise occupied. One afternoon several of the actors were walking by the hotel when they were suddenly pelted with oranges from above. They looked up. There, leaning out of a window, were the laughing faces of Mark, Peter, and Marilyn.

On the first day of shooting at Phoenix, Miss Heckart, who had flown from New York, where she had just finished playing Mrs. Carbone in *View from the Bridge*, accosted Monroe. She introduced herself and then said, "Arthur sends you his best regards."

Monroe looked at her blankly.

"You know," Miss Heckart lamely explained, "I mean Miller—Arthur Miller. He's a friend of yours, isn't he? I thought so from his mentioning you to me and giving his regards. I was in his play. You know. Miller?"

"I don't know what you're talking about," Monroe said loftily, strolling away.

The next day, Monroe drew Miss Heckart aside. "You remember Mr. A?" she inquired conspiratorially.

"Mr. A?" echoed Miss Heckart. "Who the hell is Mr. A?"

Monroe looked over her shoulder. She put a hand on Miss Heckart. "Shh, don't talk so loud," she whispered. "Remember that man we were talking about that sent me the regards?"

"Oh *him*, yeah. . . ."

"Well, I talked to Mr. A last night. He calls me on the phone every night. Nobody knows he calls me on the phone. It's a secret. I asked Mr. A if it was all right to tell you I talked to him, and he said it was fine, just fine."

"Yeah, well I'm happy to hear you and Mr. A have it all straight now."

In April, Mr. A went to Nevada for his divorce. Mrs. Miller did not contest the divorce. Mr. A took up his six weeks' residence in a secluded cabin near Pyramid Lake, 45 miles from Reno. The New York *Post*, which, in June and July, appointed itself as a benevolent angel hovering approvingly over the romance, on the theory, perhaps, that Monroe's love for Miller was a victory for liberals and a defeat for conservatives, revealed that during the time he was in Reno, Miller "spent most of his time in his cabin, writing three-fourths of a new novel." The last quarter of the novel must have given its author an unusual amount of trouble for, some four years later, the book's publication had not yet been announced. Some authors are inspired to furious outbursts of creativity by the tender passion; others are inhibited, distracted, or find writing a bore compared to love. And it isn't that actresses necessarily produce more disturbance in an author than ordinary women. D'Annunzio wrote several novels during his affair with Eleanora Duse, and Mrs. Patrick Campbell inspired Shaw to write *Pygmalion*.

When the shooting began in the studio, Monroe's insecurities troubled her. She had difficulty with lines. She blacked out in the middle of speeches. Every scene now took 10, 12, 15 takes. A movie is shot in small fragments of action, a take generally lasting no longer than two or three minutes, although the wide-screen medium has made it necessary to shoot longer takes.

Logan was appalled by the increasing number of takes. As inevitably happened, Monroe's memory lapses tended to create anxiety in the actor playing opposite her. Soon Murray began blowing lines.

He and Monroe were playing the scene in which he breaks into her bedroom while she is asleep. It is 9:00 A.M. and time for all human beings to get up. Murray's line was, "Wake up, Cherie, it's nine o'clock, no wonder you're so pale and white."

Monroe insisted on playing the bedroom scene naked. Since her success in *Niagara,* she had always played bedroom scenes, or rather scenes in which she is under the covers in a bedroom, *au naturel.* She came on the set in a terry-cloth robe. She got under the sheet. She raised it like a tepee. Then one hand appeared, flinging out the robe. Entirely nude, she stretched out under the sheet, her face and shoulders showing.

Murray, understandably confused, read the line as "Wake up, Cherie, it's nine o'clock, no wonder you're so pale and scaly."

Logan shouted, "Cut."

Monroe smiled. "Don," she said, "you made a Freudian slip. You said *scaly* instead of *white*. That's very good. That means you're getting the emotion of the character subconsciously."

"How do you figure that?" Don asked.

"Well, you know how you're supposed to feel sexy about me?

Well, *scaly* is like a *snake,* and a *snake* is a phallic symbol. See? You know what a phallic symbol is, Don?"

"Know what it is?" replied the insulted Murray. "I got one!"

One of the difficulties in portraying moments of intimate emotion in Cinemascope is that the screen is wide but not tall. In a tight close-up, a face looks distended and squashed. Logan wanted to get in close during the great love scene between Cherie and Bo in the diner toward the conclusion of *Bus Stop.* He wanted to get in extremely close, as had been done in silent films, so close one could see the magnified lips and eyes of the actors. Krasner said that with the conventional six-inch lens you couldn't shoot any closer than six feet. Logan said he wanted to get in close enough to see the fuzz on the cheeks and the veins in the eyeballs. Krasner said he would try a diminishing lens, the kind used for a shot of a small prop—a calling card or a teacup, for instance. In this way, one could get within inches of the face.

To make clear the point of what follows, I must explain that movie craftsmen use the word "establishing" to denote a shot that sets a locale or indicates a motivation. An "establishing shot" indicating, for instance, that the action is taking place in Manhattan, might be a shot of the New York skyline.

Now, Monroe had been excited by the experiment of a tight close-up in Cinemascope. As Krasner and his operator were training the camera on Murray and trying it out, she couldn't hold her excitement in. At this point, the operator, sighting Don Murray's image in his finder, called out, "I can't see the top of his head."

Monroe cried out, "Well everybody knows he's got one. It's been established!"

The most difficult sequence to do was the one in which Monroe speaks to Hope Lange on the bus, returning from the rodeo. Cherie explains how she's being abducted by a maniacal cowboy. She asks Elma (Hope Lange) to help her escape from his clutches. It was almost a monologue for her—solid masses of speech. In the course of her speech, Cherie tells the sordid story of her relations with various men, and reveals her dreams and her aspirations. She has to convey to us not only a lifetime of poverty and frustration but a half-defined desire for love, a wonderful love. "I want a guy who'll treat me with respect and have a regard for me, 'sides all of that lovin' stuff."

This was the most difficult challenge that Monroe, as an actress, had had. She could not just deploy her cinema mastery, distill her sexual mystery and put it into visual images of her eyes and lips and body. She had to use words, long blocks of them, sentences, paragraphs. She had to act as an actress in the theatre acts.

The sequence went badly. Time after time she fluffed lines. Time after time Logan yelled "Cut," and then her mood was broken as the electricians relighted the scene, the make-up man put on new make-up, the wardrobe women fixed her costume. The first day Logan didn't even have one possible take. Nor the second. Nothing had been printed. What was wrong with Monroe?

"She needs more time," Mrs. Strasberg said.

"She's had plenty of time," Logan said. "Why can't she remember her lines?"

"But she knows them letter-perfect."

"Go over them again with her tonight. I hope she gets over whatever the hell's bugging her."

The next day, as Logan was in the middle of a suggestion, Monroe suddenly walked away from him. He wondered if she hadn't been sparked into a mood of enthusiasm and wasn't anxious to get on the bus set and try it before the camera. Perhaps she wasn't being rude or indifferent. Perhaps when he thought she was blacking out in a reading, she was feeling her way slowly to the emotions behind the lines. What if the time she needed was time to secrete the emotions and they came slowly, with delays every few lines? He remembered how sometimes, in the midst of a scene, she'd suddenly ask, "Can I have a moment to think?" And she'd go off by herself and brood about something. Perhaps it was true that she knew the lines and was seeking the reality behind the lines.

He suspected that inherently Monroe was a stage performer. She had developed her artistry in the cinema, and developed it to a purer essence than anybody since Garbo. But the nature of camera acting was as unnatural to her as it was natural to Garbo. A film is a series of pictures and the action is placed within a frame, just as a painted landscape or a portrait exists within a picture frame. Acting in the movies was emotionally frustrating to Monroe because she had to keep fixed positions, marked out on the set. If, because of a spontaneous reflex of emotion, she moved out of the marked position, then the composition in the frame was disturbed. The camera, trying to follow her, stumbled into a badly arranged composition. Or she might be cut out of the frame entirely, or part of her body might be missing.

Logan had also noticed that when the camera was rolling, Monroe, unlike most movie actors, had a tendency to keep on talking and moving as long as he didn't say, "Cut." He decided he must find a way to prevent her from worrying about whether she was right on the mark or standing in the wrong position. The sensitive recording camera caught even the most subtle bodily changes. When it caught the blank look or the look of indecision, the reality of the character faded. When Monroe made a mistake, she blushed or frowned, and the camera caught it. Logan believes that in Monroe, side by side with the actress, is a critic; if she doesn't measure up to the critic, she blushes or looks sick. But instead of indicating that she had gone to pieces, it might mean that she was on the verge of being good.

That afternoon, Logan told Krasner to put the camera on her during the bus sequence and keep it on her. There would be no cries of "cut." And so it went. The camera kept on grinding when she halted in the middle of a sentence, it kept on grinding when she went blank, and Logan just murmured to her to go on and said something encouraging or handed her a prop. This technique meant that every foot of film had to be printed, because she did dozens of bad takes intermingled with good ones. The entire day's work and the next day's work had to be printed. Logan said, "We printed ten times as much film as we'd normally have printed, but now I had one moment after another where Marilyn had been freed from pressure and her emotions rose to the surface."

Whether Marilyn Monroe possesses the skill and the imagination to portray Medea, Lady Macbeth, Camille, Cleopatra, Blanche Dubois, and the other tragic heroines of dramatic literature is yet to be proved, but in *Bus Stop* she showed she was an actress of impressive range. Her Cherie is a complex character of many subtleties and nuances. From the moment of her first appearance, through all the sequences and the final culmination, she truly sustained this pathetic, illusion-ridden creature.

Monroe's first appearance in a film is generally an exciting pictorial experience. The one in *Bus Stop* is superb. Using the camera cleverly, Logan shows Monroe inside of three frames: the frame of the film; the frame of a window, several stories up, from which

O'Connell is looking down into a back alley; and then the third frame of an open window in which he suddenly glimpses the unexpected vision of Marilyn. Knees drawn up, in a kimono, she balances, wearily smoking a cigarette. There are many unforgettable moments like this in the film. Monroe singing "Old Black Magic," operating light switches with her feet, deploying a green scarf in an absurd imitation of a night-club chanteuse; flirting with Bo in a stable; at the arena; snowbound in Grace's Diner, when she reaches an intensity during which Bo comes to give her the respect she craves and they kiss. As he whispers to her, their heads close together, their torsos stretching over the counter, we see her great eyes discovering his love; her left hand crumpled over her mouth is drawn away, and as it is drawn one sees a thread of saliva from her lips to her fingers. The front office ordered the shots retouched to remove the saliva. Logan insisted it remain. It remained.

"I consider," he says, "that this is one of the greatest acting moments of intimacy in all movie history."

For the first time, the reviewers paid tribute to Monroe's acting ability. Bosley Crowther wrote: "Hold onto your chairs, everybody, and get set for a rattling surprise. Marilyn Monroe has finally proved herself an actress in *Bus Stop*."

She was now "a genuine acting star, not just a plushy personality and a sex symbol as she has previously been." I happen to believe that she had been acting for a long time, since *The Asphalt Jungle* in 1950. Her myth-making publicity, while helping to fabricate mass madness for her, also disposed the critics to see her film performances as a form of strip-teasing rather than as deliberately contrived acting performances.

In *The Saturday Review,* Arthur Knight expressed the new turn in critical reaction: "Speaking of artists, it is beginning to appear that we have a very real one right in our midst. . . . In *Bus Stop* Marilyn Monroe effectively dispels once and for all the notion that she is merely a glamour personality, a shapely body with tremulous lips and come-hither blue eyes. . . . For Miss Monroe has accomplished what is unquestionably the most difficult feat for any film personality. She has submerged herself so completely in the role . . . that one searches in vain for glimpses of the former calendar girl. . . ."

Even John McCarten unbent slightly: "Playing opposite Mr. Murray is Marilyn Monroe equipped with a rich Southern accent and a nice sense of the humorous possibilities of her role."

Since 1953, Monroe had enjoyed the admiration of film critics in England, France, and Italy. Being able to detach her work from her myth, they correctly gauged it as a true art expression. In *Cahiers du Cinéma*, July, 1957, Barthelemy Amengual wrote virtually a panegyric: "Marilyn Monroe promises to re-create the star of Garbo, after having already re-created the quality of Pola Negri. . . . With her [Monroe] I again recover the innocence of my eager adolescent heart when the silent films gave such lovely experiences."

He said that Monroe has "transposed into film the essential conquest of modern sculpture—the taking possession of space. . . . Cherie is not a realistic copy of the American female alone. By means of her omnipresent body, she becomes a creature no longer of this world."

There still remained one great prize: the Academy Award. That she did not win it in 1956, that she was not even nominated, was a bitter thing to her. Logan says, "It's a disease of our profession that we believe a woman with physical appeal has no talent. Her performance that year was better than any other. It was a classical film performance."

Ingrid Bergman won the 1956 "Oscar" for the title role in *Anastasia*.

28 Hysteria in Connecticut

Monroe returned to New York on Sunday, June 3, 1956. She had celebrated her thirtieth birthday the previous Friday. Asked how it felt to be thirty, she replied, with an unmistakable air of grace and authority, "Kinsey says a woman doesn't get started until she's thirty. That's good news—and it's factual too."

She didn't think it was too late to get started as a woman. She would be Miller's wife and bear his children and be the thoughtful mother she herself had never had. After *The Sleeping Prince*—she expected that to be the crowning glory of her career—she would retire and make Arthur the center of her interest. She would be the servant of his moods and crises, the sharer of his artistic burdens, the romantic companion, the good mother. But Arthur loved her for what she was, rather than as the imaginary wife-mother of middle-class mythology. Acting was vital to her. If she denied that for his sake, she would eventually hate him for it. So he rejected any idea of her retirement. She had enough life force for all things.

He was waiting for her at the Sutton Place flat when she got in from the airport. He said it was time she met his family. Up to now, not even his family had known he was engaged to Monroe. He telephoned his mother, Mrs. Gittel Miller, and said he wanted to bring a girl over to meet her that night. She said that would be nice. They drove to a frame house on 1350 East 3rd Street, near Avenue M, in Flatbush. Marilyn was dressed simply in a gray skirt and a high-collared black blouse. Her golden hair was covered by a scarf. She wore no make-up. She looked decorous. Arthur introduced her to his father and mother.

"This is the girl I want to marry," he said.

Marilyn kissed Miller *père*. Then she clasped Mrs. Miller about the neck and fell to kissing and hugging her. She wept with happiness. Mrs. Miller, overcome by sentimentality, also cried with joy. Marilyn asked if she could call Mrs. Miller "mother." Mrs. Miller embraced her and said she felt as if Marilyn were a daughter to her.

Tears streaming down her face, Monroe said, "For the first time in my life, I have somebody I can call father and mother."

She was going to enter the Jewish faith, she went on. And she did. In her conversion to Judaism, Monroe anticipated two other movie beauties, Elizabeth Taylor and Carroll Baker. She took instruction in the Reformed branch of Judaism. Rabbi Robert Goldberg, a leading New England cleric, tutored Monroe in the history of the Jewish people and the main tenets of the faith, and later performed the wedding ceremony. Whether Monroe's conversion stemmed from a desire to please Arthur's parents, or arose from a mystical experience, we do not know. Neither do we know to what extent her conversion has altered her daily habits. The stringent dietary and ritualistic observances which Orthodox Judaism places upon the Jewish housewife—for instance the necessity for two different sets of china and flatware, one for meat and one for dairy meals—is not part of the Reformed belief, nor are there precise theological dogmas to which one must adhere.

There are three subjects Monroe will not discuss. Motherhood, politics, and religion.

For about two weeks, the news of the engagement remained a secret from the public. On June 20, the New York *Post* reported definitely that Miller and Monroe were going to take the leap sometime before July 16, when she had to be in England to start shooting her next film.

And now the dam broke. Miller had lived a solitary sort of life. The world burst in on his privacy. As long as he was married to Marilyn Monroe, he would never be able to live far from photographers' flashbulbs, the impertinent questions of reporters, the prying stories in magazines and newspapers. There was nothing he could do about it.

Like detectives stalking criminal prey, the press staked out Monroe's apartment around the clock. Meanwhile Miller, who had never been called before a committee even in the heyday of the Communist investigations, was now summoned before a committee investigating the "unauthorized use of United States passports." Monroe did not go to Washington with him. Miller said he was willing to sign the State Department affidavit of non-Communism. He said he would not "support now a cause or movement which was dominated by Communists." He stood on the principle that while he would answer every question about his own literary and political activities—and he did, often at eloquent length—he would not reveal the names of any other persons with whom he had had any political contact in the past. "I could not use the name of another person and bring trouble on him," he said. In the course of the testimony there was only one fleeting reference to Monroe. Miller said he had applied for a passport to go to England "with the woman who will then be my wife." The inquiry lasted three hours, and what it all had to do with the unauthorized use of American passports has never been elucidated.

Miller returned to Manhattan late the same night. The journalistic posse was still on duty in Sutton Place, in the street, in the lobby, in the elevator, in the corridor outside Monroe's flat. The next day Miller and Monroe answered questions at an outdoor press conference on 57th Street. Miller forced himself to smile for the photographers and posed obediently with his arm about her. Now would the journalistic Javerts release him? They would not. They still stalked 2 Sutton Place. They weren't going to miss that marriage, whenever and wherever it took place. He did manage to get Marilyn, his two children, and his mother away in a station wagon. They were bound for Roxbury, Connecticut. But another posse of reporters was waiting at Roxbury. Miller begged the press for a few days of privacy. If he and his fiancée were left alone, they would answer all questions at a press conference on Friday. The treaty was signed.

During this period, Mrs. Miller came to know her future daughter-in-law. "She opened her whole heart to me," Mrs. Miller says. Marilyn said she wanted to become part of the Miller family. She asked Mrs. Miller to teach her the fine points of preparing cold borscht, gefülte fish, chopped liver, potato pirogen, chicken soup with matzoh balls, and other Jewish delicacies. Mrs. Miller and she set to work in the kitchen. (By July, Marilyn was able to report that she had made a borscht so wonderful that Arthur said it had the authentic home flavor.)

The Friday morning of the press conference, the dogs of journalism and television bayed again outside the Roxbury house. I was there. This was my first direct contact with the hysteria that envelops a star at certain periods. It was chilling. One could see why Miller was afraid of us. Monroe was a native of that queer country in which it is taken for granted that one's personal life exists to be exploited for the titillation of the masses. But Miller was like a foreigner going into the jungle and having to get used to the growl and howl of jungle beasts and the frightful tropical bird screams.

On all the roads leading to the intersection of Old Tophet Road and Goldmine Road, where the Miller place was located, scores of automobiles were parked. Hundreds and hundreds of men and women—I would guess as many as 400—were straggling about the property, waiting for Monroe to emerge. The sun beat down. We sweated until our clothes were damp. The errand on which we had all converged was childish if you stopped to think about it. Was this marriage really of such importance to the modern world? Must every phase of it be recorded in words and pictures?

And yet here we were, the historians of the quotidian, some with the pencils and the folded copy paper, some with the Speed Graphics and the Leicas, some with the motion-picture cameras on tripod, waiting, waiting, waiting. People from the magazines, the wire services, the newspapers of ten states, the weeklies and the monthlies; from England, France, Germany, Italy, all rights including the Scandinavian; all sweating, waiting, waiting, thirsty, parched, starving, no coffee, trading morsels of gossip, trading rumors: *No they aren't in the house.* . . . *Yes they are.* . . . *They're in New York.* . . . *They're already married.* . . . *No they're not.* . . . *They're with his cousin up the road, Morton Miller.* . . . *No they're not, they took a plane to Europe.* . . . *No they didn't.* . . .

At three minutes to one, by my watch, a green Oldsmobile stopped short on a hill near the house. A tall man in a white shirt leaped out of the car. It was Miller. He ran down the hill and then up the other hill into his house. Close on his heels flew Monroe in a yellow sweater, her bosoms bouncing as she ran, faster, faster, down one hill, up the other hill, into the house. A girl standing near me, a correspondent for an English newspaper chain, said there were splotches of blood on the sweater.

"I think something's wrong," she said.

A cousin of Miller's, Morton Miller, who had been driving the Oldsmobile, stepped out of the car. We closed in on him. "There's been an accident," he said, "it's bad." His face looked bad. "They were following us. This white car was following us. There's a turn in the road. It's sharp. We slowed up and made the turn. You have to slow up. It's a sharp turn. We heard a crash. Behind us. We pulled over. We went back. There was a photographer and a girl. She was thrown out on the road. We tried to do what we could for them. She's bleeding. Arthur's calling the hospital now. God, she's cut all over." He started to cry. I felt ashamed. A messenger from a photo agency mounted his motorcycle and went up the road to take pictures. When he came back he said, "My stomach wasn't strong enough. I put a blanket on her. The bleeding . . ." The girl died in the hospital that afternoon. She was Myra Sherbatoff, American correspondent of *Paris-Match*.

But the machinery of publicity ground on. Monroe changed out of the bloodied sweater. The swarm of us, like flies to a carcass, flew to the accident and then flew back to the house. We congregated on the patio and grounds behind the house. The photographers got set. The reporters thought about questions to ask. The newsreel men wandered about, taking light readings, setting up tripods. The net sagged in the tennis court. The swimming pool was dry. The children's playground was deserted. The heat was relentless. It was hot under the trees, too. A sleepy basset hound, tethered to an oak tree, watched us with detachment.

Arthur's parents sauntered out of the house and Arthur and Marilyn joined them. Everybody lunged toward them. It was chaotic. Then Milton Greene took command. There would be 20 minutes for the newsreels, 20 minutes for the still photographers, 30 minutes for the reporters. Miller looked like a man in shock. Marilyn looked outwardly serene in a gold blouse and a black skirt cinch-belted. The photographers shouted at them as if they were models: "Put your head on his shoulder." . . . "Look over here." . . . "That's good—one more." . . . Click-clack. Plates shoved in. Plates yanked out. "Just one more." . . . "That's great." . . . Marilyn, look over

here." . . . Click-clack. Click-clack. "Say, Arthur would you smile?"
. . . An unlit cigarette drooped between Arthur's lips. What should
he smile about? He tried to keep some dignity in the obscene riot.
He didn't lose his temper. "How about a kiss, Marilyn?" . . . "Get
in a little closer." . . .

Miller's anger betrayed itself only in his clenched jaws.

Later, I asked Monroe whether Arthur Miller would take an active part in Marilyn Monroe Productions, Inc.

"Oh, no," she assured me, "absolutely not. My company, well,
that's business. My husband is pleasure."

They were secretly married that night by a municipal judge in
White Plains, New York. They were married again by Rabbi Goldberg on Sunday at the home of Miller's agent, Kay Brown. It was a
double-ring ceremony. The rings were from Cartier's. Lee Strasberg
gave the bride away. Miller expressed the fervent wish that the
world would go back to what it had been doing before he had fallen
in love with Marilyn.

29 He Was a Very Parfit Angry Knight

The girl who flew to Japan in 1954 was Marilyn, the dream girl of the automobile mechanic. The woman who flew to England on July 13, 1956, was Monroe, and she had become a star.

Traditionally, any actor who is billed above the title of a film or play is a "star." In this sense, Monroe was a star when Jerry Wald put her name above the title of *Clash by Night*. But the word "star," like the word "love," is too often profaned. The billing is irrelevant. Nor can "star" be expressed in terms of publicity, glamour, wealth, even talent. An actress may possess great talent and still not be a star. A star is a different breed of cat—and is accepted by society as a different breed. She is imperial. She is imperious. She wields great power. She exerts a mysterious fascination upon masses of people. She embodies a charismatic quality. She becomes more than human.

Marilyn's transition from the sex symbol to the star occurred during the period between her divorce from Di Maggio and her marriage to Miller. During these two years, she had succeeded in enlarging the dimensions of her artistry. She had radically changed her personality; to be more precise, she now was able to profess openly what she secretly believed. Her fears of moral sanctions and her guilts had diminished; she now reveled in the pleasures and powers of her position and had the courage of her narcissism. Her new husband worshiped at her shrine. He did not seek to bring her to earth. In fact, he gradually became her greatest fan.

They traveled to London with 27 suitcases, of which 24 were Monroe's, not to speak of wardrobe trunks sent by cargo ship. Their luggage weighed in at 597 pounds. At Idlewild, they paid $1,500 in excess charges—more than the price of their fare. The usual hubbub surrounded them at the airport. They gave a farewell interview in a private lounge. Monroe sparkled with animation. She said she looked forward joyously to being directed by Laurence Olivier. Miller looked as if he had not had a decent night's sleep in weeks. He was quoted as saying, "We both need more privacy and quiet. I hope we will find it in Britain. Being married to a girl like Marilyn Monroe is like living in a goldfish bowl." Later he denied having made the remark.

At the Roxbury conference, I had put several questions to Miller about his forthcoming work. I wondered when his next play would be ready for presentation. He told me it was almost completed and that Kermit Bloomgarden would produce it in the spring or fall of 1957, probably the fall. He would not discuss the theme of the play. He said he expected to do a final rewrite of it in England. He expected also to rewrite some sections of *A View from the Bridge*. His novel, whose title he would not reveal, was almost completed and he hoped it would be published in 1957.

I asked him if the novel and the play concerned marriage and divorce. He looked at me and his expression of solemnity did not waver. He said it was his habit never to discuss in advance the plot of any of his works. From the fact that he did not deny the conjecture, I reasoned that, in view of the emphasis on the wife-husband-younger woman pattern of his last two plays and his obviously intense feeling about Monroe, it was likely that both works dealt in some way with variations on what had become the obsessive theme of his later work. Just as his first two plays revolved about the obligations of father to son, so the next two centered on the obligations of husband to wife. . . .

On the basis of Monroe's publicity and her film imagery, the average Englishman had constructed in his mind a conception of Marilyn as the delectable female animal. Tom Ewell, being no impossibly handsome god, was a masculine figure with whom any Englishman could identify. *Seven Year Itch* had been a sensation in England. In June, a London weekly printed a special Marilyn Monroe edition, the first edition of this sort it had got up since Queen Elizabeth's coronation. Souvenir shops and tobacconists stocked reproductions of the *Monroe Desnuda*. She was also available on scarfs, ties, serving trays, and glasses.

Miller was not altogether a real figure to the English, either. He was lionized as a heroic St. George who had slain the dragons of McCarthyism. In the view of the *New Statesman and Nation* crowd, Miller occupied a higher rank as a creative artist and an intellectual than he actually held in his own country, where he was either disregarded or derided by the academic "higher critics" and the literary-quarterly brethren who make and break aesthetic reputations.

The Millers did not know that Sir Laurence was not popular with the gentlemen of the English press. He was "unco-operative." Sir Laurence abhorred columnists. The London columnists, or calumnists, are even more powerful than their Hollywood and New York counterparts. They write in a wittily scurrilous style that is to Winchell or Parsons as Evelyn Waugh is to Hemingway. Since his *Henry V*, Olivier had barred newspapermen from the studio. "I don't care to have such persons breathing down my neck," he said. Recently, Olivier had been paid $25,000 for endorsing a cigarette on television. Paul Tanfield, the *Daily Mail*'s waspish columnist, had nicknamed him Sir Cork Tip.

The plane set down in London at ten to eleven on Saturday morning, and the usual stampede ensued. The welcoming committee of Sir Laurence and Lady Olivier was swamped in a hysterical mob of reporters and movie fans and intellectuality fans. A photographer crashed into a newsreel camera, knocking it off its tripod. Another one lost his balance and fell at Monroe's feet. He was promptly trampled by other photographers who crushed his hands and feet.

"Are all your conferences like this?" Lady Olivier inquired.

"Well," Monroe said, "this is a little quieter than some of them."

The Oliviers and Monroes got into their limousines, and with a cortège of some 30 cars, containing the reporters, drove to Parkside House in Englefield Green, which the Millers had rented from Lord Moore. When they arrived at the Georgian mansion, Monroe flinched. "I thought from the way they said it was a cottage, it was going to be a cottage," she said. "This is more like a palace." Sir Laurence explained that in England the term "cottage" referred to any one-family house not in the city.

An impromptu press conference took place in the dining room. Was she wearing a girdle? She was, for a change. To keep her stockings up. She loved living in the country.

"You know, the birds and the bees," she said, clarifying her pastoral taste. "And the trees and, well, just nature. I love nature. I think riding a bicycle is the best way to see nature. I think I am going to buy a bicycle."

"Why, that is not necessary," Sir Laurence murmured. "I'll lend you mine, sweetie."

"Oh thanks, Larry," she said, "thanks a lot."

England was breathless with excitement. The London *Evening News* palpitated, "She is here. She walks. She talks. She really is as luscious as strawberries and cream." The *Daily Worker* raved over her beauty and found her one of the few pleasant aspects of American capitalism. Addressing delegates to the International Whaling Commission, meeting in London, G. R. H. Nugent, joint parliamentary secretary to the Ministry of Agriculture, Fisheries and Food, stated, "Marilyn Monroe has obviously come to England to dispute the saying of our great literary man, Dr. Johnson. He adjured us never to believe in round figures. One has only to take one look at her to see the truth that round figures do exist." She was invited to be the patroness of a cricket match for charity at Tichborne Park and to taste the rockbound solitude of the island of Aran; the Scottish knit-goods industry was preparing for her a lifetime collection of hand-knit cashmere twin-set sweaters; a group of "teddy boys," or English hipsters, invited her to join them for a bit of fish and chips in Penge, a London suburb; the *Daily Sketch*, in an effort to be helpful, presented her with a fine bicycle.

Parkside House was on ten acres of rolling greensward. Pathways wound through neatly clipped hedges. The entire property was walled in. A squad of four police guards was on constant duty during the day to keep intruders away.

When Miller told several reporters to quote him as saying, "Thanks, England, thanks for leaving us alone," the *Daily Mail* retorted, "England had little choice."

Out for a walk in the village, Monroe asked a group of persons gathered around, "Is there anybody here from Scotland?"

"Why?" an old lady wanted to know.

"I've got a Scotch name. Monroe is a real Scotch name."

They thought she was as mad as a hatter, and a bit standoffish, too.

Discordant notes were struck. A press conference, for which Monroe Productions had rented a ballroom at the Savoy Hotel, went badly. The questions came quickly, and they were barbed with spite and suspicion. What role would she most like to play?

"Lady Macbeth," she said.

They snickered. She looked pained. "Well," she said trying to recover the fumble, "please quote me right. I don't mean I'd like to play her right now, but sometime."

Did she still sleep only in Chanel #5?

"Considering I'm in England now," she said, deftly turning the steel, "let's say I am now sleeping in Yardley's Lavender."

"Are you really studying acting?"

"Yes. I'm serious about it."

"What inspired you to study acting?"

"Seeing my own pictures," she said, smiling gaily. That was a good sally, and it drew a friendly burst of applause.

From the back of the room, somebody called out, "Can you give us your tastes in music?"

"I like, well, jazz, like Louis Armstrong, you know, and Beethoven."

"Oh, Beethoven? What Beethoven numbers in particular, Miss Monroe?" the inquisitor said, coming down ironically on the word "numbers." There was a deathly hush in the room. She looked helpless. Everybody was waiting for her answer.

"I have a terrible time with numbers," she said, floundering helplessly. "But I know it when I hear it."

"What is your definition of an intellectual?"

"Oh, go look it up in a dictionary," she said, trying to rally, but the quip fell flat.

"Do you still believe in the seven-year itch?"

She looked dismayed. "I don't know what that means. The picture or the play?"

"The idea."

"What idea was that?" she asked.

"The idea behind the cinema."

"I never did understand that," she said, lamely.

Neither Miller nor Monroe satisfied British expectations. He was neither the clever, epigrammatic man of letters nor the romantic poet and lover. He was reserved, and though the English cherish reserve in themselves they do not admire it in others, considering it rather a privately owned national trait. A London friend told me, "Arthur makes a bad impression here. Cold as a refrigerated fish in his personal appearance. Not like a hot lover, more like a morgue keeper left with a royal cadaver."

Monroe, whom this friend found to be a woman with a "Japanese water-flower personality," remained a dry, shriveled paper thing. Her references to Lady Macbeth and Yardley's were strenuous attempts to make the English feel that she was one of them. But they were not amused. They would have been amused by a woman playing a film temptress who is in real life a highbrow and able to cite the opus number of her favorite late Beethoven quartet or articulate her interpretation of Lady Macbeth. But Monroe can't talk about such matters. They would have been even more amused if she had turned out a happy-go-lusty Aphrodite. They eagerly awaited those celebrated *double-entendres,* those Monroeisms, but Monroe was neither talkative nor witty. Socially, the Millers struck the Mayfair and Belgravia set as hoity-toity. They refused invitations and did not extend any. Monroe had other things on her mind. Before the first week's shooting was over, she was facing the most acute directorial crisis of a career in which directorial crises had been abundant.

For some time, Olivier had been bracing himself for the encounter. During the spring, Logan had written him a letter every week. "I kept warning him," Logan says, "that he mustn't expect disciplined stage deportment from her. He wouldn't get it. She's not a domesticated animal. She's a wild, untamed animal. I remember writing Larry once, 'You must be more than usually patient with her. Allow her mistakes. Lots of them. Print all the film you possibly can. She'll lose her inner blocs and be free to give you a wonderful performance.' "

Olivier replied, in a letter, that he was ironing himself out "nice and smooth."

Olivier, although exploding with rage many times, tried to hold himself in. Jack Cardiff, cinematographer of *The Sleeping Prince,* says: "Sir Laurence was marvelous with her. He had been warned in New York: 'Never shout at her. Never show you are cross. She'll have a nervous breakdown and you won't get any work done at all.

She'll be off six weeks.' So he would never raise his voice. She would sometimes walk over and talk to Mrs. Strasberg, just when he was trying to persuade a big scene out of her, and he'd just take it quietly and wait for her to come back. Or she'd be late. He never once, at least in my hearing, said anything even faintly cross to her. And it was a difficult picture to make."

But the actor Olivier was in conflict with the director Olivier, and the director had to lose out. For Monroe's personality on a screen is incandescent. Her star's radiance dims the other lights around her. Dame Sybil Thorndike, who played the Dowager Queen, became aware of this when she saw the daily rushes the first time. She said recently: "When working, on the set, I thought, surely she won't come over, she's so small scale, but when I saw her on the screen, my goodness how it came over. She was a revelation. We theatre people tend to be so outgoing. She was the reverse. The perfect film actress, I thought. I have seen a lot of her films since then, and it's always there—that perfect quality.

"She has an innocence which is so extraordinary; whatever she plays, however brazen a hussy, it always comes over as an innocent girl. I remember Sir Laurence saying one day during the filming: 'Look at her face—she could be five years old!'"

Monroe tires out her leading men because she gets better with every retake while they get weaker. Olivier, the actor, was put on edge by her slow way of "making contact" with the character, by her waiting for the mysterious chemical process by which she distilled her sexual essences. He was threatened by the mystical fact that by the most languorous and seemingly artless of techniques she was putting him in the shade.

It was not unnatural that Olivier the director should have unconsciously tried to protect actor Olivier's interests. The mistake had been to commission him as a director. Originally, Olivier was to co-star and George Cukor was to direct. Olivier agreed to co-star, provided he could read and approve the screenplay. He also wished to direct the film. He said that if Monroe Productions let him direct the film, he would not need to approve the script. Strasberg advised Monroe to accept Olivier as a director. He has since said: "Sometimes I help people make certain decisions and then people cross me up and behave in a way that I don't expect. Why does Olivier say he had difficulty with her? I would say she had difficulty with him.

Though it was her company that was producing the movie, she had very little say about it. She had given Larry all the rights of cutting and editing. It was he who insisted on the coronation sequence. This could have been one of the best films ever made. The picture wasn't romantic enough. Larry has no right to say he had a terrible time with her. I was there. We had a terrible time with him. He just wouldn't listen. Paula had nothing to gain by telling him his performance was too artificial and that some good honest sentiment would help it enormously.

"And he wanted Marilyn to imitate, of all people, Vivien Leigh's performance. An English girl playing an American part, and he wanted Marilyn to imitate Vivien Leigh. On the set, he took everything as a personal slight when it wasn't. He never let Marilyn find her performance. He gave her orders and expected her to obey. He played the Regent too coldly in the early scenes, and this made a romantic atmosphere unconvincing later. Larry's conception of a good performance is an artificial performance. That's exactly what we thought wouldn't come over on the screen. The screen did not have to imitate what he had done on the stage. The screen permits a more flexible, wide-ranging, intimate approach."

There were other psychological currents in maelstrom on the set. Increasing tension developed between Olivier and Mrs. Strasberg, who had come over to coach Monroe. Mrs. Strasberg not only worked over Monroe's lines and actions in private, but she was also on the set and frequently was consulted by Monroe. Each morning, Monroe went through peculiar hand-shaking exercises for about 15 minutes before starting to act. She did these under Mrs. Strasberg's guidance. During the day, Mrs. Strasberg was seen feeding Monroe pills of varied colors.

Some of Olivier's anxiety became focused on Mrs. Strasberg. He decided that Monroe's unstable temperament was encouraged by her coach's coddling. He ridiculed the exercises and the pills. The pills were variously vitamins, tranquillizers, sedatives, or anodynes. Nobody took the trouble to explain to the director that Monroe suffered from long and painful menstrual periods.

She became seriously sick during the second week of shooting and missed two days. Was this psychosomatic? Was she pregnant? Or was it due to all the caviar and champagne with which she'd been stuffing herself? She had been playing the supper sequence of the film. This takes place when the Regent of Carpathia (played by Olivier), visiting London for the 1911 coronation, is impressed by the charms of Elsie Marina, an American chorus girl. He invites her to the legation for a party. She comes, expecting a grand ball, and then sees that it is going to be supper à *deux* with a seduction to follow. She was required to drink champagne and eat caviar and cream trifle. The wine, the sturgeon eggs, the cream were genuine, for being now a Stanislavskyite, Monroe would brook no little bread balls dyed black in place of Beluga caviar. The caviar came from Fortnum & Mason's and cost $12 a small jar. In two days of retakes Monroe consumed $60 worth of caviar, not to speak of endless glasses of wine. But, no, it couldn't be that her stomach was too proletarian for such food and drink. Since one illness or another troubled her continually, even when she was eating nothing richer than tea and biscuits, Olivier concluded this was a species of psychological warfare.

He believed that Monroe used Mrs. Strasberg when she wanted to show displeasure with him. Often, while he was explaining to her how he wanted her to say a speech, she would suddenly stride away, leaving him open-mouthed. She would go straight to Mrs. Strasberg, get a pill or two, and hold a whispered discussion.

Olivier had noticed that first Monroe would dilate warmly over a scene when she saw the daily rushes and then, or so it seemed, she would talk it over with Mrs. Strasberg or Hedda Rosten and begin complaining about the scene. Mrs. Rosten, the wife of Miller's oldest friend, had become Monroe's friend. She had come over as a secretary and companion to Monroe.

At any rate, Olivier conceived an intense hatred of both Mrs. Strasberg and Mrs. Rosten. He jeered at Marilyn's "entourage." The entourage included her huge bodyguard, former Scotland Yard Superintendent Roger Hunt. From the time she went outdoors in the morning until she returned home, Hunt never left her side, unless she had to go to the ladies' room. A photographer from the *Daily Mail* had got into Pinewood studio and managed to shoot a picture of her. Hunt seized the camera and confiscated the plate. It became known as The Sleeping Print!

Olivier put heavy pressure on Greene to get rid of Mrs. Strasberg and Mrs. Rosten. Mrs. Rosten was sent home in September and Mrs. Strasberg in October. But this did not help. "The production office thought they were being clever," Cardiff says, "but they weren't clever at all. Marilyn came to hear about this ruse, and she promptly had a breakdown!" This lasted almost a week, and after another week of argument (Greene was constantly pleading with Monroe and Olivier, "But let's finish the picture first and fight later. We've got to finish the picture"), Mrs. Strasberg was recalled from exile.

One day, when Monroe was being insufferably slow about everything, Olivier said something about speeding things up a bit. Mrs. Strasberg said, "You shouldn't rush Marilyn. After all, Chaplin took eight months to make a movie."

Olivier looked from Monroe to Mrs. Strasberg to Greene. He didn't say a word. But his expression indicated that the analogy between Monroe and Chaplin was possibly the most nauseating remark he had ever heard or was likely to hear.

Desperately, Greene said, suddenly, "All right, let's take eight months on *The Sleeping Prince*."

"Oh, no," Monroe said. "How can you think of such a thing? I must be in New York by Christmas."

Meanwhile, an embittered feeling was building up between Greene and Miller. Back in New York, I had heard rumors in October that Miller was persuaded that Greene was ruining his wife's career. I heard that Green was going to be euchred out of Monroe Productions and be replaced by Miller. I cabled Miller, querying him about this rumor and trying to find out more about the play he was completing or rewriting. He cabled the following reply on October 24:

"I HAVE NO CONNECTION WITH MARILYN MONROE PRODUCTIONS BEYOND FACT THAT ITS PRESIDENT IS MY WIFE I HAVE NO MORE THAN THE NORMAL FAMILY INTEREST IN MY WIFE'S BUSINESS AFFAIRS AND AM HAPPY TO STATE THIS WORKS OUT FINE RUMORS OF CONFLICT BETWEEN MYSELF AND MILTON GREENE ARE SPACE FILLERS FOR UNIMAGINATIVE COLUMNISTS THERE WAS NEVER ANY THOUGHT OF MONROE PRODUCTIONS FILMING A VIEW FROM THE BRIDGE I AM NOT WRITING A COMEDY BUT A DRAMA AND IF THERE IS A PART FOR MARILYN I WILL BE THE BEST SERVED PLAYWRIGHT IN HISTORY BUT I AM UNABLE TO WRITE WITH AN ACTOR OR ACTRESS IN MIND SO WE SHALL HAVE TO WAIT AND SEE—

The idea that he could be married to Monroe and retain a creative life apart from hers was an illusion. All experience to the star, even the experience of love, even the experience of husband and of children, is subordinate to herself as the central reality in a world where all other people are shadowy figures—applauding her, betraying her, adoring her. She is the star of her private life as well as the star of her films. A star could not long endure a playwright who wrote a play in which the major role was not intended for her. A woman who could accept her husband's autonomy would perhaps be more of a woman, but less of a star. As time went on, Miller's actions went far beyond "the normal family interest" in his wife's "business affairs" and artistic problems. One witness, a publicity man in New York connected with the firm then publicizing Monroe, once described to me how he had come to see Monroe with an assortment of new still photographs for her approval. She asked Miller to join the conference. He studiously examined each picture and then handed down his critical opinion of their worth and publication prospects. The publicist, an admirer of Miller's plays, was stunned. He felt that a great man had debased himself. Once, Milton Greene, entering Monroe's dressing room, observed Miller neatly snipping out newspaper items about her and pasting them into a scrapbook. Herbert Kamm, a fan-magazine writer, has told how, in 1958, he witnessed Miller helping his wife choose between four swatches of satin from which an evening gown was to be made: turquoise, champagne, kelly green, and burgundy red. In the four years since his marriage, Miller has published only five pieces: a short story about three rootless men in Nevada, a short story about an adolescent boy, and the scenario for a radio play about juvenile delinquency, all three in *Esquire;* an essay on playwriting in *Harper's;* and a sentimental *causerie* for *Life.* This essay served as an introduction to a series of photographs of Monroe posing—in color—as Theda Bara, Lillian Russell, Clara Bow, Marlene Dietrich, and Jean Harlow. "Her beauty," wrote Miller of his wife, "shines because her spirit is forever showing itself."

The first intimation Miller had that his wife demanded the whole of his emotions came that August, 1956, in England. His daughter fell ill. He flew back to the States, expecting to stay for several weeks. Monroe was in despair. She came down with one of her vaguely psychic disorders and could not go to the studio. She didn't recover until Miller cut short his visit and returned to her. She had to hold the first place in his heart at all times.

On October 10, the London *première* of *A View from the Bridge* took place. In a new version and staged with less artificiality than in New York, this play took the critics by storm. It was a huge success. But the first-nighters were taken, not with Miller, but with Monroe. The Millers attended the opening with the Oliviers. Though this was her husband's great night in England, Monroe did not wear a simple black gown. She wore a blood-red strapless satin gown that fitted her like a layer of skin. Her alabaster breasts were displayed to the world. She was the evening's sensation. "Marilyn Monroe's close-fitting dress turned the London opening of her husband's latest play into a near riot," reported the Associated Press. Criticized for the impropriety of her dress, Monroe said she had worn red because red was Miller's favorite color and "I am a movie star. If I were in black, it wouldn't be me."

Did Miller feel outraged because his wife had spurred the population into a frenzy—when it was his play they should have concentrated on? On the contrary. He was delighted with her beauty and the attention it was paid. In a curious public statement, he lauded her beauty, hurled a shaft at the hypocrisy of a culture which covertly enjoys nudity and pretends disgust at it, and attacked the homosexuality of many dress designers who try to make women "look like something they're not. Why should someone like Marilyn pretend to be dressing like somebody's old aunt?"

In October, I interviewed Mrs. Strasberg in New York about the relationship between the Millers. She said, "I have never seen such tenderness and love as Arthur and Marilyn feel for each other. How he values her. I don't think any woman I've ever known has been so *valued* by a man."

Before departing for England, Greene had been offered $500,000 for his 49-per-cent interest in Monroe Productions. He spurned the offer. How could anything ever come between him and the president? Miller? Why, Miller was too absorbed in his own works. Who but Greene would have the time to be a vice-president in charge of Monroe's temperamental fluctuations and passionate outbursts?

But the best-laid plans of vice-presidents go agley. In September, by transatlantic telephone, Greene assured me that whatever issues existed were superficial and were being compromised nicely. "I'm very happy here," he said, "and Marilyn is very happy, and Miller and I are good friends. He's only been on the set once. And I will never sell my stock in the corporation."

Greene now says that he had a premonition that Miller was going to participate actively in Monroe Productions when he saw Miller keeping her scrapbook. Could he believe his eyes? Was this the author of *Death of a Salesman*? His eyes had not deceived him.

Miller also began taking an interest in the quality of Monroe's scripts. Greene and Miller differed violently over Rattigan's screenplay. Miller found it excellent. Greene wanted it extensively revised to include scenes of Monroe singing and dancing. Greene also imputes an ignoble motivation to Miller's campaign to displace him: greed. "He didn't want anybody to share any part of Marilyn's income no matter how much he had done for her," Greene says bitterly.

As relations between Olivier and Monroe got stickier, Greene, trying to intervene, trying to make peace between them, found himself accused of being on Olivier's side and stabbing Monroe in the back. He got extremely depressed. So did Olivier. By now, Monroe was openly and sarcastically addressing him as "Mister Sir." Gone was the "Larry" of yesteryear. One day when Monroe failed to appear on the set, both Greene and Olivier got so depressed they went into his dressing room and polished off a fifth of whisky in the short space of an hour. Columnist Tanfield remarked he was willing to give odds of "37-23 ½-37 ½ to 1 that they'll never film together again."

The Millers rejected all social invitations from the theatrical and society sets. There was one English home, however, to which they were willing to be invited. That was Buckingham Palace. In a long list of assignments which Alan Arnold, an English publicist, was asked to carry out, there was this confidential memorandum: "Investigate proper occasion for Marilyn to meet members of the Royal Family."

Arnold called this to Olivier's attention. Sir Laurence, who could easily have arranged Monroe's presentation at court, happily drew a thick line through the command. Arnold therefore did not pursue the scheme. Late in October, at a formal reception following the Royal Film Performance, the queen of the movies came face to face with Queen Elizabeth.

The Queen remarked, "You are my neighbor, Mrs. Miller. How do you like living at Windsor?"

Monroe was slightly confused. She had been sure the Queen lived in that great stone fortress in London, guarded by red-uniformed grenadiers with fur busbys.

"I don't understand," she said. "I thought we lived at Englefield Green and you lived at Buckingham Palace."

"You see," the Queen explained, "we often live at Windsor Castle, and that makes us neighbors, doesn't it? What do you think of the place?"

Monroe screwed up her forehead. "Oh," she breathed, "I think I see what you mean. Oh, Windsor Park. Yes, Windsor's a lovely place. Why, we have a permit to bicycle in . . . in *your* park."

"How long will you be here, Mrs. Miller?"

"About two weeks more, I think. We must leave as soon as the picture is finished." Then Monroe swooped downwards and made a fine curtsy.

"That's a very proper curtsy," the Queen said.

"Curtsying isn't difficult for me now," Monroe said. "I learned how to do it. For this picture, I have to do it three or four times."

Princess Margaret now joined the conversation. "Do you really ride a bicycle, Mrs. Miller?"

"I really do love riding a bicycle," she assured Princess Margaret. "But I haven't had much time lately to do it, I'm sorry to say."

There was a widespread feeling that Monroe's love of cycling was a publicity myth. The hounds of Fleet Street were on Monroe's traces, and they snapped, barked, and bit at her all during that fall. She was criticized for untidy coiffure and garish clothes, for bad manners and stand-offishness, for *lèse majesté* to England's foremost actor, Sir Laurence Olivier. She had got herself the worst press that any actress ever had in England. On the set, she had engendered bad feeling by her lateness and by her coldness to the technical personnel at the studio. She did not say good morning. She did not say good night. She quarreled with the wardrobe department and with the cameraman. She set an all-time record for tardiness, even for herself, when she appeared for a 9:00 A.M. appointment at 6:20 P.M., which was nine hours and twenty minutes late.

At a gathering of the entire company, after the film was done, Monroe apologized for having been "so beastly" to everybody. She said, "I hope you will all forgive me. It wasn't my fault. I've been very, very sick all through the picture. Please—please don't hold it against me." She didn't say much to Greene. They were hardly on speaking terms.

As they left England on November 20, one newspaper said that "her triumphal visit to Britain ended today on a note like the thud of a soggy crumpet."

A well-informed London source explains the débacle: "The English public felt she was being stand-offish. A thing it hates. She didn't seem to know the common touches which Winston Churchill or, to take a star, Gracie Fields know. The little touches, like eating fish and chips with some cockneys; or having a lark with some sailors. She was like a bunch of beautiful grapes seen through a plate-glass window—luscious but untouchable. It would have been so easy for her. She could have done it on her ear. And if she'd done it against Sir Laurence's wishes, all the better, so long as she'd smile and make a little sweet joke of it. She didn't have to be so formal. It's the British who are supposed to be so stiff, but Marilyn Monroe outclasses us. She was about as approachable as a crown jewel."

The time had passed when she would humble herself to buy the public's love. Oh, she knew all the wiles to seduce that anonymous, glutinous aggregation of libido. She knew the lies to tell and the repartee with which to charm, she knew the poses and the droll little *gaffes* to make as if by accident, and just when to be sentimental and pull at the heartstrings. But she didn't want the public's love, for it was no love really. She had had to do it once. Now she had the power. She didn't need to scrape affection from the public.

For now she was a star.

A star tends to be autocratic, believing that only she is of any real consequence in the world. This conviction carries within it the seeds of artistic self-destruction. The film, more than any other performing art, is a collaborative enterprise, and one, moreover, in which the professional actor is not the *sine qua non*. Interesting films have been made with non-objective drawings (Mclaren), animal cartoons (Disney), natural phenomena (Cousteau), and non-professional actors (Flaherty's *Nanook of the North*, Rossellini's *Open City*). But usually the film's principal partners are the actors, the scenarist, the cinematographer, the director. Though the star may be unique, and even, like Monroe, irreplaceable, it is the director who is the moulding power of the film. It is possible, by skillful editing and cutting, to induce emotional reactions in the audience without the movie actor's acting at all. In *The Liveliest Art*, Arthur Knight describes the famous experiment of the Russian director Lev Kuleshov: "Kuleshov obtained a close-up in which Mozhukin appeared perfectly expressionless. This same shot he inserted at various points into another film—once in juxtaposition to a plate of soup, once next to a child playing contentedly with a teddy bear, and again next to a shot of an old woman lying dead in her coffin. Audiences shown the experimental reel praised Mozhukin's performance—his look of hunger at the bowl of soup, his delight on seeing the child, his grief over the dead woman."

An extreme conception of the film as a director's art holds that the director uses the camera the way a painter uses a brush and that the actors are inanimate models posing for the artist. This was valid for the silent film, but the sound film is not so completely a plastic art. It is partly a dramatic art. Therefore the words of the screenwriter and his scenes of action contribute to the movie; the actress who can build a character is important; the cinematographer is not a dumb tool. This brush has a soul of its own. Milton Krasner's photography in *Bus Stop* and *Seven Year Itch* and Jack Cardiff's in *The Prince and the Showgirl* were vital in conveying the mysterious phosphorescence of Monroe.

What sometimes happens to the movie star is that she comes to believe that, since the audience is collected to see her, she is the movie. Not the director, not the plot, not the words and ideas and the character. Only she. She may select stories as vehicles for her grandeur without regard for the film as a whole. She may insist on directors who placate and flatter her, instead of stubbornly insisting on hard work.

In the 50 years of the film, only one star's ego was immense enough to encompass other egos, only one star's genius was so divine that it did not feel threatened by other geniuses. This was Chaplin.* He was the acting star. He wrote the scene outline and plot, he wrote the dialogue, he composed the music, he directed the film, he edited and cut the printed takes. Chaplin has the actor's imagination

---

* Chaplin's self-destructive autocracy manifests itself in his personal life—in his relations with women and with the social order.

—but he also can think like a writer, sing like a musician, and paint like a painter.

Whatever Chaplinesque mystery Monroe has on the screen, she is not, as yet, a "universal" woman. For all her sensitivity to music, painting, and literature, Monroe has no sense of story form or graphic unity. And a film cannot be a glorification of the star; it is nothing if it is not a dramatic whole, in which she is one part, enacting a role invented by a writer and realized by a director.

The paradox of the star underlay Monroe's clashes with Olivier. Olivier himself was a star—a star threatened by a rival star. So *The Sleeping Prince*—whose title was changed to *The Prince and the Showgirl*—was a film without a director. It was a disappointment both to the admirers of Olivier and those of Monroe.

It opened at Radio City Music Hall on June 13, 1957. The reviews on the whole were devastating. Crowther found "both characters . . . essentially dull." Zinsser criticized Monroe for playing Elsie without "fine shadings. This is a dumb affable showgirl and nothing more." And John McCarten continued to be at no loss for disparaging words: "Apart from the whimsicality of teaming up England's leading actor with a young lady whose dramatic experience has been largely confined to wiggling about in Technicolor pastries cooked up in Hollywood, it offers little in the way of diversion."

A minority of the critics thought otherwise. Two of the most discriminating reviewers, Archer Winsten of the New York *Post* and Justin Gilbert of the New York *Mirror,* were pleased. Gilbert wrote, "The film emerges as the season's sparkling comedy surprise." Winsten, who had previously been impervious to her charms, said, "As for Marilyn Monroe, she has never seemed more in command of herself as person and as comedienne. She manages to make her laughs without sacrificing the real Marilyn to play-acting. This, of course, is something one can expect from great, talented, practiced performers. It comes as a most pleasant surprise from Marilyn Monroe, who has been half-actress, half-sensation."

In retrospect, the negative judgments seem to me unfair. *The Prince and the Showgirl* is an excellent high-comedy film, with many moments of filmic charm. Even when I first saw it, I was impressed with Monroe's sensitive portrayal of the emotional and intellectual changes in the girl's character. The first supper scene was one of the choicest pieces of high comedy on film that year. Olivier, his face a glacial mask, his monocle tightly held, did a pretty piece of playing the arrogant Balkan regent. Monroe, playing with shadings of tenderness, naïveté, and Yankee shrewdness, was a perfect counterpoint. Getting drunker and drunker on vodka and champagne, and encouraging Olivier's game out of curiosity to see how royalty went on the make, she was eloquent. Her disillusionment at the lack of candlelight and romantic music was marvelous. Olivier's bad temper and his hurriedly arranging for dim lights and a gypsy violin off-camera was terribly funny, as was Monroe's passing out on the sofa after some scuffling with Olivier. The following night there is another supper scene—but now the positions are reversed. It is Monroe who is on the make for Olivier! Both seduction scenes, in my estimation, rank with the finest high comedy in movies. The film as a whole may suffer from inconsistencies, but when Monroe's gift for tenderness and laughter is given rein—as in the interplay with Sybil Thorndike and the Regent's son—she is in superb form.

If the characters seemed dull, it may be because 30 per cent of the film was tedious and the tediousness seeped over into that 70 per cent of the film which sparkled. For this, not Olivier the actor, but Olivier the co-producer-director-editor must be blamed. In order to impart a specious quality of realism, it was decided to intercut newsreel scenes of the Queen's coronation into this film, which took place in 1911 during George V's coronation. The pageantry and sweep of English history, which stirs Olivier's imagination in a *Henry V,* is merely a distraction in a story about a man and a woman involved in a sudden passion. The coronation scenes distract from the period flavor of Rattigan's story.

Both the screenplay and the direction were too enslaved to the original dramatic version. Olivier tended to set up his camera scenes as if he were staging a play. The film settles down into a static succession of immobile scenes. And yet, for all the immobility, the film will live for the electrifying counterpoint between these two personalities.

Visually, Monroe never looked so exquisite or so innocent, like a flower between bud and bloom, a rose opening after a light rain in June, a few beads of moisture on its fragrant petals. Monroe might come to believe that her partnership with Milton Greene was of no financial value, but could she doubt that the virginal radiance he had seen in her, back in 1953, he had helped directors and cameramen to capture for all time on film in *Bus Stop* and *The Prince and the Showgirl*?

30 Sorrow by the Sea

During the early summer of 1957, the natives of Amagansett, a peaceful hamlet far out on the eastern end of Long Island, between East Hampton and Beach Hampton, delighted in taking visitors on a morning tour of their village. As their cars passed a weather-beaten brown-shingled Cape Cod house, they would slow up. They would point to a blonde sun-glassed girl, whose comely physique was in contrast to her old khaki shorts and man's white shirt, worn tail out. If it was the middle of the morning, the girl was usually engaged in working about a small garden. The residents would ask the visitors who they thought the girl was. Usually the visitors could not guess, although they confessed she looked vaguely familiar.

To their astonishment, they learned that the girl was Marilyn Monroe.

Monroe had found a haven here. Nearness to the ocean gave her peace. She loved to watch the breaking waves and to run into the water. The Millers had rented the house for the summer. It was a mile from the beach.

Monroe was a star, Monroe was a goddess, but when she played, she did simple and natural things.

Now that the fever and fret of England were behind them, Marilyn responded to Arthur's devotion with a full heart. In the early mornings or at twilight, they would drive to the beach and surf-cast for an hour. They fished together, swam together, walked together on moonlight evenings. A year had not dulled the sharpness of their feelings. Their sense of excitement with each other had deepened.

That summer Monroe loved being Mrs. Miller. She marketed at the supermarket, cleaned the house, and cooked the meals.

During the weekdays, Miller wrote from nine until one. He was still making revisions on the play he had hoped to have completed in time for a 1956 production. He had now written over 1,000 pages of visions and revisions—enough to have made eight plays. Perhaps his work was complicated by the fact that what he wanted to say was not entirely clarified in his own mind. The experiences of the last three years had profoundly altered his views on the human condition. In an essay, "The Creative Agony of Arthur Miller," * Miller's friend the novelist Allen Seager observed that the former Marxian now believed that man could not be reformed by the "passage of wise laws, the election of competent officials, or any organized gestures whatever." Miller now saw mankind's problem as primarily a "failure of love."

Was there more to Miller's "creative agony" than a change of philosophy? How time-consuming was the business of being the husband of a great star and immersing oneself in her professional crises? From the moment he married Marilyn, Miller was by her side, actively participating in her career. Yet, at least during the phases of composition, a playwright must exclude everything but his characters from his consciousness.

Could he ever exclude her from his mind? Did he want ever to exclude her, even if he could? She was everywhere. Even in his study he could not leave her behind, for the principal decoration there was two large photographs of Marilyn on the wall above his desk.

In 1957, Miller burned the 1,000 pages of manuscript of his play. He began again from the beginning. In two years, he wrote 3,000 new pages, which he attempted to distill into a final script of about 120 pages. "I don't know whether I'll get it on this season," he told Arthur Gelb of the New York *Times,* in September, 1959. Seager, who was privy to Miller's confidences, had stated, "It is practically certain that Kermit Bloomgarden [Miller's producer] can go ahead and rent a theatre for the 1960 season." But the new play was not completed in time for 1960–61.

Monroe had lived up to the plan she had formulated in 1955. She

* *Esquire,* October, 1959.

went to Los Angeles only during the shooting of a film. She did not, however, buy a house in Brooklyn. The Millers lived in an elegant apartment at 444 East 57th Street in Manhattan. They participated in the strenuous social and cultural life of the city. They were to be seen frequently at the theatre and at the art-film houses. They attended dinners, cocktail parties, and receptions for visiting celebrities from Europe. They gave parties themselves. With the aid of her well-organized husband, Monroe had begun to function as a domestic animal of sorts. The Millers had two secretaries, a maid, and a cook. Monroe was not the dream wife of her ancient fantasies, she was not the shirt-collar ironer and sock darner, but she had become a sophisticated New York woman, delighting in social life and intelligent conversation. At her parties, she was a charming and hospitable hostess.

When they were not at the shore or at their Roxbury, Connecticut, estate for the summer, the Millers entertained in a large living room, decorated to Monroe's taste. Its principal color motif was white— white walls, white draperies, thick white carpet, white furniture, a white piano. The one dramatic contrast was a large nude statue, cast in black metal, by William Zorach, which Monroe had chosen. The nude, one of those angular creatures, is contorted against an abstract tree trunk. One night, Walt Kelly, the artist who draws the Pogo cartoon, was visiting the Millers. He questioned whether it was anatomically possible for a woman to twist herself into the awkward stance of Zorach's nude.

"Why," Monroe said, smiling, "it's easy."

Kelly, a fine-arts practitioner as well as a cartoonist, disagreed.

"Well, I can do it," she said, throwing her head back proudly.

"I don't believe it," Kelly said.

She got up and walked to a wall. She closed her eyes thoughtfully and then quickly arranged her body against the wall in a pose similar to that of Zorach's nude.

Kelly looked skeptical. Had her body, under the dress, really duplicated the impossible position?

"Oh yes, yes," Monroe said. "Here, see for yourself."

She nonchalantly guided Kelly's fingers along the outline of her flanks wedged against the wall. It was indeed so. Monroe had not forgotten what she knew of the human anatomy and the female bone structure. Her command of her body was still as sure as it had been in 1945 when she had been the pride of the Hollywood Blue Book Models Agency.

It was during the summers, usually, that Miller was able to give himself up most completely to his play. That summer of 1957, at Amagansett, he had been working at a rapid pace, except on weekends when his parents came or his children, and there were outdoor barbecues and games on the beach. Sometimes friends came for the day. Jim Proctor, an old friend of Miller's, describes his impressions of the couple: "I don't think I ever saw two people so dizzy with love for each other. Having known Arthur a long time as an introspective guy, it was well, like a miracle, to see him so outgoing. She made all the meals, and she's a hell of a cook. She even baked bread. I remember once she was preparing noodle soup. She made the noodles. She made this dough and rolled it out flat, cut it into strips. I happened to come into the kitchen and she was drying the noodles with her portable hair dryer! That night we had a great meal. Bluefish soufflé with fresh caught fish, oh, and this noodle soup, and a chocolate meringue pie."

Monroe thought all the barriers to her happiness were overleaped finally. She had become pregnant. The complications of her professional life were dissolved. In March and April, after a series of conferences, Greene had been forced to sell his stock in Monroe Productions for $85,000 ($415,000 less than he had been offered for it eight months before). Monroe said that "my" company had not been organized to "parcel out forty-nine per cent of my earnings to Mr. Greene for seven years." They had been, she said, at "odds" for "over a year and a half," and he had "made secret commitments without informing me." She has never stated what these commitments were. Greene denied he had made any commitments, secret or otherwise, without consulting President Monroe. Anyway, Greene was out of the picture. She was in complete control of herself. And she wasn't in a hurry to get back before a camera. The studio wanted her to play Jean Harlow in a biographical film about the platinum blonde and to do a remake of *The Blue Angel*. The opportunity to do Grushenka in *The Brothers Karamazov*—the role that had become the symbol of her emancipation from Hollywood—was lost when Maria Schell played it. "I thought Maria was wonderful in it," Monroe said, graciously. She didn't think Kim Stanley was so wonderful in *The Goddess,* a film by Paddy Chayefsky about the unhappy personal life of a lonely, neurotic girl who becomes a movie star and marries a famous professional athlete. It was widely believed that the heroine was modeled after Monroe. Miller attempted to dissuade Chayefsky from doing the film, and there were threats of an injunction to halt its release. The film, except for its touching opening scenes, was unreal and melodramatic, and the heroine bore little actual resemblance to the personality of Monroe.

On Thursday morning, August 1, as Monroe was weeding her garden, Arthur, working inside, heard her screaming. She was doubled over in pain. He carried her into the house and laid her on the couch. The doctor told him to get an ambulance at once and rush her to the hospital in New York. Arthur rode in with her, holding her hand as she lay on the stretcher, her face writhing in agony, and wiping away the sweat on her forehead as she twisted about. It took four hours to get to the hospital. She was given sedation and placed in surgery. One of those unusual, but not uncommon, accidents had taken place in a Fallopian tube, one of the pair of small ducts which lead from the ovary to the uterus. Fertilization had occurred, as is normal, in this oviduct. But the ovum had remained there, instead of passing into the uterus. Marilyn was in danger of rupturing at any moment. In an hour, perhaps two hours, she would have died.

Waiting for her as she lay on the operating table, Miller's love was heightened by the fear that he might lose her. He wanted to express his love to her, and it was during these anxious hours that he resolved to give her the best thing a playwright can give to the woman he loves. He would write a screenplay for her. He had written only one screenplay, *The Story of G.I. Joe,* in 1943. While he and Marilyn had been in England, Miller had written a short story, *The Misfits,* which had recently been accepted for publication by *Esquire.* (It was to be published in the October, 1957, issue.) The narrative was a sensitively written piece about three men who, out of tune with the society in which they live, are attempting desperate maneuvers to come to terms with their need for freedom and independence. The three characters around whom the story centered were Guido Raconelli, the pilot of a dilapidated monoplane; Gay Langland, a forty-six-year-old cowboy, separated from his wife; and Pence Howland, twenty-two, a young rodeo performer. Rosalyn, the wife of Langland, is described as a girl from the East—warm, affectionate, sexually promiscuous. She does not appear directly in the magazine story. The story tells of the three men and their efforts to capture wild horses in the mountains of Nevada. The men sell the horses to canners of dog food. The time is the present. The style has a quality of descriptive beauty and a haunting sense of the melancholy of life that had not been so vividly expressed in any of Miller's work since *Death of a Salesman*. There are overtones of social bitterness—men of great spirit, like the wild horses, are roped by a society, are chopped up, as it were, into canned meat for dogs—and there is a vague intimation of Miller's new theme of the "problem of love" in the barely suggested triangular relationship between Langland and his wife and the young Pence, who has apparently had a liaison with Rosalyn.

It was this story, then, that Miller began to occupy himself with when he took his wife back to Amagansett. She lay in the sun and got back her strength, and he wrote in the mornings and in the afternoons read her what he had written. The character of Rosalyn was expanded. She became the central character of the story, the focus of the anxieties of the three men. She would not be Langland's wife in this version. She would be a woman, still from the East, who had come to Reno for a divorce and who had remained in Nevada—a lonely disoriented human being. For Monroe as an actress, the part of Rosalyn Taber would be, of all her roles, the most satisfying to her ego as well as the most challenging to the subtleties of her artistry. Except for an elderly confidante, Isabella, played by Thelma Ritter, Monroe was to be the only woman in the film. And each of the three men was in love with her, each in a different way, and each seeking in her the fulfillment of his special need. In Rosalyn, for the first time in his work, Miller had created a truly interesting and feminine character. The essence of her character was a burning vitality and thrust, and she was moved constantly by an immense pity; like Monroe herself, Rosalyn has, as the mainspring of her experience of love, the sensation of pity. She responds with pity to the various emotional scars of the three men, and, like Major Scobie in *The Heart of the Matter*, she finally chooses the person most wounded by living. But her instinct for life and her overmastering pity extend beyond the love of men. She is suffused by that "reverence for life" of which Albert Schweitzer has written.

What was the whole of the original magazine story—the pursuit and the capture of the mustangs, the story ending as the horses lie lonely and tethered in the dusk—becomes the climax of the screenplay, as Rosalyn opposes the senseless killing of the horses, and Gay Langland, the leader of the expedition, opposes Rosalyn.

In its breadth of conception and beauty of dialogue, *The Misfits* was almost the equal of Miller's best work in the theatre, and it was, compared to the average screenplay, a masterpiece. In June, 1958, Miller read the play to his friend Frank Taylor, who had been a Hollywood producer for several years and was now the editorial director of Dell Books, a paperback reprint publisher. Taylor was fascinated by the scenario and said that the ideal director for it was John Huston. He knew Huston and sent him a script. Huston agreed to direct *The Misfits*, and, some months later, Miller persuaded Taylor to produce the film. Clark Gable was cast to play Langland, Montgomery Clift was Howland, and Eli Wallach, Raconelli.

For Monroe, the film would mean the closing of several circles. There was, first, her reverence for Huston. She had never forgotten that it was he who had seen into her depths and crystallized her first good performance. Although the role of Angela had been a small one, Monroe often said that she thought Huston had been her best director and that her favorite performance was the one in *The Asphalt Jungle*. An actress will frequently, for personal reasons, place a higher value on certain performances than the critics. In her own opinion, Monroe always felt that her two best dramatic performances had been the last scene with Calhern in *The Asphalt Jungle* and the scene of her cracking up in *Don't Bother to Knock*. All that came afterward—even *Seven Year Itch, Bus Stop, The Prince and the Showgirl, Some Like It Hot*—she considered not as perfect, in terms of her individual artistry, as these two films. In *Bus Stop*, for instance, she felt that her finest piece of acting, the scene in which she talks about her early life to Hope Lange on the bus, had been improperly edited by Josh Logan. So, to play a major role in a film of importance under Huston's direction was the consummation of a ten-year wish. For a long time she had wanted to play opposite Gable, for she not only looked up to him as a masterful movie performer but believed that the elements of their personalities would combine into a fiery thing on film. Wallach, of course, was her closest friend in the Actors' Studio, and she admired his comic gusto. Clift had become a dear personal friend. Just as Wallach's bonhomie brought out the good-humored liveliness in Monroe, Clift's thoughtful wryness appealed to the dark side of her nature. Often, when her husband did not wish to attend a theatrical *première* and Clift was in town, it was he who escorted Monroe.

But, above all, to work on *The Misfits* would mean a close collaboration with the man she loved as well as the author she admired. It would deepen the relationship of a marriage that had already given her more tenderness than she had ever expected to find in her life. And so Miller wrote and rewrote the screenplay, fashioning her part to her personality and her acting style. Love had changed the writer who, only a year before, had said that he could not write with "an actor or actress in mind."

Financially, *The Misfits* would be the most profitable of her films. She would receive an advance payment of $750,000 against 15 per cent of the gross receipts. The film was to be made entirely on location near Reno, Nevada, in the summer of 1960. But there were still two films to come before that.

After she left the hospital, that summer in 1957, Monroe suffered a fit of melancholia that nothing could shake. Miller thought it would be good for her to face a camera again as soon as possible. Billy Wilder had been writing to her about a story he was playing with. The story took place during Prohibition, and she would play a ukulele-strumming singer with an all-girl band. Wilder said he was reluctant to expand the idea into a screenplay unless she would play Sugar Kane, a boop-boop-a-doop vocalist. Miller told her the film would take her mind off her accident; she should do it. Wilder could be trusted to make a good film. It wouldn't hurt her to have a box-office success after the failure of *The Prince and the Showgirl*. Even she, even Wilder, did not suspect how successful *Some Like It Hot* would prove to be.

31 *Some Like It Hot*

The screenplay, written by Wilder and I. A. L. Diamond, skated on perilously thin ice. Justified by plot exigency—for Tony Curtis and Jack Lemmon are in danger of being murdered—the two leading men are robed in women's clothes. They speak in falsetto and "camp" as openly as the Duc de Charlus. Transvestitism is an ancient basis for farce—*Charley's Aunt* is the most famous example. But the magnified intimacy of cinema could have made it disgusting. Yet because Monroe's co-stars masquerade as women, scenes of sophisticated sex play would pass the Production Code censorship. The scenario was one of the wittiest and most daring of the 1950's. It abounded in *double-entendres*, unbelievably racy dialogue and scenes —for instance, the fantastic drinking party in which 12 girls climb into Lemmon's upper berth, a scene as wildly comical as any in a Marx Brothers film. It was because of the borderline quality of the story that Wilder was reluctant to do it with anybody but Monroe. Nobody but Monroe projected the mixture of innocence and provocativeness that the film required.

The interior scenes were shot at the Goldwyn Studios on North Formosa Avenue in Hollywood. Monroe arrived in July, about two weeks before shooting was to get under way. There were to be rehearsals and the usual make-up and wardrobe tests. To her dismay, Monroe learned that *Some Like It Hot* was to be in black and white. She objected. So obdurate was she about the use of color that she had insisted on a clause being written into the 1955 contract with

2oth that all her studio films must be in color. For two days Wilder argued that in color the film would be objectionable. He had run color tests of Lemmon and Curtis in female costume and heavy make-up of rouge and lipstick. They looked gruesome, with an eerie "greenish" unwholesomeness about them. He ran the color tests to prove it. Marilyn conceded.

Whatever alterations in her had been effected by marriage, psycho-analysis, and the Actors' Studio, Monroe's tardiness was still un-changed. One day, Wilder scheduled tests for wardrobe, make-up, and coiffure. Curtis and Lemmon were on 11:00 A.M. call, Monroe on 1:00 P.M. At half past three, she swept into the studio. By the time she was ready for the camera, it was ten after six. She went to the sound stage. It was deserted. Wilder had sent the crew home at six. He himself had departed a few minutes later. He would condone an hour or two of lateness, but he would not stand for this intolerable degree of it. He expected to work standard union hours of nine to six, five days a week. A day's shooting may cost as much as $25,000. After 6:00 P.M., the actors and crew go on double time. Besides, when Monroe was late, the other actors became restless and nervous.

Asked if Monroe had been habitually late, Tony Curtis laughed bitterly. "Late? Look, if we had a nine A.M. call, she'd make it by eleven. That was on her good days. On her bad days, she didn't show up until after we came back from lunch. She had days when she didn't make it till three. I didn't see Wilder lose his temper with her once. I remember once, Billy said something to her, quite tact-fully—a suggestion about a line reading—and she said, 'Don't talk to me now. I'm thinking about how I'm going to play the scene.' But he kept himself under control."

From the first, Monroe got on Curtis's nerves. He reacted by be-coming more and more hostile to her. He could not endure her end-less procrastination. She was feeling her way slowly into her soul and drawing up sense-memories, but he didn't care. She had always worked slowly. Now she worked even more slowly, and the results were even more powerful.

Four years after Wilder had told me that he feared the Actors' Studio would destroy her, I revisited Wilder. Did he think the teach-ings of Lee Strasberg had been harmful?

"No," he said, "there I was wrong. She has become a better actress, even a deeper actress, since Strasberg. But I still believe she was developing herself naturally and would have become greater as she matured, even without him. I still say she was encouraged in bad habits. You see, Strasberg doesn't have to stand on the set and direct her. Now it takes Monroe even longer to get her work done. If we were working alone with her, it would be all right. But she's working with other actors. She wears them out. Before, she was like a tightrope walker who doesn't know there's a big pit down there she could fall into. Now she knows about the pit and she's more careful on the tightrope. She's more self-conscious. I'm still not convinced she needed training. God gave her everything. The first day a photographer took a picture of her, she was a genius."

I do not happen to agree with this opinion. One has only to contrast Monroe's stiff gestures and strained vocal tones in *Don't Bother to Knock* with her poise in *How to Marry a Millionaire,* made 18 months later, after Monroe had been coached by Natasha Lytess, to see how she absorbed education. Again, though Sugar Kane is as disarmingly lovely as The Girl Upstairs, we can see with how much more freedom Monroe explores the later character and how much more sense of reality she has developed, although Sugar is as fantastic a character as The Girl.

The Strasberg Method, which seeks to overcome the actor's inhibitions by training him to introspect scientifically, did multiply Monroe's desire for takes. On many scenes, she needed 30 and 40 takes, and one unfortunate day it required 59 takes to get a scene right! Normally, Wilder gets his scene on the first or second take indoors, and by the tenth take outdoors.

Playing opposite Monroe was a painful experience for Curtis. A disciplined film star, who prepares himself for each day's work by memorizing his lines and knowing the action, Curtis is, in Wilder's words, "terrific in the early takes, say his first three or four takes." As take followed take, Curtis would dry up. Monroe, on the other hand, grew more expressive. To compound his difficulty, in some of their scenes together he had to wear high heels and uncomfortable padding under the dress.

Sometimes there was no rational basis for Monroe's "blowing" her lines. In one scene she enters the hotel room where Lemmon and Curtis, disguised as women, are staying. The action called for her to open the door, say, "Where's the bourbon?" and then open and close bureau drawers in search of a hot-water bottle containing bourbon.

She couldn't get the line right. She'd say, "Where's the whiskey?" or "Where's the bonbon?" or "Where's the bottle?" In despair, Wilder finally pasted slips of paper with the line WHERE'S THE BOURBON written on them into every drawer. He changed the action so she would first open drawers and then speak the line. She still went up in her lines!

Her acting habits are mysterious. Scenes which would be difficult for most actresses, like the upper-berth scene, she plays with ease. When the company went on location to Coronado Beach, California, to shoot the Miami Beach sequences of the film, Monroe played the outdoor scenes without missing a line or having any problems—despite the fact that strangers were watching the operation. Yet a fairly simple piece of action like an entrance and an uncomplicated line like "Where's the bourbon?" gave her much trouble.

Wilder always printed several of the early takes and several of the later takes. "When I come to cut the film," he explains, "I look at the early takes. Curtis looks good on those and Monroe is weak. On the later takes, she is wonderful and he is weak. As a director, I must disregard his best takes and use her best takes. So this makes Curtis mad at her. But you have to go with Monroe, even if other actors suffer, because when Monroe is on the screen the audience cannot keep their eyes off her."

One evening, some of the cast—though not Monroe—were watching the rushes of the yacht sequence. Curtis, lolling on a couch in the mahogany-paneled lounge of a yacht, played the scene in a droll pastiche of Cary Grant. He is posing as a rich man's son who suffers from a frigid libido. Girls cannot excite him. Monroe decides to cure him of this ailment by kissing him and making love to him. On the fifth kiss, the treatment succeeds admirably.

In the darkness, somebody said to Curtis, "You seemed to enjoy kissing Marilyn." And he said loudly, "It's like kissing Hitler."

When the lights came on, Paula Strasberg was crying. "How could you say a terrible thing like that, Tony?" she said.

"You try acting with her, Paula," he snapped, "and see how you feel."

During much of the shooting, Monroe was reading Paine's *Rights of Man*. One day, the second assistant director, Hal Polaire, went to her dressing room. He knocked on the door. He called out, "We're ready for you, Miss Monroe."

"Drop dead," she replied.

When the apparent contradiction between her admiration for Paine and her rudeness to Polaire was pointed out to Wilder, he shrugged his shoulders. "Maybe she doesn't consider that directors and assistant directors have rights," he said. Then he paused thoughtfully. "Or maybe she doesn't consider us men."

Miller did not interfere in the making of the film in any way, either by suggesting script revisions or by criticizing the rushes. Late in November, he came to Wilder. Monroe had again become pregnant. He said, "My wife is pregnant. Would you go easy with her, Billy, please? Could you let her go at four-thirty every day?"

Wilder blazed up. "Look, Arthur," he said curtly, "it is now four o'clock. I still don't have a take. She didn't come on the set till half past eleven, and she wasn't ready to work until one. I tell you this, Arthur, you get her here at nine, ready to work, and I'll let her go—no, not at four-thirty—I'll let her go at noon."

Arthur looked at Wilder. He rubbed his chin. He opened his mouth as if to say something. Then he swallowed. "I see," he said quietly. He turned and walked slowly away. He looked very sad.

Monroe lost her second baby on December 17, 1958, this time through a miscarriage in the third month of her pregnancy. But she would not give up so easily. In June, 1959, she went to the Lenox Hill Hospital for what was described as "gynecological surgery of a corrective nature." To give birth to her own daughter, to whom she could be the loving mother for whom she had yearned when she was a little child—this was, of all the desires that raged in her, the strongest. And she would not be balked of this desire. She would wrestle with nature for the child she wanted. . . .

Some Like It Hot ran hundreds of thousands of dollars over the budget. Walter Winchell estimated the amount at $500,000! The production cost totaled $2,800,000. Wilder gave an interview to Joe Hyams in which he criticized Monroe's lateness. Wilder said, "I'm the only director who ever made two pictures with Monroe. It behooves the Screen Directors Guild to award me a Purple Heart." Hyams inquired whether his health had improved after the completion of *Some Like It Hot*. "I am eating better," Wilder replied. "My back doesn't ache any more. I am able to sleep for the first time in months. I can look at my wife without wanting to hit her because she's a woman."

Would he like to do another cinema with Monroe?

"Well," Wilder replied, "I have discussed this project with my doctor and my psychiatrist, and they tell me I'm too old and too rich to go through this again."

Upon reading the interview, Miller wired the director. His wife had been insulted. There must be an apology. Wilder sent a wire stating that he was sorry about the incident and had not meant to hurt anybody's feelings. Miller insisted upon a public apostasy. In all, six telegrams were enchanged. In the final wire, which Miller did not answer, Wilder said:

DEAR ARTHUR IN ORDER TO HASTEN THE BURIAL OF THE HATCHET I HEREBY ACKNOWLEDGE THAT GOOD WIFE MARILYN IS A UNIQUE PERSONALITY AND I AM THE BEAST OF BELSEN BUT IN THE IMMORTAL WORDS OF JOE E BROWN NOBODY IS PERFECT UNQUOTE SINCERELY BILLY WILDER.

Some Like It Hot was an instantaneous hit with the critics and the public. It was so popular that before the year ended it was brought back for reruns in the movie houses. Wilder, who has made such films as *Sunset Boulevard, Sabrina,* and *Lost Weekend,* said, "*Some Like It Hot* is the biggest hit I've ever been associated with. It has already grossed over ten million dollars, and by the time the figures are in from the worldwide distribution it will go beyond fifteen million dollars—maybe twenty million. I believe that from the box-office viewpoint it is the most successful film comedy ever made."

John McCarten was still reluctant to praise Monroe. In a long, favorable review, his only reference to her was in this sentence: "Mr. Curtis . . . is trying to impress a dipsomaniacal singer played in sprightly style by Marilyn Monroe." The box-office statistics in *Variety,* the weekly trade paper of show business, revealed that in April, May, and June, 1959, *Some Like It Hot* was the most popular movie in the United States. It was Monroe's twenty-third film and the first one out of which she would make a fortune, because she had been paid a guarantee against her eventual payment of 10 per cent of the gross earnings of the film and so stood to gain two million dollars from the enterprise. *Variety* summed up Monroe's uniqueness in the movie industry: "She's a comedienne with that combination of sex appeal and timing that just can't be beat."

Some Like It Hot was popular in England, on the continent, in Latin America, the Near East, the Middle East, the Far East. Since the public ideal of the eternal feminine varies so much from one country to another, from one culture to the next, it is one of the deepest mysteries of the Monroe *mystère* that her filmic imagery haunts the dark Turk in Istanbul; the slight, sensitive Japanese in Tokyo; the Parisian *boulevardier;* the polite Englishman; the romantic Pole and the sensual Italian; the hot-blooded *señor;* and the impassive Scandinavian. Her appeal to the masculine id is universal.

In February, 1957, Iraq had officially banned exhibitions of *Bus Stop* on the grounds that it was "dangerous to boys and young men." The Moslem was as vulnerable to her beauty as the Christian. That had been proved several years previously when a young Turk became so crazed while watching Monroe in *How to Marry a Millionaire* that he had slashed his wrists. A copy of the *Monroe Desnuda,* the one called *Golden Dreams,* had been hung in 1952 in the municipal assembly of Mogi, Japan, in order to "rejuvenate the assemblymen." And the Kansas Board of Review had censored 105 feet out of the yacht sequence in *Some Like It Hot,* for she was as stimulating to the young men of Kansas as she was to those of Iraq.

And if the 2,500 members of the Motion Picture Academy of Arts and Sciences had never nominated her for an Academy Award (they had also failed to bestow an Oscar on Chaplin and Garbo), formal recognition of her conquest had come from Europe. She achieved a certain immortality in November, 1957, when a life-sized statue of her in the costume of Elsa Marina was placed on exhibition in Madame Tussaud's Wax Works in London. The film artists of France and Italy named her the "best foreign actress" of 1958 for her performance in *The Prince and the Showgirl.* The Italian Cultural Institute awarded her its David di Donatello prize—a gold plaque under a reproduction of Donatello's statue of David. And Georges Auric, the noted composer and president of the French Film Academy, presented her with the Crystal Star, an enormous and lovely *étoile* of hand-carved crystal which is the Gallic equivalent of our "Oscar."

Ladies of the Chorus (1947).

Love Happy (1948). Marilyn Monroe; Groucho Marx.

All About Eve (1950). Anne Baxter; Bette Davis; Marilyn Monroe; George Sanders.

Never was Marilyn's innocence and experience more poetically expressed than in this shot from *The Asphalt Jungle* (1950).

We now realize that during her career Marilyn was playing with—and against—some of the most powerful screen presences of our time—from George Sanders and Louis Calhern in the beginning to Laurence Olivier and Clark Gable at the end, with Robert Tynan and Robert Mitchum and Richard Widmark along the way. Here is Marilyn with Louis Calhern, as the mob lawyer who is utterly entranced by her in *The Asphalt Jungle* (1950).

Let's Make It Legal (1951). Macdonald Carey; Marilyn Monroe; Zachary Scott; Claudette Colbert.

Clash by Night (1951). Robert Ryan; Marilyn Monroe.

With Charles Laughton in "The Cop and the Anthem" episode of *O'Henry's Full House*. Laughton, who like all masters of the acting art was fascinated with the mystery of her radiance on screen, wanted to play opposite her in a full-length comedy, but he and Billy Wilder could never find the right story (1952).

Don't Bother to Knock
(1952). Elisha Cook,
Jr.; Richard
Widmark; Marilyn
Monroe.

Gentlemen Prefer Blondes (1952).

Monkey Business (1952) Marilyn Monroe; Cary Grant.

Roller skating with Cary Grant in *Monkey Business* (1952).

Niagara (1952). Marilyn Monroe; Joseph Cotten.

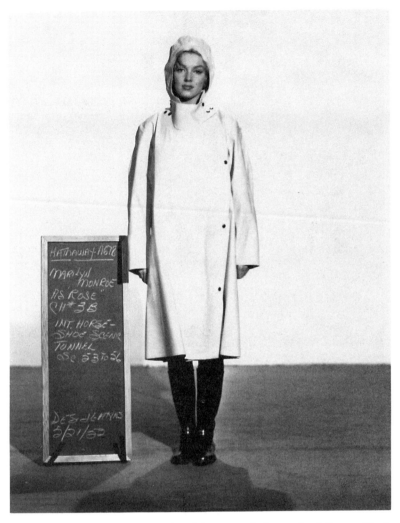

A rare unpublished shot of Marilyn doing a wardrobe test for *Niagara*. She is modeling the yellow slicker and rain hat she eventually wore in the film. She raised objections to the ensemble, but once she boarded the *Maid of the Mist* for the actual shooting she was glad she had the protection—which is standard for all visitors to the falls. By the way, the motel in which Miss Monroe and Joe Cotten—as husband and wife on a honeymoon—occupied has since been torn down. Until it was, Monroemaniacs went to Niagara Falls not for honeymooning but for retracing her steps during her breakthrough film (1952).

We're Not Married (1952).

How to Marry a Millionaire (1953). Cameron Mitchell; Marilyn Monroe; Betty Grable; Lauren Bacall.

Robert Mitchum gets rather brutal toward her in *River of No Return*, but no more so than director Otto Preminger (1953).

River of No Return (1953). Rory Calhoun; Marilyn Monroe.

There's No Business Like Show Business (1954). Mitzi Gaynor; Marilyn Monroe.

The Seven Year Itch (1954). Tom Ewell; Marilyn Monroe.

Of course, the skirt-blowing still from *The Seven Year Itch* is the most copied of all movie stills, yet this is, to me, an equally delicious photo, from the piano duet scene with Tom Ewell (1954).

Bus Stop (1956).

The Prince and the Showgirl (1957). Sir Laurence Olivier; Dame Sybil Thorndike; Marilyn Monroe.

For me, this glimpse of Olivier and Monroe in a scene from *The Prince and the Showgirl* expresses a mood of subtle and romantic sexual bliss which seems to have disappeared from most of the films in the late 1980s. This particular shot was excised from the final cut, yet it was so tender and romantic that it was used in the advertisements (1957).

A glorious moment from *Some Like It Hot* during the upper berth sequence, in which Jack Lemmon was somehow able to make room for Marilyn and a dozen other women—or so it seemed. The Pullman version of the famous Marx Bros. shipboard crowd-in-a-room sequence (1959).

Some Like It Hot (1959).
Tony Curtis; Marilyn Monroe.

Let's Make Love (1960).

Here is a rare and hitherto unpublished still of Marilyn in an intimate moment with Clark Gable in *The Misfits*. The scene was cut, but this still survives (1960).

32 All Things to All Men

Is there something unique in the cinematic image of Monroe? Are we dealing here with the sex symbol of a generation of bosom worshipers? Is Monroemania a symptom of an Oedipal epidemic?

There is much more in the meaning of the Monroe phenomenon. In *Metaphysics of the Love of the Sexes,* Schopenhauer explains the essence of love as sexual attraction; he explains sexual attraction as the male's evaluation of the woman as child-bearer; consequently, sexual attraction inheres in a woman's potential for motherhood, in her bosom and hips. Yet art and experience say otherwise. Cranach's tubercular nudes, for instance, or the flat-chested, flat-hipped flappers of the 1920's, suggest that men at times have found even the breastless and hipless female desirable. In our own time, the Monroe era was a period in which the gamine type of Audrey Hepburn and the classic Grecian beauty of Grace Kelly were also adored. So I do not believe that any one woman or any single type of woman can become the sex symbol of her time.

I am not even sure that I know exactly what a "sex symbol" is, anyway. The phrases "sex symbol" and "love goddess" have been incessantly used, not only apropos of Monroe, but of Rita Hayworth, Ava Gardner, Elizabeth Taylor, Gina Lollobrigida, and Brigitte Bardot. A "love goddess," as I understand the term, refers to a deity, an idol, or a priestess who performs during fertility rituals, fructifying the soil or the womb by magical processes. The religious element, in the sense of the supernatural presence, operates

337

here, whether in a primitive or civilized paganism. Now, nobody has suggested, as far as I know, that attending a Marilyn Monroe film will overcome sterility in the female or that the presentation of *Some Like It Hot* in Kansas will prevent droughts and improve crops.

A "sex symbol" would imply something that represents the sexual force, the sexual act, or the sexual instinct. It makes as much sense to talk of a voluptuous actress as a "sex symbol" as to say that a beautiful painting is an "art symbol." And if "sex symbol" be equated with "ideal woman" or "ideal sexual partner," then the phrase is even more absurd. Different men have found certain women anaesthetic, while other men have found these same women stirring. Between 1950 and 1960, ladies with such varying physiques and temperaments as Susan Hayward, Judy Holliday, Doris Day, Brigitte Bardot, Elizabeth Taylor, Joanne Woodward, Eva Marie Saint, Jeanne Moreau, and Ingrid Bergman have inflamed the blood of twentieth-century man.

And if, as Freud said, "anatomy is destiny," then why Monroe—why not another female with the same dimensions of hips and breasts or even larger ones? The studios sought physical duplicates of Monroe—Jayne Mansfield, Diana Dors, Sheree North, Mamie Van Doren—but the duplicates could not achieve the original's success. Nor did those great Italian ladies, so well endowed with mammary and steatopygous qualities—Sophia Loren, Silvana Mangano, Gina Lollobrigida—acquire the mystical hold that Monroe had over audiences and even over persons who had never seen a Monroe film.

An interview with Vladimir Nabokov was published in *The American Weekly*, October 4, 1959. The questions asked of the novelist illustrate the misconceptions, and Nabokov's reply leads us to the real issue:

"What about the American sex symbols—Marilyn Monroe and Jayne Mansfield? Do they represent sex for the author of *Lolita*?

"Says Nabokov: 'Well, first of all, Miss Marilyn Monroe is one of the greatest comedy actresses of our time. She is simply superb. Miss Mansfield I've never seen. But the usual concept of the bosomy female does not represent sex from my point of view. Sexual appeal seems to me something far more subtle than that."

The nature of Monroe's appeal must be sought in what she is and what she acts out. Even painted nudes, when they are good—Botticelli's Venus or Titian's Venus of Urbino or Goya's Maja Desnuda—are not inanimate lumps of breast-flesh and thigh-flesh. If they have excited generations, it is because the artists painted the souls of these women through subtleties of expression and posture. It is even more true that in paintings that move and tell a story it is the spiritual essence of the woman that draws us to her.

Authorities, of varying degrees of authority, have been aware of something special about Monroe. In his *America as a Civilization,* Max Lerner chooses 13 of the "icons" of the movie audience over a 50-year span of movie history. Monroe is one of the elect. On another occasion, Lerner went to Hollywood to write a series of columns, and he told how he liked to search out "interesting minds wherever I can find them." He intended to interview Monroe and discuss intellectual matters with her. He wrote a column describing such an interview with Monroe. James T. Farrell had seen Monroe as a girl triumphing over economic deprivation. He thought her alliance with Arthur Miller a wonder to behold; Miller was the "poet of frustration" and Monroe's life was the victory of a proletarian over social and economic "frustration."

Norman Mailer has said that Monroe is one of the few actresses "I still have some real curiosity about." Unlike Farrell, Mailer did not regard Monroe's marriage as a fine thing. He found it disturbing. He did not think Monroe should be married to anybody. She belonged to all men. She was a strange, wild, off-centered creature, who represented the sexual element in a mystical and unorthodox form, and she ought not to be organized into the conventional patterns of a bourgeois culture. "This whole thing about her feeling she has to get married and have children and be normal and well-adjusted," Mailer told me once, "I blame it on psychoanalysis." Mailer had lived in Hollywood for a year while attempting to get a scenario produced he had written in collaboration with Jean Malaquais. Fascinated by the psychology of the movie actress, he wrote, in the character of Lulu Meyers in *The Deer Park,* one of the best descriptions in literature of this species of humanity. Lulu Meyers is a composite of three actresses, none of whom, by the way, is Monroe. "These psychoanalysts," Mailer said, "convince actresses they're frigid or narcissistic and they have to be like everybody else. They're not. I mean, Marilyn came up like ten thousand other girls, but she came out of it and she is different. The psychoanalysts want to take her difference away from her."

Paddy Chayefsky, on the other hand, views the movie star as the victim of parental rejection who is seeking mass-audience love as a substitute and whose salvation lies in love and a happy marriage. Chayefsky has denied that the character of Rita Shawn in *The Goddess* was based on Monroe, but since Rita's husband was an athlete addicted to television, suspicions were aroused.

It is curious that almost any man can find an element in Monroe to correspond to his interests. Lerner finds a woman with whom to discuss "ideas," Mailer a blonde hipster, Farrell a *femme du peuple*, Nabokov a comedienne of sex, Chayefsky a love-starved victim. And there is something, either in Monroe's past history or in her complicated personality, in her eerie intellect, in her being rejected and seeking the love of older men, that lends a certain rationale to each of these responses to Monroe, just as there are two good reasons to justify those who see her as the ideal physical mate for bearing children.

In *Movies: A Psychological Study*, Martha Wolfenstein and Nathan Leites developed a thesis, based on an analysis of 19 American films, especially *Gilda*. They said that "current American films have produced the image of the good-bad girl. She is a good girl who appears to be bad. She does not conceal her apparent badness, and uncertainty about her character may persist through the greater part of the film. The hero suspects that she is bad, but finally discovers this was a mistaken impression. Thus he has a girl who has attracted him by an appearance of wickedness, and whom in the end he can take home and introduce to mother."

The study was published in 1950, just when Monroe was creating a new variation on this theme.

Though Wolfenstein and Leites did not analyze the most interesting or artistic films of that period, nor explore specific movie personalities and acting styles, their thesis is valid. I have made my own catalogue of cinematic Good Girls, Bad Girls, and Good-Bad Girls. Before 1930, Hollywood tended to segregate its leading ladies into either blatantly physical sirens—who portrayed sexuality as a force disastrous to mankind—or blatantly noble, almost asexual angels, blessing men with their tenderness and self-sacrifice. The Goods—

Norma Shearer, Lillian Gish, Jean Arthur, Katharine Hepburn, June Allyson, Deborah Kerr, Greer Garson—we still have with us, of course. Curiously enough, the Bads are fewer—Theda Bara, Pola Negri, Jean Harlow, and Marlene Dietrich. The largest number are the Good-Bads, but they had existed in Hollywood long before *Gilda*. Garbo was fundamentally a Good-Bad, as were Gloria Swanson and Clara Bow. Lana Turner, Rita Hayworth, Joanne Woodward, Susan Hayward, and Elizabeth Taylor still uphold the tradition.

But there is a fourth category. It had flourished for a long time. It is composed of movie heroines who do the things that the Bad Girls do but are not bad themselves and do not become revealed at the end to be Good Girls: Ginger Rogers, Carole Lombard, Claudette Colbert, for instance. They played in high comedies and freely expressed the idea that sex was good for you. The laughter they aroused dissolved the anxiety that, in life or art, usually infused sexual relations for American audiences.

Monroe's great invention was the playing of a frankly sexual, frankly voluptuous, frankly interested woman who was not evil, not dangerous, not destructive—and playing her without the ironies of a Colbert or a Lombard. Because of the primal innocence inside the Venus body, she was authentic. Her imitators were not authentic. She had begun the evolution of this character in her own life, in her struggle to reconcile the contradictions between what she felt and what her moral mentors believed she ought to feel, and she gradually built up the character with the aid of a series of responsive directors. She intimated this character in *The Asphalt Jungle*, in 1950, and expanded the conception in *Gentlemen Prefer Blondes*. In her later films she could venture on the most dangerous territory without shocking audiences or suggesting that she was morally depraved. She could tell the man who loved her that she had been sexually promiscuous (*Bus Stop*). She could seduce the hero (*Prince and the Showgirl*). She could portray an alcoholic girl of loose morals and a desire to marry a rich man (*Some Like It Hot*).

In 1955, Delmore Schwartz suggested a movie version of the Garden of Eden "free of all morbidity: Miss Monroe plays Eve; the serpent, Raymond Massey, comes along with the apple, which is turned down by Miss Monroe as Eve, who declares she is getting along fine with Adam, is happily married and needs no fruit; and then either the serpent is sent away like an obstreperous salesman or Eve uses all of her female wiles to seduce the serpent into eating the apple himself, thus eliminating Satan, purging the universe of evil, and bringing about the most overwhelming, total and conclusive of all the happy endings Hollywood has ever filmed."

The age, I believe, welcomed Monroe because the emergence of the character she created coincided with a fundamental change in man's conception of woman's role in sexuality. The distinction between "good women" and "bad women" had been eroded by 75 years of propaganda and social change. By 1950, the ideal woman, in American society and even in Europe and parts of the Orient, was becoming the mistress-wife.

Is not Monroe the image *par excellence* of this new woman? She is voluptuous, but she admires Dostoevski. She devotes endless hours to making herself look beautiful, but she reveres children and the home, and she cooks well and bakes her own bread. She, or the character she plays (which is partly she and partly a product of her imagination), experiences sex as a pleasurable act, and yet she is no wanton, for her libido arises out of love and pity and she is faithful to one man. That it is men, all over the world, rather than women, who have taken Monroe to their hearts may be a sign that, after all, men have come to cherish this new woman.

33 Full Circle

Again, she was in a sweater. They were shooting the big production number of *Let's Make Love* on sound stage 11 at 20th Century-Fox, and Monroe was wearing a sweater for the sequence. On the set, everybody stared admiringly at her; 22 years before, her classmates had stared at her when she had worn that first sweater. Life often seems like one of those canon songs that never ends but recommences with the same chord. *Plus ça change, plus c'est la même chose,* and there's nothing new under the sun.

Yet if familiar chords were sounding in 1960, the notes were not in the old order. The chords were, so to speak, inverted. Certain persons and things out of the past recurred, but they had changed. And she had changed in some ways, so that her response to each chord was altered by time and her growth, by her achievement of a success and power exceeding her most extravagant childish fantasies.

In the sweater, she was singing and dancing the Cole Porter standard, "My Heart Belongs to Daddy." It was a six-minute sequence; a long time by the cinema clock. It was her most complicated and lubricious number since "Heat Wave" in *No Business Like Show Business.* A chorus of eight male dancers took part in the number with her. They hurled her about from one to another. She leaped, she gyrated, she writhed, she sinuously maneuvered herself to the frantic rhythm. She was magnificent. She was beautiful. She was "hot." She was Monroe.

Under that sweater, a sheer leotard sheathed her like a dark epidermal layer. As Monroe whirled in rising momentum, she came to a climax and suddenly pulled off the sweater and flung it away from her, like a strip-teaser casting the final undergarment into the wings. . . .

The more things are the same, the more they change. Like the sweater. The sweater was not machine-made and sold at a department store like the one she had borrowed in 1938. This one was hand-knit of rich cashmere. Costume designer Dorothy Jenkins had ordered it for Monroe in Dublin, Ireland. It cost $75. Monroe's prodigious physical exertions were so intense that, after each take, the sweater was wet with perspiration. Four extra sweaters had to be air-expressed from Dublin.

Monroe, as Jane Russell observed years before, worked more strenuously than anybody else in a production.

Monroe's hair became so soaked that between takes a hairdresser had to towel it dry, comb it, and set her coiffure again.

Her art is a product of her sweat as well as her fancy. And she sweated profusely during the 11 days it took to get this six-minute sequence on film. And, yet, when the takes were spliced, when they were cut and edited, Monroe would look free and natural and so exuberant that audiences would imagine that the action came easily and spontaneously.

But nothing had ever come easily to her—not her beauty, not her personality, not her acting. Facing the gaping camera eye still did not come easily. Under the beautiful mask was a grave inquietude. She still asked herself, "What am I afraid of? Do I think I can't act? I know I can act but I am afraid. I am afraid and I should not be and I must not be." * Before the camera she paid with more than sweat; she paid with the hoarded coin of her emotional reserves.

And the dancing—this did not come spontaneously. She was not really a dancer. She mimicked the intricate design of the choreographic routine, down to the movements of the eyes, as they were done

---

* An actor playing in *Let's Make Love* picked up a notebook in which Monroe had been absently scribbling during a lull in the shooting. He found these words written by her. Reported by Richard Gehman in *The American Weekly*, May 1, 1960.

by the dance director and his assistant. When the music played, Jack Cole and Maggie Banks moved in rhythm to it, and Monroe copied their motions, looking now at one, now at the other, depending on where her positions had been marked on the floor. The sequence was shot slowly, in 15-*second* takes—an ordeal for Monroe and for Cole.

Cole, too, was a recurrent motif. He had been madly devoted to her since he had directed her dances in *Gentlemen Prefer Blondes*. He had been one of the first to see her possibility, to exploit it, and to make it come through on film. She never forgot anybody who had helped her professionally. She had asked for Cole to direct her musical numbers in *Let's Make Love*. Her wishes—even her whims—were now almost the law of the lot. Buddy Adler was as anxious to please her as Zanuck had been to discipline her.

Cole had envisioned her years before as Nana. She still had not played Nana. The heroine of *Let's Make Love* was named Amanda Dell. The author was not Zola, but Norman Krasna, the man who had persuaded RKO not to conceal the identity of the calendar girl.

The director was the man whom Cole had formerly praised to her: George Cukor, most celebrated of the so-called "women's directors." She had insisted upon Cukor before she would agree to star in *Let's Make Love*. Cukor had directed Garbo in *Camille*, Hepburn in *A Bill of Divorcement*, Harlow in *Dinner at Eight*, Norma Shearer in *Romeo and Juliet*, Ingrid Bergman in *Gaslight*, Crawford in *A Woman's Face*.

And her producer was a familiar chord: Jerry Wald, now grown into a mandarin—older, stouter, blander. His recent films had been *Peyton Place* and *The Best of Everything*, films which expressed the trite Hollywood conception of sexuality as a destructive force in human affairs.

To Wald, Monroe had not basically changed since he had cast her as box-office bait in *Clash by Night*. She was still ambitious. She was still galvanic. She was still driven by a compulsion to work. "She's one of the few stars who doesn't act as if she's made it," Wald explained. "She does not coast. She worked harder in *Let's Make Love* than she did in *Clash by Night*. She's still the same person."

Instead of Natasha Lytess who stood on the sidelines during the making of *Clash by Night* there was now Paula Strasberg, but that was a familiar strain, too; there was always a woman standing *in loco parentis* to Monroe, whether it was Grace McKee Goddard, Ana Lower, or now Paula Strasberg.

Before a take, Monroe still vigorously shook her fingers. The gesture had irritated Olivier and baffled Wilder. Wilder likened it to a person shaking water off his hands. Cukor compared it to a pianist getting ready to play a concerto. "She closes her eyes while she's doing it. Sometimes, she begins shaking her wrists after the cameras are rolling and I've said 'action'! I have to say 'action' again, and she doesn't seem to hear me, and I say, 'Oh, come on, Marilyn, let's go,' and it seems to me that she doesn't like me to interrupt her." But Cukor was polite, he was gentle, he was delicate, he never raised his voice. The successful "women's director" behaved with the concentrated devotion of a man in love with a woman; he overflowed with kindness, compliments, and small attentions.

When Monroe looked around the set, she could see her husband standing there. "He worships her," one of the technicians remarked one day. He worshiped her so much that he had rewritten Krasna's script to fatten her role. (Krasna had emigrated to Switzerland for three years and so was not available for rewrites.) Gregory Peck, originally cast to play opposite her, felt that his role was too much diminished, and he resigned. For many weeks, production was suspended as Wald frantically sought a new leading man. He attempted to secure Rock Hudson from Universal in exchange for a loan-out of Monroe. (According to Louella Parsons, Universal wanted Monroe to star in a film about Freud. Miss Parsons did not reveal whether Monroe would have portrayed Mrs. Freud, Anna Freud, or one of those early patients who suffered from the conversion hysterias. The project collapsed when MCA, her agents, demanded for her services $500,000 against 15 per cent of the gross earnings of the film.)

Eventually Yves Montand, the French actor and singer, agreed to play Jean Marc, a billionaire who falls in love with Amanda Dell, a young actress playing in an off-Broadway musical revue. Monroe had admired Montand since she had seen his one-man show on Broadway in September, 1959. Later, Montand, together with Mrs. Montand— the lovely and gifted Simone Signoret—had come to Los Angeles, where he was booked into a theatre. In Paris, Montand had played Proctor in the French version of *The Crucible*. The Millers and the Montands were in every way congenial.

Unlike Di Maggio, Miller did not shun the set. He came almost every day. He went to the projection room with Monroe when she looked at the daily rushes. During the first weeks of shooting, Cukor and the film editor joined these expeditions. Whenever Cukor expressed a preference for one of several takes—and there were, as always, a great number of takes—he found Monroe debating his judgments. He softly justified them. Monroe defended her views. Miller added his thoughts. Finally, Cukor did not go with the Millers. He saw the "dailies" alone, during his lunch hour. Monroe saw them in the evening, after she had completed the day's shooting.

Miller was by her side when she examined still photographs for publicity. She studied each print through a magnifying glass, as carefully as she had examined her first awkward commercial photographs when she had been a young model. She "kills" more publicity stills than anybody else: 90 per cent of them are condemned. A photographer who has worked with her explained that she has a good sense of photography, "but she's so goddam particular, she drives you the hell out of your mind. Nobody wants to work with her. It's too frustrating."

At the lunch hours, in the 20th commissary, everybody gossiped about Monroe. "There are six pictures shooting at Fox," an actor remarked in May, 1960, "but all we talk about is Marilyn Monroe." The rumors and the innuendoes flew. *Monroe insisted on a closed set today. . . . Why was the set closed? She's fighting with Cukor. . . . She's fighting with Montand. . . . No, she's in love with Montand. . . . They're having a romance. . . . She had a fight with Miller. . . . They're splitting up. . . . She's in love with Vaughan. . . . She missed two days last week. . . . No, she didn't. . . . The set is closed down tight as a drum. . . . It's running a million dollars over the budget. . . .*

A frequently heard remark was that Arthur Miller was wasting his talent as Monroe's cavalier, and wasn't it a pity? But a man does not live to please dramatic critics or provide material for the lectures of professors of drama. And who shall say, if Miller now gives himself to the writing of screenplays, that he may not attain greater artistic heights than he has in the theatre? The film at its best is as viable a form of expression as the play. What if this collaboration of Monroe and Miller were to culminate in cinematic masterpieces?

Or who can say that Miller will not write good plays or that Monroe will not star in them?

Again the pattern of the past. After the first week of shooting, Cukor found that Monroe's lateness and days missed because of illnesses were no legends. How could *Let's Make Love* be completed on time? Logan's solution in *Bus Stop* had been to keep the camera on her continuously. Cukor employed two cameras at once. One for medium shots and one for close-ups.

And Monroe's insecurity was still there. It was manifested after every take. She always wanted "one more take."

Cukor acceded to her requests and printed them. Wilder found Monroe stronger in her later takes. Cukor did not. He was able to ignite her at once, and she was good in the early takes. He preferred her earlier takes when he came to cut the film.

Monroe was one of the happy few in the movie colony invited to attend the banquet given for Khrushchev at the 20th Century-Fox commissary in 1959. The guests were asked to be at the Café de Paris at noon. Billy Wilder entered at eleven-forty-five. He saw that Monroe was already seated.

"At last," he said to those at his table, "a man who can get Marilyn to come on time. Now I know who should direct all her pictures —Nikita Khrushchev."

After the spirited debate on free enterprise versus Communism between Spyros Skouras and Khrushchev, the guests of honor made their way past the tables to go outside. Skouras halted at Monroe's table. He introduced her to the commissar, who bowed politely as Monroe blushed. Skouras cried, "Kiss her. Kiss her. Kiss her." The translation was lost in the hubbub, and Khrushchev did not kiss her, an action that might have affected the course of modern history. The entourage passed. Then Joshua Logan, who was at the table, recognized Mikhail Sholokhov, the novelist. Sholokhov had glowered all through lunch. He had sulked in the other cities the party had visited. Logan stopped Sholokhov. He said, "This is Marilyn Monroe." Sholokhov looked grim. "She is one of our leading American movie actresses, Mr. Sholokhov," Logan added. Sholokhov looked bored.

Then Monroe suddenly spoke. "My husband," she said proudly, "Arthur Miller, the playwright, sends you his best wishes."

The information was translated. Then the novelist beamed a smile at her. "Ah," he murmured, "yes, Arthur Miller, your husband, yes, I am honored, a very great man, your husband, we think of him highly in my country."

Monroe's eyes shone. It was a moment of personal triumph over Hollywood.

One more chord from the past resounded. Marilyn's mother was still alive. She was now called Mrs. Eley—Eley was the name of her second husband. At a hearing before a Los Angeles court on December 3, 1959, Inez Melson, who had once been Monroe's business manager and was still a friend, was appointed "conservator" of Mrs. Eley's affairs. Evidence was submitted that Monroe approved of the appointment. Mrs. Melson testified that Mrs. Eley "is confined to a sanitarium and cannot handle her own affairs." According to Mrs. Melson, Mrs. Eley lives comfortably and happily in a rest home on the outskirts of Los Angeles. She has made what psychiatrists call a "social recovery."

"She is perfectly well," affirms Mrs. Melson, "but not well enough to live alone. She is not in a mental hospital now. She does not require custodial care. Marilyn's mother likes to read a lot and she sews and knits. Marilyn sees her often. I don't know how often. She is happy about her daughter's success and is proud of her."

Hollywood has never understood Monroe. Hollywood has never honored her. But now it respects and fears her. At her disposal, night and day, there is a limousine and chauffeur, supplied by the studio. The limousine brings her to the studio, and it drives her right up to the sound stage. It is parked close to the stage door, so close it is barely possible to open the door.

"I think it is there all the time so Marilyn can have escape three yards away," a studio executive speculates. "I think the limousine is an escape symbol to her."

After the day's work she escapes with her husband to the luxuries of a private bungalow on the rear terrain of the Beverly Hills Hotel. The studio pays the enormous rent for the bungalow.

Now, at thirty-four, Monroe has it all—the Beverly Hills Hotel, the limousine, the stardom, the fame, the wealth, the celebrated and adoring husband.

But no one of these, nor even all of them together, though they are the outward and delicious trappings of success, represent her essential victory. Marilyn Monroe's great achievement has been the making of herself and the imposition of her will and her dream upon a whole world. Joseph Conrad wrote that when we are born we fall into a dream. Norma Jeane Mortenson, called Norma Jean Baker, fell into the most extravagant of dreams. She made it come true. She made it come true by making herself. She made herself beautiful. She made herself an artist. She triumphed in that arena where the loveliest women of the world contend fiercely for the prizes.

In one sense, then, her life is completed, because her spirit is formed and has achieved itself. No matter what unpredictable events may lie in her future, they cannot change who she is and what she has become. And there will be many surprises and alterations in her life ahead; there will be, in Hart Crane's phrase, "new thresholds, new anatomies."

In her heart is a questing fever that will give her no peace, that drives her on "to strive, to seek, to find," and then to strive and seek again. Her soul will always be restless, unquiet.

Epilogue (1961)

The two, whom God had joined together on Friday, June 29, 1956, were officially put asunder four years, three months, and thirteen days later, on another Friday, November 11, 1960. A brusque communiqué from Marilyn Monroe's minister of public information transmitted the news: *A spokesman for actress Marilyn Monroe and playwright Arthur Miller announced today that the couple had amicably parted. Miss Monroe will file for divorce but has made no immediate plans for consulting an attorney. She has just returned from California, where she co-starred with Clark Gable in "The Misfits."*

Monroe's *envie d'ailleurs*, her restless and romantic demand that everyday life be shaped in the contours of great beauty, without the monotonous trivialities of ordinary existence, had, finally, disposed her to cast away her third husband. Even as Madame Miller, she remained Madame Bovary, dominated by her fantasies. In the end, the Madame Bovaries of the world are always alone, and if they cannot ever learn to compromise with their impossible dreams, they eventually learn to compromise with their loneliness, as Garbo did, or they die.

Monroe has not told us of the miseries of her third marriage; perhaps some of these will be enumerated in her divorce petition.

Others are as clouded to herself as the world. Does she ponder them during the nights when sleep doesn't come, there in her white apartment on 57th Street, does she go over and over them with her lady psychoanalyst on Central Park South?

Five days before the public announcement, Miller told his parents that he and Marilyn were separating because "it could not go on this way." And when his mother wanted to know if perhaps there was a chance for a reconciliation, he replied grimly: "No, there's no hope for us."

But what way was "this way"? And why was there no hope and in what sense? Did he imply there was no hope for them either together or separated? Or no hope as a wife and husband? Had the sundering come about because he could not give her the passionate heights she expected from her lover and companion? Did she seek experiences in her friendships with Yves Montand and Montgomery Clift that she had not found with the somber, introspective writer? Or did Miller begin demanding periods of solitude for the contemplation that the literary process requires? Did he, at last, get tired of her passion for unwittingly excluding other people's desires because there was nothing within her field of awareness except her own desires? Had her emotional and time-consuming demands upon him finally drained him? Had he finally become enraged by his creative frustration—for in the five years since he had fallen in love with her, he had written only one work of any great consequence and that a screenplay for her?

"From the very first," wrote Oscar Wilde to Alfred Douglas in *De Profundia*, "there was too wide a gap between us. You had been idle at your school, worse than idle at your university. You did not realize that an artist, and especially such an artist as I am, one, that is to say, the quality of whose work depends on the intensification of personality, requires for the development of his art the companionship of ideas, and intellectual atmosphere, quiet, peace and solitude. You admired my work when it was finished: you enjoyed the brilliant successes of my first nights, and the brilliant banquets that followed them: you were proud and quite naturally so, of being the intimate friend of an artist so distinguished: but you could not understand the conditions requisite for the production of artistic work. I am not speaking in phrases of rhetorical exaggeration but in terms of absolute truth to actual fact when I remind you that during the whole time we were together I never wrote one single line."

But the analogy between the two playwrights, although significant in some ways, is not quite perfect. Monroe did not, like Wilde's parasitical friend, drain away his money to pay for fine houses, servants, good wines and food, clothes, and furs. She had paid for her own clothes and furs and vodka and luxuries. During the marriage she had earned about $2,000,000 and had worked constantly, making four films.

And there were not many brilliant first nights and brilliant banquets for her with Miller; there was only one event of this sort, the London *première* of *A View from the Bridge*. So there were no crescendos of acclaim as followed the opening of *Death of a Salesman*, no tributes, no prizes, no garlands. The fact that he ceased to be productive partly because of the quality of their relationship could not alter her sense of disappointment. Before he was hers, he had been like a rare jewel in a window, glittering with prestige; afterward he became like an ordinary piece of beveled glass. Had the crises that are part of the life of an actress slowly gnawed away at his talent? Had the talent, over the years, gotten rusty from disuse? Why had the stream of plays dried up? What had tarnished the distinguished reputation? In a letter dated November 19, 1960, Allan Seager, who had been Miller's English instructor at the University of Michigan and remained his friend, and, as we have seen, had been an observer of the playwright's "creative agony," gives us a glimpse of the home life of the Millers. He wrote:

> The last time I heard from Art Miller was in July and he said that as soon as "The Misfits" was in the can, he was going to take his girl and go to Europe but Europe came to him, and took his girl apparently. She is a smart girl, but it occurs to me that much of her experience with men has been like a whore's, business that is, and she may have had very little actual emotional involvement with anyone and when a smooth Frenchman is politely flirtatious, she goes overboard. That big white apartment of hers on 57th Street was not a love nest—it was the home of an industry, and Art sort of wandered around without a necktie, keeping out of the way. I went up there at three in the afternoon one time. Marilyn was in a wrapper, her hair done up in those big aluminum curlers, wolfing down a steak. "I'm terribly sorry," she said. "But I've got to run. Sitting for *Life*." She ran. Art said, "Am I going to see you for dinner, honey?" She didn't know.

Up till two or three weeks before the rupture, Miller expected the marriage to continue. In a conversation with a friend of mine during the filming of *The Misfits*, he said they were still in love and that the scandal over Yves Montand had been manufactured by gossip columnists. He did express a certain resentment over the influence that Lee Strasberg and Mrs. Strasberg exerted over his wife and seemed to believe that this influence was the chief disruptive element in the marriage. He believed that Marilyn had now achieved a degree of personal development that made the ministrations of Paula Strasberg quite superfluous. Mrs. Strasberg, during the making of *The Misfits*, was constantly in attendance—on the set and away from the set. Originally the Millers had stayed at the Mapes Hotel and Mrs. Strasberg was at the Holiday Hotel. In September, at Monroe's behest, they moved out of the Mapes and into the Holiday so that Monroe's coach and confidante could be available at all times. Miller came to resent Mrs. Strasberg as intensely as Di Maggio had resented Natasha Lytess. A curious physical parallel exists between Di Maggio, Miller, and Montand. They resemble each other. Somebody has said, "If you put Di Maggio, Miller and Montand in baseball suits and sent them to the outfield, you wouldn't be able to tell them apart."

I regard as wide of the mark Seager's speculation that Europe, in the body of Montand, had come to Monroe and commanded her heart. Romantic she is, but naive, in the sense of Isobel Archer or Daisy Miller or the other Henry James innocent American heroines seduced by Europe and the Europeans—that she is not. I know that she admired Montand as an artist and was thrilled by the rhythms and the energies of his performances. She was enchanted, also, by his physical force and sexuality. But she did not fall in love with him. He could not have been the attendant lord that Monroe requires in a man. During the filming of *Let's Make Love* there happened what often happens when two actors play scenes of love: the imagination they have mastered for their craft deviates from make-believe into reality, but it is still acting and both parties are subtly aware of it, although the knowledge is not directly expressed even to themselves. Miller, during the shooting of *Let's Make Love*, was in Ireland for a month, for conferences with John Huston. Simone Signoret, Mrs. Montand, had had to return to Paris and later was in Italy for a long time, playing in a film. The friendship between Monroe and Montand could now flower into an amorous game of thrust and counterthrust, which all persons, even happily married, can enjoy, if only as a diversion from the tedium of work, and the repetitive nature of film acting, the long periods of waiting for a shot to be set up and lighted, the takes and the retakes, surely make it one of the most laboriously boring of employments. Yes, flirtations are delightful, and to flirt in a new style, to have to develop new romantic ripostes to meet Montand's technique, which was fresh to her, must have been stimulating to Monroe, jaded on a long diet of Americans. How seriously did she take it, after all?

Montand did not take it seriously. He told Hedda Hopper, in September 1960 when the gossip about the supposed affair had taken on worldwide proportions, that there was nothing serious between himself and Monroe and that he had no intention of divorcing Mme. Montand. He described Marilyn as a sweet, simple girl, free of guile, who had perhaps mistaken certain of his gestures and tender words. "Perhaps I was too tender," he confessed. "But I thought she was as sophisticated as some of the other ladies I have known. Had Marilyn been sophisticated none of this would have happened."

As Montand sings it, in one of his favorite *chansons*, "*Moi, j'aime bien vivre comme ça.*"

Can Montand's ego have been so profound that he believed she had mistaken the game for the real thing? Yes. He was not quite so worldly as he pictured himself, nor was she as naive as he imagined. Perhaps he was not habituated to *l'amour americain*. For Monroe it was also a divertissement. She finds diversion in the company of actors. Several times during the filming of *The Misfits*, she flew down to Los Angeles on weekend trips to see her West Coast psychoanalyst and diverted herself with Montand. She also diverted herself with Montgomery Clift, with whom she went to San Francisco one weekend, with the agreeable cognizance of Miller, a man who does not suffer from the sense of property values in one's wife that is commonly found among more bourgeois husbands. On another evening, the entire company of *The Misfits* was invited to attend a performance by Frank Sinatra at the Cal-Neva Lodge, not far from Reno, where the company was in residence. Monroe was enormously taken by Sinatra's charm and physical *bonhomie* and she telephoned Jerry Wald and said she must do a picture with Sinatra very very soon. A member of the company took a dim view of these diversions and was afraid that Miller was becoming a helpless Emil Jannings in the hands of a strumpet Marlene Dietrich in a revival of the Josef von Sternberg classic *The Blue Angel*. And Eli Wallach, who played the aviator in *The Misfits*, became annoyed with Monroe when she ventured some disparaging remarks about Miller's literary incompetence during a birthday party for John Huston. Wallach told her that she had displayed cruelty and bad manners in speaking to her husband so in front of the group. Monroe did not take kindly to this criticism, even from Wallach, and their friendship cooled.

No, it was not the attentions of other men that ended the marriage. Rather it was an increasing, though to her indefinable, frustration during the five months of shooting *The Misfits*. Without any conscious intention on Miller's side—as we have already noted, the composition of this screenplay was a dedicated expression of love for his wife— Clark Gable became the most prominent figure during the filming process. A jealousy arose in the marriage, but it was an artistic jealousy, I believe.

Gable's role in *The Misfits* was to be the last of his career. Several weeks after the shooting was over, Gable suffered a heart attack and subsequently died. Louella Parsons has raised the question as to whether the strain of playing opposite Monroe—for she experienced her usual need of retakes and suffered her usual *mélange* of psychic and somatic ailments, one of which hospitalized her for several weeks —had exercised Gable's auricles and ventricles to the breaking point. More likely it was the high elevation in which most of the film was shot—in the mountains—and the fact that he was playing an extremely complex character and that for long stretches the setting took place in desert country where the temperature remained at 105 to 110 degrees day after day. Artistically and commercially, John Huston is one of the most successful directors in the American cinema, his films including *The Maltese Falcon, The Treasure of the Sierra Madre, The Asphalt Jungle, The Red Badge of Courage,* and *The African Queen.* Not through any conscious act on his part, Huston tended to be drawn more to Gable and Gable's challenge in the film than to the work Monroe was doing. What seems to fascinate Huston most as a director are the conflicts between man and man and between man and nature. Huston is not a "woman's director," as are George Cukor, Billy Wilder, and Josh Logan.

Huston is intrigued by a man's greed, a man's toughness, a man's amorality. Huston's *Beat the Devil*, one of the most original screen comedies in years, is probably also one of the most amoral. When an interesting woman character appears in a Huston film—Mary Astor's unscrupulous ice-cold murderess in *The Maltese Falcon*, for instance, or Katharine Hepburn's characterization in *The African Queen*—she is a woman who behaves like Huston thinks men really behave—that is, with courage, with a disdain for moral qualms, with ruthless cunning, with greed, with tireless physical strength. The tender love scene, the rising sequence of delicately photographed images painting an emotional rapport between a man and a woman culminating in a kiss, an embrace—this is not Huston's idea of what the movies are about. Huston is the "man's man." So was Gable. So, ironically enough, is Arthur Miller. Miller has not written one love scene—in all his plays. In its original short story form, as we have noted, *The Misfits* was concerned only with three men and their capturing of wild horses. The character Monroe played in the film, Rosalyn Taber did not appear in the short story.

Although, to express his love for her, Miller undertook to transform his short story into a lovely screenplay, conscious intentions and the urgings of the will cannot compel a writer to write something that does not arise out of his depths. Bend himself as much as he might, Miller could not write a "woman's movie." Nor could Huston help to create to Monroe's satisfaction the sort of character that she plays so exquisitely—that luminously fragile creature, mingling the voluptuous and the tender, the naive and the worldly, the innocent soul in the ageless Venus. Yet Monroe had asked for Huston as her director—and indeed her work in *The Misfits* is superb, but it is Huston's version of Monroe we see here, it is a different Monroe, and, on the whole, the film tends to be Gable, Gable being the first of her leading men to hold the center of the screen when playing together with her. Monroe had been led astray by the fact that her first important role, which had opened the way to her success, was in *The Asphalt Jungle*. What she forgot was that Angela was a whore—a whore with a golden heart, but a whore. In the cinematic ideology of Huston, women are divided up either into masculinized heroines (Hepburn in *The African Queen*) or beautiful whores (Astor in *The Maltese Falcon*). It was inevitable that in the translation of *The Misfits* from the mimeographed pages of the screenplay to the film, the focus became the character of Langland, being played by the most skilled of all the American outdoor he-man virtuosos. It is extraordinary how few American movie actors can play romantic lovers and how many of the tough-guy genre, who became inarticulate when faced with a girl—Gable and John Wayne, Gary Cooper, Marlon Brando, Tony Curtis. Of Monroe, Gable said, shortly before his death: "I think she is something different to each man, blending into him somehow to supply the things he seems to require. All men are different and she is different to all men, but in a sense she is the same thing to them all—their pride. I think this is her secret."

As we have seen, the men with whom Monroe has gotten deeply involved are older than she is and seem to occupy the role of a crypto-father. Except for Fred Karger, her first love, however, the other men have been of the stern and manly type. It is not that Marilyn does not aspire to moments of lyrical sweetness in love, but the gentle poetic lover does not seem to be able to arouse her lust. Your romantic lover has an element of the female in him; there is that in his temperament that attunes him to a woman's craving for lovely words and music and flowers and caresses from the fingertips. But it is the type of the brute —flashing with violent passion—with which Marilyn finally comes to rest. A characteristic almost all of Monroe's *amants* have had in common is a passion for hunting, fishing, the chase, killing, a ruthless lack of sentimentality.

And here another paradox comes into play, for to the same degree that brute force excites her, it also repels her, since she is terribly squeamish and feels an empathy for animals, for all small suffering helpless creatures.

And finally, whatever be the complex hungers of a father complex, no man can for long persist in father-substitution when he loves a woman, since sexual love is often a selfish appetite that seeks its own appeasement, and in some of its moods and perhaps its best moods, it is direct, spontaneous, and literally rapacious. So if it is a protective security she desires, she cannot have this for long. She wishes to be dominated by a stronger man, but she resists domination and is resentful of physical brutality. She feels that she is not loved if her husband does not participate in every phase of her artistic struggles and neurotic turmoil—and yet if he does this at the cost of his own ego, she comes to lose respect for him and her desire disintegrates. Her first husband, James Dougherty, thought her dreams naive and her ambitions foolish, and he could not remain subordinated to her. Her second husband, Joe Di Maggio, accepted her status and her long hours at the studio, but he wanted to limit her activity and he himself did not want to participate directly in the problems of her work or her conflicts with her colleagues. That did not do for her. But her third husband, Arthur Miller, gave her an extremity of devotion, of attention, of total surrender to the requirements of the frenetic daily life of a star, and the business of the household came to revolve solely around Marilyn Monroe. And this was not enough. Nothing can ever be enough, for reality is never the equal of her fantasies and she demands that it equal or exceed her fantasies.

There are some persons, including several acquainted with Miller, who do not believe that Miller surrendered everything in marrying Monroe. Those persons believe that he was undergoing that unpleasant transition, commonly called "writer's block," in which one is unable to function for long periods of time and in which one seeks a violent change of activity and new scenes during which one can regroup one's inner forces and prepare oneself for a fresh attack; Miller, perhaps, may have welcomed the excuses that his wife's career presented to evade the temporarily onerous duties of the writer. A Moscow dispatch, published in Los Angeles on December 26, 1960, gives us another interpretive nuance, although it is less Marxist–Leninist than anti-feminist. In an article published in *Nedjela*, a youth weekly, Marilyn Monroe was criticized as a destructive product of the American way of life, along with chewing gum and Coca-Cola. She had lived a hard life, the writer said, and had learned the ways of *The Asphalt Jungle* and had then applied them in her rise to power, sacrificing one husband after another. "She found in Miller," according to the article, "what she lacked. She exploited him without pity. He wrote scripts for her films and made her a real actress. Marilyn paid him back. She left him. Another step in her climb to the stars. Another broken life on this path." What this essay lacks in factual accuracy, it more than compensates for in sentimental banality of the most *petit-bourgeois* character. Is it possible that already, in the Soviet Union, the male is quavering under the impact of equal rights and that the concept of woman as destroyer, as shrike, is becoming popular?

Perhaps, for a great star of the combination of paradoxical and conflicting desires as Marilyn Monroe, there will never be, there can never be, an enduring love for another person. Perhaps Monroe must come to terms with herself and accept a sort of alienation from the common stream of humanity, accept her essential loneliness, as Garbo came to accept her loneliness, and live out her life in the solitariness of her private dreams, her rich fantasies, making contact with the human race only through the way of her art. Her soul will always be restless and unquiet.